THE NINE DAYS' QUEEN

LADY JANE GREY AND HER TIMES

BY

RICHARD DAVEY

EDITED, AND WITH INTRODUCTION, BY
MARTIN HUME, M.A.

ILLUSTRATED

First Published in 1909

ISBN-13:
978-1981814824

ISBN-10:
1981814825

NOTE: Original pagination can be found throughout this publication

AUTHOR'S NOTE

My object in writing this book has been to interest the reader in the tragic story of Lady Jane Grey rather from the personal than the political point of view. I have therefore employed, more perhaps than is usual, what the French historians term *le document humain* in my account of the extraordinary men and women who surrounded Lady Jane, and who used her as a tool for their ambitious ends. The reader may possibly wonder why in several of the earlier chapters Lady Jane Grey plays so shadowy a part, but I deemed it impossible for any one who is not very familiar with our History at this period to understand, without having a complete idea of the chain of conspiracies that preceded and rendered possible her proclamation, how a young Princess, not in the immediate succession to the Crown, came to be placed, if only for nine days, in the towering position of Queen of England. These conspiracies were four in number. The first was that of the Howards and the Catholic party against Queen Katherine Parr. The second, the conspiracy of the Seymours against the Howards, which ended in the downfall of the great House of Norfolk, whereby Edward Seymour was enabled to proclaim himself Lord Protector of the Realm. The third plot was that of Thomas Seymour to cast down his brother Edward from his high station, and, if possible, to usurp the same for himself—a strange story of folly and intrigue and overvaulting ambition which ended in one of the most terrible fratricidal tragedies to be found in the history of the nations. Fourthly, the removal of the brothers Seymour from the scene enabled John Dudley, Duke of Northumberland, to work his own will and to prepare the way, during the last days of Edward VI, for his daughter-in-law, much against her will, to usurp the throne.

I have consulted every available document, as well in ourviii national archives and private libraries as in those of foreign countries, concerning Lady Jane and her friends and foes, the better to paint as vivid a picture as possible of the times in which they lived.

I need scarcely add how greatly I appreciate the honour Major Martin Hume has conferred upon my work by his scholarly Introduction, which gives so succinct and deeply interesting an account of our foreign politics at a most momentous period of English history. To him, to Dr. Gairdner, to Earl Spencer, to Earl Stamford and Warrington, and to many other gentlemen and friends, including the officials at the State Paper Office and the British Museum, I beg to tender my sincere thanks for their courtesy and for the valuable information with which they have helped me to complete my picture of one of the most interesting periods in our national history.

I cannot, moreover, allow this opportunity to pass without recording, with sincere gratitude and affection, the aid which I received, when I first thought of writing this life of Lady Jane Grey, from the kindness of my old valued and lamented friend, Dr. Richard Garnett.

RICHARD DAVEY

200 Ashley Gardens, London, S.W.
5th September 1909.

CONTENTS

Introduction

CHAP.
- I. Bradgate Hall and the Greys of Groby
- II. Birth and Education
- III. The Lady Latimer
- IV. The King's Household
- V. Mrs. Anne Askew
- VI. The Howards and the Seymours
- VII. Henry viii
- VIII. Concerning the Lady Jane and the Queen-Dowager
- IX. The Queen and the Lord High-Admiral
- X. The Lady Jane goes to Seymour Place
- XI. The Education of Lady Jane
- XII. John Dudley, Earl of Warwick
- XIII. The Fall of the House of Somerset
- XIV. The Lady Jane marries the Lord Guildford
- XV. On the Way to the Tower
- XVI. The Lady Jane is proclaimed Queen
- XVII. The Nine Days' Reign
- XVIII. The Last Days of Northumberland
- XIX. The Trial of Queen Jane
- XX. The Supreme Hour!
- XXI. The Fate of the Survivors

Appendix

LIST OF ILLUSTRATIONS

Henry Grey, Duke of Suffolk
From the Painting by Joannes Corvus, in the National Portrait Gallery

Queen Katherine Parr
After the Painting formerly in the possession of Horace Walpole

Henry viii in 1547
From an old Engraving

Roger Ascham's Visit to Lady Jane Grey at Bradgate
After the Painting by J. C. Horsley, R.A.

John Dudley, Duke of Northumberland
From an Engraving by G. Vertue

Edward Seymour, Duke of Somerset
From an Engraving after the Painting by Holbein

Supposed Portrait of Lady Jane Grey
Formerly in the Collection of Col. Elliott of Nottingham, and now at Oxford University. From an Engraving after the Painting by Holbein

Edward vi
From an Engraving by G. Vertue

Lady Jane Grey by Wyngaerde
The earliest engraved Portrait of her, from a Picture said to be by Holbein, now lost

Queen Mary at the Period of her Marriage
From the Painting by Antonio Mor, in the Prado Museum. (Photograph by R. Anderson)

Portrait of the Lady Frances Brandon, Duchess of Suffolk, and her Second Husband, Adrian Stokes, Esq.
Probably by Corvinus, property of Col. Wynn Finch

INTRODUCTION

The tragedy of Lady Jane Grey is unquestionably one of the most poignant episodes in English history, but its very dramatic completeness and compactness have almost invariably caused its wider significance to be obscured by the element of personal pathos with which it abounds. The sympathetic figure of the studious, saintly maiden, single-hearted in her attachment to the austere creed of Geneva, stands forth alone in a score of books refulgent against the gloomy background of the greed and ambition to which she was sacrificed. The whole drama of her usurpation and its swift catastrophe is usually treated as an isolated phenomenon, the result of one man's unscrupulous self-seeking; and with the fall of the fair head of the Nine Days' Queen upon the blood-stained scaffold within the Tower the curtain is rung down and the incident looked upon as fittingly closed by the martyrdom of the gentlest champion of the Protestant Reformation in England.

Such a treatment of the subject, however attractive and humanly interesting it may be, is nevertheless unscientific as history and untrue in fact. An adequate appreciation of the tendencies behind the unsuccessful attempt to deprive Mary of her birthright can only be gained by a consideration of the circumstances preceding and surrounding the main incident. The reasons why Northumberland, a weak man as events proved, was able to ride rough-shod over the nobles and people of England, the explanation of his sudden and ignominious collapse and of the apparent levity with which the nation at large changed its religious beliefs and observance at the bidding of assumed authority are none of them on the surface of events; and the story of Jane Grey as it is usually told, whilst abounding in pathetic interest gives no key to the vast political issues of which the fatal intriguexiv of Northumberland was but a by-product. To represent the tragedy as a purely religious one, as is not infrequently done, is doubly misleading. That one side happened to be Catholic and the other Protestant was merely a matter of party politics, and probably not a single active participator in the events, except Jane herself, and to some extent Mary, was really moved by religious considerations at all, loud as the professions of some of the leaders were.

Mr. Davey has given in the vivid pages of this book a striking picture of the Society in which the drama was represented and of the persons who surrounded Lady Jane Grey in the critical period of her unhappy fate; and this of itself enables a wider view than is usual to be taken of the subject. But, withal, I venture to think that an even more extended prospect of it may be attained and the whole episode fitted into its proper place in the history of England, if supplementary consideration be given to international politics of the time, and especially to the part which England aspired to take in the tremendous struggle for supremacy which was then approaching the end of its first phase on the Continent of Europe; a struggle in which not only the two most powerful nations in Christendom were engaged and the two greatest monarchs in the world were the leaders, but one in which the eternally antagonistic principles of expansion and repression were the issues.

It is too often assumed that the system of political parties in English Government dates only from the rise of Parliament as the predominant power in the State in the seventeenth century, since, by the open opposition and the public discussion of rival policies in the Legislature, the existence of different groups of statesmen then became evident to the world. But at least it may be asserted that, from the time when the two first Tudor kings sought the aggrandisement of England by placing their power in the balance between the great Continental rivals, two schools of English politicians surrounded their sovereign, each intent upon forwarding the alliance which seemed to them wisest in the interests of the country and their own. When, however, the political rivalry of France and the Emperor was accentuated by the introduction of religious schism in the contest, by the boldxv defiance of Luther and the spread of the reformed doctrines, the political parties in the English Court were divided more distinctly than ever by the new element introduced; and, despotic as the Tudor sovereigns were, the apparently personal and fickle character of their policy, which proves so puzzling to students, really arose in nearly every case from the temporary predominance in their counsels of one or the other school of thought represented in their Court. It is only by recognising this fact that the strange and sudden changes which took place in the reigns of Henry VIII and Edward VI can be made comprehensible, and by it also the rise and fall of Lady Jane Grey can be seen in its true light.

During the last twenty years of the reign of Henry VIII his bewildering mutations of policy and of wives were the result of efforts on the part of rival sets of politicians to utilise his brutal sensuality and inflated pride to their respective ends. With him, as with the most of them, religion was a mere stalking horse for other interests. The traditional and more Conservative party, which usually leant towards the imperial alliance, naturally took the Catholic side, the established nobility such as the Howards backed by the Catholic bishops being contrasted with the more recently ennobled men, aided by bureaucrats like Cromwell and by the reforming churchmen. Thus it came to be understood before the end of Henry's reign that the men in the English Court most favourable to emancipation from the Papacy were generally speaking the advocates of a French alliance, whilst those who clung to the orthodox view of religion favoured the traditional adherence to the house of Burgundy. It is true that the men on both sides were equally eager to participate in the plunder of the Church and in filching the commons from the people of England; and that both parties included men who were ready to profess themselves faithful Catholics or ardent reformers as their interests demanded at the time. But the political aims of the respective parties were quite distinctly divided, notwithstanding religious affinities, for the Emperor was just as desirous of having Protestant friends in England as the King of France was willing to accept Catholic support there. The object of the English sovereigns, it must be recollected, was usually somewhat different fromxvi that of their bribed councillors who had their own interests to serve. The aim of Henry VII and Henry VIII, and especially of Elizabeth, who alone was successful in attaining it, was so to distribute the weight of England's influence as to avert any coalition of the two great Continental powers against her, rather than to become the permanent tool of either; the efforts of Charles V, and his French rival being respectively directed towards preventing England from throwing in her lot with their enemies.

Until religious bitterness infinitely complicated the question, and finally led to the long state of war with Spain, the side which commanded most sympathy amongst the English people at large was unquestionably that which favoured a cordial understanding with the sovereign of Flanders and Spain. The country had been in close antagonism with France on and off for centuries, the proximity of the coasts and the aspirations of the French to dominate the Channel represented a constant danger and source of anxiety, and it was instinctively felt in England that the time-honoured policy which bound her to the monarch who was able when he pleased to divert the aggression of the French by threatening any of their land frontiers, was the safest friend of this country. The English merchants who found their richest markets in Flanders and Spain, and who were in chronic irritation at the French piratical attacks upon their commerce, were equally anxious for a friendship which they looked upon as the best assurance against a war which they dreaded; so that the chief English advocates of the French connection were usually those whose adherence to the reformed religious doctrines overbore their political interests, and the newer nobility and politicians who found themselves at enmity on social and other grounds with the traditional conservatives.

It must not be forgotten that both France and the Emperor strove ceaselessly to gain friends amongst the English councillors. Immense bribes found their way into the pockets of ministers and secretaries of State, in many cases regular yearly pensions being settled upon influential political supporters, and by means of flattery, social attentions, and promises, the ambassadors in England of the rival powers became centres of intrigue to influence English policy inxvii favour of one or the other. The goal to which both the rivals directed their eyes was one in which, curiously enough, England had no interest whatever, namely, the hegemony over Italy; but England which by activity on the northern coasts of France or on the Scottish border could weaken the French power for harm in other directions, could enable the Emperor at any time to check his enemy's Italian ambitions; whilst with England as her friend France could brave the imperialists, certain that she would not be taken in the rear, especially when, as she usually managed to do, she had enlisted on her side the Turks on the Hungarian frontier and the Lutheran princes and towns of Germany.

The marriage of Henry VIII with Jane Seymour was looked upon by the Imperialist Conservative party in England as a victory for their cause. Her brother, Sir Edward Seymour, had been in the Emperor's service, and Jane had supplanted the hated Anne Boleyn, whose sympathies were, of course, entirely French. It is true that later Seymour, a parvenu noble, be it recollected, was driven into the anti-papal camp mainly by the antagonism of Norfolk and the older nobles who led the Conservative party, but, notwithstanding his Protestantism, he never wavered in his attachment to the imperial alliance and his opposition to French interests.

When the death of Henry VIII made Seymour, as Duke of Somerset and Protector, virtually ruler of England with Paget as his principal minister, both of them were almost servile in their professions of devotion to the cause of the Emperor; and made no secret of their distrust of France with which a hollow and temporary peace had only been recently patched up. Somerset harried the Church and changed religious forms ruthlessly; his greed was insatiable and the devotional endowments were looted without compunction, the Catholic bishops were treated with stern severity, and even the schismatic Catholicism of Henry VIII was cast aside in favour of an entirely new creed and ritual. Norfolk was kept in the Tower, Wriothesley was disgraced and the Catholic Conservative nobles were warned not to stand in the Protector's way. But through it all Somerset and Paget were politically the sworn servants and friends of the Emperor, pledged to discountenance any attempts of thexviii French to injure him: whilst Charles V on his side, much as he deprecated the religious changes, could no more afford to quarrel with Somerset than he could with Henry VIII, twenty years before when he contumeliously repudiated his blameless Spanish wife and scornfully threw off the papal supremacy which was the keystone of the imperial system.

Submissive as were the words of Somerset and Paget to their imperial master1 not by words alone but by acts also they sought to serve him as against France. The strong policy adopted by Somerset towards Scotland, and his defiant attitude at Boulogne, then temporarily held by the English against the payment of a great ransom, served the Emperor's turn excellently at a period when he was at grips with his Lutheran subjects, at issue with the Pope and faced by a series of dangerous French intrigues in Italy. That the French themselves understood this perfectly well is seen by the desperate efforts they made to conciliate Somerset and win him to their side. Early in July 1547, only five months after his accession to power, Somerset told the imperial ambassador in strict confidence, when the latter was complaining of his religious innovations, that the special French envoy, Paulin—"immediately after the death of King Henry had striven to win him, the Protector, to the side of France by means of a large annual pension, which, as was only right, he had always declined. Notwithstanding this, however, Paulin, the last time he came hither, was instructed to offer him the assignment of the pension, which he had brought with him already signed and sealed. But with all these offers and grand promises of the French to divert the English Government from their alliance with your Majesty (the Emperor), he said he would always remain constant and loyal to you, knowing well that the strict preservation of the ancient alliance was so important for both parties." Even a month previous to this Somerset had informed the ambassador that the French had greatly scandalised him by offering him as an inducement to join France, in an offensive and defensive alliance, the cession of the Emperor's Flemish province to England when it had been conqueredxix by the allies, Boulogne at the same time to be restored to France.

What wonder that the Emperor's reply to this was to send flattering autograph letters to Somerset, assuring him of his unalterable regard, but saying not a word about his Protestant proceedings. "Of course," continues the Emperor, writing to his ambassador, "the Protector would naturally refuse to accept the pension from the French, if only in the interests of duty and decency. The goodwill he displays towards us must be encouraged to the utmost by you on all occasions, and you must lose no opportunity of confirming the Protector in these favourable sentiments." Somerset and Paget were therefore from first to last "Emperor's men" and opponents of French interests, that is to say advocates of the same policy as that identified with the older nobles and Catholics, most of whom were now under a cloud in consequence of their religion or in consequence of their personal enmity to Somerset whom they regarded as a greedy, unscrupulous interloper.

From the first days after the death of Henry VIII, it had been seen by close observers that personal and not political rivalry alone was likely in the future to bring about a split in Somerset's Government. The imperial ambassador, writing less than a fortnight after Henry's death, says that whilst Hertford (Somerset) and Warwick (Northumberland) would apparently be supreme in authority, "it is likely that some jealousy or rivalry may arise between them because, although they both belong to the same sect, they are nevertheless widely different in character: the Lord-Admiral being of high courage will not willingly submit to his colleague. He is in higher favour with the people and with the nobles than is the Earl of Hertford, owing to his liberality and splendour. The Protector, on the other hand, is not so conspicuous in this respect, and is looked down upon by everybody as a dry, sour, opinionated man": the sequel to this being that both these nobles with Paget and Wriothesley should, in the opinion of the ambassador, be "entertained" by the Emperor "in the usual way."

Before many months had passed, as we have seen, it was recognised by the Imperialist party that Somerset and Pagetxx were their fast friends and that the rising personal opposition of Dudley had adopted, not unnaturally, as its policy that of a *rapprochement* with France. It would, of course, be untrue to say that Dudley's attack upon Somerset had for its sole object the substitution of one international policy for another. Dudley, like his rival, was in the first place ambitious and self-seeking; but it was necessary for both of them, in order to serve their ends, that they should obtain the cooperation and support of one or other of the two main currents of public opinion, the adhesion of both rivals to the advanced Protestant practices in religion being dictated in the first place by their need for the money and patronage that the religious confiscations provided, and, secondly, by the great predominance of the reformed doctrines in and about London. But Somerset having embraced the Conservative or Imperialistic policy, and infused, under the influence of Catholic Paget, some consideration for the professors of the old faith into his reforming zeal, it was incumbent upon Dudley, who wished to overthrow him, to adopt in both respects an entirely opposite policy.

It is the fate of most Governments to be judged by results, and it was a comparatively easy matter for Dudley to pick holes in Somerset's management of affairs. The debasement of the coinage and the consequent dislocation of business and the terrible distress it caused, the enclosures of the commons and the process of turning customary copyholds into tenancies at will, had reduced the people of England to a condition of misery such as they had never seen before. The cruel confiscation of the monastic properties had deprived the sick and the poor of their principal source of relief, the drastic changes in religion had produced indignation in the breasts of many citizens, whilst slackening the hold of authority generally and promoting lawlessness. When to all this is added the grasping selfishness of Somerset personally, and above all the success of the French arms before Boulogne, attributed to the parsimony of the Protector, it will be seen that Northumberland had a large area of discontent upon which to work for support against his unpopular rival. But even so, it is improbable that he would have ventured to take so bold an action against the Protector asxxi he did, but for the consciousness that he had behind him the support, moral and financial if not military, of France and the Lutheran enemies of the Emperor.

When the loss of the English forts protecting Boulogne made negotiations for peace necessary, a French Embassy was sent to London, and a keen observer present at the time2 thus records what was evidently the public impression of events—"It was suspected that the principal object of this embassy was to bribe them (*i.e.* the English Government) to make war on the Emperor. Whilst these ambassadors were there they were greatly feasted by the Earl of Warwick (Northumberland) and the Grand Master (Paulet, Marquis of Winchester) much more than any other of the lords; for it appears that the French ambassadors could not gain the ear of the others—The King of France found out from his ambassadors which of the English lords showed more leaning towards France and against the Emperor. These were the Earl of Warwick and the Grand Master (of the Household), and it is believed that the King (of France) wrote to them warning them against the Protector and the Earl of Arundel who were plotting their destruction." If this contemporary belief was well founded, as it probably was, the overthrow of Somerset is proved to a great extent to have been an international intrigue promoted and probably well paid for by France.

As the observer already quoted remarks, the sequel of the Embassy which thus ensured Northumberland's neutrality in favour of France was the almost immediate declaration of war by the French King against the Emperor, and the wholesale plundering of the imperial subjects at sea. Seen in this light, therefore, Northumberland's complete change of England's policy, his truckling to France, his merciless measures against Catholics, although, as events proved he was a Catholic at heart himself, his imprisonment of Paget the Emperor's humble servant, and his ostentatious disregard for the imperial friendship, his whole attitude indeed, assumes a new aspect. His ambition was boundless for himself and his house; but it must have been evident to him that it could only be successfully carried into effect if he had behindxxii him a strong body of public opinion in England itself, and the countenance of one of the great continental powers. Both these desiderata he had in the earlier months of his domination; and if Edward VI had died or had been despatched late in 1551, or in the earlier weeks of 1552, it is quite possible that Northumberland might have carried through his great conspiracy successfully.

But the eighteen months that elapsed between the execution of Somerset and the death of Edward were fully sufficient to prove to the people of England that they had cast off the yoke of a King Log to assume that of a King Stork—Northumberland's overbearing arrogance and roughness had offended everyone with whom he came into contact: his colleagues dreaded and hated him, especially after the marriage of his young son Guildford to a lady of the Royal house in the direct line of succession had to some extent opened the eyes of men to the magnitude of his aspirations. The condition of the country, moreover, instead of improving under his rule was considerably worse even than it had been under Somerset. The coinage had now reached its lowest point of debasement, the shilling containing only one quarter of silver to three quarters of copper, and even was ordered by decree to be only valued at half its face value. The gold had all left the country and foreign trade was killed by the lack of a decent currency. Labour, driven from the land by the wholesale conversion of the estates from tillage to pasture, crowded the towns clamouring for food, and the disgraceful treatment of the Princess Mary by the ruling minister had aroused a strong feeling against his injustice and tyranny.

The Emperor was at war with France and the Lutherans, and was obliged to speak softly to Northumberland. Again and again he tried to win him over to his side, and the ruler of England knew full well that, whatever he might do he was safe from any overt interference from the imperial power. But for this fact it is certain that Northumberland would not have attempted the bold stroke of disinheriting Mary and placing Jane Grey and his own son upon the throne of England. When Edward VI was known by him to be sick beyond recovery Northumberland, with an eye to the near future, endeavoured to conciliate the Emperor somewhat andxxiii to bring about peace upon the Continent. His object in doing so was twofold—first to persuade Charles that he was still a potential friend; and, secondly, to set his French friends free from their war with the Emperor, and so enable them at the critical moment he foresaw to come to his aid in England if necessary. The English trading classes were by this time in a fever of indignation against the French for their piratical interference with English shipping, and Northumberland must have known that with this and the fear aroused by the French successes in the Emperor's Flemish dominions—always the key of English policy—even he could not for very long withstand the demand of the English people to help the Emperor against his enemies. It was Northumberland's misfortune that he was obliged to deliver his blow against the legitimate English succession in this state of public affairs. The Emperor and his ministers were keenly alive to the situation, and although they were of course not yet aware of the details of Northumberland's intended *coup d'état*, they feared that the Princess Mary might by his influence be excluded from the throne. This of course would have been a serious blow to the imperial cause; for it would in all probability mean the permanent adhesion of England to the French alliance. But Charles had swallowed so much humiliation to keep England friendly in the past that he was not disposed now to be too squeamish. He did not know how far his enemies the French had gone in their promises of support to Northumberland when Edward should die, but if by blandishments and conciliatory acquiescence he could win the friendship of England he was willing to smile upon any occupant of the throne or any power behind it who would keep to the old alliance and turn a cold shoulder to the French.

As soon as it was known in the imperial court that Edward was approaching his end the Emperor's ambassadors hurried over to England with instructions to conciliate Northumberland at all costs, and to assure him that the Emperor's affection for England and its young King was much greater than that of the King of France. "But," continues the Emperor's instructions, "if you arrive too late and the King is dead, you must take counsel together and act for the best for the safety of our cousin the Princess Mary, and secure, if possible, her accessionxxiv to the Crown, whilst doing what you judge necessary to exclude the French and their intrigues. You must endeavour also to maintain the confidence and good neighbourship which it is so important that our States should enjoy with England ... and especially to prevent the French from getting a footing in the country, or of gaining the ear of the men who rule England, the more so if it be for the purpose of embarrassing us."

News had already reached Flanders of Northumberland's intention to exclude Mary from the throne on her brother's death, and although the Emperor saw that in such case the life of his cousin would be in grave peril, especially if French aid, as was feared, were given to Northumberland, the principal efforts of the imperial envoys were to be directed to assuring the English government in any case that the Emperor was their friend and not France; Northumberland was to be persuaded that the Emperor had no thought of proposing a foreign husband for Mary; and that any match chosen for her by the ruling powers in England would be willingly accepted by her imperial kinsman. In short, the envoys were to promise anything and everything to secure the throne for Mary, even to endorsing the religious changes effected under Edward. But failing success in this it is made quite clear that the Emperor was willing to accept Jane Grey or any other sovereign who would consent to regard him as a friend and exclude French influence from the country.

The French were just as much on the alert to serve their own interests, and Northumberland, knowing how unpopular the French were at this juncture, and how much his supposed dependence upon them was resented, was extremely careful not to show ostensibly any leaning towards them. But as soon as he heard, late in June, that the imperial envoys were coming to London he came specially from Greenwich to the French ambassador's lodging at the Charterhouse to inform him that the Emperor was sending an embassy. "I doubt not," writes the French agent to his King, "that they will do their best to interrupt the friendship that exists between your Majesty and the King of England. I will keep my eye upon them and will leave no effort untried to subvert them."

xxv Edward died on the very day that the imperial ambassadors arrived in London, though the death was kept secret for some days afterwards, and it soon became evident, both to the French and the Imperialists, that Northumberland had prepared everything for the elevation of Jane Grey to the throne. At this juncture, which called, if ever one did, for prompt and bold action, only one of the several interests took a strong course, the Princess Mary herself. It is quite evident that everyone else had deceived himself and was paralysed in fear of action by another. Again and again the French ambassador expressed a belief that the coming of the imperial envoys portended an active interference on the part of the Emperor in favour of Princess Mary; and Northumberland and his council, notwithstanding all the protestations of the imperial envoys, were of the same opinion; whereas we now see that the Emperor was quite willing to throw over Mary, and even the Catholics, if only he could persuade Jane Grey and her government to join him against France.

When Mary's bold defiance of the usurper was announced, the Emperor's envoys, whom many believed to be forerunners of a strong foreign armed force to aid her, had nothing but shocked condemnation for her action. They considered her attitude "strange, difficult and dangerous"; and predicted her prompt suppression and punishment. In reference to the suggestion of her Catholic friends, that imperial aid should be sent to her, the envoys, who were supposed to be in England for the purpose of forcing her upon the throne, could only say to their master, "Considering your war with the French, it seems unadvisable for your Majesty to arouse English feeling against you, and the idea that the Lady will gain Englishmen on the ground of religion is vain." Serious remonstrances were sent to Mary herself by the imperial envoys, pointing out the danger and the hopelessness of her position in the face of Northumberland's supposed strength, and they laboured hard to dissuade the Duke from his idea that they had been sent to England to sustain Mary's cause.

Nor was the Emperor himself bolder than his envoys. He instructed the latter to recommend Mary, "with all softness[xxvi] and kindness," to the mercy of Jane's government, but they were to make it quite clear that he would strike no blow in her favour, and would receive with open arms any sovereign of England who would not serve French interests. Mr. Davey has indicated in the present book the eagerness with which the great imperial minister, Don Diego Hurtado de Mendoza, greeted Guildford Dudley as King of England. That Mendoza, one of the most trusted and ablest of the Emperor's councillors, could take such a step without knowing that it would not, at least, be against his master's policy is inconceivable: and all through it is clear that, if Mary had waited for effective help from her imperial cousin, Jane Grey might have reigned for a long lifetime.

Just as the Emperor was paralysed in his action by the fear that he might alienate England from his side, so France allowed discretion to wait upon valour for fear of driving the English government irretrievably into the arms of the Emperor. When the news of Mary's rising came to London the French ambassador bitterly deplored Northumberland's want of foresight in not having seized the person of the Princess in time to prevent it. He confessed that Northumberland was excessively unpopular, but believed that his possession of the national forces would enable him to crush Mary and her malcontents. But he took care not to pledge himself too deeply to Jane, and whilst full of sympathy and good wishes for Northumberland's success always kept in touch with some of Mary's friends. Neither the French ambassador nor the English council really understood the Emperor's attitude. When the council communicated to the imperial ambassadors Jane's succession, they haughtily told them that it was known they were here to force Mary upon the throne, and that a new sovereign now having been successfully proclaimed, the sooner they left England the better. The French ambassador, writing to his king at the same time, remarked that the imperial ambassadors had informed the English council, that rather than submit to Jane's wearing the crown to Mary's deprivation his master would make friends with the French on any terms and would deal with Jane in a way which she would not like.

It is almost amusing, now that we have the correspondence[xxvii] of all parties before us, to see how they all deceived themselves. The Emperor, as has been said, would not lift a finger to help Mary, even when she was in the field with a strong armed force, for fear of alienating hopelessly the sovereign of England whoever he might be; the King of France, whilst giving the same sort of hesitating implied support to Northumberland and Jane as Charles held out to the Princess Mary, would give no effective help for the same reason that tied the Emperor's hands. Both sides, indeed, were waiting to greet success without pledging themselves to a cause which might fail.

But the person who miscalculated most fatally of all was Northumberland himself. He had been during the whole time of his rule the humble servant of France. He had violated the treaty of 1543, by which England was bound to side with the Emperor in case his territory was invaded by France, and he stood between the throne and Princess Mary who it was known would serve the cause of the Emperor and her mother's country to the utmost. He was obliged, as has been shown, to cast his hazard when the public opinion was strongly against him, the commercial classes of England well nigh ruined, the labourers in a worse condition than had ever been known before, and the nobility jealous and apprehensive. Knowing this, as he did, it is difficult to believe that he would have dared to take up the position he assumed unless he had persuaded himself that, as a last resource, French armed aid would support him. That such a thing was not remotely probable is now evident from the correspondence of the French ambassadors. They were only full of sorrow for "this poor Queen Jane" and feared for the fate of their unfortunate friend the Duke of Northumberland. And yet London itself was in a panic, born of the conviction that 6000 French troops were on their way to keep Jane upon the throne; Northumberland, in fact, presumably believing that his past services to France had deserved such aid, had actually sent and demanded it of the King. If it had been afforded in effective time the whole history of England might have been changed.

We know now, although none knew it then, that the Emperor would have greeted with smooth assurances the[xxviii] victorious Jane and Northumberland, and would have deserted his cousin Mary until a turn of the wheel gave her hopes of success again. There was, indeed, nothing to prevent Henry of France, but groundless fear of his rival, from sending to England the small force necessary to keep Jane upon the throne and defeat Mary. But time-serving cowardice ruled over all. The edifice of Northumberland's ambition crumbled like a house of cards under the weight of his unpopularity alone, and when Mary the victorious entered into the enjoyment of her birthright, the Frenchman who had plotted and intrigued against her in secret, vied with the imperial ambassadors who had stood by, unsympathetic in the hour of her trial, in their professions of devotion to her and her cause. The people of London, overwhelmingly Protestant as they were, greeted the Queen with effusion and had few words of pity for poor Jane, not because they loved the old observance but because they dreaded the French, and hated Northumberland the tyrannous and unjust servant of France. In the country districts, too, where Catholicism was strong, the enthusiasm for Mary was not so much religious, for all the people wanted was quiet and some measure of prosperity, as expressive of joy at the hope of a return to the national policy of cordial relations with the sovereign of Flanders, which in past times had ensured English commerce from French depredations and the English coast from French menaces, with freedom from the arrogant minister who had harassed every English interest and had reduced to ruin all classes in the country.

The unhappy Jane, a straw upon the rushing torrent, was not raised to her sad eminence that the Protestant faith might prevail, though that might have been one of the results of her rule, nor was she cast down because Catholicism was triumphant, but because the policy which her dictator, Northumberland, represented was unpopular at the time of Edward's death, and the English sense of justice rebelled at the usurpation and its contriver. Mary, in addition to her inherent right to the succession, which was her strong point, had only her own boldness and tenacity to thank for the success which she achieved. The Emperor, notwithstanding all his sympathy and the enormous importance[xxix] to him of her success, did nothing for her until she was independent of him, and only promised her armed aid then in case the French should attempt to overthrow her by force.

Northumberland fell, not because the country at large and London above all, was yearning for the re-submission of England to the Pope, but because the eighteen months of his unchecked dictatorship had made him detested, and because he overrated the boldness and magnanimity of the King of France. The English public, by instinct perhaps more than by reason, believed in the ideal policy of Henry VII: that of dexterously balancing English friendship between the rival continental powers, making the best market possible for her moral support, keeping at peace herself and adhering mostly to the more prosperous side without fighting for either. Such a policy required statesmanship of the highest order, and Elizabeth alone was entirely successful in carrying it out. Somerset and Northumberland both failed because they were unequal to it. Each of them took the minister's view rather than that of a monarch. They were party leaders, both of them, and incapable of adopting the view above party considerations which marks the successful sovereign. They pledged themselves too deeply to the respective foreign alliances traditional with their parties; and in both cases, as a penetrating statesman would have foreseen, their allies failed them at the critical moment.

Mary's tragical fate was the result of a similar short-sighted policy. When she determined against the wishes of her people and the advice of her wisest councillors, Catholics to a man, to hand herself and her country, body and soul, over to Spanish interests, she ceased to be a true national sovereign; the nice balance upon which England's prosperity depended was lost, the love and devotion of the people turned to cold distrust, and failure and a broken heart were the result. Not until Elizabeth came with her keen wit and her consummate mastery of the resources of chicanery was England placed and kept firmly again upon the road to greatness which had been traced for her by the first Tudor sovereign.

MARTIN HUME

THE NINE DAYS' QUEEN

CHAPTER I
BRADGATE HALL AND THE GREYS OF GROBY

There is no more picturesque spot in England than Bradgate Old Manor, the birthplace of Lady Jane Grey. It stands in a sequestered corner, about three miles from the town of Leicester, amid arid slate hillocks, which slope down to the fertile valleys at their feet. In Leland's *Perambulations through England*, a survey of the kingdom undertaken by command of Henry VIII, Bradgate is described as possessing "a fair parke and a lodge lately built there by the Lorde Thomas Grey, Marquise of Dorsete, father of Henry, that is now Marquise. There is a faire and plentiful spring of water brought by Master Brok as a man would judge agyne the hills through the lodge and thereby it driveth a mylle." He also informs us that "there remain few tokens of the old castelle," which leads us to believe that at the time of Lady Jane Grey's birth Bradgate was a comparatively new house. The ruins show that the mansion was built of red brick and in that severe but elegant form of architecture known as the "Tudor style." Worthy old Leland goes on to say that Jane's paternal grandfather added "two lofty towers at the front of the house, one on either side of the principal doorway." These are still remaining.

In Tudor times the park was very extensive and "marched with the forest of Chartley, which was full twenty-five miles in circumference, watered by the river Sore and teeming with game." Another ancient writer tells us, in the quaint language of his day, that "here a wren and squirrel might hop from tree to tree for six miles, and in summer time a traveller could2 journey from Beaumanoir to Burden, a good twelve miles, without seeing the sun." The wealth of luxuriant vegetation in the old park, the clear and running brooks, that babble through the sequestered woods, and the beautifully sloping open spaces, dotted with venerable and curiously pollarded oaks, make up a scene of sylvan charm peculiarly English. Here cultivation has not, as so often on the Continent, disfigured Nature, but the park retains the wild beauty of its luxuriant elms and beeches that rise in native grandeur from amidst a wilderness of bracken, fern, and flags, to cast their shadows over heather-grown hillocks. On the summit of one of the loftiest of these still stands the ruined palace that was the birthplace of Lady Jane Grey. The approaches to Bradgate are beautiful indeed, especially the pathway winding round by the old church along the banks of a trout-stream, which rises in the neighbourhood of the Priory of Ulverscroft, famous for the beauty of its lofty tower. When Jane Grey was born, this Priory had been very recently suppressed, and the people were lamenting the departure of the monks, who, during the hard winter of 1528, had fed six hundred starving peasants.

Bradgate Manor House was standing as late as 1608, but after that date it fell into gradual decay. Not much is now left of the original structure, but its outlines can still be traced; and the walls of the great hall and the chapel are nearly intact. A late Lord Stamford and Warrington roofed and restored the old chapel, which contains a fine monument to that Henry Grey whose signature may be seen on the warrant for the execution of Charles I.

A careful observation of the irregularities of the soil reveals traces of a tilt-yard and of garden terraces; but all is now overgrown by Spanish chestnut trees, wild flowers, nettles, and brambles. The gardens were once considered amongst the finest in England, Lord Dorset taking great pride in the cultivation of all the fruits, herbs, and flowers then grown in Northern Europe. The parterres and terraces were formal, and there was a large fish-pond full of golden carp and water lilies. Lady Jane Grey must often have played in these stately avenues, and there is a legend that once, as a little girl, she toppled into the tank and was nearly drowned—a less hideous fate than that which was to befall her in her seventeenth year.

3

"This was thy home, then, gentle Jane! This thy green solitude; and here At evening, from thy gleaming pane, Thine eyes oft watched the dappled deer (Whilst the soft sun was in its wane) Browsing beside the brooklet clear. The brook yet runs, the sun sets now, The deer still browseth—where art thou?"

These sentimental lines were written in the eighteenth century, when deer still browsed in Bradgate Park, whence they have long since departed. Many curious traditions concerning Lady Jane are even now current among the local peasantry. Some believe that on St. Sylvester's night (31st December) a coach drawn by four black horses halts at the door of the old mansion. It contains the headless form of the murdered Lady Jane. After a brief halt it drives away again into the mist. Then again, certain strange3 stunted oaks are shown, trees which the woodmen pollarded when they heard that the fair girl had been beheaded. The pathetic memories of the great tragedy, reaching down four slow centuries, prove how keenly its awful reality was felt by the poorer folk at Bradgate, who, no doubt, had good cause to love the "gentle Jane."

The Manor of Bradgate was settled upon the Lady Frances Brandon, Henry VIII's niece, when she espoused Henry Grey. It had been inherited by the Greys of Groby, Lady Jane's paternal ancestors, from Rollo, or Fulbert, said to have been chamberlain to Robert, Duke of Normandy, who gave him the Castle of Croy in Picardy, the ruins of which are still to be seen not far from Montreuil-sur-Mer. It was hence he derived the surname of de Croy, afterwards anglicised to de Grey. This Rollo accompanied William the Conqueror into England, and was settled, soon after the Conquest, at Rotherfield, in Oxfordshire. The first of the family to be noticed by Dugdale is Henry de Grey, to whom Richard I granted the Manor of4 Grey's Thurrock, in Essex, which grant was confirmed by King John in the first year of his reign. The descendant of this nobleman, Edward de Grey, was summoned to Parliament in 1488 in right of his wife's barony of Ferrers of Groby, and his son John, afterwards Earl Rivers, who was slain in the battle of St. Albans, married the beautiful daughter of Sir John Woodville, subsequently the Queen of Edward IV. Bradgate is thus associated with two of the most unfortunate of England's Queens: Elizabeth Woodville, who passed much of her life in its leafy glades; and Lady Jane Grey, who first saw the light in the stately red brick Manor House of which the crumbling ruins are now so beautiful in their decay.

Jane Grey's grandfather, Thomas, the eldest son of Elizabeth Woodville, was summoned to Parliament on the 17th October 1509 as Lord Ferrers of Groby, his mother's barony, and to the second Parliament in 1511 as Marquess of Dorset. He was a man of great note. In the third year of Henry VIII's reign he had charge of the army of 10,000 men sent into Spain to assist the forces invading Guyenne under the Emperor Ferdinand. This force returned to England without doing service. We next hear of the Marquess figuring at the jousts with Charles Brandon, Duke of Suffolk, Lady Jane's maternal grandfather, on the occasion of the latter's adventurous journey to France to bring back Mary Tudor, widow of Louis XII of France, whom he subsequently married. The Marquess was also sent to Calais to attend Charles V to England; indeed, he was very conspicuous throughout the early years of Henry's reign. King Hal paid him the compliment of calling him "that honest and good man"—a title which he thought he richly deserved, since he signed the celebrated letter to Pope Clement VII touching the King's divorce. He died in 1530, and was succeeded by his eldest son, Henry, Lady Jane's father. The inheritance of this nobleman included the Marquisate of Dorset and the baronies of Ferrers,4 Grey, Astley, Boneville, and Harrington, besides vast estates in Leicestershire and other parts of England. Henry Grey, though his portraits show him to have5 been a very good-looking man, did not enjoy a good contemporary reputation for ability or strength of character. During the brief reign of Edward VI he became the patron of the Swiss Reformers and was adulated by Bullinger and Hill. His name will be found attached to many of Henry VIII's anti-papal decrees, and so long as that monarch lived, he was a staunch "Henryite" or schismatic, professing belief in all the doctrines of Rome save and except papal supremacy. In 1531, when the clergy were threatened with *præmunire* and mulcted in a fine, as a punishment for their too close attention to pontifical interests, young Henry of Dorset, who had just come to his own, displayed great energy in carrying out the King's wishes and supporting his attempt to get himself acknowledged supreme head of the English Church. He also evinced considerable courage in connection with Henry VIII's resistance to the excommunication of the Pope, launched against him after his marriage with Anne Boleyn. Such zeal in his sovereign's service undoubtedly led to his advancement and paved the way to his marriage with the King's niece, the Lady Frances Brandon. He may have owed much to the counsels and influence of Cromwell, to whom he carried a letter of introduction from his mother,5 when he first went to London as a lad of seventeen, immediately after his father's decease. The Dowager recommended her son very earnestly to "Master Cromwell," pleaded his youth, and besought that worthy, then all-powerful, not to take heed of certain ill-natured reports concerning alleged wilful damage to the priory buildings of Tylsey, where she was then residing.5

The good lady couches her letter in very humble terms, but does not enlighten us fully about the nature of the "damage" to which she refers, or by whom it was done. She seems, at any rate, to be in a terrible fright lest the tale should injure her son's prospects with the all-powerful Chancellor. Some little time afterwards the Marchioness wrote another letter to Cromwell complaining of her son's undutiful behaviour to her. It is dated from the "House of Our Lady's Passyon"6 (the Priory of Tylsey), and begins:—

6

"My Lorde,—I beseeche you to be my good lorde, consyderyng me a poor wydo, so unkyndly and extreymly escheated by my son."

This curious epistle, now in the British Museum, is much defaced and in parts illegible. The name of the person to whom it is addressed is undecipherable, but, taken in conjunction with two other letters previously addressed to Cromwell by the same correspondent, there can be little doubt as to its destination. Her son had evidently withheld some property intended for her under her husband's will. Whether he mended his manners and paid her the money, we know not; but as the Dowager is occasionally mentioned as attending Court functions in company with her daughter-in-law, it seems probable that the ultimate issue of the difficulty, whatever it was, was satisfactory to her.

Margaret, Dowager Lady Dorset, became one of the greatest ladies of the Court in the latter years of the reign of Henry VII and during a part of that of Henry VIII. She was in much request, it seems, at royal christenings, for not only was she specially invited to that of Mary Tudor, afterwards Queen Mary I, but she enjoyed the signal honour of carrying the infant Elizabeth to the font. She was invited to perform a like office at the baptism of Edward VI, but this time she was unable to be present, and wrote to make her loyal excuses, pleading that some of her household at Croydon had been attacked by the "sweating sickness." It is probable that she had no desire to attend, for she had been the intimate friend of Anne Boleyn, and could hardly have felt kindly towards Jane Seymour.7 Her place was filled by the Marchioness of Exeter, who eventually, after the execution of her luckless husband, was sent to the Tower on a flimsy charge of treason, and kept there until Mary I's time.8

A singular point in the history of Jane Grey's forbears is that her father, in his hot haste to marry into the royal7 family, set aside, without the slightest scruple, his legitimate wife, Lady Katherine Fitzalan, daughter of the Earl of Arundel. Some writers say he was simply "contracted," not married, to this lady, who never demanded her marriage rights, but retired into a dignified obscurity. None the less her family resented the affront offered their kinswoman, and it was Thomas, Earl of Arundel, this discarded lady's brother, who acted as Dorset's Nemesis, and at last betrayed him into the hands of his enemies.

Lady Jane Grey's maternal grandfather was, as he wrote himself in the famous quatrain referring to his marriage with the King's sister, descended from "cloth of frieze." He was the grandson of a London mercer who had married a lady allied to the great houses of Nevill, Fitzalan and Howard, and his father had fought and fallen at Bosworth Field in the cause of Henry VII. In recognition of his services, Henry attached young Charles Brandon to the person of his younger son, Prince Henry, who was of similar age to himself. Thus began a friendship which was only severed by death. In appearance the Prince and his comrade were singularly alike: both were tall and stalwart, both with red hair and fair complexions, and they were equally skilful and agile in sport and manly pastimes. Charles was more intellectually gifted than Henry, but there was little to choose between them as regards their execrable views of moral responsibilities and their laxity in respect of their marriage vows.

As this last characteristic of Charles Brandon, Duke of Suffolk, touches somewhat upon the legitimacy of Lady Jane Grey's descent, a short summary of his matrimonial vagaries may be pardoned here. He was contracted in marriage early in life to Anne Browne, a daughter of Sir Anthony Browne, Governor of Calais, by his wife Lady Lucy Nevill, daughter of George Nevill, Duke of Bedford, brother of Richard, Earl of Warwick, "the King maker." In 1513 he was bold enough to flirt most outrageously with, and seek in marriage, one of the greatest ladies in Europe, Margaret of Austria, the widowed Duchess of Savoy, aunt of the Emperor Charles V. But though Margaret fell in love with him, such a match was soon seen to be impossible, even by the lady herself, and Brandon came out of the affair most ungallantly. For this or some other reason never clearly[8] explained, Brandon set aside his contract with Anne Browne, notwithstanding that by the laws of the period it was considered as binding as the completed marriage ceremony. We next learn that a probable reason for his unchivalrous conduct was a chance that suddenly offered itself to him of marrying the Lady Margaret, the rich widow of Sir John Mortimer of Essex. Charles and his mature consort—there was a difference of nearly thirty years between them—did not abide long together, for he presently endeavoured to annul this marriage on a plea of consanguinity, the Lady Margaret being sister to the mother of his neglected bride, Anne Browne, and consequently her aunt, a complication which surely ought to have been discovered at an earlier stage of the proceedings. Having settled this matter for the time being to his own, but certainly not to the lady's, satisfaction, he remarried his discarded wife, Anne Browne, in the presence of a great concourse of relations and friends. By this lady he had two daughters: Mary, who became the wife of Lord Mounteagle; and Anne, who married a connection of the Greys, Viscount Powis. Their mother died in 1515, and Brandon soon afterwards contracted himself in matrimony with the Lady Elizabeth Grey, daughter and heiress of Viscount de Lisle. Whether through the interference of Lady Mortimer or not it is impossible to say, but it is certain that Lady de Lisle refused to carry out her side of the contract, and the match was broken off. Brandon, with the consent of Henry VIII, filched from the poor lady her title of Lisle, which he forthwith assumed. In due time the lady gave her hand to Edmund Dudley, father of the fateful Duke of Northumberland. It was probably when in France, and in attendance upon King Henry, at the time of the negotiations for the marriage of the King's youngest and most beautiful sister, Mary, to the prematurely aged Louis XII, King of France, a hideous victim to elephantiasis, that Charles made so strong an impression upon that ardent Tudor princess that she swore by all the saints that she would not wed the French King unless it was thoroughly understood she was to marry whom she chose after his death, which took place within eighteen months of the marriage. The romantic story of how Brandon, now created Duke of Suffolk, wooed and married the royal widow within a fortnight of the King's[9] death, and whilst she still wore the white widow's weeds of a French King's Consort, is too well known to need recapitulation here, nor need we enter into the details of the gorgeous ceremonies of remarriage that took place at Greenwich, in the presence of King Henry, Queen Katherine of Aragon, and their Court, soon after Mary and Suffolk had landed in England. The Duke of Suffolk took his bride to spend their honeymoon in his magnificent mansion in Southwark, known as Suffolk Place, which he had recently inherited by the death of his uncle, Sir Thomas Brandon. It must have been about this time that the friends of the Lady Mortimer, and probably that lady herself, began to spread rumours abroad that made both Charles and his consort anxious as to the validity of their marriage and the legitimacy of their offspring. Indeed, even at the time of his clandestine wedding in the Chapel of the Hôtel de Cluny (now incorporated in the Museum of that name), he had felt very uneasy about the matter, and, foreseeing his peril, wrote to Wolsey, beseeching his assistance and advice on a matter of such vital importance, which, however, was not decided so easily as Charles expected. It was not until 1528 that Wolsey dispatched a somewhat garbled account of the matter to Pope Clement VII, then in exile at Orvieto, where he received Cardinal Campeggio and the English envoys who came to him with the first negotiations for the divorce of Henry VIII from Katherine of Aragon. Trusting in the evidence which Wolsey sent him, the Pope, by a special Bull (dated 12th May 1528), annulled the marriage of Brandon with the Lady Mortimer, on the plea of consanguinity, and at the same time declared valid that of her niece, Anne Browne, and legitimized her two children. The Bull further stated that Lady Mortimer and her friends were "liable to ecclesiastical censure if they made any attempt to invalidate the decree" making valid Brandon's marriage to Anne Browne and Mary Tudor. The importance of this decree, which was first read out to the people in Norwich Cathedral in 1529 by Bishop Nyx, can readily be imagined when we remember that it was not delivered until after the Queen-Duchess had given birth to two children. Her only son, the Earl of Lincoln, died in infancy, and the Lady Frances became in due time the Marchioness of Dorset and mother of Lady Jane Grey. On10 the other hand, the legitimacy of the Lady Eleanor Brandon, the younger daughter, who was born after the publication of the papal decree, was never disputed, and moreover, before she entered upon her sorrowful career, the Lady Mortimer was dead. That considerable doubt was entertained as to the validity of Brandon's marriage with the Queen-Dowager is proved by a variety of facts too numerous to be detailed, but one of which is very significant. Late in the first half of Queen Elizabeth's reign, the validity of the claims of the Lady Mounteagle and her sister, the children of Brandon and Anne Browne, to be considered legitimate, was ventilated in the Court of Arches, and after much deliberation confirmed. Although the legitimacy of these ladies, both of whom were long since deceased at the time of this trial, had nothing to do with the legal position of Mary Tudor as the wife of the Duke of Suffolk, it was none the less an indirect test of the right to the throne of her granddaughters, the Ladies Katherine and Mary Grey.

From these briefly resumed facts it is not difficult to understand that although King Henry VIII highly approved of his bosom friend's conduct, his subjects held Charles to be an arrant rascal. His treatment of his beautiful royal wife was on a par with his low conception of his moral obligations. He neglected her, spent her money, and lived openly with a notorious woman known as Mrs. Eleanor Brandon, by whom he had an illegitimate son, Charles, who is said to have been the well-known jeweller to Queen Elizabeth, and whose son, or grandson, Gregory Brandon, was, according to tradition, the headsman who executed Charles I.

Lady Jane's grandmother, Mary Tudor, was a most amiable and long-suffering princess, who after a somewhat secluded life in Southwark withdrew to Westhorpe Hall. Here she died on 24th June 1533. Her two daughters—the Lady Frances, who had recently married the Marquess of Dorset; and the Lady Eleanor, soon to be the bride of Henry, Lord Clifford, eldest son of the Earl of Cumberland—were with her at the time of her death, but the Duke was absent in London, and so too was the Marquess of Dorset, her son-in-law, attending at the coronation of Anne Boleyn. The Queen-Duchess was interred in Bury St. Edmunds, Henry VIII and Suffolk paying the11 expenses of a gorgeous alabaster monument to her memory, "full of little saints and angels," which was destroyed soon after, during the wreck of the glorious Abbey Church at the time of the suppression of the monasteries. The remains of the Queen were then removed to the parish church, where they still rest, a marble tablet put up in the early nineteenth century being the only memorial of Mary Tudor, Dowager Queen of France and Duchess of Suffolk.

Within three months of the Queen's death (September 1533) Suffolk married a fifth wife, the Lady Katherine Willoughby d'Eresby, who, it seems, was his ward and only fifteen years old. She was a great heiress, and what made her marriage all the more singular was the fact that she was a daughter of that Doña Maria de Sarmiento who, as Lady Willoughby, was the friend and attendant of Queen Katherine of Aragon. It must also be remembered that Queen Katherine had no more bitter enemy than Suffolk. This Duchess developed into a very pretty woman, of great wit and character, and a staunch supporter of the doctrines of the Reformation.

The Lady Frances Brandon was born at Hatfield, then a palace of the Bishop of Salisbury, who had afforded her mother hospitality; for it seems that the Queen-Duchess was obliged to halt here, for reasons easily understood, on her way to Walsingham Priory, whither she was bound on a pilgrimage. There is still extant a very curious account of the baptism of the Lady Frances in the parish church of Hatfield, which was hung with garlands for the occasion. The Lady Anne[9] Boleyn, aunt of the ill-fated Queen Anne of that ilk, stood proxy for Queen Katherine of Aragon as sponsor.

In 1533–4 the Lady Frances was married, notwithstanding his afore-mentioned "contract" to the Lady Fitzalan, to Henry Grey, Marquess of Dorset. The wedding took place at Suffolk Place, Southwark, and the religious ceremony in the Church of St. Saviour, now the cathedral of the new diocese. No very great pains seem to have been taken with[12] the lady's education, except in the matter of what we should call "sports," in which, it seems, she was very proficient.

The Lady Frances was a handsome woman, however, but somewhat spiteful and wholly unscrupulous. In a well-known portrait, dated after her second marriage, she is represented as a buxom, fair-haired, well-featured matron, with a very sinister expression in her light grey eyes. Her eldest child was a son who died of the plague when a baby, and the three children who survived were all girls—the Ladies Jane, Katherine, and Mary Grey. Lady Jane Grey, as we shall see, had little cause to feel deep affection for either of her parents, but least of all for her mother. The Lady Frances seems to have been cast, so far as her heart went, in a mould of iron. Even the bloody deaths of her husband and her eldest daughter, and the wretchedly precarious existence of her two remaining children, did not affect her buoyant spirits, since she enjoyed her life to the end. It would be difficult to define her religious opinions. She was a schismatic under Henry VIII, and under Edward VI she appeared a zealous Protestant and so intimate with the famous Reformer Bucer that when he died she petitioned Cranmer to obtain a pension for his widow. She became a pious Papist in Queen Mary's time, and died a prominent member of the Church of England as by law established, under Elizabeth.

The Lady Eleanor Brandon, Henry VIII's niece and Lady Jane Grey's only maternal aunt, married, as we have said, Henry, Lord Clifford, to whom she was united in 1537 at the Duke of Suffolk's palace in Southwark. The Lady Eleanor gave birth to two sons and a daughter. At the time of the Pilgrimage of Grace (in 1536) she was staying at Bolton Abbey, which Henry VIII, after confiscating it from the Church, had presented to Lord Clifford; and had it not been for the chivalry and bravery of Christopher Aske, the rebel leader's brother, she would have suffered at the hands of the infuriated "pilgrims." By dint of a bold night ride, Aske aided Lady Eleanor to fly from Bolton Abbey and reach a place of safety. In 1542 her husband succeeded to the Earldom of Cumberland on the death of his father, and five years later (November 1547) Lady Eleanor passed away at Brougham Castle and was laid to rest in Skipton Church.

HENRY GREY, DUKE OF SUFFOLK

FROM THE PAINTING BY JOANNES CORVUS IN THE NATIONAL PORTRAIT GALLERY

13 It will be seen by this rapid sketch of her forbears on both sides that Lady Jane Grey might, without exciting surprise, have developed a character strongly sensual and unscrupulous. That she did not do so, apart from the fact that her early death perhaps prevented the full development of her character at all, was probably owing to the rigid and severe nature of the education to which she was subjected. The influence of Erasmus and the fashion of the newly revived classical learning had in the childhood of Jane Grey firmly seized upon the higher classes of England; and the ladies of royal and noble birth, schooled in the stern pietism of *The Instruction of a Christian Woman* of Luis Vives, which they all studied in Latin or in English, and, steeped in the classic moralities, they became prim and self-suppressed in expression and behaviour. It is likely enough, indeed, that in most cases this prudishness of attitude was but skin deep; but in the case of the hapless Jane, who was little more than a child when she was sacrificed, no other

impression of her personality than this was left upon the world. We may picture the tiny demure maiden pacing the green alleys and smooth sward of Bradgate, with her Latin books and her exalted religious meditations, a fervent mystic, with no knowledge of the great world of greed, ambition, and lust, of which she, poor child, was doomed to be the innocent victim.

CHAPTER II
BIRTH AND EDUCATION

Lady Jane Grey was born at Bradgate Old Manor10 in October 1537, most probably in the first days of the month, for Prince Edward, her cousin, came into the world on the 12th,11 St. Edward's Eve, and three days later Henry, Marquess of Dorset, attended the royal christening, which he would scarcely have done if his own wife, a member of the royal family, had not been safely delivered. His15 presence in London can be traced in the State Papers from the date of Prince Edward's birth until the first week in November. Lady Jane's christening took place, as was then the custom, within forty-eight hours of her birth, in the parish church, with all the ancient rites. Some writers state that the babe was carried to the font by her grandmother, the Dowager Marchioness; but this good lady, as we have already seen, was unable at the time to leave her sick household at Croydon. She sent her new granddaughter a rich bowl with a chiselled cover. It was the custom at that time, when a baptism took place, for the whole family, godfathers and godmothers and guests, to walk in procession from the mansion to the church. As is still the case in Catholic countries, the number of sponsors in pre-Reformation times was unlimited. All these worthy people brought gifts of more or less value, according to the nearness of their kinship and the length of their purses. The Marquess, if he was present, would certainly have worn his robes of state and "carried the salt." At the church door the christening company was met by the clergy, and after a short prayer the child was named.12 The officiating priest on this occasion was either Mr. Harding, then chaplain at Bradgate, or else Mr. Cook, Rector of the parish. After being named, the child was carried to the font, which stood in the middle of the church under an extinguisher-like canopy, richly carved and painted, which pulled up and down, so as to keep the holy water clean. In those days the back of the head and the heels of the infant were immersed in the water,13 the present ceremony of sprinkling having only been introduced into this country from Geneva by the Reformers during Elizabeth's reign. The infant was also anointed with chrism on the back and breast, a very ancient ceremony, the abolition of which caused considerable controversy and some persecution in the reign of Henry VIII. This anointing, or unction, which was performed within the sacred edifice, was16 followed by the presentation of the gifts of the various sponsors.14 Abundant hospitality in the shape of sweet wafers, comfits, spiced wine, or hippocras was dispensed in the porch, not only to the invited company, but to the promiscuous village crowd that elected to attend the function; and at last the procession, with the infant wrapped in a sort of shawl of rich brocade, returned to the mansion, where a dinner was served to the guests and to the members of the household.

The life of an English child in olden times, especially in the upper classes, was by no means the ideal existence it has now become. A careful study of contemporary records proves that the barbarous and filthy system of swathing or "swaddling" an infant was almost universally practised. We may take it for granted that the baby Jane Grey was swathed or "swaddled" according to the prevailing English fashion, from her armpits to her knees, and was thus able at all events to move her tiny hands and feet, a privilege denied her infant contemporaries on the Continent. So late as 1684, Madame de Maintenon, writing to Madame de Présné, who had just been delivered of a son, beseeches her to "adopt the English method of allowing her infant's limbs free play," and stigmatises the French custom of "tight swaddling" as "abominably dirty and unhealthy."

The Lady Frances certainly did not nurse her own baby; it would have been considered most indecent for a woman of her rank to suckle her offspring. A foster-mother was engaged, and it is likely enough that the good woman who supplied little Jane Grey with the sustenance nature had intended her to derive from her parent, was that Mrs. Ellen who, seventeen years later, attended her beloved foster-child on the scaffold.

In her eighteenth month the child was weaned, and this was attended by some considerable ceremony. In the morning Mass was said in the presence of the whole family, including the foster-mother and the child, who was blessed with holy water. This finished, the company returned in procession to the hall and forthwith sat down to a copious banquet.

17 The archives of Sudeley Castle contain an interesting description of an aristocratic nursery in the first half of the sixteenth century. Queen Katherine Parr, having married Admiral Lord Thomas Seymour, lived at Sudeley, where she died in September 1548, after giving birth to a child, for whom was provided an apartment very elaborately furnished with tapestry, and containing everything a modern infant of the highest rank could possibly want, all in silver or pewter, and, moreover, a "chair of state" hung with cloth of gold.

The Lady Frances's nursery was, no doubt, fitted up quite as luxuriously as that prepared for the infant of Queen Katherine Parr; but no inventory of its contents has been handed down to us. Nearly all the toys commonly used in England at this period were made either in France or Holland, and closely resembled those grotesque playthings which were our grandparents' delight: wooden dolls with roughly painted heads and jointed limbs, hobby horses, hoops, and even toy soldiers mounted on movable slides. Jane must have had an abundance of these nursery treasures, besides an oaken cradle with rockers and also a sort of little perambulator, wherein she might be carried to take the air in the park and gardens. She had a complete household, consisting of Mrs. Ellen, two under-nurses, a governess, two waiting women, and two footmen. Sometimes, but very rarely, the voice of nature may have prompted her mother and father to play with her and enjoy those exquisite moments of purest love common alike to prince and peasant. Her babyhood may have been fairly happy, but when that ended, the stern training which prevailed in every aristocratic family of the period began in all its severity: long prayers, tedious lessons, and that terrible "cramming" system which as often as not engendered premature physical decline and even imbecility. The tiny princess, from her third year upwards, was dressed like a little old lady, in miniature reproduction of her mother, coif and all complete, an exceedingly irksome garb for so very small a child. Even when full-grown, Jane, like her sister Katherine, was of very diminutive stature; and their youngest sister, Mary, was an actual dwarf, "not bigger, when over thirty, than a child of ten."

18 The greater part of the Lady Jane's15 infancy was spent at Bradgate with her little sisters—Katherine, two years her junior; and Mary, six years younger than herself. A Mrs. Ashly, sister or sister-in-law to the Mrs. Ashly, or Astley, who acted in the same capacity to Princess Elizabeth, was appointed to attend as governess upon Jane and her sisters; but of this lady little is known, whereas Elizabeth's governess is, of course, frequently mentioned as a woman of great importance. It was evidently not until the Lady Jane had been named in Henry VIII's will as a possible successor to his throne that any particular attention was paid to her instruction, and then only for purely political purposes. Her two sisters received but an ordinary education, and Jane herself must have been between nine and ten years of age when she was handed over to Queen Katherine Parr to begin her more important studies. No doubt the Dorsets secretly intended their eldest daughter to become Edward VI's consort and to rule the kingdom through her, and her education therefore became a matter of great importance to them, as they wished her to be thoroughly equipped to hold the high station they desired her to occupy. In religion she was to be exceedingly Protestant, but in social matters her training was most varied, including music and classical and modern languages, even Hebrew and, if we may credit some of her enthusiastic eulogists, Chaldee!!

The royal birth of the Marchioness of Dorset and the great wealth of her lord placed their family in a very exceptional position in the county. Here, as also in London, they maintained semi-regal state. No one could compete with them, and although they received much company, especially at Christmas time, they rarely mixed with their neighbours, and when they did so condescend, they were invariably received with all the ceremony due to royalty. When, for instance, the Marquess of Dorset and his lady visited Leicester, they were entertained with great ceremony. In the archives of that city for 1540 there is a charge of "two shillings and sixpence for strawberries and wine for my Lady Marchioness's[19] Grace, for Mistress Mayoress and her sisters." Also, on the occasion of another visit, "Four shillings" were paid "to the pothicary for making a gallon of Ippocras,[16] that was given to my Lady's Grace, Mistress Mayoress and her sisters, and to the wives of the Aldermen of Leicester, who gave the said ladies, moreover, wafers, apples, pears, and walnuts at the same time." From another record, of the city of Lincoln, we learn that the Dorset family when on its way to London frequently put up at the White Hall Inn for the night, their expenses being paid by the town. There is also an entry specifying the expenses for entertaining the Lady Jane Grey when on her way to London and on her return journeys through Leicester to Bradgate in 1548 and 1551.

There was much in the stately mode of life led by our great aristocracy in the sixteenth century which has not even now passed altogether out of fashion. At certain seasons of the year, it appears, the family resided in the main building of the mansion and kept up a state almost equal in magnificence to that of a royal Court. A great number of servants—as many as eighty or a hundred—were maintained, and these, being very ignorant, often formed a rather disorderly crew. They received very small wages; but as they wore brilliant liveries, and served as an escort to their masters when they went abroad, they made a highly picturesque appearance. Few people, even in the upper circles of society, could read or write with ease; and as there were no newspapers and scarcely any books, no correspondence, and but few visits to fill up leisure time, the men's sports were mainly those of the field, so that large hunting and hawking parties were the general order of the day. The ladies were frequently invited to share these pursuits; and the Lady Frances was well known in Leicestershire in her day as a great huntress and a skilful archeress.

[20] Hospitality, if barbaric, was none the less sumptuous. Tablecloths and napkins were already in use, and "damask" was pretty generally to be seen in the houses of the wealthy; while the plate belonging to the great nobility was not only very costly, but exceedingly artistic in design. Then as now, it was the custom to pass the winter months in the country and the summer in London. During the hunting season Bradgate was thrown open to a throng of guests, and since the mistress of the house was niece to the reigning sovereign, many of these were of princely rank, including Princess Mary, who was on very friendly terms with her cousin Frances and her children. It is not at all unlikely that when the family gathered in the great hall of an evening, dances, masques, and other pastimes of a more boisterous kind, described as "romps and jigs," were indulged in. On occasion, players were summoned from London, and displayed their skill in representing those rough and unformed plays which delighted our ancestors until the more shapely Elizabethan drama came into being.[17]

People rose and retired to rest earlier in Tudor days than we do now, especially in summer, when breakfast was served as early as six o'clock, dinner at ten, and supper at five. Tea and coffee were as yet undiscovered, and light home-brewed ale was the usual breakfast beverage. Such very young ladies as Lady Jane Grey would be served at this meal with a cup of hot milk and sometimes with a sort of mead, or barley water, heated and spiced. During Lent breakfast consisted of bread, with salt fish, ling, turbot and eels, fresh whitings, sprats, beer and wine. At other seasons there were chines of beef, roast breast of mutton or boiled mutton, butter, cooked eggs, custard, pies, jellies, etc., as well as chickens, ducks, swan, geese, and game.[18] Dinner came at noon, and it was customary in large country houses to close the gates while the whole establishment sat down, according to rank, in the great hall. Sometimes a slight alteration was made, two tables being set in the dining-room, at the first[21] of which sat the lord and his family, with such titled guests as they might be entertaining, while the second was occupied by "knights and honourable gentlemen." In such a case the tables in the great hall were generally three, the first for the steward, comptroller, secretary, master of the house, master of the fish-ponds, the tutor—if one was attached to the family—and such gentlemen as happened to be under the degree of a knight. In a very large household it frequently happened that as many as a hundred and fifty or two hundred people would sit down to eat at one and the same time, but in most castles, halls, and manors the ladies of the family, excepting on state occasions, ate apart from the men, a separate table being laid for them, and for the chaplain, in the ladies' chamber, while two others were laid in the housekeeper's room for the ladies' women. The Lady Frances usually partook of her dinner in solitary state, waited upon by young gentlewomen and, when they were old enough to do so, by her two elder daughters, who stood on either side of her until she had finished, when they in their turn sat down and were served by gentlewomen. In their infancy, the children, attended by their nurses and gentlemen and women, dined with the housekeeper in her chamber.

All meals were somewhat disorderly, for, forks not being in general use, it was the custom for the gentlemen to pick the daintiest scraps out of the common dish with the tips of their fingers, and place them gallantly upon the platters of the ladies seated nearest them. It was considered ill-bred to lick one's fingers after this act of courtesy. Proper behaviour was to wipe them daintily upon a sort of napkin or serviette, sometimes, as in Japan, made of tissue paper.

Grace was said both before and after meals, and as most large houses had several chaplains and a choir for the service of the chapel, it was usual for one of the priests, accompanied by three or four of the choristers wearing their surplices, to enter the hall and solemnly chant the *Benedicite* or Grace, which until Edward VI's time invariably concluded with a petition for the release of the souls in Purgatory. It was considered impolite to talk during a repast unless addressed by the master or mistress of the feast. The chaplain was employed to read aloud either the Gospel of the day or a22 chapter from that enlivening work *The Martyrology*. Occasionally a minstrel was invited to sing an interesting ballad or tell a story; otherwise the clinking of the knives was the only sound heard during meals, which, however copious, were invariably dispatched with the utmost speed. In proportion to the amount of meat very little bread was consumed. "The English bolt their food in dead silence," remarked the Venetian Ambassador Giustiniani, "and, bread being dear, eat very sparingly of it. They throw their chicken bones under the table when they have sucked them clean."

When supper, a meal which corresponds with our late dinner, was over, evening prayers were said, and soon afterwards, on ordinary occasions, everybody retired to rest. It should be remembered that artificial light was exceedingly costly and inadequate, as indeed it remained until the beginning of the later half of the nineteenth century. Many who are still in the prime of life can remember the rush tallow dips made and used in old-fashioned country houses and farms in their childhood. In the sixteenth century these were the only lights to be had, except oil lamps and wax candles imported at immense expense from France and Italy, and only kindled on high days and holidays.19 Resin torches were burnt in the great hall; but many complained of the stench and smoke, so that an early departure to bed was not only wise but necessary.

It may perhaps be concluded that we who live at the beginning of the twentieth century would have found life in an English manor in Tudor days insufferably dull and monotonous. Yet there were compensations. Outdoor exercises were many and various. There was the tennis-court, bowls and quoits were much in vogue, and our forefathers practised many other excellent sports, some of which we might well revive. There was hawking, then in the zenith of its popularity;23 hunting, archery, slinging, mase or "prisoner's bars," wrestling, tennis, of which game Henry VIII was exceedingly fond; fivestool ball, football, and golf. Cricket does not seem to have been known, at all events under its present name; but there were a score or so of other popular games and sports, some of which, such as duck-hunting, dog-fighting, and cock-fighting, were exceedingly barbarous. The cruel sport of trying on horseback to pull off the greased head of a living duck or goose suspended by the legs from a cross beam was exceedingly popular at this time.20 Edward VI, in his *Journal*, mentions it in an entry dated 4th June 1550: "Sir Robert Dudley, third surviving son of the Earl of Warwick, was married this day to Sir John Robsart's daughter, after which marriage there were certain gentlemen on horseback that did strive who should first carry away a goose's head that was hanged alive on two cross-posts." Can we imagine the whole Court of England, King included, assisting at this childish and cruel spectacle?

The Marquess of Dorset and his family did not spend the whole year at Bradgate; political and social duties brought them a great deal to London, especially in the early spring and summer months. In London they inhabited a mansion at Westminster, not far from Whitehall Palace. The town residence of the Marquess of Dorset was not, as usually stated, situated in Grey's Inn. At no time did his branch of the family of Grey possess property in or near the Inn which bears their name; it belonged from a remote period to the house of Grey de Wilton, who sold it, in Edward IV's time, to the Carthusians of Sheen, from whom it was confiscated at the Dissolution and subsequently granted by the Crown for the purpose which it still serves. Thus Grey's Inn did not fall to Lady Frances, although she was presented by her uncle the King with nearly all the other property owned by the Carthusians in and around London. It has also been said that the Marquess of Dorset had a house in Salisbury Place, Fleet Street, but this is another popular error. This property passed to the *Earls* of Dorset in 1611 and is connected, not with Lady Jane and24 her family, but with many worthies of the seventeenth and eighteenth centuries. Henry, Marquess of Dorset, had his town residence on the Thames above Whitehall,21 precisely where stood, until quite recently, Dorset Place—the name by which the house was known in Lady Jane's time. After the execution of Suffolk it was seized by the Crown and eventually, in the last days of the sixteenth century, cut up into three separate houses, one of which was inhabited by John Locke the philosopher, who died in it. By a curious coincidence, Locke had previously lived at Salisbury Square. Dorset Place must have been a very large house; we know from contemporary evidence that it had a fine garden and a broad terrace overlooking the Thames. Here Lady Jane Grey certainly lived for a good many months of her life, and here she formed the acquaintance of the Reformers Bullinger and Ulmer, or ab Ulmis. She may also have lived for a time in yet another house owned by the Marquess, near the Temple, of which no trace now exists.

The Dorsets were in the habit, especially in the winter season, of paying country visits to their numerous relatives—to Princess Mary at Newhall; to the Lady Frances' stepmother, Katherine, Duchess of Suffolk, at Wollaton; to Dorset's sister, the Lady Audley, at Walden; to his orphan wards and cousins the Willoughbys, at Tylsey; and to Lady Jane's paternal grandmother, the Dowager Marchioness of Dorset, either at her house at Croydon or at Tylsey, where at one time she presided over the household of the young Willoughbys.

The entertainment of such important personages must often have been a doubtful pleasure to hosts of limited means, for they never stirred abroad without a numerous escort of male and female servants and a guard of thirty or forty retainers mounted on horseback and armed to the teeth. Carriages were but little used as yet, and people of quality had to journey from place to place on horseback, the elderly ladies being provided with the quaintest but most inconvenient and perilous of side saddles, while the young girls and children25 rode pillion either in front of or behind their nearest male relatives or some trusty yeoman. In cold or damp weather the ladies and children and their female attendants travelled in a huge and very heavy covered vehicle22 not unlike a Turkish *araba* or a modern omnibus in shape. This was furnished with leathern curtains and lined with mattresses and cushions, and could often contain as many as twelve persons, six on either seat facing each other. To protect themselves from the cold the ladies wore cloaks and vizors, or "safeguards."23 The first genuine statute for repairing roads dates only from

1668. Before that the roads were, like those of modern Turkey, universally execrable, and over them this ponderous vehicle, with its enormous wheels, moved at a snail's pace: it is not surprising that most people preferred the hackney, even in winter time. Yet in spite of all its inconveniences, this old-world fashion of travel was not without charm, especially in genial weather, when the passage of a lordly cavalcade added much to the life of our highways and verdant lanes and lent to the ever lovely English landscape a picturesqueness and a gaiety which modern civilisation can never hope to restore. On the other hand, delicate folk must have dreaded these excursions, and it is not surprising to learn that on one occasion, in 1550, after a ten hours' ride in very bad weather to Newhall, on a visit to Princess Mary, the Lady Jane was taken very ill, and kept her room for many days.

The Dissolution of the monasteries and the general troubles of the Church had no doubt greatly attenuated the quaintness of English life on the high roads by the time Jane had attained girlhood. No longer did the Lord Abbot or Prior, with his princely train of ecclesiastics on their gaily caparisoned horses and mules, pass through the leafy lanes on their way to pay visits of duty or ceremony. Lady Jane can never have seen the Abbot of Leicester, for instance, he who attended the death-bed of Wolsey, go forth with all his monks to pay his respects to the Prior of the rich house of Ulverston, for both abbeys were suppressed before she was a year old. She was26 not familiar with the begging friars, with their sacks and their jokes; and the pardoner, the palmer, and the pilgrim had also faded into the near past long before she began to toddle on the green slopes of Bradgate. Still she must have often witnessed the procession on Corpus Christi, when her own native village was enlivened by garlands of flowers and on every house front hung a linen sheet decked with bunches of bright flowers. She may even have walked with the rest of the children of high and low degree in the annual procession of Our Lady on Assumption Day, for throughout the reign of Henry VIII this festival was observed.

The roads were still full of colour in the summer months, with packmen and peddlers, troops of armed men—not unfrequently dragging along between them some poor wretch, tied by the wrists, to his fiery doom at Leicester or London—with travelling caravans, with itinerant mountebanks and jugglers, and occasionally with a troop of showmen hastening to exhibit dancing bears or learned dogs and pigs at some neighbouring village fair.

The suppression of the monasteries had a disastrous effect on travelling in Henry VIII's time, comparable only to what would happen nowadays if all the first-class hotels in the country were suddenly closed. The Marquess and Marchioness of Dorset, as they journeyed with their children from Bradgate to London, must have heartily regretted the hospitality they had enjoyed in their own young days at many a lordly abbey and wealthy priory now laid in ruins. The inns were picturesque enough, but none too luxurious; still the beds were generally comfortable, and the cooking, according to the taste of the day, was excellent. Conti, an Italian traveller who visited England some few years after Henry VIII's death, was much struck by the cleanliness of the parlours and the softness of the feather beds he met with in our country hostelries. The fare, too, he found abundant, and the wines, "sack," and beers often of superlative quality—facts to which Shakespeare has not failed to allude. The innkeepers were great gainers by the Dissolution, for such rich travellers as did not care to trouble their peers looked to them for board and lodging now that they were no longer able to put up at a religious house. We may be sure that the Dorsets and their people27 were familiar and welcome guests at all the chief inns along the roads they travelled.

Aylmer, who became Bishop of London in Elizabeth's time, is usually described as Lady Jane's earliest tutor. This is a patent error, for Aylmer, who was born in 1521, would have been far too young, in Jane's infancy, to be appointed tutor to the children of the Marquess of Dorset. It is more likely that Dr. Harding, who was chaplain at Bradgate when Jane was born, had the honour of teaching his patron's daughters their alphabet. He was reputed a learned man, and posed at one time as a staunch Protestant; but he resembled his employers in having a chameleon-like facility for changing the colour of his opinions according to the state of the religious barometer in regal quarters. Under Henry VIII he was a schismatic and a firm believer in transubstantiation and in the wisdom of invoking saints; when Edward came to the throne he turned *quasi*-Calvinist. Very early in Mary's reign he became, much to the unspeakable horror of Lady Jane, a penitent Papist. Aylmer, a far more estimable man and a greater scholar, appeared on the scene at Bradgate as tutor after the accession of King Edward, when Jane was in her twelfth year and ripe to receive his learned instruction in theology and classic lore.

CHAPTER III
THE LADY LATIMER

No task is more congenial to the earnest student of history than that of tracing the origin of some important event, and following its gradual development from a trivial incident to its culmination in a great matter destined to alter the fortunes, and even change the faith, of an entire nation. If we would reach a thorough comprehension of the chain of events which led up to the proclamation of Jane Grey as Queen of England, we must now leave her to pursue her Greek and Latin studies and broider her samplers at Bradgate, while we trace the earlier fortunes of those who so ruled her destiny as to compel a simple-hearted and naturally retiring girl to accept a station which, by the time she was constrained to relinquish it, brought her to the lowest depths of misfortune and transformed the regal diadem which she herself had never coveted into a crown of martyrdom.

The Lady Latimer, better known in history as Queen Katherine Parr, influenced the fortunes of Lady Jane Grey more than is usually imagined, for it was to her care that the ten-year-old child was committed (after it had been proposed by the Seymour faction that she should become Queen-Consort of Edward VI and head of the Protestant party in England), in order that her education might be directed and her mind bent towards "the new learning" of which Katherine was secretly a supporter.

Born in 1513 at that lordly Kendal Castle whose ruins still command one of the loveliest prospects in Westmoreland, Katherine Parr, though a simple gentlewoman, could boast royal blood—that of our Anglo-Saxon kings, inherited from her paternal ancestor Ivo de Talbois, who married Lucy, the sister of the renowned Earls Morcar and Edwin. She was also29 of Plantagenet descent through her great-great-grandmother Alice Nevill, sister to Cicely Nevill, Duchess of York, a lineage that made her cousin four times removed to King Henry VIII himself. We will not enter in detail into the many alliances of the Parr family with the Nevills, Stricklands, Throckmortons, and Boroughs, but we are safe in describing it as a wealthy and honourable county stock, much looked up to in those days.

Katherine's father, Sir Thomas Parr, married, when his bride was but little over thirteen, Maud Green, daughter of the rich Sir Thomas Green of Boughton and Greens-Norton in Northamptonshire. Lady Parr had a sister, Mary, who, when a mere child, married Lord Vaux of Harrowden, and, dying without issue, left her splendid fortune to her sister Maud. Lady Parr's eldest son, born before his mother was fifteen, was the celebrated Sir William Parr, ultimately Earl of Essex and Marquess of Northampton. Her next child mated with Mr. William Herbert, who was raised to the peerage in 1551 by Edward VI as Earl of Pembroke six weeks before the death of his wife. Katherine, the third and youngest child of Sir Thomas and Lady Parr, was destined to occupy the perilous position of sixth Queen-Consort to King Henry VIII. When she was a mere child, the proverbial gipsy-woman predicted that "she should one day wear a crown, and not a cap; and wield a sceptre, not a distaff."24 Sir Thomas Parr died in London in 1517, leaving very scant provision for his two daughters, the bulk of his fortune having been settled upon his wife and son; but both young ladies married wealthy men, and thus were not seriously affected by their lack of means. Anne married at fifteen; and Katherine, long before she was fourteen, was led to the hymeneal altar by Lord Borough of Cantley Hall, Gainsborough, Yorkshire. The bridegroom had already been twice married, and so great was the disparity of age between the couple that Lady Borough was wont to call her eldest stepdaughter "little mother." Two years after her marriage Katherine became a widow with a very handsome dower. Much of her time of mourning was spent at Sizergh Castle in Westmoreland, the seat of her kinsfolk the Stricklands, where she left several fine specimens of her skill as a needlewoman—notably a gorgeous white satin quilt embroidered30 with gold—which are still preserved in an apartment known as Queen Katherine's Room.

We are fortunate in possessing a good many portraits of this lady, and at least one wonderful miniature, formerly in the Strawberry Hill Collection, and which now belongs to Mr. Brocklehurst-Dent of Sudeley Castle. This contains a likeness of Henry VIII painted in a space not bigger than a pin's head, on a tiny medallion suspended round the Queen's neck. A strong magnifying glass is required to do justice to the beauty of this microscopic miniature within a miniature, probably the smallest ever executed. Judged by all these portraits and by contemporary descriptions, Katherine Parr must have been a pretty little woman with delicate features, an intellectual brow—too amply developed for beauty—fox-coloured eyes, and a rather cunning expression about the thin yet flexible mouth. When her body was disinterred in 178625 it was found not to be decomposed, and measured exactly five feet and three inches. The hair, very long and curling naturally, was of a fine golden auburn.

QUEEN KATHERINE PARR

History does not record the names of the tutors who assisted31 Katherine Parr to acquire her remarkable education and numerous accomplishments. We may suppose that some priest or monk chaplain at Kendal or Sizergh instructed her in Latin and Greek, in both of which languages she was proficient. She may have learnt French from Mr. Bellemain, French tutor to Prince Edward, a pronounced Huguenot, who, notwithstanding his unorthodoxy, was in high favour at Henry's Court, received a pension from Edward after he ascended the throne, and walked in the young King's funeral procession. She mastered the language sufficiently to be able to write it and speak it correctly, and even to record her sentimental impressions in tolerable verse. Amongst the MSS at Hatfield there is a curious French poem, partly written by Katherine and partly by another, probably her teacher. It opens with the following verse in the Queen's handwriting:—

"Considerant ma vie miserable Mon cœur marboin, obstine, intraitable, Outrecuide tant, que non seullement, Dieu n'estimoit ny son commandement."

The concluding verse runs:—

"Qui prepare vous est devinement Ainsi que le monde eust son commencement Au Pere au Filz au Saint Esprit soit gloire Loz et honneur d'eternelle memoire. Finis."[26]

Katherine's handwriting, though clear and legible, is not to be compared with that of Elizabeth, King Edward, and Jane Grey, who very probably took lessons in the then much esteemed art of caligraphy from Dr. Cheke, chief tutor to the Prince, or from Ascham, both famous for the beauty of their penmanship.

Although very worldly, Katherine Parr was much preoccupied with theological disputations, and a distinctly evangelical tone pervades her literary remains; it is nevertheless certain that during the lifetime of her second[32] husband, Lord Latimer, she was, or pretended to be, a Catholic, and that during the few years of her married life with Henry VIII she was a schismatic or "Henryite." Tact and prudence were her leading characteristics, and she was both amiable and conciliatory, though she could, when angered, be extremely vindictive. Thomas Cromwell's downfall, usually attributed to the machinations of Katherine Howard, was in reality mainly due to those of Katherine Parr, for she it was, as we shall presently see, who opened Henry VIII's eyes to the prodigious rapacity and unpopularity of his favourite chancellor.

Lord Latimer, the lady's second spouse, like Lord Borough, had been twice married, and when he took her to wife was already the father of several children. The date of this marriage has not been handed down to us, but as Latimer lost his second wife in 1526, it could not have taken place earlier than 1527. He was a staunch Catholic of the belligerent sort, and a prominent leader of the Pilgrimage of Grace, an insurrection that broke out in the North of England in 1536 in consequence of the popular displeasure at the suppression of the monasteries and sequestration of church property. The peasants, suddenly deprived of the monks' accustomed charity and driven to desperation, began a local crusade, which soon assumed large proportions, their ranks being joined by a great number of noblemen and gentlemen belonging to the old faith, amongst them the Archbishop of York, Lord Nevill, Lord Darcy, Lord Latimer, Sir Stephen Hamerton, Sir Robert Constable, a certain mysterious individual who called himself the "Earl of Poverty," and Robert Aske, who though of mean extraction was nevertheless considered by the rest of his party as their nominal general. These motley pilgrims increased in numbers as they swept southwards in picturesque confusion; but despite the enthusiasm of their members, they seem to have been ill-disciplined and badly organised, and were presently dispersed at Dunstable, thanks to the conciliatory attitude of the Duke of Norfolk, whom the King had empowered to treat with these rebels and disband them. Latimer, who had been elected their spokesman, withdrew almost immediately and returned to London, where he soon afterwards resumed his post as Comptroller of the King's Household. After this excursion into open revolt against[33] his sovereign, Lord Latimer evidently deemed it prudent to keep himself very much in the background: he did not join the second Pilgrimage of Grace, which broke out in the following February (1537) and terminated in the execution by sword and fire of some seventy of its more prominent members, among them old Lord Derby, who was over eighty-three years of age.

When in London, Lord Latimer inhabited a house situated in the churchyard of the Charterhouse. The Chartreuse, as it was then called, was rather a fashionable place of residence, being not far distant from Clerkenwell, which in King Henry's time was a sort of Court suburb, such as Kensington became in the eighteenth century. From a letter still extant, it would appear that Lord Latimer, like many a modern nobleman and gentleman, was in the habit of letting his mansion furnished when he himself was absent at Snape Hall, his country seat in Yorkshire. Sir John Russell, Lord Privy Seal, who looked meek enough27 but was popularly known as "Swearing Russell" on account of his profane language, wrote in January 1537 requesting Latimer to allow a friend of his to have the loan of his house in the "Chartreuse" during his absence. Latimer dared not refuse, but his answer betrays his reluctant compliance with the request and some temper at the favour having been asked:—

"Right Honourable and my especial good Lord,—After my most hearty recommendations had to your good Lordship. Whereas your Lordship doth desire ... [effaced] of your friends my house within Chartreuse churchyard, beside so ... [effaced] I assure your Lordship the getting of a lease of it costs me 100 marcs, besides other pleasures [*i.e.* "improvements"] that I did to the house; for it was much my desire to have it, because it stands in good air, out of press of the city. And I do alway lie there when I come to London, and I have no other house to lie at. And, also, I have granted it to farm [*i.e.* "have let it"] to Mr. Nudygate,28 son and heir34 to serjeant Nudygate, to lie in the said house in my absence; and he to void whensoever I come up to London. Nevertheless I am contented if it can do your Lordship any pleasure for your friend, that he lie there forthwith. I seek my lodgings at this Michaelmas term myself. And as touching my lease, I assure your Lordship it is not here; but I shall bring it right to your Lordship at my coming up at this said term, and then and alway I shall be at your Lordship's commandment, as knows our Lord, Who preserve your Lordship in much honour to His pleasure. From Wyke, in Worcestershire, the last day of September.—Your Lordship's assuredly to command,

"John Latimer"

"To the right honourable and very especial good lord, my Lord Privy Seal."29

Lord Latimer died in February 1543, a twelvemonth after the execution of Queen Katherine Howard, leaving his widow the manors of Nunmonkton and Hamerton for life, and his mansion in the Charterhouse for as long as she should remain a widow. As soon as her husband was safely buried in St. Paul's Churchyard, Katherine began to indulge her leaning towards what was then known as the "new learning"; and her house became the resort of the leaders of a movement which was eventually to complete the Reformation in England. These gentlemen were wont, it is said, to assemble at regular intervals and hold conferences on religious subjects in the presence, not only of Katherine and her household, but of a select circle of great ladies, among them Katherine's sister, Anne Herbert, and the charming Katherine, Duchess of Suffolk, the fourth wife of Lady Jane's singular grandfather, who were only too willing, notwithstanding the risk they ran, to sit at the feet of a Coverdale, a Latimer, or a Parkhurst. Religion, however, sat lightly on this clever Duchess, who—so brilliant, witty, and amusing are her letters—might well claim to be the precursor in the epistolary art of Madame de Sévigné. To these pious gatherings of the widow Latimer came likewise the haughty and turbulent Anne Stanhope, Countess of Hertford, who in due time, as wife of the Protector, was to be35 Duchess of Somerset and Katherine Parr's arch-enemy; Lady Denny,30 wife of Sir Andrew Denny, Privy Councillor to Henry VIII; the Lady Fitzwilliam,31 wife of Sir William Fitzwilliam, and acknowledged to be one of the ablest women of her time; and the Lady Tyrwhitt,32 who came very near martyrdom for her heretical opinions, in the last year of Henry's life. The Countess of Sussex,33 second wife of Henry Ratcliffe, Earl of Sussex, was likewise one of Lady Latimer's *intimes*. This lady's alleged familiarity with the black art eventually led to her being charged with witchcraft, in 1552, and imprisoned in the Tower, from which durance she was delivered six months later by order of the Duke of Northumberland. The Marchioness of Dorset may also have assisted at Lady Latimer's religious exercises, which, although noticed by her contemporaries as matters of general knowledge, seem to have temporarily escaped the unpleasant attention of King Henry's chief heretic-hunters. The Lady Frances was certainly on the most friendly terms with Lady Latimer, and so too was Princess Mary.

Another guest there was at the Charterhouse who probably came when the house was quiet, the voices of the preachers[36] hushed, and the great ladies returned to their respective domiciles. This was Sir Thomas Seymour, the late Queen Jane's second brother, who was considered the Adonis of the Court. Lady Latimer seems to have been deeply enamoured of his good looks and stalwart figure; but it is not unlikely that it was her rich dower, rather than herself, that tempted Sir Thomas. Be this as it may, the intimacy which began about this period, paved the way to the tragic close of the handsome courtier's chequered career. Seymour appears to have proposed to the widow three months after Lord Latimer's death, and she seems to have rejected him "pleasantly," saying "some one higher than he had asked her to be his wife." For all that, Sir Thomas had certainly made a deep impression on her heart, a fact all the more remarkable since he was in every way the opposite to herself: she was learned and sedate—he was gay and profligate; the lady loved rich but sober attire—the gentleman blazed with brilliant satins and silks and cloth of gold and silver, setting his brother courtiers the fashion as to the wearing of their jewels and the number of feathers they should sport in their caps. Still, the advantage of the alliance was obvious, for though not a rich man, he was a great favourite with the King, his potent brother-in-law, and further, he was the second member of the rising house of Seymour, which many predicted—in the event of any accident happening to His Majesty, whose health was fast declining—would at once assume a preponderating position at his successor's Court.

But although Lady Latimer must have been acquainted with every detail of the conspiracy organised by the Seymours against the house of Howard, of which the first fruit was the revelation of the unfortunate Queen Katherine Howard's misconduct, she does not seem to have hesitated for a moment in her determination to become Queen of England, even at the sacrifice of her passion for Thomas Seymour, which, all-absorbing as it was, never diverted her from the two great objects of her ambition: her own political influence, and the ultimate advancement of the Reformation. She cannot be described as a Protestant, for in her time that word was not yet coined. During her second husband's lifetime she must have concealed her "advanced views," and when she became[37] Queen she was—outwardly at least—a schismatic, who attended as many as three and four Masses daily. Henry VIII rarely heard less than three, and sometimes as many as five Masses every day, and what is more, obliged every official of his Court and household, high and low, to do the same. How she first attracted his attention has never transpired; but as a great Court lady she must have been in frequent and immediate relations with the sovereign. The first mention of her personal dealings with King Henry is connected with trouble in the Throckmorton family. Owing to some dispute over their respective country seats, Coughton Court and Oursley, which were contiguous to one another, her maternal aunt's husband, Sir George Throckmorton, had incurred Cromwell's ill-will. Cromwell, with a view to ruining his opponent, went so far as to accuse him of conspiring against the King's supremacy in ecclesiastical matters. According to an MS. ballad still preserved in the Throckmorton archives, Lady Latimer interceded with His Majesty for her uncle, and obtained full justice for him. At the same time she contrived the overthrow of Cromwell, whose title of Essex was eventually conferred upon her brother, Sir William Parr, who married Anne Bourchier, only daughter of the last Earl of Essex of the original branch.

The divorce—based on the futile plea that the King did not find Anne of Cleves physically attractive[34]—which followed six months after Henry VIII's pompous marriage with that lady was accepted by the philosophical Dutchwoman in a spirit that proved her practical sense to be stronger than her sentiment. A noble mansion in the country, a dower of £4000 a year, and precedence over all the great ladies of the Court, the Princesses Mary and Elizabeth excepted, struck her as more desirable than an anxious and uncertain struggle to38 retain the crown matrimonial which, under somewhat similar circumstances, had proved so sorry a possession to Queen Katherine of Aragon. None the less, the Reformers took Anne's humiliation—she was a Lutheran princess—in much the same spirit as that which possessed the Catholics at the time of the momentous divorce of Queen Katherine. The accommodating "daughter of Cleves," as she now styled herself, continued to receive friendly visits from the King even in the halcyon days of his brief matrimonial alliance with Katherine Howard, and shortly after that wretched woman's execution an influential party appears to have been bent, in Reformation interests, on reconciling King Henry with his repudiated spouse. Anne herself seems to have been not at all averse to the scheme; and Marillac, the French Ambassador, who favoured it, found her on one occasion quite hopeful—"in the best of spirits," and "thinking only of amusing herself and of her fine clothes." But when the matter of a reunion between the King and his discarded wife was formally proposed to Cranmer by the Duke of Cleves' Ambassador, it met with a flat refusal. The Archbishop knew the good-natured lady's character too well to doubt that she was never likely to influence the King or be of the least use in furthering the Reformers' interests. In the meantime, Parliament had urged Henry, for his "comfort's sake," to take unto himself another wife; and at the same time, as if to keep him out of the way, Sir Thomas Seymour was sent on an embassy to the Queen of Hungary, and did not return to London until some days after Katherine Parr's wedding.

The earliest intimation in the State Papers of the King's connection with Katherine is in a letter from Lord Lisle, afterwards Duke of Northumberland, to Sir William Parr, dated Greenwich, 20th June 1543:—

"My lady Latymer, your sister, and Mrs. Herbert be both here in the Court with my Lady Mary's grace and my Lady Elizabeth." Quite a friendly party!

On 22nd June 1543 the gorgeous State barges streamed up the Thames from Greenwich to Hampton Court. On 10th July Cranmer issued a licence for the King to marry Katherine, Lady Latimer, "in any church or chapel without39 issue of banns," and two days later Henry VIII led Lord Latimer's widow to the altar of an upper oratory called "the Quynes Prevey closet" at Hampton Court Palace. After Low Mass, said by Bishop Gardiner, the consent of both parties was pronounced in English. The King, taking the fair bride's right hand, repeated after the Bishop the words: "I, Henry, take thee, Katherine, to my wedded wife, to have and to hold from this day forward, for better for worse (*sic*), for richer for poorer, in sickness and in health, till death us do part, and thereto I plight thee my troth." Then, unclasping and once more clasping hands, Katherine likewise said, "I, Katherine, take thee, Henry, to my wedded husband, to have and to hold from this day forward, for better for worse, for richer for poorer, in sickness and in health to be bonayr and buxome in bed and at board, till death us do part, and thereto I plight unto thee my troth." The putting on of the wedding ring and offering of gold and silver followed, and after a prayer the Bishop pronounced the nuptial benediction.

At the wedding were present, amongst others, Lord Hertford and his Countess; Sir Anthony Browne; Joan, Lady Dudley; Katherine, Duchess of Suffolk; Lord John Russell; the King's niece, the Lady Margaret Douglas; Mrs. Herbert, the Queen's sister; and last but not least, the Princesses Mary and Elizabeth, to whom their stepmother made handsome presents of money. There is no mention of the Dorsets attending the wedding, though both were in London at the time. Everybody seemed delighted, even Wriothesley, who went so far as to write to Suffolk, then with the army in the north, that "on Thursday last the King had married the Lady Latimer, a lady in his judgment for virtue and winsomeness and gentleness most mete for His Highness, who never had such a wife more agreeable to his harte than she is." Katherine herself informed her brother, Sir William Parr, that "it had pleased God to incline the King's heart to take her as his wife, which was to her the greatest joy and comfort that could happen."

Wriothesley enclosed this letter in one of his own in which he entreated Parr to make himself worthy of such a sister as the new Queen. Chapuys wrote to the Emperor on 27th July: "My lady of Cleves has taken great grief and despair at the King's espousal of this last wife, who is not, she says, nearly 40 so beautiful as she, and besides that there is no hope of issue, seeing that she has been twice married before and no children born to her." Richard Hills, "Heretic Hills," as they called him, in a letter to Bullinger, the Swiss Reformer, who subsequently became the friend of Lady Jane Grey, and dated from Strasburg on 26th September, makes the following very characteristic comments on the King's sixth marriage:—

"No news but that our King has, within these two months as I have already written to John Bucer, burnt three godly men in one day. In July he married the widow of a nobleman named Latimer, and, as you know, he is always wont to celebrate his nuptials by some wickedness of this kind."

The victims alluded to are known as the "Windsor martyrs." They were men in humble circumstances named Parsons, Testwood, and Filmer.[35] A fourth, John Marbeck, who was organist at St. George's Chapel Royal, was, it is said, reprieved at the instance of Dr. Casson, Bishop of Salisbury, and of the Queen, who is also credited with having saved the life of Dr. Haines, Dean of Exeter, of Sir Philip Hoby and his wife, and of Sir Thomas Carden, who had been denounced by Dr. London as spreading heresy even within the precincts of the palace. The result of the Queen's action was that London and Simmonds, his coadjutor, were condemned for perjury, and sentenced to ride round Windsor with their faces to the horses' tails—a humiliating punishment which is said to have caused Dr. London's death—no great loss to humanity.

To save human life and to alleviate suffering is a meritorious[41] act that brings its own reward; but in spite of this, and although the newly made Queen was thus enabled to realise her own influence, she must have found her honeymoon a season full of dread, revealing as it did the terrible insecurity of lives dependent on the fiat of so capricious a tyrant as her royal mate.

CHAPTER IV
THE KING'S HOUSEHOLD

Not Solomon in all his glory—nor Sultan Suleyman the Magnificent of Istambul—was lodged more sumptuously than Tudor King Henry VIII of England. When Katherine Parr espoused the much-married monarch, she found herself mistress of a score of royal palaces, each furnished in a manner not unworthy of the splendour of Aladdin after that fortunate youth had gained possession of his magic Lamp, and served by the most numerous retinue ever brought together in this ancient kingdom of ours. The Venetian envoys, accustomed to the luxury and artistic elegance of the Queen of the Adriatic, were fairly dazzled by the sight of the treasures Henry gathered about him. Although within the space of a few brief years he suffered vandal hands to rob his country of more noble abbeys, churches, libraries, and works of art than had been destroyed by time and foreign and civil war combined since William's Conquest, the King's own artistic sense was highly developed, and he revelled, with a glee that sometimes verged upon the childish, in pomp and luxury and all things rare and beautiful.[36] To the confiscated collections of Wolsey he added the spoils of a hundred monasteries, and the Inventory of his effects, taken a few days after his death,[37][43] fills two enormous folio volumes preserved among the Harleian Papers in the British Museum. It is written in a round, legible hand, on the finest paper of the period, and a glimpse of its contents cannot fail to excite the longing of the *virtuoso* and to stir the imagination as effectually as any brilliant page of description in the *Arabian Nights*. A perusal of these bulky tomes facilitates some partial conception of the extraordinary magnificence of the Court at which Lady Jane Grey figured as a child, and whence, no doubt, she derived that taste for "costlie attire, music and other vanities," which was to evoke the unfavourable criticism of her Puritan friends at Zurich and Strasburg, who exhorted her, if she really desired to save her soul, to forswear all such trash, and imitate "the simplicity in dress and modesty in demeanour" practised by her cousin the Princess Elizabeth. We find hundreds of entries touching bedsteads, tables, card or playing tables, chairs, couches and footstools of carved ebony, cedar-wood, walnut, or oak, inlaid with mother-of-pearl, ivory, or rich metal wirework, and upholstered in silk, satin, velvet, or Florence brocade, fringed with gold, and even with strings of seed-pearls. Persian and Turkish carpets, silks and woollen, covered every available space in corridor, gallery, hall, and bedchamber, and there is mention of one especially wonderful carpet "of silk," probably Persian, "nine yards long by two and a half wide." One chamber was decorated with "101 yards of white satin embroidered and fringed with gold," while the walls of another were panelled with purple cloth of gold, *i.e.* purple silk shot with gold.

There must have been some hundreds of complete sets of the costliest tapestries and arras in the various royal palaces. Wolsey, whose passion for tapestry as a mural decoration became quite unreasonable, collected scores of the finest specimens the looms of Italy and Flanders could produce and lavish outlay secure. After his fall these remained as he had left them at Hampton Court, where we still admire the splendid series representing the "Story of Abraham," designed by[44] Raphael's pupil, Bernard van Orly, and another of yet earlier date illustrating the "Triumphs," of which three, those of "Death," "Renown," and "Time," occupy their original positions in Henry VIII's Great Watching or Guard Chamber. As we gaze on their faded beauty, we should remind ourselves that the immense quantity of gold thread wrought with infinite care and taste into their composition, and now tarnished, glistened in King Henry's time in all the glory of its freshness. In the Audience Chamber at Whitehall many a great Ambassador may have envied the arras hangings, representing the "Acts of the Apostles,"[38] from designs by Raphael presented to the King by Pope Leo X when he gave him the proud title of "Defender of the Faith."

The walls of three State rooms at Hampton Court were hung "with cloth of gold, blue cloth of gold, crimson velvet upon velvet, tawny velvet upon velvet, green velvet figury, and cloth of bawdekin," a regal material woven partly of silk and partly of gold. Some of the chief tapestries at Whitehall represented the "History of Our Lady," the "Story of Ahasuerus and Esther," the "Crucifixion," the "Story of Apollo and Daphne," "St. George and the Dragon," "Hawking and Hunting Scenes," the "Siege of Jerusalem," and many other like episodes in sacred and profane history and in mythology. The King would order a score of sets of tapestry at once, and would spend a sum equal to £10,000 or £15,000 of our money upon them. The overflow of tapestries, "picture-hangings," Oriental silks, Genoa velvets, Florence[45] and Venice brocades, curtains of French lace, Chinese silks, and costly furniture, went to the State rooms of the stern old Tower; to Windsor—where a few remnants of Henry VIII's belongings still remain; to Woodstock, to Richmond, to Greenwich, to Oatlands in Surrey—where Prince Edward often lived; to Newhall to Havering atte Bower—the chief country seat of Princess Mary; to Hatfield and Enfield Chase—where Princess Elizabeth spent her girlhood; to the Queen's dower-houses at Hanworth and Chelsea; and above all, to that marvel of the age, the new Palace of Nonesuch, which Henry had built him at Cheam, Surrey.[39] At Whitehall there were scores of cupboards crammed with gold and silver plate, and there were ivory and ebony cabinets with crystal doors, in which glittered strange Italian jewels, and curiosities from all parts of the then known world. In none of Henry's palaces does there seem to have been a gallery exclusively devoted to pictures, such as would be found in most contemporary Italian and French royal and princely residences; but there were plenty of pictures or "painted tables," as the Inventory quaintly calls them, in nearly every chamber. In 1540 Holbein's great fresco in the King's Privy Council Room at Whitehall, representing King Henry VII and Queen Elizabeth of York in the background, with Henry VIII and Jane Seymour standing in front, was a comparatively recent work. The illustrious artist, who died in London of the plague in 1543,[46] had also designed the ceiling of the "Matted Gallery," and covered the walls of the Chapel Royal with frescoes and arabesques.

The King's appearance, as he developed from boyhood to manhood and middle age, might have been studied in scores of presentments of him, to be met with at every turn: here, a plump little boy, by Mabuse; there, a singularly handsome fair-haired young man by Paris Bordone; and yonder, a full-length portrait by Hans Holbein, in which it was evident that His Majesty was beginning to "put on flesh." In the Audience Chamber was a "table" of the monarch painted by Bartolomeo Penni, wherein the "peepy eyes" and the bloated cheeks of his latter years were only too faithfully portrayed. Though there were portraits of nearly all the King's contemporaries, including one of Charles VIII of France and another of Charles V, besides a round dozen of Francis I, the likenesses of the five queens who preceded Katherine Parr had all been carefully removed, or, as in the case, of Anne Boleyn and Katherine Howard, destroyed. A cabinet full of relics of Queen Jane stood, however, in the anteroom of the King's bedchamber at the Tower; and at Westminster, in a picture-book, there was a portrait of this Queen with another of the King facing it on the opposite page. Among the great "tables" at Whitehall were the "Virgin and Child," by Leonardo da Vinci,[40] given to the King by Francis I in exchange for a picture by Holbein; "St. George and the Dragon,"[41] by Raphael; "Christina of Denmark,"[42] by Holbein, full length; a portrait, "Like unto Life," of "Thomas, Duke of Norfolk,"[43] and "one table of the King's Highness trampling upon the papal tiara, whence issues a serpent with seven heads snorting fire. In the King's hand is the Bible, and a sword whereon is written *Verbum Dei*."[44]

If the art of painting was well represented in the King's many palaces, that of music was even more cherished. Page[47] after page in the Royal Inventory is devoted to "double" and "single" virginals, with cases inlaid and encrusted with ivory and mother-of-pearl or adorned with arabesques of gold, studded with gems; while of lutes and flutes, rebecks and viols, there seems to have been a perfect arsenal. Then there was a library of over a thousand precious volumes, a sort of perambulating feast of reason, for in the Household Expenses we find various sums of money disbursed from time to time for the removal of boat-loads of books from one palace to another. The number of gold, silver, bronze, crystal, and glass chandeliers, sconces, and candlesticks distributed among the royal residences baffles belief. Each of the two hundred and eighty-four guest-chambers at Hampton Court boasted a bedstead hung with the richest silk and satin, with a gorgeously embroidered and wadded counterpane to match, an Oriental carpet, and a toilet set, ewer, basin, and candlesticks complete, of massive silver; while one closet at Whitehall was stored with an immense collection of the choicest German and Venetian glass. Such, in fact, was the King's mania for collecting things rich and rare that, in spite of the hopeless and suffering condition of his health, he was still "buying," down to the ultimate week of his life, and some of his last purchases seem never to have been paid for by his successors.

These contemporary accounts of the Household of Henry VIII strike the student by their marked resemblance to similar descriptions, by such writers as Sagrado and Knowles, of the quaint and numerous population of the Seraglio in the palmy days of the Ottoman Khaliphats. The Tudor King, like the Grand Turk, had four battalions of pages—pages of the Outer and of the Inner Court, of the King's Antechamber, and of the King's Presence Chamber; and yet a fifth contingent was attached to the service of the Queen. These lads, some hundreds in number, had their captains and even their school-masters; they were mostly of good family, and were apparelled, according to their rank, in wondrous State garments either of satin, green and white, the colours of the house of Tudor, or else of royal scarlet and gold. There was a legion of Grooms of the Wardrobe, Keepers of the King's Horse, Sports and Pastimes, of his Harriers and Beagles, Sergeants-[48]at-Arms, Sergeants of the Woodyard, Sergeants of the Bakehouse, Sergeants of the Pantry, Sergeants of the Pastry, Sergeants of the Trumpeters, Yeomen of the Wardrobe, Yeomen of the Armoury, Yeomen of the Buttery, Yeomen of the Chamber, Yeomen of the Chariots, of the Cooks, of the Henchmen, Stables, and Tents. The Royal Chapel was served by a full complement of chaplains, sub-chaplains, organists, and choir-boys. There were apothecaries, physicians, astronomers,[45] astrologers, secretaries, ushers, cup-bearers, carvers, servers, singing-boys, virginal players, Italian singers and English madrigalists, and a perfect orchestra of players on the lute, the flute, the rebeck, the sackbut, the harp, the psalter, and all manner of instruments.

Full fifty cooks and twice as many scullions worked in the spacious kitchens, and in 1544 we hear of a French pastry-cook of good repute who rejoiced in the very pleasing and appropriate name of M. Doux. A regiment of gardeners and under-gardeners trimmed the pleasaunces and kept the King's orchards in order.

The dresses and costumes of this army of picturesque, though often quite useless, folk, numbering some thousands or so, were sufficiently costly to account in part for the straits of the Royal Exchequer. Their wages and silks and satins cost the nation, in the last year of Henry VIII's reign, £56,700—against £17,280 in the last year of that of his father; a prodigious increase—when we take into consideration the relative value of money—and sufficient to explain the depletion of the coin.

HENRY VIII IN 1548

FROM AN OLD ENGRAVING

Scarlet, or rather deep red, was the predominant colour of the garments of King Henry's retainers, but dark blue and orange, with the white and light apple green of the house of Tudor, were not lacking, and added to the kaleidoscopic aspect of the courtyards and staircases, galleries and audience chamber, in the stately residences of "bluff King Hal." One Venetian Ambassador, commenting on the order kept at the English Court, declared that "everything is regulated as by clock-work, and no one ever seems to be out of his place."49 When the King condescended to walk abroad, he was attended by a host of superbly attired courtiers, by his grand equerries and chamberlains, the Grand Master of his Horse, his almoners, ushers, and physicians; his fool—Will Somers46; his pages, and even by a favourite musician or so. In the last years of his life, owing to his increasing infirmity, Henry was sometimes carried upon the shoulders of six sturdy noblemen, in a kind of *sedia gestatoria* like the Pope's. At His Majesty's approach every knee was bent, and many who particularly desired to conciliate his favour "grovelled" face downward as Orientals before some Eastern despot. The officials and serving-men who prepared the table for His Majesty's meals made an obeisance each time they passed the vacant chair wherein the monarch was presently to seat himself. The Queen-Consort, and the Princesses, his daughters, knelt whenever they addressed him. In brief, King Henry, having filched from Peter some of Peter's pontifical prerogatives, exacted the same sort of homage as that paid to the Roman Pontiff, and turned himself from mortal into a sort of demigod or idol. But foreigners and Catholics noted that though people knelt as he rode past, His Majesty bestowed no blessing upon them. This slavish etiquette continued throughout the reign of Edward VI,47 but was modified when Mary renounced the titular position of Head of the Church. Elizabeth, however, demanded, and, what is more, received, *quasi*-divine honours from her subjects.

Yet another point of resemblance between the Courts of England and the Ottoman at this period: Whitehall, like the50 Seraglio, was gay and brilliant on the surface, but in each case there was an undercurrent of terror and suspicion. The Tudor Court swarmed with spies and informers, and often a thoughtless jest, a careless remark, spitefully retailed at headquarters, would send men or women to the Tower, or even to the stake. Folks went in fear and trembling lest what they had said overnight in their cups might be brought home to them with appalling consequences in the morning. This state of abject and habitual fear engendered habits of whispering and talking apart and an atmosphere of mystery, in spite of which the gossip and rumours of the King's own chamber passed to the pages, grooms, and serving-men in the courtyards below, and thence to the general public, as rapidly as news flies nowadays by telephone and telegraph.

There can be no doubt that Jane Grey, the daughter of one so closely connected with the throne as was the Marchioness of Dorset, must often have mingled in the gaudy crowd that thronged her grand-uncle's palace. Henry was as "fond of children as he was of pastry," although, for obvious reasons, he did not display any overweening affection for his own offspring. This engaging little niece, now about six years of age, is likely to have found favour in the monarch's sight, and Jane Grey, for all we know, may even have throned it on her dread relative's august knee. Cranmer's hand, too, must have rested in benediction upon her head, and she may, perchance, have won the smile of Gardiner and of Bonner. She must often have heard the sick King, who had lost his own fine voice, accompany his favourite fool, Will Somers, on the lute, in some song or hymn of his own composition. She must have been familiar with the two Seymour brothers; with the dreamy face and austere manner of the Earl of Hertford, and the bluff good-nature of Sir Thomas. She may even have been tossed in the strong arms of John Dudley, at this time Lord High-Admiral of England and Viscount de Lisle, reputed a "magnificent gentleman," but otherwise of secondary importance. Wriothesley, Rich, and foredoomed Surrey and his father, old Norfolk, must often have watched her run along, clinging to her portly mother's trailing brocades as she passed on her way to and from the King's cabinet, and may even have whispered51 one to the other that the little damsel would surely be as good a match for young Prince Edward as the Scottish Queen's daughter, Mary Stuart. In the apartment of her grand-aunt the Queen, where that busy little lady nestled like a sultana among her innumerable soft pillows and cushions,48 encased in cloth of gold and silver, the child Jane must have heard much evangelical counsel from the erstwhile widow Latimer, who found some consolation in the gorgeousness of her thraldom for the loss of her handsome lover, Sir Thomas Seymour.

The Queen's lodgings were parted from the King's by a short corridor, and nearly all her windows overlooked the Thames. Here Katherine Parr played the housewife, and in the midst of her tapestries and brocades and her "stretches" of silver and gold cloth, made poultices for Henry's ulcered legs, wrote her pious treaties on probity and prayers, and probably counted the hours till the Lord in His mercy should deliver her royal spouse from his sore sufferings. In these rooms, perhaps, Jane Grey sat for her miniature to Lavinia Tyrling; Bartolomeo Penni may here have limned her diminutive but very pretty features; and we fancy we can see Mr. Crane or Mr. John Heywood, His Majesty's chief virginal players, teaching her the notes upon the King's "favourite virginal," the one "enlaid with gold and mother-of-pearl." In the last months of Henry's life, when Lady Jane is known to have been much with Katherine Parr, the little girl may have listened with delight to the wonderful warbling of the King's Italian singers, Alberto of Venice, Marc Antonio Galiadello of Brescia, or Giorgio da Cremona, as they vainly endeavoured to soothe the sufferings of the dying monarch by their elaborate *cadenze*.

Queen Katherine soon made her influence felt at Court. She could not control the violent passions of her wayward lord, but she did in a measure modify them, and steered her own course amid the shoals of regal existence with consummate52 skill. No breath of scandal ever sullied her fair name, though Thomas Seymour, back from his convenient mission to Hungary, was appointed her Chamberlain, and must have been a good deal in her company. Even her worst enemies never ventured on that track. When at a later date they planned a blow, which they hoped would prove fatal to the Queen, they selected her religious leanings, not her love affairs, as their fell weapon. Katherine Parr, to her credit, lost no time in reconciling the King with his hitherto neglected daughters. Princess Mary was near her own age, and had been intimate with her when she was Lady Latimer. The Emperor's Ambassadors praise "the new Queen for her kindness to the daughter of Katherine of Aragon,49 who now takes her proper place at Court." Elizabeth, too, was summoned from her suburban retreat, but had not been many weeks under her father's roof ere he became so exasperated by her pert obstinacy that he summarily ordered her back to Enfield. In a few weeks, however, Katherine patched up the quarrel, and on 24th July 1544 Elizabeth wrote Her Majesty, in Italian, a most graceful letter of thanks for her good offices.50 Edward was too delicate to be much in London, but none the less his stepmother looked after his health with so much "gentleness" that she soon won his sincere affection and lasting goodwill. He wrote her letters in Latin, French, and Italian, addressed to his *charisima Mater*, and full of praise for her beautiful penmanship, which, on comparison, proves greatly inferior both to his own and to that of either Elizabeth or Jane Grey. Katherine induced her stepdaughter Mary to assist in the translation of Erasmus's *Paraphrase of the Four Gospels*. The Princess selected that of St. John, and when the work was finished, an amusing correspondence ensued as to the propriety of the future Queen of England placing her name, as translator, on the frontispiece. "I see not why you should reject the praise deservedly yours," argued the Queen; and53 the Princess at last allowed the editor of the work, the learned Dr. Udall, to allude to the fact that "the most noble, the most virtuous and the most studious Lady Mary" had a hand in its success.51

To occupy her own leisure, Queen Katherine devoted herself to the composition of a quaint book entitled *The Lamentations of a Penitent Sinner*, a pious work which gives us, at least in one passage, a lucid idea of the methods employed by Her Majesty to keep her hold over her extraordinary husband, among which gross flattery was by no means the least. A copy of this work was once in the possession of John Thelwall, and was sold at the death of his second wife. It contained a curious autograph, indicating that it had been given by the Queen to her "dear cosyn, Jane Grey," who no doubt read it with veneration and delight. In this tiny volume Henry had the satisfaction of being likened unto Moses leading the Children of Israel out of bondage. "I mean by Moses, King Henry VIII, my most sovereign favourable lord and husband, one (if Moses had figured any more than Christ) through the excellent grace of God, meet to be another expressed verity of Moses' conquest over Pharaoh (and I mean by this Pharaoh the Bishop of Rome), the greatest persecutor of all true Christians than ever was Pharaoh of the Children of Israel."

As may well be imagined, Queen Katherine Parr did not fail to use her influence to obtain prominent positions about the Court for her own kith and kin. Her uncle and Chamberlain, Sir Thomas Parr, was created Lord Parr of Horton; her brother was raised from the rank of Baron Parr of Kendal to be Earl of Essex, in lieu of the lately decapitated Thomas Cromwell; and her brother-in-law, William Herbert, was knighted. These gentlemen received their new dignities in the Chapel Royal, but were not entertained in one of the apartments spread with Persian carpets. Their dinner was served in the choir-boys' mess-room, in which a fresh litter of rushes was strewn for the occasion—a curious fact, which leads one to conclude that the acting master of ceremonies expected the party to indulge in libations which might result in some injury to Oriental rugs but were not likely to do much54 damage to fresh rushes costing 3s. 6d. the litter. Parr had to pay 40s. for his new paraphernalia, and the choir-boys got 10s. for singing after the dinner.52

On 14th July 1544 King Henry sailed from Dover for France to superintend in person the approaching siege of Boulogne. He left our shores in a vessel with sails made of cloth of gold, the glitter of which does not appear to have added to the ship's speed, for the King did not get to Calais for nearly twenty-four hours, although the weather was fine, and the sea calm—probably too calm. The last time he had crossed the Channel, on his way to the Field of the Cloth of Gold, Henry had acted the part of pilot, garbed in nether garments of cloth of gold, and had blown the pilot's whistle as loud as any trumpeter. This time he was too anxious and enfeebled to play at all. His Majesty was attended by his brother-in-law, the Duke of Suffolk, also a very sick man; by Sir William Herbert, who acted as his spear-bearer, by the Duke of Norfolk, the Earl of Surrey, the Spanish Duke of Alberqurque, John Dudley, the Lord High-Admiral, afterwards Duke of Northumberland, and half the English nobility. Before his departure he appointed the Queen Regent of England and Ireland, with power to sign all official and State documents, this being almost the first occasion on which a Queen-Consort of England held so responsible a position. The Earl of Hertford was to be Her Majesty's constant attendant, but should he chance to be temporarily absent, Cranmer was to remain with her, and with these two, Sir William Petre and Lord Parr of Horton, her Grace's uncle, Wriothesley, and Gardiner, Bishop of Winchester, were to sit in council.

During this regency Katherine kept aloof from politics and occupied herself principally with assisting the University of Cambridge and with the royal children, who were left in her charge. Princess Mary, who was an almost constant guest during the King's absence, and Princess Elizabeth, were both invited to join the circle at Oatlands, where Prince Edward was residing, and whither, owing to an outbreak of the plague, the Queen herself soon retired. From the55 various suburban palaces in which she was residing, Katherine addressed letters almost daily to the King, giving him accounts of the health and the doings of his children; and the monarch vouchsafed in return to write most approvingly of all she did. Towards the middle of August the Lady Dorset and her daughter, the Lady Jane Grey, came to Oatlands for a few days' visit. This was perhaps the first and probably the only time spent by Lady Jane and Prince Edward under the same roof. The royal kinsfolk may have lived a very quiet life, spending their days in the gardens and park, and their evenings either listening to the singing of Princess Mary, who is reputed to have had a magnificent contralto voice, or to Princess Elizabeth's playing upon the virginals, an art in which she already excelled. The Queen may perchance have favoured the company with a chapter or so from some one or other of her remarkably dull theological compositions. There is no evidence that she was a musician, and she does not seem to have been infected with the prevailing Court vice—gambling—in which even the pious Princess Mary indulged, frequently losing much more than she could pay—as demonstrated by the Household Books of Henry VIII.

Boulogne capitulated to Suffolk on 16th September, after a lengthy siege, and on the 18th, the King, accompanied by the Duke of Alberqurque, representing his ally the Emperor, received the keys of the city from his brother-in-law's hands, and made what he was pleased to consider his triumphal entry into the town. But he rode through a city untenanted and in ruins; even the magnificent Cathedral had not been spared, and the townsfolk, who had fled for security, as they hoped, to Hardelot and Etaples, were massacred, man, woman, and child, by the allied Spanish, German, and English troops. English historians have been reticent in dealing with the siege of Boulogne,53 and the majority have passed56 very lightly over the disagreement which soon broke out between our King and his ally the Emperor.54 Charles now urged Henry to join him and march on Paris. Henry, who knew his troops to be enfeebled by hardship and suffering, and moreover felt himself far too ill to supervise fresh military operations, would go no farther, more especially because he feared to infuriate the French King, who might at any moment ally himself with his former enemy the Emperor Charles, and thus form a Catholic coalition absolutely inimical to the policy of the English King. Henry's hesitation undoubtedly saved the city of Paris. Seeing the Emperor's troops approach the capital, Francis roused himself for a moment from the lethargy in which he had been plunged, and once more became the hero of Marignano. The King's attitude and the bravery of the Dauphin, who was covering the capital with 8000 men, stimulated the drooping spirits of the Parisians, and, with their usual heroism, they prepared to offer a stout resistance to their foes. They even made merry at the expense of their two arch-enemies, ridiculing the gouty Emperor and caricaturing the corpulent English King—a proof, if one were lacking, that the fatal diseases destined eventually to carry Henry off had already made sufficient progress to excite general attention. Queen Eleanor, the neglected wife of Francis I, foreseeing the horrors to which the capital and its inhabitants were exposed, determined, without consulting her husband, to plead personally with the Emperor. Accompanied by a Spanish monk named Guzman, she proceeded to the Imperial tent, and casting herself upon her knees before Charles, then writhing in agonies of gout, obtained terms from him, thus averting a siege which must have cost rivers of blood. The peace then concluded was none too satisfactory, so far as England was concerned, since it stipulated that Boulogne was to be restored in the space of six years, during which time the place lost us in money and men far more than it was worth. Never, indeed, was57 there a more futile expedition than this, nor a greater waste of money. The much-talked-of sails of cloth of gold wafted the King home on 1st October 1544. In London he was received with little enthusiasm, or none at all. The nation was disappointed by the terms of the peace, the army was disorganised, Norfolk already out of favour, and Surrey, accused of insubordination, was openly disgraced. Boulogne was left in the hands of Jane Grey's future father-in-law, Lord High-Admiral John Dudley.

The health of Lady Jane's maternal grandfather, Charles Brandon, Duke of Suffolk, failed him completely soon after his return to England. He seems to have suffered from a complication of disorders not unlike those which were afflicting his brother-in-law, the King. After the siege of Boulogne, he appears to have been of very little use, and eighteen months later he retired with his Duchess to Guildford Castle "in much suffering and pain." There is a portrait extant of Charles Brandon, taken at this time, which represents him seated in a large armchair, his head bound up in a sort of nightcap, and his swollen and gouty feet, one of which rests on a stool, enveloped in bandages. The bloated face bears a weird resemblance to Henry VIII. Brandon died at Guildford in 1546 after a long illness, during which he was nursed by his Duchess and his two daughters, the Ladies Frances and Eleanor, the former of whom brought her eldest daughters, Jane and Katherine, with her. By his will Charles Brandon left, after deducting a rather meagre dower for his wife, the bulk of his vast fortune to his two sons, with remainder to his daughters in unequal shares, the Lady Frances, in the case of the death of her two brothers, inheriting considerably more than two-thirds of her father's lands and money. He desired to be buried in Lincolnshire, but Henry, overlooking this request, caused his body to be conveyed to Windsor, where it was interred with great pomp in St. George's Chapel, in the presence of his family and of a multitude of courtiers.

CHAPTER V
MRS. ANNE ASKEW

It was in the latter years of Henry VIII's reign that Stephen Gardiner, Bishop of Winchester, conceived his scheme for the reconciliation of England and England's monarch with the Roman Pontiff. Although a less astute intriguer than his powerful opponent Cranmer, Gardiner, who was apt to lose his temper and blurt out things best kept to himself, was a man of marked ability, one of whom his crafty master made frequent use, playing him off against the Archbishop, and so retaining the balance of power in his own jealous hands. Cranmer was at this period using his influence with Henry to abolish the use of Latin in the Mass, preparatory to the eventual introduction of the Book of Common Prayer and the early and total abrogation of the Eucharistic Service in the Roman sense. Yet the wily Churchman knew right well that so long as the King lived there was but faint hope of this change. For His Majesty clung to the doctrine of Transubstantiation closer than to any other tenet; not so much on account of his faith—did he believe anything?—as because, in the days of his youth, he had indited a work in defence of the Catholic doctrine of the Sacraments, which, so his clergy had averred, proved him wiser than Solomon himself, and which Pope Leo X had favourably compared with the writings of St. Augustine and Gregory the Great, rewarding the royal author with that title of "Defender of the Faith" which is still a cherished appanage of British royalty. Henry had even made belief in the Sacrament of the Altar a principal Article amongst the famous Six, any denial of which was punishable with death. Yet, if the King had searched Cranmer's study at Lambeth at the very moment when that wily prelate was professing to accept his beliefs from his King,[59] as submissively as though the monarch had possessed the infallible powers of his own Maker, he might have laid his hand on a bulky correspondence between the Primate and every Lutheran and Calvinistic leader in Germany and Switzerland—with Calvin, Bullinger, Œcolampadius, Osiander, Dryander, Bucer, and the rest. Gardiner, on his side, was in communication with Cardinal Pole, Charles V, the Pope, and the entire papal party at home and abroad. This duel between the papal leader and the Reformers, then, was the true basis of all political undertakings at this momentous crisis. The rival parties were really preparing themselves for the departure of the dying King, and aimed at controlling the inevitable Protectorate, necessitated by the minority of his successor, a lad of nine summers. Had Gardiner, the Howards, and the Catholic party won the day, history would have had little, perhaps nothing, to record concerning Lady Jane Grey. Her name, like that of her accomplished friend Lady Jane Seymour, daughter of Lord Hertford, would have been lost, buried in the spent sands of the past.

The decline of the King's health began in the summer of 1541–2, when he was attacked by a dangerous tertian fever, from which, thanks to his powerful constitution, he partially recovered.

At the time of his marriage with Anne of Cleves he was again in poor health, and during the proceedings for the King's divorce from his Dutch consort, Cranmer laid great stress on the fact that although she had shared his chamber for six months, the bride was still to all intents and purposes unwed. At the siege of Boulogne, as we have seen, Henry was terribly altered, and the French ballad-writers jested about *le cercle de fer*, which, they averred, kept his ungainly carcass together. Queen Katherine was probably espoused rather as a skilful nurse than as a wife, in the ordinary acceptance of the term, and a most assiduous attendant she proved, kneeling for hours at a time rubbing his swelled legs and dressing his many ulcers. It would be unjust to the Queen's memory to attribute this wifely devotion to none but selfish motives. But her contemporaries shrewdly guessed that, while fulfilling her wifely duty, she did not fail to work in her own interest, and that of her friends, with her own peculiar skill and tact. She[60] certainly wished to be appointed Regent during Edward's minority, and would gladly have excluded the Howards, Wriothesley, Gardiner, Rich, and the whole Catholic element from the King's sick-room, while doing all she could to strengthen the hand of the Seymours, maternal uncles of the future King, who were intent on ruling his kingdom for him on strictly anti-papal lines. In the spring of the year 1546 the King had a bad relapse, and day by day the grey shadows of approaching death deepened on that broad and bloated countenance. He would not have the grim word mentioned in his presence, and any courtier who appeared before him dressed in mourning[55]—even for the nearest kin—was driven in fury from his sight. None the less, he realised that he had not many months to live. It was imperative, therefore, if any reconciliation with Rome was to be effected before the new reign began, that no time should be lost, and that some sharp and decisive blow should overthrow the influence of the Queen, now the chief intermediary between her sick spouse, Cranmer, and the Seymours. But Katherine, in spite of the notoriety of her intimate friendship with Sir Thomas Seymour, was far too clever to give her enemies any chance of blasting, or even smirching, her reputation. With respect to her religious opinions, which were distinctly heterodox, she was less guarded, however, and her enemies had good reason to believe that if they could convince the King, beyond any doubt, that she was in correspondence with those whom he was pleased to term "heretics," she would never be able to weather the storm her treachery must inevitably raise in the King's resentful breast.

Henry, whose brain remained astonishingly active, notwithstanding his infirmities, had never been so irritable and ferocious as during the last few months of his life. He was like a half-dead rattlesnake, which may recover life and spring afresh upon its prey at any moment. Never were the fires at Smithfield so active as in 1546. Early in this year six poor wretches were sent to the stake—three Catholics; the other three, Reformers. To demonstrate the impartiality[61] of their merciless judge they were all chained together. People scarcely knew what they must believe or what disbelieve, to escape execution. The King's informers were always at work, spying upon the sayings and doings of people in every rank of life; and the wonder is that the Queen and her ladies were not caught in some imprudent admission or other, and convicted. At last, however, in the early spring of 1546, an incident occurred which brought Katherine's foes their longed-for chance of effecting her downfall.

Anne Askew, second daughter of Sir William Askew, or Ayscough, of South Kelsy, Lincolnshire, was born at Stallingbrough, near Grimsby, in 1521. When about fifteen years of age, she was married, without her consent, to Mr. Thomas Kyme, a Lincolnshire squire and neighbour, who had been previously "contracted" to her elder sister. During her early wedded life Mrs. Kyme appears to have been happy enough, and became the mother of two children. She presently occupied herself in studying the newly translated Scriptures, and shortly after imagined she had a divine mission to preach the gospel and correct what she deemed the theological errors of her neighbours, especially on the subject of the Lord's Supper, concerning which she held Genevan views.

After a few years of discomfort, Mr. Kyme, who, according to the latest researches, entertained contrary religious opinions to those of his wife, began to complain of the scanty enjoyment he derived from her society. She was perpetually "gadding up and down the country, a-gospelling and a-gossiping, instead of looking after her children." Anne is described as a handsome and daring young woman with a good deal of native wit and ability, and was evidently the prototype of not a few ladies of our own time, who prefer public life and controversy to domestic duty and retirement. She even took upon herself to read and comment on the New Testament in the nave of Lincoln Cathedral, where she was often to be found surrounded by an interested or amused group of priests and people. This state of things no Dean or Chapter could be expected to endure, and one fine day Mrs. Kyme found herself forcibly ejected from the sacred edifice. After this incident, she must have had some unusual disagreement with her husband, for her relations persuaded her to leave the town, and she travelled[62] to London, where she soon made herself conspicuous as a preacher of the new learning, and secured several distinguished converts. She lodged in a house near the Temple, and one of her neighbours, Mr. Wadloe, a hot Catholic, who began by deriding her behaviour, ended by admiring her "godliness"; to use his own expression—"At mydnyght when I and others applye ourselves to sleape, or do worse, Mrs. Askew" (she had resumed her maiden name), "begins to pray, and ceaseth not in many howers after," doubtless to the edification of such of her neighbours as suffered from insomnia.

By dint of perseverance, and also, it may be, through her connections, Anne Askew formed the acquaintance of several great ladies of the Court, and is said to have obtained, through the offices of the Duchess of Suffolk, an interview with the Queen, to whom, in the presence of her ladies, notably Lady Tyrwhitt, Lady Lane, Lady Denny, and the little Lady Jane Grey,56 she offered some copies of Tyndale's version of the New Testament, and certain tracts arguing against Transubstantiation, which were subsequently found in the Queen's own closet and in the possession of the King's "Suffolk nieces."

It was in March 1545 that Mrs. Askew was first arrested on a charge of heresy and taken to Sadler's Hall, where she was denounced to the civil authorities and taken before the Lord Mayor, who in the course of his examination questioned her as to the probable changes in a consecrated wafer after a "mowse" had swallowed it, whereupon she "made no answer but smiled," and was committed to the Counter. That much-abused man, Bishop Bonner, appears to have taken an interest in her case, and endeavoured to save her from an awful fate. He granted her a private interview and drew up a form of recantation which she signed in the following ambiguous terms: "I, Anne Askew, do believe all manner of things contained in the Catholic Church and not otherwise." On this, Bonner, whose patience had been severely tried,—for Anne was very sharp-tongued and uncompromising,—waxed wroth, and taking her by the shoulders, pushed her out of the chamber. Her next friend was Dr. Weston, afterwards Bishop of Westminster, who got her liberated on her own security; and for some months we hear no more about her, except that she63 was busy preaching and distributing her tracts secretly. On 10th May 1546 both Mr. and Mrs. Kyme received a summons to present themselves within a specified time before the Privy Council, then sitting at Greenwich, and they accordingly appeared on the 19th of the following June before the Chancellor of the Augmentations, Sir Richard Rich, the Bishops of Durham and Winchester and a number of other noblemen and gentlemen, and were put through a severe cross-examination.57 Anne, we learn, received this summons in London, but her husband came to town on purpose to attend. Kyme got off with a caution, on his promise to return forthwith to Lincoln, and remain there. His wife, in open court, declared she would never again recognise him as her husband. He went back to Lincoln, and we lose sight of him. All we know is that he died, where he is buried, at Friskne in 1591.

Anne Askew was eventually arraigned before the King's Justices at Guildhall for speaking against the Sacrament of the Altar, contrary to the Statute of the Six Articles. This time she appeared with two other "heretics," one of them that singular personage Dr. Nicholas Shaxton, ex-Bishop of Salisbury, whose pupil she is said to have been. Shaxton, a Norfolk man by birth, was one of the Commission appointed by Gardiner in connection with the divorce of Katherine of Aragon, and during the proceedings he so favoured the King's view that he eventually became almoner to Anne Boleyn and Bishop of Salisbury. At a later date he preached Zwinglian doctrines concerning the Eucharist, got himself into serious difficulties with Archbishop Cranmer, and was forced to relinquish his see. After a time he became a notorious "gospeller," and was finally arrested with Anne Askew and a man named Christopher White. The lady and White were both sent to Newgate; but the former recanted, and so escaped a fiery ordeal. Shaxton did the same, obtained his pardon, and was actually ordered to visit Anne in prison, and persuade her to follow his example. But, weak woman though she was, Anne was made of sterner stuff than the ex-prelate. "It were better for you you had not been born than do that which you have done," cried she; and, crestfallen, her former friend and tutor left her presence. Her condemnation followed immediately afterwards. It was64 presently noticed that Anne enjoyed more creature comforts in prison than the customs of Newgate allowed. She explained the matter by saying that "her maid went abroad into the streets and made moan to the prentices and they did send her money!" But her persecutors refused to believe this story, and so one afternoon, not long before her martyrdom, she was conveyed to the Tower, taken to the torture chamber, and there racked in the presence of Lord Chancellor Wriothesley, Sir Richard Rich, Sir John Barker, and Sir Anthony Knyvett, Constable of the Tower. Hitherto no one had been tortured in England for conscience' sake, this terrible resource being solely employed to extract information from persons suspected of treasonable practices. Wriothesley, exasperated at his failure to elicit direct information or satisfactory answers from his victim, turned the screws himself, after Knyvett had refused to order her to be further tormented by the official executioner. Sir Richard Rich lent his hand to the Chancellor in this merciless task, and so, to use poor Anne's own words, she "was nigh dead."[58]

Dr. Lingard and other historians have cast doubt upon the veracity of this horrible story, but the scene is described by Anne herself in her "Narrative," dictated a few days before her death, and published at Marburg, in the Duchy of Hesse, in 1547, with a long running commentary by John Bale, afterwards Bishop of Ossory. In his *Three Conversions of England*, the Jesuit, Father Parsons, who had access to much information and evidence long since destroyed or lost, not only confirms the truth of the torture episode, but adds that it was ordered by the King himself, who, hearing of the intercourse between his Queen and Anne, "caused her to be apprehended and put to the rack, to know the truth thereof. And by her confession he learned so much of Queen Katherine, as he had purposed to burn her also, if he had lived." Parsons goes on to say that "the King's sickness and death, shortly ensuing, was the chief cause of her escape." Mrs. Askew bravely endured the most horrible torments rather than betray her friends' trust, and[65] only yielded so far as to admit that whilst in prison she had received ten shillings, delivered by a man in a blue livery. She thought the money had been sent her by the Countess of Hertford, but was not sure. She had a further sum of eight shillings at the hand of a footman in a purple livery, and believed it was a gift from Lady Denny. Questioned if she knew Lady Fitzwilliam, the Duchess of Suffolk, Lady Sussex, or any other great ladies of the Court, she evasively answered that she "knew nothing about them that could be proved." She does not seem to have been questioned point-blank as to whether she had ever had any direct dealings with the Queen. Wriothesley may have thought he had already obtained sufficient information for his purpose. However that may have been, the stout-hearted lady was sent back to Newgate, there to spend her last three days of life, which she occupied in writing and dictating the "Narrative" to be found among Dr. Bale's writings.[59]

On the eve of her execution Anne Askew and three men who had been condemned for heresy at the same time as herself were visited in the little parlour at Newgate by George Throckmorton and his brother, who were kinsmen of the Queen—a rather suspicious circumstance. They were cautioned in time, and thus escaped being arrested on a charge of heresy, which might have proved fatal to themselves and their royal cousin. John Louthe, the Reformer, who has left us an account of the meeting, also came, at great risk to himself, to encourage the unfortunate Anne. Mrs. Askew, with an "Angel's countenance and a smiling face," talked "merrily" with her unhappy companions, John Laselles, who had been a gentleman in attendance upon the King, and is supposed to have been the individual who betrayed the secrets of Katherine Howard; Nicholas Bolenian, a priest from Shropshire; and John Adams, a tailor. They talked on religious subjects until it was time to separate. The next day, 16th July, Mrs. Askew and her three fellow-prisoners were taken from Newgate to Smithfield. So dislocated were the poor lady's limbs that she had to be carried to her doom in a chair. Cranmer, seeking to throw the full odium of the horrible[66] business on Gardiner, kept much in the background in the whole matter of Anne Askew. He did not attend the ecclesiastical commission which condemned her to the stake; but for all that his signature is affixed to her death-warrant. Six years later, another martyr, Joan Bocher, one of the last of his many victims, reminded the Archbishop that he had martyred her friend Anne Askew for teaching more or less the same doctrines he now preached himself.

In the 1563 edition of Foxe's *Martyrs* there is a most curious engraving, probably after an original drawing, representing the burning of Anne Askew and her companions. The spectators are kept back by a ring fence within which we see the stake, and a quaint pulpit, from which Dr. Nicholas Shaxton, duly restored to grace, preached a sermon, supporting the very dogma for denying which he had been prosecuted but a few days previously. Anne is shown dressed in white; one side of the pyre is entirely devoted to her, while the three men, apparently naked to the waist, are bound together, on the side opposite the pulpit. The concourse of people appears enormous; the mob seems to seethe round the scaffold, loll out of the surrounding windows, and even swarm on the opposite roofs. On a raised bench, under a canopy, sit Wriothesley, Rich, the Dukes of Norfolk, Surrey, "Swearing Russell," and the Lord Mayor. These worthies, it appears, were sorely perturbed by a rumour that there was an unusual amount of gunpowder on the spot, and were very much afraid of a dangerous explosion. Their terrors were swiftly allayed when Bedford informed the company that the explosive in question was merely a number of small bags of gunpowder concealed about the persons of the victims with the object of shortening their sufferings.

At the very last moment Mrs. Askew was offered a pardon on condition that she recanted and gave up the names of her high-born friends. She refused: the Lord Mayor shouted *Fiat justitia*, and the faggots were lighted. Presently the fire crackled. A quick succession of explosions followed, the smoke concealing the wretched victims from sight. When the flames and smoke died down only the charred and blackened remains of four human beings could be descried. Clouds had been gathering; a peal of thunder rolled, and heavy drops of[67] rain soon dispersed the throng. The show was over, and the home-returning spectators chatted as they went, blaming or praising the deed, according to their individual view. The horror of it does not seem to have affected them much, although among the Reformers and the better classes of all creeds expressions of hearty indignation were not lacking. But the masses were accustomed to such sights of horror, and so, indeed, were our own immediate forbears, until public executions ceased and the death sentence was carried out in the courtyards of the prisons. We have indeed progressed in these matters since 1546 and even since 1868.

A few days after the burning of the unfortunate Lincolnshire lady, Foxe tells us, Wriothesley, Gardiner, and Rich waited on the King, and so persuaded him that Anne had made damaging revelations concerning the Queen's intercourse with heretics that Henry "proposed to burn her also." His Majesty, in his rage, actually signed a warrant for the arrest of his offending Consort and handed it to Wriothesley. That worthy let the paper drop in a corridor or gallery close to the Queen's apartment. One of her servants picked it up and carried it to Her Majesty, who was so terrified by its contents that she fell into violent hysterics. Her apartments were close to the King's, and Henry, overhearing the outcry, and probably disturbed by the noise, sent to inquire what was amiss. The Queen's physician, Wendy, informed the messenger that Her Majesty was dangerously ill, and her sickness, to his reckoning, caused by sudden and extreme distress of mind. Whereupon the King sent word that she was not to trouble herself further, as no ill was intended to her. Greatly comforted by this reassuring message, Katherine presently felt herself sufficiently recovered to receive a visit from her husband, who, at great personal inconvenience, caused himself to be conveyed into her apartment in his chair. Nothing could have been better calculated to revive the drooping spirits of the scared Consort than the sight of her august spouse in a good humour. The following evening she was well enough to return the King's visit. She was accompanied by the Lady Tyrwhitt, her sister the Lady Herbert, by the King's niece the Lady Jane Grey, and by the Lady Lane, who bore the candles before Her Majesty. The King welcomed the Queen[68] and her company very courteously, and, bidding her be seated, in a cheerful tone entered into a controversial conversation with her. He possibly wished to "draw" his Consort upon certain theological questions; but she shrewdly observed that "since God had appointed him Supreme Head of the Church it was not for her to teach him theology, but to learn it from him." "Not so, by St. Mary," said the King, "you are become a doctor, Kate, to instruct us, and not to be instructed of us, as oftentimes we have seen." "Indeed, indeed, Sire," quoth the Queen, "if your Majesty so conceive, my meaning has been mistaken, for I have always held it preposterous for a woman to instruct her lord." "If," she continued, "I have occasionally ventured to differ with your Highness on religious matters, it was partly to obtain information, and also to pass away the pain and weariness of your present infirmity with arguments that interested you." "And is it so, sweetheart?" replied His Majesty, "then we are perfect friends," and thereupon he kissed her and gave her leave to depart.

The day appointed by her foes for the Queen's arrest chanced to be fine and the sun shone brightly. The King sent for her to take the early air with him on the garden terrace overlooking the Thames. Katherine came, attended as before by her sister, the Lady Herbert, the Lady Lane, the Lady Tyrwhitt, and the little Lady Jane Grey. They had not been long walking up and down in the sunshine before the Lord Chancellor, with forty of the guard, entered the garden, expecting to carry off the Queen to the Tower—for no intimation of the change in the King's intentions had reached him. Henry received his minister with a burst of furious invective. Bidding the Queen and her ladies stand apart, he called up Wriothesley and cast every evil name he could think of at him, commanding him, finally, to "avaunt from his presence and never show his face again till he was summoned." Wriothesley, crestfallen and humbled, was about to withdraw, when the Queen advanced and interceded for him: "Poor soul, poor soul!" quoth the King; "thou little knowest, Kate, how ill he deserveth this grace at thy hands. On my hand, sweetheart, he hath been to thee a very knave!" So the disappointed minister departed, and Henry walked up and down the terrace69 again, leaning on his Queen and followed by her escort of ladies. Although Wriothesley's part in this tragi-comedy seems to have been overlooked, the King is said never to have forgiven Gardiner his share in the matter. A little later, notwithstanding the royal prohibition, both conspirators presented themselves with their colleagues. The King forthwith reminded Wriothesley in his most forcible manner that he had ordered him never to show his face again, and above all never, on any pretext whatever, to bring "that beast Gardiner" along with him. "My Lord of Winchester," replied the cunning Wriothesley, "has come to wait upon your Highness with an offer of benevolence from his clergy." The King being as usual in great need of money, began to listen more benignly, allowed Gardiner to present the address, and finally accepted the bribe.60 But he took no further notice of the Bishop, and is said to have struck his name off the list of his executors within the next few days. He also cancelled that of Thirlby, Bishop of Westminster, because, said he, "he is too much under the influence of Gardiner."61 Queen Katherine may have had a hand in this affair, and after the revelation of the treachery which would fain have destroyed her she very likely took the opportunity of letting the King know more concerning the machinations of Gardiner and Wriothesley than was good for their credit or likely to serve their influence.

The details of this formidable but abortive plot against Katherine Parr rest mainly on the authority of Foxe. But it must be remembered, by those inclined to doubt the "Martyrologist," that at this time he had attained his thirtieth year, he was in touch with most of the personages named, and was consequently in a position to obtain the information which he wove into his famous narrative—not, we admit, without considerable embellishment and exaggeration, introduced to suit the taste of his readers—from living witnesses. Foxe also made liberal use of Paget's statement during the proceedings70 for Gardiner's deprivation, which took place early in Edward's reign. All the Elizabethan and Jacobean historians of Henry VIII—Herbert, Parsons, Holinshed, Strype, Speed, Oldmixon, and others—reproduce the story with slight emendations and additions from Foxe. No direct confirmation of it is to be found indeed in the State Papers, but this is not surprising, for such matters were not usually set down in writing. Nevertheless, it is hinted at.62 Nor do the Ambassadors seem to have known anything about it. Father Parsons, who, like Foxe, obtained much of his information at first hand, introduces the incident in his *Three Conversions of England*, a book written to refute some of Foxe's errors, and adds that although Foxe lays "all the cause of the Queen's trouble upon Bishop Gardiner and others, and though the King did kindly and lovingly pardon her, the truth is that the King's sickness and death were the chief causes of her escape, for had the King found her guilty he would have commanded her also to be burned."

Speed, possibly mistaking Lady *Lane* for Lady Jane, introduces the King's little niece on this occasion, not only as a witness of the reconciliation of the royal couple, but in the character of a candle-bearer before the Queen. Jane Grey, being a Princess of the Blood, could never have been in *attendance* upon the

Queen, and she was too small a child to be laden with a pair of heavy branch candlesticks. Lady Lane, on the other hand, was certainly in the Queen's Household at this particular juncture. She was Her Majesty's cousin-german, being the daughter of her uncle, Lord Parr of Horton, and wife of Sir Ralph Lane of Orlingby, Nottinghamshire. Still, since the fact of her being present is mentioned by so many almost contemporary writers, we may conclude that Lady Jane was a witness of the dramatic scenes that took place between King Henry and his terrified Consort, and may herself, in after life, have narrated the incident to some friend of Foxe or immediate forbear of Parson's informant. Gardiner's disgrace does not seem to have been quite as complete as Foxe has been pleased to represent it, and he was in close enough contact with those in power to be selected as chief celebrant at the King's Requiem.

71 That the King was completely reconciled to his wife is proved by the conspicuous part he assigned her in the splendid series of festivities in honour of the French Envoy, who arrived in August, when the Court had removed to Hampton Court. Not only was her apartment refurnished with sumptuous tapestries, but her wardrobe was renewed, and the King presented her with a quantity of magnificent jewellery, which, after his death, gave rise to considerable misunderstanding and trouble.

These festivities in honour of Monsieur d'Annebault, Francis I's special Envoy, were the last flicker of the pageantry of Henry VIII's reign, and revived for a week something of the brilliance of the Court of England in the great days of Wolsey. For the first and only time, Prince Edward, as heir-apparent, played a conspicuous part. On Monday, 23rd August, the boy-prince rode out towards London to meet the Ambassador, attended by the Archbishop of York and the Earls of Hertford and Huntingdon, and by a retinue of "five hundred and forty persons in velvet coats, and the Prince's liveries wore sleeves of cloth of gold, and half the coats embroidered also with gold, and there were the number of eight hundred, royally apparelled." D'Annebault, who came to ratify the peace recently concluded between the sovereigns of France and England, was accompanied by a suite of two hundred gentlemen, who were all lodged at the King's expense and entertained in the most hospitable manner. His Majesty was not well enough to receive the Ambassador on his arrival, but he received him in audience on the following day, after which monarch and Ambassador proceeded to the Chapel Royal, where, during Mass, they solemnly received the Host together.63 Then followed six days of banqueting, hunting, and merry-making, masques, and mummeries, "with divers and sundry changes, inasmuch that the torch-bearers were clothed with gold cloth, and such like honourable entertainments, it were much to utter and hard to believe." On these occasions the Marchioness of Dorset and her daughter, the Lady Jane72 Grey, were present, and Prince Edward danced with his little cousin, who also tripped it with young Lord Edward Seymour, the Lord Hertford's eldest boy. When the Ambassador took his leave, Henry made him a present of silver plate to the value of £1200. After his departure the dying King seems to have led a very quiet life at Hampton Court and Whitehall. The end was visibly approaching. His feet and hands were abnormally swollen; dropsy had set in, and he was probably also suffering from an internal tumour. Even his most fervent admirers were obliged to confess that in appearance, at least, he had assumed somewhat of the aspect of a monster; but music still charmed the suffering monarch, and the last Household Books of his reign contain various items of payments to musicians and madrigal singers.

Note.—Dr. Gairdner makes the following comments on this subject in his Preface to vol. 21, part i. of the Calendar of State Papers for 1546 (published in 1908): "But one word may be permitted here about that dreadful incident, the racking in the Tower. It took place *after* her (Anne's) condemnation, the object being to elicit from her information about persons at the Court who it was suspected had been her allies in promoting heresy. Besides others whose names are given, against whom she positively refused to utter a word, she was probably expected to accuse Queen Katherine Parr herself; for Parsons (*Three Conversions of England*, ii. 493) is no doubt perfectly correct in saying that the well-known incident related by Foxe, about this Queen, when she stood in real danger from a charge of heresy, was connected with the affair of Anne Askew. But Parsons is certainly wrong in saying that the King would have burned Katherine Parr also if he had lived. For though her heretical propensities were no secret, she survived the King, and he himself for fully six months survived Anne Askew. More probably the Queen was saved by Anne's refusal to commit anyone except herself."

CHAPTER VI
THE HOWARDS AND THE SEYMOURS

The collapse of the conspiracy against Katherine Parr led to an immediate counter-plot on the part of the Seymours and their allies to compromise the Duke of Norfolk and his son, Surrey, and thereby frustrate the aspirations of the Catholics, of whose party Norfolk was the acknowledged chief. A previous attempt to inflict irretrievable damage on the credit of the Howards had partially failed, though the unsavoury revelations connected with the arrest and execution of Queen Katherine Howard had covered the illustrious name with obloquy, and almost every conspicuous Howard in England had been sent to the Tower,64 on the charge of having concealed the Queen's previous immorality from the King's knowledge when he proposed to marry her. At that moment Norfolk and his son only escaped by taking Henry's side against their miserable kinswoman. But the Duke never regained his full influence over his master, and, despite his great services, both as statesman and warrior, lived on, to use the expression of one of his contemporaries, "like the bird that is wounded i' the wing." Yet he was a great power in the politics of those days, for though the Catholic party was of but small account at Court, a good two-thirds of the people remained firmly attached to the ancestral faith; this was the case more especially in the rural districts, where the vast majority clung to the dogmas and ceremonies of the ancient Church, and only awaited an opportunity to assert their74 preference. For the matter of that, it was shown very early in Queen Mary's reign that the Protestant fervour of the official world, being a matter of policy rather than of conviction, was not to be relied on. The majority of that aristocracy which had so eagerly accepted the extreme reforms assented to by Edward VI was to be seen, a few weeks after his death, parading the streets of London, taper in hand, in the wake of the revived processions of Corpus Christi and Our Lady.65

Thomas Howard, third Duke of Norfolk, was one of the most conspicuous figures in Henry's reign. He may not, perhaps, have been as astute a statesman as has been asserted, but he showed remarkable qualities as a capable peacemaker on the occasion of the Pilgrimage of Grace; while as a warrior he had no rival, and proved himself a hero on Flodden Field. If anything, he was excessive in his loyalty to the King, and he would even seem to have sunk all sense of his own dignity and importance, humbling himself utterly before the monarch whose assumption of *quasi*-divine attributes he had aided and abetted. Thus, when his niece Anne Boleyn was tried and executed for misdemeanours she was certainly not proved to have committed,66 he, at her royal assassin's command, pronounced the death sentence, and with his son, the young Earl of Surrey, who sat at his feet, holding the Earl Marshal's baton in his hand, was actually present at her execution. When, some few years later, Norfolk's other niece, Katherine Howard, was proved guilty of many serious offences, both before and after marriage, Norfolk sat in judgment upon her and would have witnessed her death too but for an attack of gout which kept him a prisoner. Two days after the execution he penned an abject letter to the King apologising for "the naughtiness of his said niece, the late Queen."67 In person, Norfolk was a dark, handsome75 man, of moderate stature, with piercing eyes and an exceedingly intelligent countenance. Holbein has left us several magnificent oil portraits of him, and at least one noble drawing, now in the Windsor Collection. He was fairly educated, a good Latin scholar, and a patron of art. His first wife, Princess Anne Plantagenet, the King's aunt, died young in 1512. The day on which he espoused his second,68 the handsome Lady Elizabeth Stafford, was an evil one for him. The alliance was one of convenience on his side and of compulsion on hers. His duchy had been greatly impoverished by the attainder of his father, the second Duke, after Bosworth, and the luckless Buckingham's daughter was possessed of a handsome fortune in money and wide lands. She had been previously contracted to Ralph Nevill, afterwards Earl of Westmoreland, to whom she was greatly attached and with whom she kept up a correspondence till the end of her life. Although she bore her husband five children, the Duchess of Norfolk suffered some neglect at his hands, her rival being a certain Bess Holland,69 a gentlewoman in her service. The mortification caused by this outrage drove the poor Duchess to the verge of distraction. She seems to have been a naturally conscientious, if narrow-minded, woman, of an exceedingly high-strung and excitable temperament. We should describe her nowadays as an "impossible" person, whose lack of tact and outbursts of uncontrollable rage not only alienated her husband's affections, but deprived her of her children's love as well as of her servants' respect.

Of all the men of his time, Surrey, this ill-used lady's son, was the most accomplished. He was an excellent Latin, French, and Italian scholar, and well versed in ancient and modern literature. No one could excel him in tourney or joust—not even John Dudley, afterwards Duke of Northumberland,76 who had exceeding skill with the sword and spear, and than whom scarce one could pull a bow with surer aim. Surrey danced more lightly than Thomas Seymour, who prided himself on the "altitude of his pirouettes," and the King himself in his singing youth did not warble a sweeter note. No Englishman since Chaucer had so enriched our literature with verse all redolent of those sweet-scented fields and lanes, meadows and gardens amid which the poet's muse loved best to linger. An Elizabethan critic well described him as "a poet new crept out of the school of Dante, Petrarch, and Ariosto," and "coming nearer to Ariosto" than to either the prophet of Florence or the inspired singer of Vaucluse. Though of but medium height, Surrey was so graceful and well-proportioned as to seem taller than he really was. There is a portrait of him at Hampton Court, most probably by Guilliam Streete, which gives us a fair idea of this prince for a fairy-tale. The face is full of youthful charm: the eyes hazel, frank, and winning; the cheeks rounded and flushed with rosy health; the hair a darkish chestnut; the slight moustache of the colour of ripe corn. His costume is superb. The young Earl stands before us garbed from head to foot in red velvet, softened by bands of brocade and sarsenet, the only white spot visible being the silk shirt open at the neck, and even that enriched with a dainty arabesque wrought in gold stitchery. On his well-shaped head rests a jaunty cap of crimson velvet with a feathered plume of the same tint.

There was much that was purely personal in the violent animosity displayed by the Seymours against the Howards in general and against Surrey in particular. The Seymours, although of far more ancient and well-ascertained lineage than either the Brandons or the Boleyns, were not of the great aristocracy, but, in a sense, what the modern French would call *arrivistes*. Had it not been for the accident which raised their sister Jane to the towering position of Queen-Consort, the Seymours would probably have remained what they originally were, mere country squires of excellent lineage, reputed to be remotely connected with royalty. Their father,70 Sir77 William St. Maur, or Seymour, of Wolf's Hall, Wiltshire, had on one occasion entertained King Henry VIII; and their mother, Lady Seymour, by birth a Wentworth, and a lineal descendant of Edward III, was highly connected; but otherwise there was nothing in their antecedents to distinguish them from scores of other equally respectable and wealthy country gentlemen. The sudden71 elevation of their sister Jane brought them a rapid promotion, which first dazzled them and then turned their heads. Honours and positions were heaped upon them. Edward, the eldest son, was first created Viscount Beauchamp, and, after the birth of Prince Edward, Earl of Hertford; the second, Thomas, was knighted. The youngest, Henry, seems to have preferred obscurity and security to rank and risk, and lived the life of a country gentleman, married young, and merely accepted knighthood on Edward VI's accession.

The ranks of the old aristocracy had been thinned by the prolonged civil wars and the plague, and towards the middle of the century the Court was so full of new men that at the time of Henry's last illness there were only two dukes in the peerage—Norfolk, then seventy-two; and Suffolk, a lad of seventeen. The new peers, whose fortunes were mainly derived from confiscated church property, were eager to obtain recognition from the few of the old aristocracy who yet remained, and more especially from the Howards, a sturdy race, full of sap and vigour, and conspicuous in Court and State. The Duke of Norfolk was too experienced a man, both socially and politically, to permit his inborn pride of birth to display itself out of season. With Surrey it was otherwise. In his case, pride of ancestry was something more than a mere matter of vulgar boast. He regarded it with a poet's eye and imagination, and took delight in remembering that through his veins[78] flowed the blood of emperors and kings who had founded realms and dynasties, and built up the glory of a great nation. In the beginning of the fifteenth century a marriage between Robert Howard and the Lady Margaret Mowbray had brought the illustrious house into alliance with royalty. His father's first wife had been the reigning King's aunt, and his mother, Elizabeth Stafford, had a right to quarter Royal Arms on her escutcheon. With such a pedigree, and in an age when rank was paramount, Surrey conceived himself sufficiently powerful to hold his own against the encroachments of a new peerage only too eager to claim a fellowship which offended his sense of propriety.

When the Seymours first came to Court, in the heyday of their youth and good looks, they sought young Surrey's society, just as in our day new people seek that of a leader of the "smartest set." So long as they kept their place, Surrey consorted with them willingly enough; but their rapacity and arrogance jarred on him at last, and he resented their many attempts at over-familiarity. He himself, on occasion, was apt to transgress the bounds of good behaviour, and once upon a time, being in lodgings in St. Lawrence Lane, Old Jewry, and leading what he himself is pleased to call a "racketty life," went brawling about the streets at midnight with young William Pickering[72] and young Wyatt, the poet's son, casting stones into peaceful citizens' windows, and frightening them out of their wits. One night the party rowed over in a boat to Southwark, where dwelt in those days that gay and facile sisterhood whose representatives, in this year of Grace, 1909, patrol more central parts of our great city. In this fast company, our young gentlemen, evidently in their cups, behaved disgracefully. On Surrey's part such conduct was all the more unseemly since he was already married to the plain-faced, but wealthy, Lady Frances Vere,[73] Lord Oxford's daughter, to whom he declared himself devotedly attached. These escapades ended by attracting public attention, and their heroes were arrested for disorderly conduct. Thanks to their rank, they[79] were brought before the Privy Council,[74] instead of being haled before an ordinary justice, though, as ill-luck would have it, Edward, Lord Hertford, was presiding at the Council board. The opportunity of paying off a few old scores was too much for him, and he swiftly resolved to give Surrey good cause to remember him in future. A very comical and characteristic scene ensued.[75] Surrey, mimicking Hertford, who was nothing if not puritanical in his mode of expressing himself, "having ever God on his lips," assured the Council that if he had done what he had, it had been for the good of the souls of the wicked citizens of London, who were behaving more abominably than the men of papal Rome. Had he not seen them sitting round tables and playing at cards in the late hours of the night?—and was it not a godly thing to whizz a stone or so at their windows, which stone, passing silently through the air, fell with all the greater suddenness among them, thereby recalling them to a proper sense of their duties to their God, their King, and their country?[76] Mrs. Arundel, a woman of good family but greatly impoverished, who kept a sort of boarding-house for bachelors of rank in St. Lawrence Lane, Old Jewry, was the Earl's landlady, and imparted a very different colour to the episode. "Her young gentleman," she said, had frankly admitted to her that he considered these[80] pranks good jokes: but she herself disapproved of them, especially the shooting at the windows of women of light character, or "bawds," in Southwark, which the Earl, it seems, was addicted to, going by boat close to their quarters and firing off petards at the "trolls"! There was nothing for it, therefore, but to pronounce sentence. Surrey was committed to the Fleet, the most abominable of all the many vile prisons of those days, while Wyatt and Pickering, though of much inferior rank, were sent to the stately Tower, whence they were delivered in a day or two on payment of a heavy fine and promising good behaviour. How long Surrey remained in durance it is difficult to say—long enough certainly for him to compose his "Satire on the Citizens of London" and several other poems. He never forgave Seymour his share in the business, and never failed to annoy his enemy openly or covertly whenever opportunity occurred. It was quite in keeping with his character to address amatory verses with this intent to Hertford's handsome and very proud wife, who took his lines in very bad part, as so many insults to her honour. The Countess once made a scandal by deliberately turning her back upon the poet-Earl when, in August 1542, at a ball in his own father's house,77 he ventured to ask her permission to lead her out to dance.

81 Late in the summer of 1542 a very serious quarrel broke out between Seymour and Surrey, over an incident which took place in Hampton Court Park. Seymour, it was alleged, had reported against Surrey that he had openly approved of the Pilgrimage of Grace. Surrey, coming face to face with his antagonist in a glen in the park, instantly challenged him. Coats were off in a moment, and the two were in the midst of a hearty boxing-match when the guard arrived and took both into custody for violating the royal privilege and fighting within the precincts of the King's palace. The punishment for this offence, as readers of *The Fortunes of Nigel* will recollect, was loss of the right hand. All the diplomacy and influence of the Duke of Norfolk had to be exerted to avert the infliction of this terrible penalty; but, thanks to his efforts, both the hot-headed young gentlemen escaped with a sharp reprimand. Scores of similar curious instances might be quoted from the chronicles and letters of the time, to prove the depth and bitterness of the social animosity between the Howards and the Seymours. The Duke himself resented the cruel manner in which Hertford had behaved in the matter of His Grace's niece, the unhappy Katherine Howard. There can be no doubt that at one time both Cranmer and the King wished to spare her life, and would have spared it had not Hertford, in his hot haste to ruin the Howards' credit, prematurely dispatched letters to the King's Ambassadors abroad containing full details of the Queen's disgrace, with orders to hand them to the sovereigns to whose Courts they were accredited. This publicity rendered the royal clemency impossible.78

Early in the summer of 1546 the Duke of Norfolk made up his mind, in what he held to be the interests of himself and his family, to bring about a reconciliation, if that were possible, between his house and Seymour's. He fully realised that, ageing as he was, he could no longer be a match for two unscrupulous and very able men, then reaching the prime of82 life, and already holding the King's complete confidence. Further, he felt Surrey to be hopeless in all business calling for tact and diplomacy, and was convinced the persistent animosity between his son and Hertford would lead before long to some awful catastrophe. Surrey's bravery as a fighting soldier was undisputed, but as a commander his lack of reticence and his rashness had led the King's troops in France into more than one disaster; he himself had paid the penalty of his rashness before the walls of Montreuil, where he was seriously wounded and only saved from certain death by the gallantry of Sir Thomas Clere. He had then been recalled, and Hertford had been sent to take his place, a bitter humiliation to the proud Howards and one which more than anything else rankled in Surrey's soul. Yet the old Duke recognised that Hertford's bravery and tact as warrior and diplomatist had soon ended the war and obtained peace with honour for the English forces, thus raising his popularity to the highest pitch; for there was nothing the nation then desired so much as peace, at home and abroad. Hertford's brother, Sir Thomas, was, if anything, still more popular, for he had so successfully scoured the seas in quest of French galleons laden with provisions that suppressed monasteries had been converted into storehouses. The magnificent ex-church of the Grey Friars had become a wine-vault, crammed to the roof with barrels of Burgundy and other wines of the best French vintages. In Austin Friars such a stock of cheeses was stored that there was no moving in that erstwhile beautiful priory church, and the huge and splendid church of the Black Friars was literally packed with salt herring and dried cod. Wherefore the people had good reason to be well pleased with brother Thomas.

The Duke, then, without consulting his son,—and here his disastrous mistake,—obtained an interview with Hertford, and, skilfully playing on his well-known vanity and social ambition, suggested at length that a betrothal should be forthwith arranged between Hertford's eldest daughter and Surrey's eldest son, and a similar contract entered into between Lord Thomas Howard79 and Seymour's youngest daughter, the Lady Jane Seymour. His Grace, apparently in a match-making[83] mood, gave his paternal sanction to the wooing and wedding of his beautiful daughter, the widowed Duchess of Richmond, by Sir Thomas Seymour. With all these suggestions the Seymours gladly closed, making but one condition, that Surrey should accept a slightly subordinate position under Hertford's command, virtually tantamount to a tacit apology for his repeated slights, covert and open, in the past. On Tuesday in Whitsun week 1546, then, the Duke, well pleased with his own diplomacy, presented himself at Whitehall and laid his rather complicated scheme of alliances before His Majesty. Henry was graciously pleased to approve it, and willingly agreed that his daughter-in-law of Richmond should become the bride of the handsome Thomas Seymour, with whom, according to Court gossip, she was already much in love. But in all these schemes the Duke had reckoned without his host, for when he put the matter before Surrey, that impetuous poet flew into a towering rage. He would "sooner see his children dead in their coffins than married to Seymour's brats," he said. Then, turning furiously on his sister, the Duchess of Richmond, who had accompanied her father, he cried,—at least, according to that dangerous Court gossip, Sir Gawen Carew,—"Go, carry out your farce of a marriage. My Lord of Hertford is in full favour, I grant; but why not do yet better for yourself and follow Madame d'Estampes' example with King Francis. Get you into the same sort of favour with King Henry, and rule through him." This sinister advice was evidently dictated by that vein of bitter sarcasm usual with Surrey when the uncontrollable temper which he inherited from his mother mastered his common sense. It could not have been seriously meant, for nobody knew better than Surrey that the King was already more than half dead, utterly unable to trouble himself about new mistresses, and in any case not likely to select his own daughter-in-law to replace his excellent Queen-Consort and nurse, Katherine Parr. The Duchess of Richmond, however, took the jibe seriously, replied that she "would sooner cut her throat" than do "any such vile thing," and left her irate brother to his own reflections, which, when he cooled down, cannot have been particularly agreeable. He knew his sister well; she was an exceedingly beautiful woman, to whom Holbein, in his exquisite drawing,[84] has given the expression of one of Ghirlandajo's sweetest Madonnas. But at heart she was a little fiend, capable, when her passions were roused, of working dire mischief. She said little at the time, but she nursed her grievance and exaggerated its importance. She may also have felt not a little embittered against Sir Thomas Seymour, who had ungallantly refused her hand because it was not accompanied by her brother's submission. Be this as it may, "the Duchess of Richmond from that day forth hated her brother as much as she had previously loved him,"[80] and when the hour for revenge came at last, forgetful of her obligations as sister and woman, she scandalised even that unsentimental age by appearing at her brother's trial as one of the principal witnesses for the prosecution.

Meanwhile the Duke of Norfolk was at his wits' end to know how to make Hertford aware of the unfortunate results of his negotiations with his son. He was possessed of a perfect mania for putting pen to paper on any and every pretext, although, as every one who has waded through his correspondence knows, there has never been a statesman, before or since, who could indite more indiscreet and exasperating epistles. If then, as is likely, he conveyed the unpleasant news by letter, he was not the man to improve matters by a tactful manner. The breach between the Howards and the Seymours was now complete. Hertford, hurt in pride and vanity, would accept no apologies from the Duke, and the feud between himself and Surrey soon grew more bitter than ever. To make matters worse, the Duchess of Richmond made a confidant of her friend, Sir Gawen Carew, who detested her brother, and was the most inveterate gossip of the Court, as is well known to those who have read the State Papers connected with the tragedy of Katherine Howard; it was, indeed, the gossip of Sir Gawen that did most to ruin that Queen. Presently young scions of the nobility, courtiers who hated the Howards for their airs and graces and forgot the old Duke's well-known kindness to the youthful, buzzed about the King, and did their best to set him against the luckless Earl. Hertford and his brother afforded them ample assistance, supplying all necessary instructions and information; and, for all we know to the[85] contrary, the Queen may have lent a helping hand. In fact, the whole Protestant party was now roused against the Howards, the representatives of the Catholics, and determined to bring about their ruin or perish in the attempt. It had hoped the folly of Katherine Howard would have sufficed for this purpose, but the great house of Norfolk was firm enough to resist even that storm. Another pretext had to be found, and the impolitic behaviour of the poet-Earl supplied it.

Poor Surrey was no match for the low and cunning intrigues amongst which "Fate and metaphysical aid" had thrown him. Somewhere in June 1546 he was summoned before the Privy Council, severely reprimanded for what he could not possibly help, and imprisoned in Windsor Castle, where he consoled himself by writing one of his most exquisite poems. This was his "Swan Song"! By August, however, he was certainly out of durance, and apparently once more in favour with the King, for he figured as Earl Marshal at the entertainments given in honour of the French Envoy, Claude d'Annebault, taking precedence of everyone excepting members of the royal family.

Early in September he left London, and returned to his wife and children at Kenninghall, accompanied by Churchyard the poet, who was his secretary, and an extremely numerous and miscellaneous retinue, which included several Italian painters, musicians, and jesters. One of the artists, Toto, was soon engaged upon a portrait of him, which was later used to his great disadvantage; in the left-hand corner of it appeared his escutcheon, bearing among its numerous quarterings the arms of England, but so arranged that a slide could be drawn, when necessary, over the coat-of-arms. The Duke of Norfolk and my Lady of Richmond came to Kenninghall Palace about this time; but the mansion, of which not a vestige now remains, was so enormous that every member of the ducal family had a separate dwelling. The Duchess of Richmond had a whole wing to herself, which she shared with her friend Mrs. Holland. The society of those days was not so dead to all sense of propriety as not to be scandalised by this singular intimacy between the Duke's daughter and his mistress. Most people agreed with the Duchess of Norfolk "that her[86] dater's abiding ever with that drab Holland" was a "scandayul and most unnatterall." Owing to the huge size of the mansion, not much inferior to that of Hampton Court, the Duchess and Mrs. Holland may never once have come into contact with Surrey and his family; otherwise, it is difficult to account for the fact that we have no record of any fiery scene between brother and sister. The Duke seems to have spent his time very quietly, reading the books he most affected, such as Plutarch's *Lives of Illustrious Men*, Josephus's *History*, and *The Confessions of St. Augustin*.[81]

Whilst the Howard family was thus peacefully rusticating in Norfolk, gossip and slander were making headway in the metropolis and preparing poor Surrey's ruin. Sir George Blagg, the "my Blagg" of one of his finest poems, had picked a quarrel with him in the summer, and was busy as a bee spreading evil reports against him. Sir Gawen Carew had confided to every one what the Duchess of Richmond had related to him anent her brother's advice to hasten and become the King's mistress. His enemies had even pressed the Court astrologer into their service, and this functionary had actually warned the King that unless he was careful, his successor's monogram would, like his own, be "H.R." The Duke himself was not spared: he had been seen to enter the French Ambassador's house late at night and to leave it again in the small hours of the morning. A letter of his to Gardiner, then on a mission to Brussels, was intercepted—and vague though its terms were, it was held to be proof positive of Norfolk's adherence to Gardiner's scheme, as planned with Cardinal Granville, to restore the papal supremacy in England. At last, truth and lies together rolled themselves up into an ominous storm-cloud, which burst when Surrey was called to appear before the Council in London on a charge of high treason.

Some writers have attempted to extenuate Henry VIII's share in the *dénouement* of this tragedy. They plead that he was too ill at this time to know exactly what he was doing, and that, in consequence of the swollen state of his hands, he was compelled to use a stamp to sign his letters. With regard[87] to this, we know that as far back as 1st August 1546 he had commissioned Sir Anthony Denny, Sir John Gates, and William Clere to sign documents for him with a dry stamp, the signature thus made being filled in with ink. And even this is not the first time Henry had recourse to a mechanical contrivance for signing letters and State Papers. Lord Hardwick has a letter of the King's signed with a stamp and dated as early as the seventh year of his reign. Moreover, the official documents, which were drawn up by Wriothesley, are carefully annotated and corrected in pencil by Henry himself, with very full marginal notes and numerous interlineations. The handwriting is very shaky, but it is the King's none the less, and proves that if the monarch's body was infirm, his brain was as clear and his feelings as vindictive as ever. The death-warrant of the Earl of Surrey is also scribbled over on the margin with certain pencil notes in the King's own writing, proving that Henry must have retained the use of his hands to the end.

Sufficient evidence having been gathered, and Surrey being summoned to London, he left Kenninghall82 in the last days of September, and appeared before the Privy Council in Wriothesley's house in Holborn, not far from Chancery Lane, on 2nd October. His first accuser was Sir Richard Southwell, at one time in his mother's household at Kenninghall, who hated him heartily. He averred that Surrey had placed the Royal Arms of England in the first quartering of his escutcheon, thereby claiming the crown. When confronted with Southwell, Surrey, with his foolish impetuosity, and to the consternation of the Council, proposed a sort of trial by battle after the mediæval fashion. Southwell and he were there and then to divest themselves of their upper garments, descend on to the floor of the court, and indulge the Lord Chancellor and the Council with the spectacle of a boxing-match, the winner of which was to be declared innocent. The Council, needless to say, did not88 see fit to accept the fiery Earl's suggestion, and both Surrey and Southwell were temporarily detained—the Earl being not yet formally charged.

The examination of the other witnesses took place privately a few days later, before the Council but not in the presence of the prisoner. Sir Edmund Knyvyt, a son of the Lady Muriel Howard, the sister of the Duke of Norfolk, and therefore a cousin of Surrey, out of sheer spite, and also perhaps to give himself importance, accused the Earl of harbouring Italian spies in his house at Kenninghall, of affecting foreign airs, of wearing foreign costumes, and, gravest of all, of entertaining persons suspected of correspondence with Cardinal Pole and other "traitors" abroad. Then came Sir Gawen Carew with an exaggerated version of the Duchess of Richmond's story that her brother advised her to become the King's mistress, and had spoken lightly of the King's illness, and speculated as to what might occur in the event of his death; and before the week was out a score or so of other venal witnesses had concocted sufficient evidence to send fifty men to the block.

The Duke, meanwhile, tarried at Kenninghall, wondering what had happened to his son, and never imagining how bitter and relentless was the suddenly, and indeed inexplicably, developed hatred of the King, which we, however, know was stimulated by the Seymours and Cranmer for their own ends. Instead of coming up to London to help the Earl out of his difficulties, he set himself, as usual, to write confidential letters to those members of the Council upon whom he thought he could rely. These effusions were promptly shown to Hertford, with the result that His Grace himself was ordered to London with the utmost dispatch. On 12th December the Duke of Norfolk appeared before Lord Chancellor Wriothesley at his house in Holborn, near the present Southampton Buildings, and, to his unutterable amazement, found himself formally charged with high treason. He was immediately committed to the Tower, but on account of his rank and age, and to spare him the humiliation of being paraded as a prisoner through the city streets, he was conveyed down the hill, put on board a barge in the Fleet, and so to the Thames, through the arches of London Bridge,89 and onward to his ominous destination in the ancient fortress. Later in the same day Surrey too was conducted to the Tower, but he had to go on foot and through a dense multitude. To the consternation of his enemies, he was cheered all along the road, and grave fears were entertained of a rescue.83 Three commissioners were now dispatched to Kenninghall to bring the Duchess of Richmond and her friend Mrs. Holland up to town. Another embassy rode to Redbourne, to fetch the Duchess of Norfolk, who was only too delighted to come to London and blurt out all she could to the detriment of her hated spouse. By this time London could talk of nothing but the Surrey trial. In the palaces of the rich, in the hovels of the poor, in all the little taverns and drinking-houses down by the Thames, in the parlours of the great inns in Southwark and the Cheape, the conversation turned upon no other subject, and even the all-absorbing topic of the King's illness was forgotten for the time being. A touch of horror was added to the general excitement when it became known that Norfolk's wife and his daughter and mistress were to be the chief witnesses against him and his son. The Duchess did not spare her husband. Snatching at the welcome chance of avenging her wrongs, the half-witted lady grew garrulous, and confirmed everything *suggested* by those who desired to damn her lord's cause. She had but little to say, however, concerning her son, for the simple reason that she had not seen him for many months and knew nothing about his affairs. He was very "unnatturell" towards her, she declared, and so was her daughter, but nevertheless she "loved her children dearly." Her husband, she said, had leanings towards Popery, and caused his children to be brought up to deny the King's supremacy.

Mrs. Holland behaved with great discretion, considering her position and antecedents. It was true, she said, that the Duke of Norfolk had on one occasion told her that "if he had been young enough he would like to go to Rome to venerate the Veronica, an image of our Lord miraculously impressed upon a handkerchief which He had given to certain women on His way to Calvary." The Duke had bidden her[90] lay aside some needlework upon which she was engaged, to oblige the Earl of Surrey, and in a corner of which were his arms, one quartering of which was to be left blank, "probably for the introduction of the Royal Arms and monogram." She had obeyed the Duke's behest and never set needle into the work again. Before concluding her evidence, she, perhaps not unnaturally, seized the opportunity to try and clear her own reputation, and informed the Court that "the Earl detested her because she was so friendly with his sister."

The appearance of Mary, Duchess of Richmond, must have created a sensation. Her angelic beauty contrasted strangely with her spiteful and bitter nature. Like her mother, when she was once started there was no stopping her, and in her excitement she materially damaged her brother's cause, exaggerating every point against him suggested by the prosecution. With telling and dramatic effect she related the scene when he advised her to become the King's mistress. Her brother, she said, had been reading the book about Lancelot of the Lake, and had introduced that hero's arms, together with those of Anjou, into his own. He had recently had his portrait taken by an Italian artist, as already related, and had caused the arms of England to be painted into the left corner, with the monogram "H.R." surmounted by a crown, which she thought was a closed crown, like the King's. He had also appropriated the Confessor's arms, which belonged by right to the King, and the King only; he had spoken irreverently of His Majesty, and had speculated upon what might happen after his death; and, she added, "my lord of Hertford is particularly hateful to him because he superseded him at Boulogne, and indeed he detested the new nobility in general." The Council, to its credit, discarded the Duchess's evidence concerning Surrey's alleged infamous advice to her. They held it too abominable to be even probable, and it was not included in the indictment; but the rest of her evidence was considered very compromising.

On 13th January 1548 Surrey was brought on foot from the Tower to the Guildhall, which was packed to suffocation, and the charges of treacherously conspiring, together with his father, either to usurp the throne or seize the protectorate,[91] were read over to him. He made an eloquent defence, and, while denying every other item of the charge, said he had a right, in accordance with a grant made by Richard III to his grandfather, the first Duke of Norfolk, to use the arms of the Confessor; which was perfectly true—"Herald-at-Arms knew this, and was content he used them." As to his ever "having dreamed of usurping the throne," that was "mere chatter." He owned he bore Hertford no goodwill, but the fault rested with that gentleman, and was "not of my making." He was innocent on all points, he said, and called God to witness his loyalty to his King and country. In spite of all, sentence was passed upon him, and he was condemned to die on the following morning. The breathless silence with which the verdict had been awaited gave way to tumultuous protests from all sides of the Court, and it was only with great difficulty, even danger, that the hall was cleared. As the condemned Earl passed from the Guildhall to the Tower every cap was lifted, and the utmost sorrow and sympathy were displayed when the result of the trial was revealed by the sight of the executioner walking in the procession, the sharp edge of his axe turned towards the prisoner's person.

The next morning, 14th January, rose bright and frosty. A huge multitude had assembled on Tower Hill to witness the closing scene. Surrey, dressed in black velvet, looked very handsome, as with brave and elastic step he mounted the scaffold. He delivered the usual speech—a part of the grim pageant which no prisoner, male or female, ever missed—in a clear voice. He eloquently declared his innocence, forgave his enemies, and avowed his loyalty to his sovereign. He begged the prayers of all the company, and himself prayed aloud while the final preparations were being made. These done, in the midst of an awed silence, Surrey knelt to receive the fatal stroke, and with the sacred name of "Jesus" on his lips, his brave soul passed into eternity. Thus was the Court of England robbed of a gallant and magnificent gentleman, and the country of a man of genius, who, had he lived into the calmer and fostering atmosphere of Elizabeth's reign, might have left a name in literature equal, if not superior, to that of Spenser.

92 The Duke of Norfolk escaped trial, but not attainder. His dignities and estates were confiscated and distributed among his enemies. On the 27th of January his death-warrant was brought to the King; but Henry was too far gone, by this time, to be able to affix his autograph, and Sir Richard Gates stamped the document with the Royal Seal only. The deed, however, never reached its destination. Possibly it was detained by the Seymours, who may have thought that age and infirmity would soon spare them the blood-shedding of an old man. If so, they were mistaken, for Norfolk survived them both. A few hours later the King's death saved the aged Duke's. He remained, however, a close prisoner throughout the reign of Edward VI, but at the accession of Queen Mary he was liberated and all his dignities restored.

The most pitiable part of this strange episode in the history of an epoch which was one long series of domestic and political tragedies is that the Duke, in the hope of saving his life, was induced to address a shameful confession to the King. This confession His Majesty never read. It is still in existence, and must be described, even by the most merciful critics, as a very foolish and impolitic effusion. Yet that the Duke of Norfolk and his son were both conspiring—not, indeed, to usurp the throne, but to obtain the protectorate—is beyond dispute. The Seymours, on their side, though with much greater skill and diplomacy, were doing precisely the same thing.

Among our national archives and those of Norfolk House are full inventories of the estates, goods, and chattels of the Duke of Norfolk and his son, and also of the Duchesses of Norfolk and Richmond and of Mrs. Holland. Norfolk's list is valuable as affording a fair idea of the contents of a great English nobleman's house and wardrobe in the first half of the sixteenth century. In his desire to save them, the Duke had presented his vast landed estates to the Prince of Wales, who, needless to say, never got an acre of them; they were made over to the Duke of Somerset, a title assumed by Hertford on becoming Lord Protector, to Paget, and to other members of the new Government. His wearing apparel, which consisted of many garments, mostly of black or russet93 velvet or satin richly furred, and "much worn," or even "very much worn," was also seized. The Countess of Surrey was allowed one of her father-in-law's "coats" of black satin much worn, and furred with coney and lamb, which was delivered to her "to put about her in her chariot." This is probably the first mention of a carriage rug in the domestic history of this realm. All the rest of the Duke's effects, including "three broad yards of marble cloth and two pairs of old black slippers," were given to the Duke of Somerset for his use. The Protector also obtained possession of the magnificent jewelled collars belonging to the various Orders of which the Duke was a member. Paget had a "George, set with diamonds and one ruby," and Lord St. John had poor Surrey's "Order of St. Michael with its chain, studded with pearls and diamonds." The Duke left many pictures, all of a sacred character, and an enormous quantity of gold and silver plate, which was divided into equal parcels, and delivered to Somerset, Princess Mary, the Duchess of Norfolk, the Duchess of Richmond, and Surrey's widow. Somerset seized a collection of thirty-two splendid rings, but Mrs. Holland claimed the finest table diamond as her private property. His Grace had also some fifty sets of rosary beads, some of coral with paternosters in gold, others of pearl, agate, gold studded with little jewels, black enamel, and even of glass. A great quantity of these were presented to Princess Mary, to whom also went much of the altar furniture of the Duke's private chapel.

Surrey's wardrobe was as magnificent as that of any prince. There was "a Parliament robe, of rich purple velvet lined with ermine, and with a garter set with jewels upon the shoulder," and a gown "of black velvet curiously figured in gold pasmentary"; "a coat and cassock of crimson velvet, wrought with satin in the same colour, with a cloak, hat and hose to match," was most probably the identical costume in which he was represented by Streete in the picture still at Hampton Court. We read of dozens of gorgeous suits, one more splendid than the other. Somerset chose the finest for himself, and handed over the rest to his brother Henry, who had come up to town to be knighted,94 and who doubtless ultimately paraded his Wiltshire market town, decked in poor Surrey's finery, looking very much like the fabled jay in peacock's feathers. The furniture of Surrey's country house, St. Leonard's, near Norwich, which he had built after designs of John of Padua, was given to his widow, but some of the altar furniture went to Princess Mary at Newhall.

Seals had been placed on the goods and chattels of the Duchesses of Norfolk and Richmond and of Mrs. Holland, but they were lifted immediately, and the ladies received all their several properties intact.

The name of Sir Thomas Seymour does not figure in any connection, even remote, with this tragedy, and he did not receive a single coat or "night-gown,"84 whether of velvet, satin, or common cloth, belonging to either the Duke or to his son. It may be that by the time the distribution of the confiscated property took place the feud between the ambitious brothers had already begun. It was destined amply to avenge Surrey's untimely fate.

Readers may fairly ask what the story of the poet-Earl's end has to do with Lady Jane Grey? It may be replied that his death and his father's imprisonment affected her very nearly. They cleared the way for the temporary triumph of the Protestant party, and enabled Seymour to proclaim himself Protector unopposed. The close intimacy between the families of Howard and Dorset is easily traced through at least three generations in the household books of Thomas, Earl of Surrey, afterwards Duke of Norfolk.

When the Earl entertained company, the ladies and gentlemen, it seems, all dined together in the "great chamber," and there were often as many as twenty to fifty guests staying in the house. Their names include nearly all the leading aristocracy of the time, among them being Lady Jane Grey's father and mother, the Lord Marquis of Dorset and the Lady Frances; Brandon, Duke of Suffolk; the Lady Wyndham, the Lady Parker, the Lady Essex; Mrs. Brian, afterwards governess to the Princesses Mary and Elizabeth; the Lady Vere, the "old" Lady of95 Oxford,85 etc. The ladies attending on the visitors86 dined at my Lady's mess, the gentlemen in the hall. When Mr. Thomas Reddynge, a gentleman of the Duke's household, brought his bride to Tenderinge Hall for her honeymoon, "all the company dined and supped in the bride's bedroom." The little Lord Thomas Howard, afterwards Earl of Surrey, dined in the nursery.

Hospitality was exchanged between the Howards and the Dorsets almost to the end of the Duke's life. The Marquis and Marchioness of Dorset (the Lady Frances Brandon), Lady Jane Grey and her sisters, were certainly at Hunsdon87 on more than one occasion, and when the two families were in town there was, doubtless, constant visiting between them. It must be remembered that the Duke of Norfolk, being uncle-by-marriage to the King, was also uncle to the Lady Frances's mother, Mary Tudor, the royal Queen-Duchess of Suffolk. Little Lady Jane must often have sat perched on Surrey's knee and listened with delight as he whispered in her ear those tales of fairy enchantment he himself loved so well. Owing to her tender age, Jane may never have been told the details of the closing scenes of her gallant kinsman's life, but she must surely have noticed that on a certain day in January 1547–8 the curtains of her father's house were drawn, as for a family in mourning;96 that her parents moved about with pale and saddened faces; and that the servants stirred noiselessly and spoke under their breath. The shadow lay everywhere, and the various chronicles of the period afford abundant proof that there was a genuine sorrow felt in the city on the day of Surrey's death.

And there is yet another link between Lady Jane Grey and the unhappy Surrey. The name of her kinswoman, Elizabeth Fitzgerald, the "fair Geraldine," must ever be associated with that of the poet-Earl, for she is as indissolubly connected with him as is Laura with Petrarch, or Leonora with Tasso. A daughter of Oge, Earl of Kildare,88 by his wife, the Lady Elizabeth Grey, daughter of the first Marquis of Dorset, the fair Fitzgerald was a not distant cousin to Lady Jane Grey, and there were but a few years between them. She was born in Ireland, probably at Maynooth Castle, somewhere in 1528, and was brought to England whilst yet an infant. In 1533 her father died in the Tower, broken-hearted at the news that his son, whom the Irish cherished as a patriot and the English hated as a rebel, had been captured and brought to London. A few days after his father's decease, the young man was hanged at Tyburn with some seventeen other Irishmen. Henry VIII appears to have pitied the widowed Lady Kildare, who was reduced to the verge of starvation after her husband's death. A small pension was granted her, and her children were dispersed among the leading families of the aristocracy, to receive an education worthy of their rank. Elizabeth, "the fair Geraldine," an extremely beautiful child, was placed under the guidance of the Princess Mary.89 It was probably in the year 1542, whilst attending Her Highness on a visit at Hunsdon, that she first fell under the notice of Surrey, who,97 though already married, became desperately enamoured of her. The young lady cannot have been more than fourteen or fifteen at this time, but in those days this was quite a marriageable age. We have Surrey's own word for it that it was at Hunsdon he first beheld the "fair Geraldine"—

"Hunsdon did first present her to mine eyen: Bright is her hue, and Geraldine she hight. Hampton me taught to wish her first for mine; And Windsor, alas! doth chase her from my sight. Her beauty of kind; her virtues from above. Happy is he that can obtain her love!"

They appear to have met again at Hampton Court, and we seem to have evidence that the "fair Geraldine" yielded to some extent to her suitor's prayers. They danced together, no doubt, in the Great Hall, which still delights us with its lofty beauty and rich arras. They sat side by side in the oriel windows, or romped among the flower-beds of the palace garden. But the lovely Irish girl, true to her race, was chaste as snow, and when Surrey's ardour grew too hot for modest endurance, he was firmly repulsed. One thing is quite certain, that "Geraldine" was very beautiful, with Irish sea-green eyes90 and glorious fair hair. She seems otherwise to have been a very matter-of-fact young lady, who presently bestowed her hand on the rich old Sir Anthony Browne.91 After his death, in 1548, she re-entered the household of her royal mistress, and as the Lady Frances and her daughter paid several visits to their cousin, Princess Mary, in 1551, Jane Grey must often have seen the *bella ma fredda innammorata* of poet Surrey. After Queen Mary's death the "fair Geraldine" consoled herself with a second husband, in the person of Clinton, Earl of Lincoln.98 An account of her funeral still exists, according to which sixty-one old women walked in the procession, each wearing a new suit of clothes and carrying a loaf of bread, their number recording the fact that the lady they mourned had reached sixty-one years at the time of her decease.

The Duchess of Richmond seems ultimately to have repented to some extent of her wickedness. At any rate, her father left her £500 in his will—a considerable sum of money in those days—in acknowledgment of the expense and trouble she had borne to obtain his liberation, and of her care of her brother's children. She died of the plague in 1556.

It is curious that Surrey's children should have been placed under his sister's charge, since their mother, an eminently respectable woman, was living, and they were with her at the time of their father's death. She was, however, a Catholic, whereas the Duchess had for some years past rather ostentatiously proclaimed herself a Protestant. Somerset's religious opinions may have had something to do with this transaction, concerning which there is a strange legend. Three days after the Earl of Surrey's execution, Foxe, the martyrologist, was sitting in St. Paul's Cathedral, pale, haggard, and almost dying of misery and starvation. Presently a gentleman approached him and placed a considerable sum of money in his hand, bidding him be of good cheer, for that "luck was coming to him at last." A few days later Somerset appointed him tutor to the children of the late Earl of Surrey, then under the charge of their aunt, the Lady of Richmond. Notwithstanding his ardent Protestantism, Foxe was never able to completely detach the future Duke of Norfolk from the older faith; but he gave his pupil a sound and virtuous education, and won his enduring affection. This Duke shared his father's fate; he was beheaded, in the reign of Elizabeth, for espousing the cause of Mary Stuart. From him the present Duke of Norfolk is descended in a direct line.

The Countess of Surrey resided for many years at Kenninghall, but, as usual in those days, she presently took a second husband, in the person of Mr. Thomas Steyning, of Woodford, Suffolk, most likely her steward or secretary.99 She lived to an advanced age, and is buried in Framlingham Parish Church, under the elaborate monument she erected to the memory of her husband, whose remains, however, are by some believed to be still lying in the interesting church of All Hallows', Barking, near the Tower, where they were certainly interred immediately after his decapitation.

CHAPTER VII
HENRY VIII

On the night of Wednesday, 27th January 1547, Henry Tudor lay dying on that huge fourpost bedstead which Andrea Conti, an Italian traveller who visited Whitehall a few years after the King's death, described as "looking like a High Altar," so costly were its hangings of crimson velvet and cloth of gold, so dazzling its rich embroideries.92 The vast apartment was hung with rare Flemish tapestry glistening with gold thread; the furniture, of carved oak and inlaid ebony, was upholstered in glorious Florentine brocade. Curtains of "red velvet on velvet" draped the numerous windows overlooking the Thames, and the Eastern carpets that covered the floor muffled the sound of footsteps cautiously moving about the mighty couch.

The once puissant and magnificent Henry VIII, King of England, France, and Ireland, and Defender of the Faith, was now a mass of deformed flesh, eaten up and disfigured by a complication of awful disorders—gout, cancer of the stomach, rheumatism, ulcers, and dropsy. So swollen were the miserable man's hands, arms, and legs that he could only move with great pain, and then only with the aid of a mechanical contrivance. But his immense head tossed restlessly from side to side and he groaned piteously, often praying those about him to cool his parched lips with a drop of water. Though little over fifty-six years of age, the dying monarch's hair had turned quite white, and his beard,101 formerly so well trimmed, had grown scant and straggling. His steel-grey eyes looked as small in proportion to the broad, bloated face as those set in the elephant's enormous mask, but they still retained their ophidian glitter.93

The dying King had been unusually irritable throughout the weary day. At times indeed he was delirious, but on the whole his mind remained fairly clear. At about six o'clock in the afternoon he awakened out of a deep sleep or lethargy and asked for a cup of white wine, which was given him. Presently he wandered again,—the result, perhaps, of the draught of wine,—and shouted, "Monks, monks!" imagining, so it would seem, that he saw cowled forms hovering about his bed. Three times, too, and very distinctly, he cried out the name "Nan Boleyn." After that he kept his eyes fixed on a certain spot near his bedside, where, it may be, his fancy showed him the menacing wraith of his murdered wife. This outburst of feverish excitement was followed by a lull, and presently the King grew calmer and fell into a profound slumber.

The principal persons about the death-bed were the Earl of Hertford and his brother, Sir Thomas Seymour; Henry's Chief Secretary, Sir William Paget; and his Master of the Horse, Sir Anthony Browne, the only non-schismatic present. The physicians in attendance upon the King were Dr. Wendy and Dr. Owen, who had brought the Prince of Wales94 into the world, and who subsequently assisted at the death-beds of Edward VI95 and Mary. With them was Dr. John Gale,96 the King's surgeon-in-ordinary, who had waited upon Henry and his army when in France. Notwithstanding the number102 of priests attached to the Chapel Royal, there were no clergymen in the room. The Catholic party afterwards declared they had been purposely kept out of the way lest the King, whose hatred of the Papacy was purely political, might recant and make a death-bed submission to Rome. The elimination of the clerical element from the death-chamber is significant, and we have no certainty as to whether the King, who clung so tenaciously to the theory of the Church as to her Last Sacraments, ever personally received them.

Another very remarkable fact is that neither in the State Papers nor in any other contemporary accounts of the death of Henry VIII is there any mention of the Queen's presence at this time. Her Majesty had certainly been her husband's assiduous nurse until early in January, but after that we hear no more of her, and except for one or two hints to the contrary in documents connected with the household effects of the King, we might almost conjecture she had left the palace before the King passed away. The *Spanish Chronicle*, introduced to English readers by Martin Hume, which contains a great deal of what would now be called back-stair gossip, informs us, however, that Katherine Parr was summoned to the King's bedside the day before he died, and that "he thanked her for her great kindness to him," adding that he had "well provided for her." The good Queen, falling on her knees, burst into such loud sobbing that she had to be removed and conveyed back to her apartments. From the same source we learn that Princess Mary saw her father three or four days before the end, and received his blessing. Of these statements there is no confirmation in the English State Papers; they are confirmed, however, by documents in the Simancas archives and in a pamphlet published at Valladolid some three years after Queen Mary's death entitled *La Muerte de la Serenissima Reyna Maria d'Inglaterra* (Valladolid, 1562).97

The last we hear of Katherine Parr as Queen-Consort is in a letter addressed to her from Hertford on 10th January103 by her stepson, Prince Edward, in which he thanks her for a New Year's gift.98

If we trust the *Acts and Monuments*, there is direct evidence that Henry VIII deliberately omitted Gardiner's name from his testament. In the afternoon of the day before his death, Sir Anthony Browne asked him directly if "My Lord of Winchester was left out of His Majesty's will by negligence or otherwise?" He was kneeling at the moment by the King's bed and endeavouring to recall to him the Bishop's long services. The broad face of the dying King turned towards him, and he said angrily, "Hold your peace. I remember him well enough, and of good purpose have I left him out; for surely if he were in my testament and one of you, he would cumber you all and you should never rule him, he is of so troublesome a nature." If this be a truthful account of the scene, there can be no doubt that Henry realised the omission of Winchester's name from the will, which would imply a truckling to the Seymour faction; for there was now no one left to oppose their influence or expose their intrigues.

Between seven and eight in the evening of 27th January, Sir Anthony Denny, who had been watching his master very closely, thought he perceived signs that the end was approaching. Stooping over him, he whispered into the dying ear a message especially dreadful to one who, like Henry, held the mere mention of death in horror, warning him that his hour was very near, and that "it was meet for him to review his past life and seek God's mercy through Jesus Christ." The King, although in great agony, evidently understood what Denny had said, and is reported to have answered that he would suffer no ecclesiastic near him but Cranmer, who was immediately sent for. The Archbishop was at Croydon, but, being an excellent horseman, he galloped up to London, and reached Whitehall about one o'clock in[104] the morning of Thursday, 28th January.[99] He found the King almost speechless but in full possession of his faculties, and exhorted him, in a few words, to repent him of his sins and "to place his trust in Christ only." Henry pressed the Churchman's hand, and muttering the significant words, "All is lost!" immediately expired.

So passed into eternity Lady Jane Grey's great-uncle and the most extraordinary of all our kings. Even at this date it is impossible to define his true character, for whereas, on the one hand, his cousin Pole, who knew him well, likened him unto Nero and Tiberius, that painstaking historian Froude has endeavoured to prove him a well-intentioned man, whose political and whose domestic troubles especially were not of his own making, but the result of circumstance and of Court intrigues beyond his control. Between these two appreciations the truth doubtless lies. Henry VIII was beyond question a wonderful being—in whom were reflected, nay, absorbed, all the good and evil qualities of the subjects whose very Church he contrived to dominate. With all his treachery, his lust, and his cruelty, he may well have been a necessary evil, a tool in the guiding Hand that has shaped the destinies of the British Empire. He tore down the last vestiges of the Middle Ages; and if the light so suddenly admitted was too dazzling for the eyes that first beheld it, in due time it mellowed into the slowly developed liberty and progress that have placed our country at the forefront of civilisation. Our eighth Henry was the tyrant who inadvertently forced open the gate whereby Freedom was to enter.

Much as we loathe his sensuality and his cruelty, his personal extravagance that emptied the overflowing treasury left by his father and led him to debase the coin of the realm in order to replenish it, much as we may deplore his iconoclasm that destroyed a thousand abbeys, priories, and noble churches and dispersed the art treasures of ages, as Englishmen we still entertain a surreptitious liking for Bluff King Hal. His[105] magnificent appearance and the Oriental side of his nature, his six wives, his fantastic and gorgeous pageants, his outbursts of bad language, his masterfulness, his love of art and music, all appeal to the imagination and help us to convert a monarch, a very weak and poor specimen of humanity, who really had much of the vile criminal about him, into a hero of romance, and cast over his strange career something of the legendary glamour that so fascinates all students of the reign of the illustrious daughter who inherited so many of his good and evil qualities and carried on much of his chosen policy. To King Henry we owe the formation of our Army and the creation of our Navy. He abused his Parliament, but he was its first and greatest organiser. He shaped it to his own will; and it eventually shaped itself to the will of the nation.

Earlier in the evening of that momentous 27th of January Hertford and Paget had spent slow hours pacing up and down the long corridor outside the King's chamber, and consulting as to what it would be best to do as soon as the monarch was dead. Parliament, then in session, had been busy with the alleged treasonable transactions of the Duke of Norfolk, now lying in the Tower under sentence of death. His Grace, therefore, was one of the only three members of the Privy Council absent from the death-chamber: the other two were Dr. Thirlby, Bishop of Westminster, then resident Ambassador at the Court of Charles V; and Dr. Nicholas Wotton, Dean of Canterbury, recently dispatched on a diplomatic mission to France. Gardiner, whose name had been erased from the Council list, had lately returned from Brussels, and must have been communicated with at once, for to him were eventually entrusted all the arrangements for the late King's obsequies. An improvised Council was held immediately after Henry's death, and decided that the event should be kept a profound secret until the Prince of Wales was brought to London. This was cleverly managed by putting all the immediate attendants in the King's private apartments under oath; and the multitudinous household in the outer rooms performed its usual vocations as though Henry, who had long been absent from his general courtiers' sight, were still alive. The sentinels were changed, and106 everything at Whitehall went on with clockwork regularity, as if nothing unusual had happened. At about four o'clock in the morning of 28th January Hertford and his brother, Thomas Seymour, stole out of the palace, took horse, and galloped towards Hertford, where the young heir was then residing. By an oversight—or was it done purposely?—Hertford put in his pocket the key of the coffer in which the King's will was kept, and Paget had to ride out into the dark after him to obtain possession of it. At about dawn the Seymours were joined by Sir Anthony Browne, an accession which greatly elated them, for he was one of the most important leaders of the Catholic party. They reached Hertford100 a little after daybreak, and the boy Edward was instantly roused from his slumbers. They did not at once inform him of his father's decease, but rode with him to Enfield Chase, where his sister, the Princess Elizabeth, was residing with her governess, Mrs. Ashley. Here they broke the news to both of the dead King's children, who burst into tears, the Princess Elizabeth holding her young brother's hand the while. The company stayed all Sunday at Enfield, their suite being in the meantime reinforced by a numerous bodyguard, attended by which they started on the following morning for London, the boy-King riding on a milk-white palfrey between Lord Hertford and Sir Anthony Browne. As the procession passed through the villages on its way to London, the inhabitants were informed of King Henry's death. We have proof, however, that it was not known in the metropolis on the Sunday. On that day the Grey Friar's Church, which had been closed for some years and107 converted into a wine-vault, was restored to public worship by order of the late King, and his "munificence and generosity" were fulsomely eulogised by the preacher, who, however, never alluded to the sovereign's demise. Towards evening, the fact that the King was dead began to circulate among the upper classes, and next morning it was pretty generally known all over London.

At three o'clock on the Monday afternoon King Edward VI entered the capital through Aldgate, where he was met by the Lord Mayor and a great assembly of the nobility and gentry. Cranmer greeted him at the Bridge and read him an address, after which he was conducted in state to the Tower, being only fairly well received by the populace. Meanwhile, his father's body, still at Whitehall, after being "spunged," cleaned, disembowelled, and embalmed with spices, was exhibited, covered with a silken garment, to the great nobility. This done, it was sealed up in a leaden coffin and brought down into the Privy Chamber, where it lay, "with all manner of lights thereto requisite, having divine service about him with Masses, obsequies, and prayers," until 3rd February, when it was conveyed into the Chapel Royal, where Mass was said between nine and ten in the morning.

The *Chapelle Ardente* was hung with black cloth and with banners of St. George and England. Eighty huge silver candlesticks with tall wax tapers in them were ranged on either side of the catafalque. On the Tuesday, and for five following mornings, Norreys stationed himself at the entrance to the chancel and cried out at intervals to the congregation, "Of your charity pray for the soul of the most high and mighty Prince Henry VIII, our late Sovereign Lord and King." Watch was kept day and night by the chaplains and gentlemen of the Privy Chamber. Then began the saying of Masses for the benefit of the King's soul, and these were "as numerous as they were on the occasion of the funeral of his father, Henry VII." They were continued until the 13th February. Tens of thousands of Masses were said throughout the country, both in the capital and the provinces, in the cathedrals as well as in the parish churches.101 The ritual was everywhere108 absolutely Latin. In London Gardiner was the celebrant at High Mass each day, assisted by the Bishops of Durham, London, Ely, St. David's, Gloucester, Bangor, and Bath. Archbishop Cranmer was present but did not officiate. Low Masses were said in the chapel at Whitehall, at an altar erected at the foot of the catafalque, from four o'clock in the morning until ten, when High Mass was chanted, the Marquis of Dorset acting as chief mourner. In the evening there were Vespers for the Dead and Dirge and "a great attendance of noblemen and gentlemen mourners." The Queen and the King's nieces, the Marchioness of Dorset and her daughters, the Ladies Jane and Katherine Grey, the Lady Eleanor

Brandon, Countess of Cumberland, the Lady Margaret Lennox, the Duchess of Richmond, the Duchess of Suffolk, and all the great ladies[102] of the Court, were present, not only at High Mass, but at countless other Masses in the Chapel Royal. They were, however, not in the body of the Chapel, but in an upper gallery overlooking it—mourning cloaks being provided for them out of the Wardrobe.

Queen Katherine may have left the palace somewhat hurriedly,[103] for in the inventory taken immediately after the King's death there is an account of the seals being on one chamber described as full of female attire of the most sumptuous description, presumably belonging to the Queen, who certainly left behind her the jewels given her by the King to wear at the reception of M. d'Annebault, the French Envoy—an oversight that gave rise to terrible subsequent[109] dissensions between Sir Thomas Seymour and his eldest brother.

Lord Chancellor Wriothesley dissolved Parliament early on Monday, 1st February, in a neatly turned speech declaring that "their most puissant master was dead." The eventful news was received with every demonstration of sorrow, some members even bursting into tears, or pretending to do so. Then followed the reading of that portion of the King's will which concerned the Royal Succession.

By this famous testament[104] Henry provided that in case Edward died childless, and Henry himself had no other children by his "beloved wife Katherine or any other wives[105] he might have hereafter," King Edward was to be succeeded by his eldest sister Mary; and if she in her turn proved without offspring, she was to be succeeded by her sister Elizabeth. Failing heirs to that princess, the crown was to pass on the same conditions to the Lady Jane Grey and her sisters Katherine and Mary Grey, daughters of the King's eldest niece, the Lady Frances Brandon, Marchioness of Dorset. In the eventuality of the three sisters Grey dying without issue, the throne was to be occupied successively by the children of the Lady Frances' younger sister, the Lady Eleanor, Countess of Cumberland. The Scotch succession was set aside, from no personal ill-will, however, to Henry's eldest sister, the Dowager Queen of Scotland, Margaret Tudor, for he left her daughter a handsome legacy. Henry most probably omitted the name of the young Queen of Scots as heiress to the throne, and gave his preference to the daughters of his two nieces, because, although at war with the Regent of Scotland, he still hoped that the betrothal of his grand-niece, Mary Stuart, then only six years of age, to his son Edward might be arranged, and thus[110] eventually bring about the desired union of the two crowns in a natural manner. Moreover, there was the religious question to be considered. The Regent, Mary of Guise, was an ardent Papist, using all her influence, both in England and in Scotland, to thwart the English King's anti-papal policy.

Henry VIII mentioned Queen Katherine in the following eulogistic manner: "And for the great love, obedience, chastity of life, and wisdom being in our forenamed wife and Queen, we bequeath unto her for her proper life, and as it shall please her to order it, three thousand pounds in plate, jewels, and stuff of household goods, and such apparel as it shall please her to take of such as we have already. And further, we give unto her one thousand pounds in money, and the amount of her dower and jointure according to our grant in Parliament." Henry appointed the Earl of Hertford Protector of the Realm during the minority of his son, and mentioned as his colleagues all those persons who were interested in keeping him in power in order to share it with him. Gardiner's name was omitted, as already stated. The provisions of the will opposed a serious obstacle to the Earl of Hertford's ambition, for they made him fifth in order of precedence, thus placing him on a footing of equality with other executors; recognising no claim arising out of his kinship to the young Prince. Sir Thomas Clere declared that the original will was stamped, a fact which inclined so careful a writer as Mr. Pollard to conclude that the idea that a stamped will was illegal must have flashed across somebody's mind, and suggested the hasty drawing up of another, for the King to sign in autograph. The form now in the Record Office is doubtless this second one. It displays no trace of a stamp, and the two signatures at the beginning and end are not sufficiently uniform to have been impressed mechanically. In the last the up-strokes are very unsteady, and on comparing them with other signatures of Henry VIII one is justified in thinking that both were forged. It must not be forgotten, however, that the King was very ill, and failing; his hand may well have trembled.106

111 In those days the funeral of a sovereign and the coronation of his successor took place almost simultaneously, occasionally with strange results, considerable confusion arising as to the arrangements for the two ceremonies: the sombre preparations for the obsequies of King Henry, for instance, clashed weirdly with the festivities organised for the accession of his son. Matters became so confused at last that Bishop Gardiner found himself obliged to appeal to "My Lord of Oxford's Players," who were already at Southwark preparing to act a pageant and a comedy. It would be more decent, His Lordship pointed out, to sing a solemn Dirge for their master than to perform a merry play, and he besought them to desist until after the King's funeral.

In the end the Bishop had his way, and the grandeur of Henry's obsequies suffered nothing from the counter-attractions of the "green men," "morris dancers," and "mountain for the gods," which were among the items promised by the players, who produced their performance in the hall of the ex-monastery of Blackfriars immediately after Edward's coronation—doubtless to their own satisfaction and that of the public, albeit they seem to have had hard work to get the necessary cash for their "properties" out of Sir William Carwarden or Carden, the official in charge of such matters, to whom they had to frequently apply for payment.107

On Monday, 31st January, the young King entered London, and passed direct to the Tower, where, in accordance with traditional etiquette, he was to remain in semi-seclusion until after his coronation. The next day, Tuesday, 1st February, the late King's executors assembled in the great hall of the Tower, and having heard the will read from beginning to end, took the oath for the King, and Hertford108 was proclaimed Protector during the coming minority. On 4th February the Protector proceeded in state to Westminster Hall, where he assumed the offices of Lord Treasurer and112 Earl Marshal, rendered vacant by the attainder of the Duke of Norfolk. He subsequently relinquished his post as Lord Great Chamberlain to John Dudley, Viscount de Lisle, who in his turn surrendered his place as Lord High-Admiral to Sir Thomas Seymour.

On Sunday, 13th February, High Mass was again sung in the Chapel Royal by Gardiner, assisted by the Bishops of London and Bristol, and the royal coffin was removed "from the Chapell to the Chariot; over the coffin was cast a pall of rich cloth of gold, and upon it a goodly ymage like to the Kyng's person in all poynts, wonderfully richly aparrelled with velvet gold and precious stones of all sorts, holding in ye right hand a Sceptre of gold, in the left hand the ball of the world with a crosse; upon the head a crown imperial of inestimable value, a collar of the Garter about the neck and a garter of gold about the leg, with this being honourably conducted as aforesaid, was tied upon the said coffin by the Gentlemen of his Privy Chamber upon rich cushions of cloath of gold and fast bound with silk ribands to the pillars of the said Chariot for removing." It seems, however, that this image was not quite complete, for it had presently to be removed and "touched up."

The gorgeous funeral procession, which is said to have been four miles long, left the Chapel Royal, Whitehall, at about eleven o'clock on 14th February for Sion *en route* for Windsor. The weather was very fine, and immense crowds lining the streets, people of every class, holding lighted candles. Over a thousand "lights," or torches, were held by the mourners who preceded or followed the hearse containing the King's body and upon which was placed the waxen image already described. This hearse was drawn by eight black horses emblazoned with the Arms of England and of the house of Tudor, and surrounded by noblemen and knights in mourning robes, some on horseback and others on foot, holding lights and banners, images of saints, and other glistening devices and symbols. The procession passed through the streets of London by Charing Cross, Knightsbridge, Hammersmith, Chiswick, and Brentford, and, owing to its enormous length, did not reach Sion until twilight. It is gratifying to note that the vast assemblage113 of nobles and gentry was plentifully supplied with refreshments, wine, and beer throughout the whole of these very elaborate and costly obsequies, to the tune of about £10,000 of our money.

At Sion the coffin stood all night within the ruined walls of that erstwhile monastic house which had been the prison of Katherine Howard, the second of Henry's murdered consorts. The ravages of ruin to be seen there were now hidden by hangings of fine black cloth and by two great altars blazing with lights and jewels. By a curious coincidence, the body arrived at Sion on the day after the fifth anniversary of the Queen's execution, a fact which lends additional horror to the following story, related in a contemporary document now in the Soane Collection: "The King's body rested in the ruined Chapel of Sion, and there, the leaden coffin109 being cleft by the shaking of the carriage, the pavement of the church was wetted with Henry's blood. In the morning came plumbers to solder the coffin, under whose feet, I tremble while I write it," says the author, "was suddenly seen a dog creeping and licking up the King's blood. If you ask me how I know this, I answer, William Greville, who could scarce drive away the dog, told me so, and so did the plumber also."

The coffin had most likely been abandoned by the mourners, who had retired to rest for the night, and probably some gaseous explosion led to this uncanny incident, the report of which greatly increased the superstitious terror in which the late King's name was held. Thus was fulfilled, so the people said, Friar Peyto's denunciation from the pulpit of Greenwich Church in 1553, when that daring friar compared Henry to Ahab, and told him to his face "that the dogs would in like manner lick his blood."

114 This horrible occurrence, if it really took place, does not seem to have made any very deep impression on Bishop Gardiner, for no more fulsome sermon was ever preached than that delivered by him at Windsor on 16th February. He took for his text, "Blessed are the dead who die in the Lord," and, enlarging on the virtues of the late monarch, lamented the "loss both to high and low by the death of this most good and gracious King"; for whom, Sir Anthony Browne declared, "there was no need to pray, for he was surely in Heaven." Queen Katherine Parr, the King's nieces, the Lady Frances, Marchioness of Dorset, and the Lady Eleanor of Cumberland and their daughters and other noblewomen attended the obsequies at Windsor from a closet or chamber looking into the chapel, much such a one as Queen Victoria used in the Chapel Royal, Windsor, on similar occasions.

Some weird stories of supernatural apparitions were circulated all over London, especially among the Catholics. The "old King" had appeared, wreathed in flames, to an ex-Carthusian friar. Folks at Windsor had beheld him fleeing along the battlements and corridors of the castle, blazing like a meteoric ball; and he had even, so it was rumoured, paid a warning visit to his widow in the still hours of darkness.

CHAPTER VIII
CONCERNING THE LADY JANE AND THE QUEEN-DOWAGER

The will of Henry VIII conferred upon the houses of Seymour and Grey a towering position in the State which naturally brought forward into extraordinary relief the hitherto ignored name of Lady Jane. A few weeks earlier she was but the eldest daughter of the rather weak-minded Marquis of Dorset, a man whom no one seems to have held in any great consideration, notwithstanding his royal alliance and rather showy past career as a soldier under Henry VIII; to-day she was almost as prominent in the matter of the succession as the King's two daughters, Mary and Elizabeth, both of whom could easily be set aside by an ambitious faction: the elder on account of her religion, the younger on that of her somewhat doubtful legitimacy. It is not surprising, therefore, that the intrigues which were to culminate in the ruin of the unfortunate Lady Jane began almost immediately after the accession of her cousin, Edward VI; for it was at this time that the newly made Lord Sudeley, desiring to possess "two strings to his bow," embarked in a most imprudent intrigue to obtain possession of the person of the Marquis of Dorset's daughter, who, as the reversionary heiress of England, was justly regarded by both parties as a most valuable asset. The intermediary employed in this transaction was one William Sharington, a gentleman in Seymour's confidence, who was his equal in the conducting of tricksome intrigues: it will become apparent as we proceed that whenever Sudeley had any particularly difficult and dangerous matter to deal with, he invariably got some subordinate to share the danger with him. One morning, very soon after King Henry's death, Sharington appeared at Dorset Place, Westminster, to open negotiations with the Marquis about the transfer of his eldest[116] daughter into Sudeley's charge. He began by informing Dorset, apparently one of the most credulous of mortals, that the Admiral, as uncle to the King, "was like to come to great authority, and was most desirous of forming a bond of friendship with him." On the following day Sharington returned, and after assuring the Marquis that "the Lord High-Admiral was very much his friend," insinuated that "it were a goodly thing to happen if my Lady Jane his daughter were in the keeping of the said Lord Admiral." He said he had often heard his master say "that the Lady Jane was the handsomest lady in England and that the Admiral would see her placed in marriage much to his (the Marquis's) comfort."

"And with whom will he match her?" inquired Dorset.

"Marry," replied Sharington, "I doubt not but you shall see he will marry her to the King, and fear you not, he will bring it to pass, and then you shall be able to help all the friends you have."

After this visit the Marquis held a consultation with the Lady Frances, which resulted in his accepting a personal interview with Lord Sudeley.

Thomas Seymour does not appear to have had any fixed London abode in his bachelor days, but probably lived, on occasion, as Surrey did, in what we should now call chambers, somewhere in the Strand. But when he became Baron Sudeley and Lord High-Admiral, he conceived it incumbent upon him to live in a style commensurate with his increased rank, and solicited a suitable mansion from his brother, the Protector. Somerset forthwith filched Bath House, Strand, from Bishop Barlow, and presented it to his brother. This house, which must not be mistaken for Bath House, Holborn, was built in the fourteenth century and considerably enlarged and embellished in the beginning of the sixteenth; it was one of the finest mansions in London, and, with its gardens, occupied the whole space now covered by Arundel, Norfolk, and Suffolk Streets, Strand. The mansion stood on the approximate site of the present Howard Hotel. It commanded an extensive view of the Thames, and there was an orchard extending to the Strand.[110]

[117] To Seymour Place, Strand, therefore, rode my lord of Dorset, to find Sudeley walking in his garden. The two gentlemen held a most confidential conversation, in the course of which Sudeley persuaded Dorset not only to hand the wardship of the Lady Jane over to him, but to send for her then and there, and allow the young girl to take up her abode under the roof of one of the most notorious profligates of an exceedingly degenerate Court.

The Lady Jane did not arrive at Seymour Place *in formâ pauperis*. She was attended by her governess, Mrs. Ashley, by four waiting women and a number of male servants of various degrees. Sudeley's household was at this time ruled over by his mother, the Dowager Lady Seymour. Since the death of her husband, Sir John Seymour, in December 1536, this lady had kept house for her younger son, who brought her for that purpose either from Hertford or from a suburban house on a site now crossed by Upper and Lower Seymour Street, Portman Square.

There is some unexplained mystery connected with Lady Seymour which the present writer does not pretend to have fathomed. No explanation is discoverable of the strange fact that the mother of a Queen and the grandmother of a King of England seems to have been almost ignored by her son-in-law Henry VIII, by her young grandson Edward VI, by her own son the Protector, and indeed by all the great people with whom her high position must have brought her into contact. Her name is not once mentioned in connection with that of her daughter, Jane Seymour, after she became118 Queen. She did not figure at the christening of the baby Edward, and did not present the customary gifts offered by near relations on such occasions. She has left no correspondence, and there is only one allusion to her in the Household Books of Henry VIII, and none at all in those of Edward VI, which contain some reference to almost every lady of importance of the period, as receiving or presenting gifts from or to the sovereign, either personally or through attendants. We only know that her banner of arms figured, close to that of her daughter, Queen Jane, at the obsequies of Henry VIII and Edward VI; and that Henry, in 1537, during the year of his marriage with Jane Seymour, when he raised his brother-in-law Edward Seymour to the rank of Baron Beauchamp, granted him a pension of £1100 per annum, out of which he was to pay his mother an annuity of £60111—but beyond the papers connected with this pension there is only one other existing document in which her name figures, and this deals with an incident that arose after her death, in 1551, when her grandson the King was induced by the Privy Council, and by her own son, the Duke of Somerset, to countermand the wearing of official mourning for her. Beyond the fact that Lady Seymour was by birth a Wentworth, and therefore highly connected, and that in one of his letters to Lady Jane's mother Seymour represents his own as a fitting person to take the young girl under her maternal care, Lady Seymour may be said to have lived and died as much ignored as though she had been a woman of no birth and no importance.112

Of the sort of life lived by the Lady Jane during the weeks she spent at Seymour Place we know nothing, but from the alacrity with which she consented to return there at a later period we may feel justified in believing she was very happy under the charge of the mysterious Lady Seymour and her erratic and wilful son. Miss Strickland says, but without naming her authority, that Lady Seymour was one of the earliest Englishwomen of rank to adopt the tenets of the119 Reformation. If this was the case, Lady Jane Grey probably met at her house some one or other of the numerous foreign Reformers who began to invade England shortly after the death of Henry VIII. It is, however, likely that Sudeley undertook the charge of this young lady at the instigation of Katherine Parr, and that whilst at Seymour Place her education was continued under the direction of the scholarly Miles Coverdale, afterwards Bishop of Exeter, who had been appointed chaplain to the Queen-Dowager. There is some little resemblance between the handwriting of this divine and that of Lady Jane, which leads one to think he had a considerable share in directing her studies at this period.

If the Dorsets imagined they were doing themselves and their daughter a service by placing her under the guardianship of Thomas Seymour, they made a terrible mistake, for this incident was certainly at the root of that fatal animosity between the two brothers which led up to one of the most appalling tragedies in our history. In the first place, it revealed to Somerset that Sudeley was fighting for his own hand, and further, entirely upset the Lord Protector's domestic schemes and arrangements. Both Somerset and his wife had been very intimate with the Marquis and the Marchioness, his royal consort, and the young Earl of Hertford,113 their eldest son, was a constant visitor at Westminster and at Bradgate. He was an exceedingly handsome youth, described by Norton, his tutor, as "singularly like his father," who, judged by his portraits, was one of the finest-looking men of his day. So fond was the Lady Frances of the young Earl that she would call him "her son," and undoubtedly looked on him as a welcome suitor for her eldest daughter; and if there was any love romance in Lady Jane's brief life, it was certainly in connection with this youth, and not with Guildford, whom she eventually married, but whom she slighted rather than loved. The Somersets, moreover, had made up their minds that if the proposed marriage between Mary Stuart and Edward VI came to nothing, Edward should be contracted as soon as 120 possible to their youngest daughter, the very pretty and highly accomplished Lady Jane Seymour.114 Under these circumstances it may well be imagined that the Duke and Duchess were not only furious when they learned that Lady Jane Grey was already comfortably installed under their brother's roof, without their knowledge and consent, but firmly resolved that the young lady should see as little of her cousin the King as possible.

Brother Thomas had yet a greater surprise and vexation in store for Somerset and his Duchess, and even for King Edward VI himself, than the matter of the wardship of Lady Jane Grey. He was, if the truth is to be honestly told, about the most extraordinary scamp of his time. Physically he eclipsed his elder brother, the Protector, himself considered a very handsome man. In addition to a fine figure, Thomas possessed beautiful features, just escaping the long thin nose which characterised his brother's face and ruined Queen Jane's pretensions to beauty. He was dark, with a full beard, a ruddy complexion, and full brown eyes. In a word, a very fine fellow indeed, and exceedingly attractive to the fair sex, who found it hard to resist his blandishments, a cruel fact of which he was apt to boast. He danced to perfection, was first in all sports, could turn pretty verses when it suited him—and even godly ones, on occasion. His love of dress was proverbial, and in that brilliant Court of Henry VIII Sir Thomas Seymour never failed to hold his own for extravagance and magnificence. Like his brother Somerset, he could be kindly when it suited his purpose, and liberal enough to his inferiors when he desired to create a good impression. He seems to have even been a dutiful son, for, as we have said, his mother lived with him to the end of his life, and he spoke well of her.

These comparative virtues were outweighted by his evil qualities, for not even in that age of rascality and of wickedness in high places did there exist a greater ruffian than this121 seemingly polished gentleman. Thomas was one of those men who are born without a conscience.115 Henry VIII had not long been dead and the elder Seymour scarcely proclaimed Protector of the Realm when Sudeley began to realise that his own part at the Court of his nephew, Edward VI, must be quite secondary unless he could forthwith contract some royal alliance and thereby make his position equal to his brother's. So it fell out that, before the late King's body was cold, Thomas Seymour had made up his mind to marry one of the royal princesses; and ere it was buried he had offered his hand to the elder of the King's widows, Anne of Cleves. That cautious Princess promptly refused the dubious proposal, preferring her independence and present comfort to the probable sacrifice of a handsome income paid by the State for the poor pleasure of espousing a cadet of the house of Seymour. Nothing daunted by this refusal, the undismayed suitor aimed higher yet, and offered his hand and heart to Princess Mary, who thanked him, in a courteous letter, for the honour he paid her, and assured him that she had not the slightest intention of changing her state, especially so soon after her father's death. Baffled again, my Lord of Sudeley now addressed himself to the youthful Princess Elizabeth, who, according to Leti, answered him in a most becoming manner, reminding him that her father was just dead, and that it would ill become her to think of marriage at such a moment or for at least two years after so sad an event. She had not, she said, had time to enjoy her maidenhood, and wished to do so for that period at least, before embarking on the stormy seas of matrimony. Elizabeth's letter, if she really wrote it,—one can never quite trust Leti, though he lived near enough to the time to have access to papers and documents long since destroyed,—was a model of *finesse* and good taste.

The rejected, but undejected, Seymour now turned his attention to his old love, Katherine Parr, whom, as we know, he first courted when she became the widow of Lord Latimer. He must have been a good deal in her122 company in the last months of King Henry's life, and on her own admission she had not lost any of her old love for him; for in a letter, written presumably within a fortnight of the late King's death, she says, "I would not have you think that this, mine honest good will towards you to proceed from any sudden motion of passion; for, as truly as God is God, my mind was fully bent the other time I was at liberty [that is, after the death of Lord Latimer], to marry you before any man I know. Howbeit God withstood my will therein most vehemently for a time, and through His grace and goodness made that possible which seemed to me most impossible; that was, made me renounce utterly mine own will and follow His most willingly. It were long to write all the processes of this matter. If I live, I shall declare it to you myself. I can say nothing, but as my Lady of Suffolk116 saith, 'God is a wonderful man.'" In March, after Henry's death, the Queen removed to Chelsea Manor, a mansion which Henry had built as a nursery for his children and settled on her as a dower-house. Princess Elizabeth had joined her within a few days for the purpose of finishing her education under the auspices of the learned Queen. At the very time, therefore, that Seymour was intriguing to secure possession of Lady Jane Grey, he was clandestinely spending his evenings with Katherine Parr either at Whitehall or, later, when she finally removed with her household to Chelsea, at the Manor House, coming there by a lane that led from the Bishop of London's house up a path which, until a few years ago, was still in existence and associated by tradition with the names of Katherine Parr and Thomas Seymour. Some authorities assert that the two were secretly married about three weeks after the King's death, and that the Lord Admiral prolonged his visits, not leaving his wife till dawn, when she would let him out by the garden wicket, and then steal back to her room unobserved (at least, so she hoped).117 According123 to Edward VI's *Journal*, however, the marriage was not officially celebrated until May, and it was certainly not made public before the end of June 1547. The intrigues of Lord Thomas to induce the young King, his nephew, to sanction his marriage with his stepmother began by his poisoning the King's mind against his brother Somerset, and, taking advantage of the Protector's absence in Scotland, he did all in his power to make himself agreeable to Edward VI by lending him considerable sums of money. Somerset kept the royal lad very short of petty cash, so that at times he had none to distribute to such folk as strolling musicians, servants who brought him presents from his relatives, and other persons who had obliged him. Seymour, who had isolated the King, employed a man named Fowler as intermediary between himself and Edward.118 Flattered and cajoled by his uncle Thomas and well disposed by his natural affection to his stepmother, the poor little King was at length induced to write a letter advising the Lord Admiral to marry the Queen-Dowager. This extraordinary missive, which is still extant, was penned a few days after Edward had received a very curious epistle from his stepmother, then on a visit to him at St. James's Palace, in which she had dilated upon her extraordinary affection for the memory of his late father. The letter was written in Latin, and the young King's answer was in the same dead language. The King's letter is full of advice, which comes124 oddly from a lad not yet ten to a woman verging upon forty. He hopes to do what is acceptable in her sight because of, firstly, "the great love you bear my father the King, of most noble memory; then your good-will towards me; and lastly, your godliness, and knowledge and learning in the Scriptures. Proceed, therefore, in your good course; continue to love my father, and to show the same great kindness to me which I have ever perceived in you. Cease not to love and read the Scriptures, but persevere in always reading them; for in the first you show the duty of a good wife and a good subject, and in the second, the warmth of your friendship, and in the third, your piety to God."119 Very soon after writing this letter he wrote another to Her Majesty, this time in English, in which he assured her that, far from being vexed with her for marrying his uncle, he promised to aid her in the hour of need, should the alliance prove offensive to those who were in power.

In June the marriage was made public. The indignation of the Duke and Duchess of Somerset knew no bounds. They had been greatly angered over the matter of Lady Jane Grey, but no words could express their exasperation at what they were pleased to consider their brother's fresh exhibition of "indecency and wickedness." The first practical expression of their wrath was the sequestration of the jewels the Queen had left behind at Whitehall after King Henry's death. She had applied for them several times, and now wrote in a more determined strain; only, however, to receive a haughty refusal and the startling information that the jewels belonged to the Crown, whereas they really were a personal gift to her from the King at the time of the visit of the French Envoy M. d'Annebault. These jewels were never returned to Katherine Parr—a matter which roused the Lord Admiral's wrath to a culminating pitch. "My brother," he said, "is wondrous hot in helping every man to his right save me. He maketh a great matter to let me have the Queen's jewels, which you see by the whole opinion of the lawyers ought to belong to me, and all under pretence that he would not the King should lose so much, as if it were a loss to the King to let me have mine own!"120

125 Then came another unpleasant incident, in the course of which the Queen-Dowager was subjected to unfair treatment on account of her marriage. Somerset determined to force her to lease her favourite manor of Fausterne to a friend of his named Long. Katherine refused point-blank to receive this gentleman as a tenant, especially at a ridiculously low rent, and in a letter to her husband expressed her scornful indignation at the "large" offer for Fausterne which his brother had made her. Yet in the end she was obliged to accept Somerset's terms. Fausterne passed from her hands into those of Long, and was never restored to her.

It is not surprising that she felt a little "warm," as she expresses it, at the manner in which the Somersets handled her. Her position had been recognised by the King and Parliament, and yet her brother-in-law and his wife refused to acknowledge her right to precedence: the Duchess of Somerset declared that she was herself as good as Queen, since she was the consort of the King's Protector, "who was virtually the head of the Realm." Whenever Katherine went to Court, if the Duchess of Somerset chanced to be present, there was sure to be trouble. According to Lloyd, the Duchess not only refused to bear up the Queen's train, but actually jostled her so as to pass first. "So that what between the train of the Queen, and the long gown of the Duchess, they raised so much dust at Court, as at last put out the eyes of both their husbands, and caused their executions." Heylin says the Duchess was accustomed to inveigh against her royal sister-in-law in her coarsest manner. "Did not King Henry VIII marry Katherine Parr in his doting days, when he had brought himself so low by his lust and cruelty that no lady that stood on her honour would venture on him? And shall I now give place to her who in her former estate was but Latimer's widow, and is now fain to cast herself for support on a younger brother? If master admiral teach his wife no better manners, I am she that will."

Historians who, for political and religious purposes, have exaggerated the virtue and accomplishments of Edward VI, and endowed Lady Jane Grey with charms and gifts which that modest young lady never possessed, have woven a legend around her and Edward VI which would lead the uninitiated126 to believe that she was the constant sharer of his juvenile tasks and pastimes, whereas in reality it was only in the last few months of his life that she became in the least prominent at his Court. Immediately after his birth and the death of his mother Prince Edward was handed over to the care of Lady Brian,121 formerly governess to his two sisters, by whom she was greatly beloved and respected, and also to that of his dry nurse, Mrs. Sybilla Penn.122 His infancy was spent at Chelsea Manor House and at the country seats of Ampthill and Oatlands. In these places he was frequently visited by his sisters Mary and Elizabeth, and presumably also by his little cousins of the house of Grey; but when he attained his sixth year, in accordance with the peculiar views of his father on the subject of education, all female influence was withdrawn127 from him, although Lady Brian continued to preside over his household. A number of very young noblemen were selected to be his constant companions and playfellows. Among them were his cousins, the two sons of Brandon, Duke of Suffolk; the Lord Edward Seymour, afterwards Earl of Hertford; and his great friend, the one being he seems to have really loved, young Barnaby Fitzpatrick, sometimes mentioned by the Swiss Reformers as Earl of Ireland.123 His principal tutors were the extremely Protestant Dr. Richard Cox, who became Dean of Westminster in 1549 and subsequently, in Elizabeth's reign, Bishop of Ely; the learned Sir John Cheke,124 Provost of King's College, Cambridge, and his first schoolmaster; Sir Anthony Cooke; M. Jean Bellemain, his French master; and Roger Ascham, who taught him caligraphy. He also received lessons in the art of writing in the Italian or Roman type, which most nearly resembles the modern, from Dr. Croke, who had taught this art at an earlier period to the young Duke of Richmond and Queen Katherine Parr. Dr. Christopher Tye was his music master; and Philip128 Van Wylder taught him to play upon his father's favourite instrument, the lute. Lady Jane was certainly not among his circle of intimate associates, which did not even include his two sisters, although the Lady Mary was at one time officially appointed his guardian, and Elizabeth passed the greater part of the year 1546 with him at Hatfield. So little intercourse had he with his sisters after his accession to the throne that he actually only met Princess Mary three times, and Elizabeth five. As to Lady Jane, he scarcely ever saw her, unless indeed she spent a few days with him at Whitehall some weeks before his death. As soon as the Somersets were thoroughly acquainted with the true motive that had induced the Dorsets to part with their daughter, they took every precaution to prevent its accomplishment; and so little was the Lady Jane seen at the Court of King Edward that she is only once casually mentioned by that monarch in his *Journal* as being present at the great functions arranged in 1550 in honour of the Dowager of Scotland when she passed through London on her way to her northern dominions; and this was at the time that Northumberland was in favour and Somerset in disgrace.

On Thursday, 18th February 1547, the temporal Lords assembled at the Tower in their robes of estate to witness a solemn and significant ceremony. The young King having ascended his throne, and the officials of his Court taken their allotted positions about him, the doors were thrown open, and Edward Seymour, Lord Protector and Earl of Hertford, was led from the Council Chamber and conducted before His Majesty. Garter bore his letters-patent, the Earl of Derby his mantle, the Earl of Shrewsbury his rod of gold; my Lord Oxford carried his cap of estate and coronet. The Lord of Arundel bore the sword, and walked immediately before the Protector, who was supported by the young Duke of Suffolk and the Marquis of Dorset. After the usual ceremonies, Hertford knelt and was invested by his royal nephew, who put on the mantle, girded on the sword, placed the coronet upon his uncle's head, and delivered him his rod of gold. Then the trumpets sounded, and the Herald proclaimed Edward Seymour to be no longer Earl of Hertford, but now and hereafter Duke of Somerset.

129 After the Protector came the Lord William Parr, Earl of Essex, brother to the Queen-Dowager, who was created Marquis of Northampton and of Essex. Then appeared John Dudley, Lord de Lisle, who had not assumed full importance at that time, but who was presently to become the protagonist of the ominous tragedy already in preparation. The future father-in-law of Lady Jane Grey, and the Nemesis of Somerset, was a man of splendid presence, exceedingly tall, with regular and majestic features, rendered even more striking by his long beard and sweeping moustache. He entered led by the Earls of Derby and Oxford, and was presently created Earl of Warwick. Dudley was followed by Wriothesley, who was raised to the peerage as Earl of Southampton.125 Immediately after him came the majestic Sir Thomas Seymour, whom the King created Baron Seymour of Sudeley, at the same time delivering to him his patent as Lord High-Admiral of England. Sir Richard Rich, Sir John Sheffield, and Sir William Willoughby followed in succession and were created barons by the same names they had borne as knights. When the elaborate ceremony was over, a grand banquet, at which the King was not present, was offered to the new peers in the Tower. His Majesty, who was far from strong, had fainted from fatigue, and no wonder!—the function had lasted from seven in the morning till nearly midday!

In the evening of the same day (18th February) three of the handsomest men of the English Court—Somerset, Sudeley, and Warwick—rode with a small escort from Whitehall through the Strand to Baynard's Castle, the residence of Sir William Herbert, Queen Katherine's brother-in-law, one of the wealthiest men in England, served by not130 less than a thousand men, who wore his liveries. Here these three gentlemen were hospitably entertained at supper. There was much to talk over, and the party, elated by the honours so recently showered upon its members and heated by Herbert's good wine, became "right merry"—little dreaming that within two years' time Somerset would condemn his own brother Thomas to death, and that a few months later Warwick, as Duke of Northumberland, would sign the death-warrant of

Somerset, only to be beheaded in his turn for high treason a year or so later by Queen Mary's command. The Marquis of Dorset may have been of the company, and his presence would add an additional note of tragic significance—for Warwick was to become the direct cause of the deaths both of Lady Jane and of her father!

King Edward, in the meantime, remained at the Tower until his official progress thence to Westminster for his coronation. Although Somerset and his brother were in office, and the Marquis of Dorset in great favour with them, it is not probable that his cousin, the Lady Frances, or her daughters were brought to see him. His boyish Majesty was left, according to custom, in complete isolation, seen and influenced alone by his uncles, the Seymours, and by his numerous tutors (for even after his accession his lessons were continued with curious punctuality), so that, what with State functions and his education, the unfortunate lad had very little or no time for physical exercise or recreation.

On 19th February His Majesty rode from the Tower in the usual procession to Westminster before the coronation which formed a part of our regal ceremonial until the reign of James I, when it was omitted on account of the plague. Edward, garbed in silver, with a white velvet waistcoat and a cloak slashed with Venetian silver brocade, embroidered with pearls, cantered on a milk-white pony under a white silk canopy edged with silver. On either side of him rode his two uncles, the Lord Protector and the Lord High-Admiral, whilst Cranmer, dumbly riding with the Emperor's Envoy, went between him and the Venetian Ambassador. They passed through streets gay with tapestry and cloth of gold;131 whilst at the Conduit in Cornhill white and red wine ran free for the people to drink at their will, and children dressed as angels sang a quaint greeting:—

"Hayle, Noble Edward, our Kynge and soveraigne, Hayle, the cheffe comfort of your communaltye: Hayle, redolent rose, whose sweetness to reteyne, Ys unto us all such great comodity, That earthly joy no more to us can be."

At the Standard in the Chepe an erection, "like unto a tower," and hung with cloth of gold, was surmounted by trumpeters, who, after a flourish, recited the following poetic (!) effusion:—

"Ye children that are towardes, sing up and downe, And never play the cowardes to him that weareth the crowne, But always doo your care his pleasure to fulfyll, Then shall you keep right sure the honour of England still. Sing up heart, sing up heart, Sing no more downe, But joy in King Edward that wereth the crowne."

Outside the Metropolitan Cathedral there was an acrobatic display: "An argosine [Ragusan] came from the batilment of Saint Poule's Church, upon a cable, beyng made faste to an anker at the deane's doore, liying upon his breaste, aidyng himself neither with hande nor foote, and after ascended to the middes [middle] of the same cable, and tumbled and plaied many pretie toies [tricks], wherat the Kyng and other of the peres and nobles of the realme laughed hartely." In Fleet Street the King was met by Faith, Justice, and Truth, the first holding a Bible conspicuously in her hands: each of these damsels recited a long poem in His Majesty's honour. Temple Bar having been "new painted in dyvers colours," was garnished with cloth of arras and standards and flags, and seven French trumpeters "blew sweetly" to the singing of an anthem by a group of children. The customary banquet was served in the Great Hall, Westminster, and was attended by Archbishop Cranmer, most of the bishops, the ambassadors, and envoys, the nobility, the Lord Mayor, aldermen, and sheriffs.

132 King Edward stayed at Westminster Palace until the coronation, which took place on the following Sunday in Westminster Abbey. On account of the King's poor health, the service was slightly abridged, otherwise the old Catholic form was throughout adhered to; for though Cranmer preached a sermon in

refutation of Petrine claims and urged the young monarch to abolish "idolatry," he celebrated High Mass, and the incongruous function concluded with the King's "offering," as had always been done in Catholic times, at St. Edward's shrine! After the coronation there were public jousts and tournaments; and the King and Court attended at Blackfriars those very performances by the "players" which had roused the ire of Bishop Gardiner and had been postponed at his request.126 We may be certain that the Marchioness of Dorset witnessed the procession and coronation, together with her two elder daughters, Jane and Katherine, from some place of vantage set apart for the ladies of the royal family, who, however, took no active part in either the procession or the actual ceremony, it not being customary for ladies to be officially present at the coronation of a bachelor King.

Notwithstanding that Edward VI is always connected in133 the popular mind with Protestantism, and notwithstanding Cranmer's attack on "Popery" at the coronation, for quite eighteen months, if not two years, after Henry VIII's death the Church in England remained exactly as he left it. True it is, that the first Book of Common Prayer was issued in 1548, but, on the other hand, Mass was said daily in the Royal Chapel (Low Mass every day and High Mass on festivals) for the first two or three years of Edward's reign; an MS. account book of "the Treasurer of the Chamber" in the Trevelyan Papers reveals the fact that the boy-King himself heard Mass almost daily until 1549. There is every reason to believe that Mass continued to be said or sung in the parish churches also until the same year; certainly the old feasts were still observed for the first two years of King Edward's reign, especially in London. These feasts were much more numerous than those retained by the Established Church; there were the first three days in Easter Week, Corpus Christi,—when there was the usual procession with the Host through the streets,—the "Days" of St. John, SS. Peter and Paul, St. Mary Magdalen, St. James the Apostle, the Annunciation, the Nativity, the Conception, and the Assumption of the Blessed Virgin Mary, All Hallows' Day, All Souls' Day, St. Edward Confessor, Christmas Day, and the three following holy-days. High Mass of the Holy Ghost was said in St. Stephen's Chapel when Parliament met for the first time after Henry's death, the King and both Houses attending in State. All the same, things ecclesiastical were not as they used to be; there was in different churches much diversity in the matter of details—one priest would use incense, another not, and so on. In 1548, however, Compline was sung in English and the Litany of the Saints also in the vernacular.

So soon as the news that King Henry was dead was authenticated abroad, an army of foreign Reformers—Swiss, German, French, and Italian—poured into England, as a secure refuge from the persecution they endured in their respective countries. These worthies held the most varied opinions, some even casting doubt on the Divinity of Christ, and the Lutherans hating the Calvinists as cordially as they both detested the Papists. The Londoners in general, who, when not Catholics, were mostly schismatics and ever jealous134 of foreigners, did not relish this sudden invasion; but the leaders of politics and religion in England welcomed the Reformers with open arms, even overlooking their doctrinal shortcomings for the sake of their hatred of "the Scarlet Lady." Some of them—for instance, Bucer, Peter Martyr, and perhaps Paul Fagius—were awarded chairs at the Universities; whilst others, such as John ab Ulmis, Conrad Pellican, Oswald Geisshäusler (better known as Myconius), Bullinger, Martin Micronius, Bartholomew Traheron, John Stumphius, Christopher Froschover, Bernardine Ochinus, Peter Bizarro of Perugia,127 etc., were received into the houses of some of the aristocracy to teach their children "the new learning." The Marquis of Dorset, as already noted, welcomed these foreign Reformers with enthusiasm, and we shall presently learn more concerning his relations with them. He did not confine his intercourse to a mere empty display of hospitality, but kept up a regular correspondence with many of them after their return to their homes. Letter-writing seems, indeed, to have been a passion with the Reformers, and their voluminous correspondence, arranged, translated, and published by the Parker Society,128 throws much valuable light on their private characters, their politics, and their singular theological opinions. It is mostly addressed to their brethren in Basle, Zurich, Geneva, and Strasburg, or to their English patrons. According to some authorities, there were from ten to twenty thousand foreign adherents of the "new learning"—or as we might still better say, new learnings, so many and diverse were their opinions—in England during

Edward VI's reign, but the former figure is the more likely to be correct. Very many of these learned men scattered themselves abroad again when the Catholic reaction set in under Mary; but doubtless a few remained, whose descendants to this day135 worship in the Église Reformée Française, l'Église Protestante Suisse, the Dutch Church, and in the other foreign Protestant churches which are sprinkled over the metropolis, but whose congregations were materially increased after the Revocation of the Edict of Nantes.

CHAPTER IX
THE QUEEN AND THE LORD HIGH-ADMIRAL

At the time of the much-discussed clandestine marriage between Thomas Seymour and Katherine Parr, the Princess Elizabeth was a precocious girl of fifteen, not beautiful, but tall for her age, well developed, and of elegant figure. The aquiline features, which age was to harshen, were softened at this early period by the roundness of youth; and the brilliant complexion stood in no need of the artificial assistance to which the Queen so freely resorted in her later life. The splendid auburn hair—its colour may have owed something to a touch of henna—considerably heightened charms not the least striking of which were a pair of small but black and penetrating eyes, inherited from her mother, Anne Boleyn.129 Unmindful of the fact that a girl of fifteen is not precisely a baby, the Queen had encouraged the Admiral to romp with "our Eliza" in the garden and even in her bedroom. Seymour was notoriously devoid of any sense of delicacy or chivalry, and there can be very little doubt that the object of his play with his illustrious stepdaughter was to kindle a passion which might serve his purpose in case the Queen, already advancing in pregnancy, should die in childbirth—a not improbable contingency, considering her age and the fact that she had never borne a child before. At a much later date Mrs. Ashley, the Princess's governess, deposed as follows before the Privy137 Council: "At Chelsea Manor,130 after my Lord Thomas Seymour was married to the Queen, he would come many mornings into the said Lady Elizabeth's chamber before she was ready, and sometimes before she did rise, and strike her familiarly on the back, and so go forth to his chamber, and sometimes go through to her maidens and play with them. And if the Princess were in bed, he would put open the curtains and bid her good morrow, and she would go further in the bed. And one morning he tried to kiss the Princess *in* the bed and I was there, and bade him go away for shame. At Hanworth, for two mornings, the Queen was with him, and they both tickled my Lady Elizabeth in her bed. Another time, at Hanworth, he romped with her in the garden, and cut her gown, being of black silk, into a hundred pieces; and when I chid Lady Elizabeth, she answered, 'She could not strive with all, for the Queen held her while the Lord Admiral cut the dress.' Another time, Lady Elizabeth138 heard the master-key unlock, and knowing my Lord Admiral would come in, ran out of her bed to her maidens, and then went behind the curtains of her bed and my Lord Admiral tarried a long while, in hopes she would come out." Upon Mrs. Ashley's begging the Admiral to be more circumspect, because his tomfooleries were giving the Princess a bad reputation, he answered, with an oath, "I will tell my Lord Protector how I am slandered; and I will not leave off, for I mean no evil." "At Seymour Place," continues Mrs. Ashley, "when the Queen slept there, he did use awhile to come up every morning in his night-gown and slippers. When he found Lady Elizabeth up and at her book, then he would look in at the gallery-door, and bid her good morrow and so go on his way; and I did tell my Lord it was an unseemly sight to see a man so little dressed in a maiden's chamber, with which he was angry, but left it. At Hanworth, the Queen did tell me 'that my Lord Admiral looked in at the gallery-window, and saw my Lady Elizabeth with her arms about a man's neck.' I did question my Lady Elizabeth about it, which she denied, weeping, and bade us 'ax all her women if there were any man who came to her, excepting Grindal.' [This gentleman was her tutor.] Howbeit, methought the Queen, being jealous, did feign this story, to the intent that I might take more heed to the proceedings of Lady Elizabeth and the Lord Admiral."131 Mr. Ashley, husband of the above deponent, and also in Princess Elizabeth's service, concurred in his wife's opinion that the Admiral was going too far, and that the Princess was "inclined" towards him, for whenever the Admiral was mentioned "she was wont to blush to her hair-roots." That Elizabeth herself was alarmed is proved by the fact that she told Parry, her cofferer, "that she feared the Admiral loved her but too well, and that the Queen was jealous of them both; and that Her Majesty, suspecting the frequent access of the Admiral to her, came upon them suddenly when they were alone, he having her in his arms. The Queen was greatly offended, and reproved Mrs. Ashley very sharply for her neglect of duty in permitting the Princess to fall into such reprehensible freedom of behaviour." The scandalous conduct of her husband at last roused not139 only the jealousy but the apprehensions of Queen Katherine. She feared some misfortune might befall the Princess at her tender age, and felt that in such a case the blame very naturally, and not unjustly, would be cast on her; and she would be generally regarded as the author of her stepdaughter's ruin. Very quietly, therefore, Her Majesty suggested the departure of the Princess, who was forthwith sent back to Hatfield, attended by her governess and servants. Elizabeth seems to have borne her late hostess no ill-will on account of this banishment, and a few months later we see her affectionately concerned about Her Grace's health, and greatly rejoiced at the news that she had been safely delivered. Evidently a letter from the Admiral, received some days before the event, had assured her the expected child would be a boy, and it must have been on receiving this expression of opinion that the Princess indited the following quaint epistle to her stepmother:—

"Although Your Highness's letters be most joyful to me in absence, yet, considering what pain it is for you to write, Your Grace being so sickly, your commendations were enough in my Lord's letter. I much rejoice at your health, with the well liking of the country, with my humble thanks that Your Grace wished me with you till I were weary of that country. Your Highness were like to be cumbered, if I should not depart till I were weary of being with you; although it were the worst soil in the world, your presence would make it pleasant. I cannot reprove my Lord for not doing your commendations in his letter, for he did it; and although he had not, yet I will not complain of him, for he shall be diligent to give me knowledge from time to time how his busy child doth; and if I were at his birth, no doubt I would see him beaten, for the trouble he hath put you to. Master Denny and my lady, with humble thanks, prayeth most entirely for Your Grace, praying the Almighty to send you a most lucky deliverance; and my mistress [Mrs. Ashley] wisheth no less, giving Your Highness most humble thanks for her commendations. Written, with very little leisure, this last day of July.—Your humble daughter,

Elizabeth"

The phrase, "If I were at his birth, no doubt I would140 see him beaten, for the trouble he hath put you to," is as quaint as any metaphor in Shakespeare. This letter was dispatched some six weeks before the Queen's confinement. About the same time Katherine received a friendly missive from the Princess Mary, congratulating her on the rumour she hears concerning her good condition, and assuring her she will pray Almighty God to help her in her hour of hope and danger.

The unpleasant rumours as to the behaviour of "my Lord Admiral" and Elizabeth were soon well known all over London, and caused much spiteful gossip. It was currently reported that when the Princess left the Queen's house she had betaken herself to some out-of-the-way dwelling at Hackney, where a mysterious infant had been born.132 This story was so generally believed that it had an echo even during the great Queen's reign. In the twenty-first year of Elizabeth (1579), a youth who appeared at Madrid asserted himself to be the Queen's son by the Lord Admiral, and was accepted as such by the Spanish King and Court. The Lord Admiral certainly made a great impression on the young girl's heart, for long after her accession, Elizabeth, very reticent, as a rule, concerning events connected with her childhood and youth, would, in the privacy of her closet, confide to the ladies she admitted to her intimacy that "the Lord Admiral had been the only man she had ever loved; and the handsomest she had ever seen."

Perhaps the departure of Princess Elizabeth left the Queen more leisure to look after her other charge, the Lady Jane Grey, who had been removed from Seymour Place to the Manor House, Chelsea. Katherine, on account, it may be,141 of the restlessness sometimes observed in ladies in her condition, moved about a great deal during this period. Sometimes she addresses her letters from Hanworth, sometimes from Oatlands. Then, as political events rendered her husband's position less and less secure, she determined to retire to Sudeley Castle, Seymour's lately acquired seat in Gloucestershire, and to lie-in there. The journey from Hanworth must have been a troublesome one for a woman in her state of health. She travelled with her husband, Lady Jane Grey,133 Lady Tyrwhitt, six other ladies, and two chaplains. She herself was in a waggon, comfortably lined and cushioned, no doubt, and with every possible precaution to ensure her comfort, but the roads were atrocious, and the journey lasted six days. Yet the weary traveller's patience must have been amply rewarded, for Sudeley Castle in those days was one of the most splendid houses in England—a gem of Gothic architecture, furnished in the most sumptuous style. The Queen's apartments had been fitted up with as much magnificence as she would have enjoyed if she had still been Queen-Consort of England and about to present the realm with an expected heir. Her bedchamber was hung with costly tapestry, specified, in an inventory still preserved at Sudeley, as consisting of "six fair pieces of hangings illustrating the history of the Nymph Daphne." The bed had a tester and curtains of crimson taffeta, with a counterpoint of silk serge. There was another bed for the nurse, hung with "counterpoints of imagery to please the babe"—probably some stuff such as was common in those days embroidered with animals,142 birds, and little men. The outer chamber had been arranged as a day nursery, and was hung with "a fair tapestry" representing the twelve months of the year. In it was set a "chair of state" covered with cloth of gold—all the other seats were stools—and a bedstead with tester curtains and rich counterpoints, or counterpanes, as they are now called. There is still a lovely oriel window of Tudor architecture at Sudeley popularly called "the nursery window," but this cannot be the window of the nursery that was prepared for Katherine Parr's babe, for the inventory distinctly says "carpets for *four* windows in the nursery." This other "nursery window" looks out upon one of the most lovely scenes in England—the chapel where Katherine Parr sleeps in peace after her chequered life, the garden in front of it, while beyond, the lovely green of the famous woods of St. Kenelm soften into the haze of the distant horizon.

Lady Jane's room, beyond Queen Katherine's, was also splendidly furnished, and adorned with tapestries representing the history of St. Catherine. The bed was hung with blue silk, and a large piece of Turkey carpet134 covered the floor.

Queen Katherine's life at Sudeley must have been very quiet and peaceful. Local tradition tells us that she was wont, with her young charge and her ladies, to visit the poor and take an interest in her gardens. Divine service according to the rites of the Church of England was said regularly twice a day in the beautiful chapel by one of her chaplains, Coverdale or Parkhurst, and sermons were preached at least three times a day. The Lord Admiral's ostentatious absence from these pious exercises was a matter of great vexation to the Queen, and gave rise to a report that his Lordship was an atheist.135

The return of the Lord Protector from his campaign in Scotland boded no good for the Lord Admiral; the brothers had a bitter quarrel, and on this occasion it was that Seymour departed with the Queen for Sudeley. Edward had been writing to Somerset, calling him "his dearest uncle" and saying that he was well pleased with his many victories, and on the warrior's return the Admiral found himself quite driven143 into the shade. However, about a month before the Queen's confinement, he made a hurried journey to London, hoping to induce the young King to write a letter complaining of the treatment his younger uncle and the Queen were receiving from the Protector. Edward was easily persuaded to write the letter, but before the plot was thoroughly matured it was betrayed to the elder Seymour, and Thomas, arrested by the Lord Protector's order, was taken before the Council to answer for his behaviour. Threatened with imprisonment in the Tower, he made a sort of submission to Somerset, and a hollow reconciliation took place, the Protector adding a sum of £800 per annum to Sudeley's appointments in the hope of conciliating his unruly brother, who hurried back to Sudeley, where he felt himself comparatively safe; for so long as the Queen lived he could defy his foes, his wife's great rank and the well-known affection entertained for her by the boy-King sufficing to screen him even from the vengeance of the infuriated head of the house of Seymour.

On 30th August 1548 Queen Katherine bore the infant for whom such great preparations had been made. The parents had fondly hoped it would be a boy, but, alack! it was a puny girl, destined to be a child of misfortune. She cost her mother her life, and grew up to suffer the bitter pangs of poverty and neglect.

My Lord Sudeley, who had been consulting fortune-tellers and palmists about the expected child, was bitterly disappointed, for they had predicted the birth of a son. This did not prevent him from writing a very flattering account of his infant daughter to his brother the Protector. The Duke had quite recently sent his brother a very severe letter complaining of his intrigues; but the birth of the child seems to have had a softening effect, and the following letter was far more friendly, containing a courteous message to the Queen, and continuing:—

"We are right glad to understand by your letters that the Queen, your bedfellow, hath a happy hour; and, escaping all danger, hath made you the father of so pretty a daughter. And although (if it had pleased God) it would have been both to us, and (we suppose) also to you, a more joy and comfort if it had, this the first-born, been a son, yet the escape of the danger, and the prophecy and good hansell144 of this to a great sort of proper sons, which (as I write) we trust no less than to be true, it is no small joy and comfort to us, as we are sure it is to you and to her Grace also; to whom you shall make again our hearty commendations, with no less gratulation of such good success.

"Thus we bid you heartily farewell. From Sion, the 1st of Sept. 1548.—Your loving brother,

"E. Somerset"

It is a curious fact that the child was born on 30th August, and that Somerset's letter is dated the 1st of September, proving that communication was much more expeditious in those days than we are apt to imagine.

Lady Tyrwhitt, who attended on the Queen, has left a very touching account of her last hours.136 Everything seems to have gone well until about six days after the child's birth, when the Queen suddenly became delirious, and conceived a great dread and a burning jealousy of her husband. Lady Tyrwhitt says that "two days before the death of the Queen, at my coming to her in the morning, she asked me 'Where I had been so long?' and said unto me 'that she did fear such things in herself, that she was sure she could not live.' I answered as I thought, 'that I saw no likelihood of death in her.' She then, having my Lord Admiral by the hand, and divers others standing by, spake these words, partly, as I took, idly [that is, "in delirium"]: 'My Lady Tyrwhitt, I be not well handled; for those that be about me care not for me, but stand laughing at my grief, and the more good I will to them, the less good they will to me.' Whereunto my Lord Admiral answered, 'Why, sweetheart, I would you no hurt.' And she said to him again, aloud, 'No, my lord, I think so'; and immediately she said to him in his ear, 'But, my lord, you have given me many shrewd taunts.' These words I perceived she spoke with good memory, and very sharply and earnestly, for her mind was sore disquieted. My Lord Admiral, perceiving that I heard it, called me aside, and asked me 'What she said?' and I declared it plainly to him. Then he consulted with me 'that he would lie down on the bed by her, to look if he could pacify her unquietness with gentle communication,'145 whereunto I agreed; and by the time that he had spoken three or four words to her, she answered him roundly and sharply, saying, 'My Lord, I would have given a thousand marks to have had my full talk with Hewyke [Dr. Huick or Huycke137] the first day I was delivered, but I durst not for displeasing you.' And I, hearing that, perceived her trouble to be so great, that my heart would serve me to hear no more. Such like communications she had with him the space of an hour, which they did hear that sat by her bedside."

Little Lady Jane Grey was no doubt near the afflicted Queen throughout these trying scenes; but she would almost certainly have been excluded from the bedchamber when the Queen's condition became alarming. Just before the end Katherine seems to have rallied, for on 5th September she was able to make her will, leaving everything to her husband, and "wishing it had been a thousand times more, so great was her love for him." The witnesses to this will were Dr. Huycke, already mentioned, and Dr. Parkhurst, afterwards Bishop of Norwich, both men of unimpeachable integrity, who would not have signed the document if there had been anything illegal about it. Katherine Parr died on 7th September, the second day after the date of her will and the eighth after the birth of her child. She was in her thirty-sixth year, and had survived Henry VIII just one year, six months, and eight days. Her funeral took place at Sudeley Castle, according to the rites of the Church of England, on Friday, 8th September, and was the first royal funeral so celebrated in England. Dr. Coverdale was the officiant at the Queen's burial. A procession was formed of "conductors" (*i.e.* leaders) in black, gentlemen, Somerset Herald, torch-bearers, Lady Jane Grey, acting as chief mourner, her train borne by a young gentlewoman, then more ladies and gentlemen; finally, "all other following." The Lord Admiral, according to custom, did not attend his wife's funeral. The ritual was somewhat curious, and is described146 in the following terms in an MS. entitled "A Booke of Buryalls of Trew Noble Persons," now in the London College of Arms:138 "When the corpse was set within the rails, and the mourners placed, the whole choir began and sung certain psalms in English, and read three lessons; and after the third lesson, the mourners, according to their degrees and that which is accustomed, offered into the alms-box.... Doctor Coverdale, the Queen's almoner, began his sermon ... in one place thereof he took occasion to declare unto the people 'how the offering which was there done, was (not) done anything to benefit the corpse, but for the poor only; and also the lights, which were carried and stood about the corpse, were for the honour of the person, and for none other intent nor purpose'; and so went through with his sermon, and made a godly prayer, and the whole church answered and prayed with him.... The sermon done, the corpse was buried, during which time the choir sung the *Te Deum* in English. And this done, the mourners dined, and the rest returned homewards again. All which aforesaid was done in a morning."

CHAPTER X
THE LADY JANE GOES TO SEYMOUR PLACE

All Thomas Seymour's schemes and conspiracies and political and domestic intrigues were brought to nought by his wife's death, and he swiftly realised that the danger of his position was immeasurably increased by her decease. She had been an effective barrier between himself and his foes, for nothing could persuade the King to consider her otherwise than with great affection, as one of the only two persons he really loved (his young companion Barnaby Fitzpatrick being the other). Sudeley was now, metaphorically speaking, at sea in a storm, and seeking safety in any port he could discover. For a few days his troubles seem to have dazed him. He may, indeed, have loved his wife and have sincerely mourned her. There is not the slightest reason to believe that there was any solid foundation for the accusations brought against him of having ill-treated and even poisoned the Queen. A few weeks before her death, on the contrary, he swore, with one of his horrible oaths, that if any man "speak ill of his Queen in his presence, he would take his fist to his ear, be he of the lowest or of the highest." After his wife's death, Sudeley was at first inclined to break up his household and throw himself once more into public life. He even went so far as to dismiss some of his servants, and returned to Hanworth, the late Queen's dower-house in Middlesex, taking Lady Jane and her attendants with him. Hence he wrote to Dorset to say that, broken-hearted as he was at the departure of the Queen, his wife, he could not keep the Lady Jane any longer,139 and begged him to send for her. By 17th September,148 however, he seems to have cheered up considerably, for he dispatched another letter to Bradgate, which runs as follows:—

"My last letters, written at a time when, partly with the Queen's Highness's death I was so amazed that I had small regard either to myself or my doings, and partly then thinking that my great loss must presently have constrained me to have broken up and dissolved my whole house, I offered unto your Lordship to send my Lady Jane unto you whensoever you would send for her, as to him that I thought would be most tender on her. Forasmuch, since being both better avised of myself, and having more deeply digested whereunto my power [*i.e.* property] would extend; I find, indeed, that with God's help, I shall right well be able to continue my house together, without diminishing any great part thereof; and, therefore, putting my whole affiance and trust in God, have begun anew to stablish my household, where shall remain not only the gentlewomen of the Queen's Highness's privy chamber, but also the maids that waited at large, and other women being about Her Grace in her lifetime, with a hundred and twenty gentlemen and yeomen, continually abiding in the house together. Saving that now, presently, certain of the maids and gentlewomen have desired to have license for a month or such thing, to see their friends, and then immediately to return hither again. And, therefore, doubting lest your Lordship might think any unkindness that I should by my said letters take occasion to rid me of your daughter, the Lady Jane, so soon after the Queen's death, for the proof both of my hearty affection towards you, and my good-will to her, I am now minded to keep her until I next speak with your Lordship, which should have been within these three or four days if it had not been that I must repair to the Court, as well to help certain of the Queen's poor servants with some of the things now fallen by her death, as also for mine own affairs, unless I shall be advertised from your Lordship to the contrary. My lady my mother shall and will, I doubt not, be as dear unto her149 [*i.e.* Lady Jane] as though she were her own daughter; and for my part I shall continue her half-father, and more, and all that are in my house shall be as diligent about her as yourself would wish accordingly."140

To this letter Dorset replied as follows, in a particularly fine specimen of the strange orthography of those days:—

"My most hearty commendations unto your good lordship not forgotten. When it hath pleased you by your most gentle letters to offer me the abode of my daughter at your lordship's house, I do as well acknowledge your most friendly affection towards me and her therein, as also render unto you most deserved thanks for the same. Nevertheless, considering the state of my daughter and her tender years, wherein she shall hardly rule herself as yet without a guide, lest she should, for lack of a bridle, take too much the head, and conceive such opinion of herself, that all such good behaviour as she heretofore hath learned, by the Queen's and your most wholesome instructions, should either altogether be quenched in her, or at the least much diminished, I shall, in most hearty wise, require your lordship to commit her to the governance of her mother, by whom for the fear and duty she oweth her, she shall most easily be ruled and framed towards virtue, which I wish above all things to be most plentiful in her; and although your lordship's good mind, concerning her honest and godly education be so great, that mine can be no more; yet weighing that you be destitute of such one as should correct her as a mistress, and admonish her as a mother, I persuade myself that you will think the eye and oversight of my wife shall be in this respect most necessary."

Then follows a mention of the proposed scheme for uniting the Lady Jane to the King; and the letter concludes thus:—

"My meaning herein is not to withdraw any part of my promise to you for her bestowing; for I assure your150 Lordship, I intend, God willing, to use your discreet advice and consent in that behalf and no less than mine own; only I seek in these her tender years, wherein she now standeth, either to make or mar (as the common saying is), the addressing [the forming] of her mind to humility, soberness, and obedience. Wherefore, looking upon that fatherly affection which you bear her, my trust is that your lordship, weighing the premises, will be content to charge her mother with her, whose waking eye in respecting her demeanour, shall be, I hope, no less than you as a friend and I as a father would wish. And thus wishing your lordship a perfect riddance of all unquietness and grief of mind, I leave any further to trouble your lordship. From my house at Bradgate, the 19th of September.—Your lordship's to the best of my power,

Henry Dorset"141

(Endorsed)

"To my very good Lord Admiral: give this."

With this precious epistle was enclosed another, from the Lady Frances:—

"And whereas," says she, "of a friendly and brotherly good will you wish to have Jane my daughter, continuing still in your house, I give you most hearty thanks for your gentle offer, trusting, nevertheless, that, for the good opinion you have in your sister (Lady Frances herself), you will be content to charge her with her (*i.e.* charge Lady Frances with Lady Jane), who promiseth you, not only to be ready at all times to account for the ordering of your dear niece [Lady Jane], but also to use your counsel and advice on the bestowing of her, whensoever it shall happen. Wherefore, my good brother, my request shall be, that I may have the oversight of her with your good will and thereby shall have good occasion to think that you do trust me in such wise, as is convenient that a sister be trusted of so loving a brother. And thus my most hearty commendations not omitted, I wish the whole [or holy] deliverance of151 your grief and continuance of your lordship's health. From Bradgate, 19th of this September.—Your loving sister and assured friend,

Frances Dorset"142

(Endorsed)

"To the right Honourable and my very
good Lord, my Lord Admiral."

It will be noted that the Lady Frances evinces a quite sisterly affection for the Lord Admiral, adopting him as her brother; and her daughter, therefore, was to be considered as his niece.

After this correspondence, the Lady Jane was returned to Bradgate, whither she proceeded with a semi-regal escort consisting of not less than forty persons, including Mr. Rous or Rowse, controller of the Lord Admiral's household, and Mr. John Harrington, afterwards prominent at Queen Elizabeth's Court. On taking their leave of the young Princess, these gentlemen assured her that all the maids at Hanworth were expecting her back again. The wily Dorsets themselves had, indeed, made up their minds she should return, though in their heart of hearts they had something besides Lady Jane herself in view. It was somewhere about 20th September that Lady Jane arrived at Bradgate. On or about the 23rd of that month the Marquis and his spouse journeyed to London, where they met Sir William Sharington,143 Seymour's152 *âme damnée*, and the Lord High-Admiral himself. These gentlemen had a very secret business to discuss, the nature of which must now be described. The Dorsets, not then wealthy people, were deep in debt. Now Seymour was known to be rich, for, in addition to his own fortune, he had just inherited that of the Queen, and, so far, his brother had given no signs of any intention of confiscating it. The Dorsets, therefore, intimated to Sharington that he would do well to make Sudeley understand that if he desired to renew his guardianship of the Lady Jane, he must agree to give her parents £2000, £500 to be paid down at once, on account. It should be here remarked that Sudeley, by voluntarily relinquishing the care of the Lady Jane Grey, had given up his guardianship, which, by the custom of those times, gave him more than parental rights over her. It was his desire to renew his official charge that enabled the Dorsets to make this extraordinary proposal to sell him their child for what in those days was considered a large sum of money. When the game was up and Sudeley in prison, the Dorsets threw the blame of this transaction on everybody but themselves. The Lord Admiral, asserted Lady Jane's father in his deposition before the Privy Council, "was so earnestly in hand with me and my wife, the Lady Frances, that in the end, because he would have no nay, we were content that Jane should return to his house." Indeed, Sudeley, not content to treat so important a matter only through the medium of Sharington, himself appeared at Dorset's town house and interviewed the Marquis, who admitted in the above-mentioned deposition that, "At this very time and place he renewed his promise unto me for the marrying of my daughter to the King's Majesty, and he[153] added, 'If I may get the King at liberty, I dare warrant you His Majesty will marry no other than Jane.'"

Whilst Sudeley was thus pretending, if nothing more, that he was able to marry Jane to the King, could he but get possession of her, the Marquis of Dorset was inditing a letter to the Lord Protector which contained a passage referring to some negotiations he was conducting with His Highness for the marriage of Lady Jane to the Earl of Hertford, Somerset's eldest son! "Item, for the maryage of your graces sune to be had with my doghter Jane, I thynk hyt not met [meet] to be wrytyn, but I shall at all tymes avouche my sayng." Dorset's cunning must have nearly matched Sudeley's! Young Hertford was the lad mentioned in the papers of the time of Queen Mary as "contracted" to Lady Jane Grey: in later years he married her sister Katherine. Jane probably made his acquaintance in her childish days, when the Seymours lived at Whitehall and she was in residence at the "Bluff King's" Court under the wing of Katherine Parr. Hertford was also one of the band of young noblemen selected as companions for Prince Edward under the tutelage of the learned Dr. Cheke; and probably had many a romp with Jane, then a merry little girl. Later on he paid one or two visits to Bradgate, the Lady Frances conceiving such a strong affection for him that she was wont to call him her son. Here again the young people must have been much together, and their childish friendship may have inspired the Marquis of Dorset with the idea of uniting them in marriage. However that may be, he certainly got as far as corresponding with Somerset—though in the profoundest secrecy—about the matter. Was his caution due to a fear of displeasing Sudeley? What is more than probable is that the Lord Admiral got wind of the scheme, and that his desire to get Jane away from her father and his own brother and nephew was at the bottom of his readiness to pay so heavy a price to resume her guardianship, for which object he used the likelihood of her marriage with the King as a bait to catch the Marquis—who was eventually "jockeyed" by both the Seymours, for no marriage with either the King or Hertford ever took place.

Whilst Seymour was personally negotiating with the Marquis, the task of persuading the Marchioness fell to[154] Sharington. "Sir William [Sharington] travailed as earnestly with my wife," says Dorset, "to gain her good-will for the return of our daughter to Lord Thomas Seymour as he [probably Seymour is meant in this case] did with me; so as in the end, after long debating and 'much sticking of our sides,' we did agree that my daughter Jane should return to him."[144]

Their bargain with the Admiral struck, the Dorsets hurried back to Bradgate, whence they incited the dispatch of the following ingenuous letter:—

"To the Right Honourable and my singular
good lord, the Lord Admiral.

"My duty to your lordship, in most humble wise remembered, with no less thanks for the gentle letters which I received from you. Thinking myself so much bound to your lordship for your great goodness towards me from time to time, that I cannot by any means be able to recompense the least part thereof, I purpose to write a few rude lines to your lordship, rather as a token to show how much worthier I think your lordship's goodness, than to give worthy thanks for the same, and these my letters will be to testify unto you that, like as you have been unto me a loving and kind father, so I shall be always most ready to obey your godly monitions and good instructions, as becometh one upon whom you have heaped so many benefits. And thus fearing I should trouble your lordship too much, I most humbly take leave of your lordship.—Your most humble servant during my life,

"Jane Graye"

(Endorsed)

"My Lady Jane, the 1st of Oct. 1548."

With this letter the Lady Frances sent Sudeley another, in which she again calls him her "very good lord and brother": Jane considers him as "a loving and kind father," and her mother signs herself, "Your assured and loving sister, Frances Dorset"—most friendly!

It was near Michaelmas when the Lord Admiral, with a numerous retinue, including several ladies, arrived at Bradgate155 to carry the girl back with him to Hanworth. Traces of his return journey may be found in papers preserved in the Public Library at Leicester, which inform us that "beer, cold meat, and ale was provided by the Mayor for my Lady Jane and her escort, proceeding from Bradgate with the Lord Thomas Seymour, to London." Sudeley brought the £500 with him and gave it to the father who, for the sake of filthy lucre, had not scrupled to hand over his young daughter to a notorious profligate. Thomas treated the matter jovially, saying "merrily" he would take no receipt for the money, for "the Lady Jane herself was in pledge of that"; the Marquis, on the other hand, sought to endue the affair with a more respectable appearance by declaring the cash was "as it wer for an ernst peny of the favour that he [Sudeley] wold shewe unto him [Dorset]." To our eyes, there is, and can be, but one redeeming feature in the whole of this sordid transaction—the fact, proved by sufficient evidence, that Lady Jane Grey whilst under the Lord Admiral's roof was treated not only with respect, but with much kindness, and that, even allowing for the fact that letters such as that already quoted were inspired by her parents, she seems to have been genuinely attached to both Sudeley and his mother.

Had Thomas Seymour contented himself with achieving eminence in any one legitimate direction—the Navy, for instance—he might have succeeded in winning both fame and honour. But he lacked the clearness of judgment and power of reticence necessary to carry any one of his more nefarious schemes to completion, and so ended in pitiable failure. Whilst his brother was away fighting in Scotland, he had striven, and with some success, to ingratiate himself with the young King. To this end, as we have seen, he lent him various sums of money. He seized every opportunity of belittling and even calumniating his brother, the Protector, openly accusing him of conspiring against Edward's liberty, all of which the poor little King was only too eager to believe; for Somerset, with his puritanic views, had not made the boy's existence very pleasant to him, persistently treating him as a little old man, and suppressing all those amusements and sports which lads, even sickly lads, love so dearly. It is said that, on one occasion, when he came upon the King and Barney Fitzpatrick156 playing cards, he seized them in a fury and threw them into the fire. He had striven, in a word, to make Edward look at life as he saw it himself, through smoked Calvinistic glasses that robbed it of all brightness.

The Duchess of Feria relates that Queen Mary once told her Edward VI had confessed to her that he was very tired of sermons—not to be wondered at, since the poor child had to hear one at least daily on some dogmatic controversy or other, and these dull homilies often lasted a good two hours. In fact, the royal lad was bored and "prayed" to death. For more than a year after his accession to the throne he was compelled to hear a daily Mass, celebrated according to the old rites but with the Epistle and Gospel said in English. Interpolated into this Latin service was the inevitable lengthy sermon preached by men well known for their Reforming zeal, such as Canon William Barlow of St. Osyth's, in Essex, who became Bishop of Chichester in Elizabeth's reign; Dr. John Taylor; Dr. Redman, a violent opponent of the doctrine of Transubstantiation; Dr. Thomas Becken; Dr. Giles Ayre, a bitter enemy of Gardiner; and the extremely Protestant Dr. Latimer. John Knox, who came to London in 1551, also preached before the King; but by that time the Mass had been replaced by the services of the first Book of Common Prayer. Knox was in a very bad temper with the Protector at the time of his visit, and accused him of paying more attention to the building of his new house in the Strand than to his (Knox's) sermons. As time went on, poor Edward had to listen to controversies in which Cranmer, Archbishop of Canterbury, Ridley, Bishop of Rochester, and "that most zealous Papist," Heath, Bishop of Worcester (afterwards, under Mary, Archbishop of York), "debated and disputed" on such grave subjects as Transubstantiation, the Intercession of Saints, Worship of the Virgin, Prayers for the Dead, Purgatory, etc., and attend sermons preached in the courtyard of Whitehall Palace, where Gardiner delivered his last discourse on papal supremacy, which sent him to the Tower. Contemporary evidence shows exactly how the audience was grouped round the improvised rostrum built close to the walls of the palace, so that the King might hear the preacher from an open window, where he generally sat, notebook in hand, in the157 company of the Lord Protector, and of Dr. John Cheke, his tutor. Aged people of both sexes were ranged on benches close to the palace, whilst the general congregation, standing, filled up the courtyard. The learned Nicholas Udall often sat at a desk under the pulpit, taking shorthand notes of the sermon, and by his means many of the more notable of these orations have been preserved to this day. John Knox preached his last sermon before Edward VI from the pulpit at Whitehall Palace. At many, if not at most, of these pious exercises Lady Jane Grey, her mother and sister must have assisted, for it was expected that all the great ladies of the Court should attend; and consequently, in one or two old engravings of these interesting functions, we behold them, wearing their "froze pastes" or coifs, seated in rows, looking exceedingly sanctimonious, not to say bored. There are numbers of young children among them, one or two of whom have evidently fallen into a deep sleep.

Edward, extremely delicate from his birth, slightly deformed, with one shoulder-blade higher than the other, weak eyes, and occasional attacks of deafness, suffered terribly, we are told, from headaches, a fact which causes little surprise, considering the number of sermons he was forced to attend. The Lord Admiral, during the brief time he held the King's favour, altered all this. The sermons were reduced, the sports and pastimes multiplied. No wonder, then, that of his two uncles Edward VI preferred Thomas to Edward!

Hardly was Lady Jane installed at Seymour Place, whither she was removed from Hanworth as soon as the weather grew cold, than her guardian set himself to weave not one but half a dozen fresh intrigues. Once more he planned to marry the Princess Elizabeth, or, failing her, a little later on, his young ward, Lady Jane. He even endeavoured to open a fresh correspondence with the Princess, and met with some success; but the astute damsel made him a very politic response. However impressed she may have been by the Admiral's good looks, she was well aware that he had compromised her once, and was resolved there should be no second edition of the Chelsea business. Yet she had the imprudence to send his Lordship letters through her servants, and, thus encouraged, the Admiral began to make minute inquiries as to her fortune158 and the management of her affairs. He also endeavoured to find out the amount of the fortunes owned by Lady Jane Grey and Princess Mary, and, in short, of all the marriageable ladies of the royal family, not excluding Anne of Cleves. A report of these inquiries coming to the knowledge of John Russell, the Lord Privy Seal, that functionary thought it his duty to look into the matter, and seized an opportunity when riding with the Admiral through the streets of London to ask him his object point-blank. As they rode past Westminster Hall, Russell turned to Seymour, saying, "My Lord Admiral, there are certain rumours bruited of you which I am very sorry to hear."

"What rumours?" demanded Seymour.

"I have been informed," replied Russell, "that you mean to marry either the Lady Mary or the Lady Elizabeth, or else the Lady Jane."

Sudeley remained silent, and his interlocutor proceeded: "My Lord, if ye go about any such thing, ye seek the means to undo yourself, and all those that shall come of you."

Sudeley, shaking his head, denied ever having had any such intention; he "had no thought of such an enterprise." And so, for the time being, the conversation dropped. But a few days later, when the Lord Admiral was again riding with his Lordship, he said to Russell, "Father Russell, you are very suspicious of me; I pray you tell me who showed you of the marriage that I should attempt, whereof ye brake with me the other day."

Russell answered, "I will not tell you the authors of the tale, but they be your very good friends"; and he advised Seymour "to make no suit of marriage that way"—meaning with Elizabeth or Mary, or eventually with Lady Jane.

Nothing daunted, Seymour replied, "It is convenient for them to marry, and better it were that they were married within the realm than in any foreign place without the realm; and why might not I, or another man raised by the King their father, marry one of them?"—in allusion to the fact that Henry VIII had passed a law legalising the marriage of a Princess of the Blood with a subject.

Russell warned him honestly, "My Lord, if either you, or any other within this realm, shall match himself in marriage159 either with my Lady Mary or my Lady Elizabeth, he shall undoubtedly, whatsoever he be, procure unto himself the occasion of his undoing, and you especially, above all others, being of so near alliance to the King's Majesty." Then, bearing in mind the Lord Admiral's love of money, Lord Russell straightway asked, "And I pray you, what shall you have with either of them?"

Here Seymour was on his own ground: "He who marries one of them shall," he said, "have three thousand pounds a year."

"My Lord," responded Russell, "it is not so, for ye may be well assured that he shall have no more than ten thousand pounds in money, plate, and goods, and no lands; and what is that to maintain his charges and estates who matches himself there?"

"They must have three thousand pounds a year also," said the Lord of Sudeley.

Thereupon Russell lost his temper, and with some strong expressions retorted "they should *not*."

Seymour, likewise with an oath, asserted "that they *should*, and that none should dare to say nay to it."

Russell answered that he, at least, dared "say nay" to the Lord Admiral's greed, "for it was clean against the King's will." And so they parted.

These inquiries about the royal ladies' fortunes became known to the Protector, possibly through Russell, and thus the whole intrigue was brought to light.

Lady Jane at Seymour Place and in the possession of the Lord Admiral was already a stumbling-block in the way of Somerset's own matrimonial schemes for his own son, and the discovery of the underhand manner in which Thomas had endeavoured to supplant him in the King's affections goaded the elder man to fury. But Sudeley had grown reckless, and he openly defied his all-powerful brother, and vaunted his determination to oust him at any cost from his high seat.145 He boldly set about ingratiating himself with160 the yeoman class, which was embittered against Somerset on account of his exactions; and Dorset, now his willing tool, also strove to secure a following among the farmers and gentlemen, on bad terms with the existing Government. The ladies of the Court, who hated the arrogant Duchess of Somerset, were flattered into a friendly feeling for the Lord Admiral and what he was pleased to consider his just cause. To keep up his influence, he had secretly bought over a hundred manors and stewardships, and he had arranged with his scoundrelly friend, Sharington—who, to save his skin, turned traitor—to secure sufficient ammunition and arms to store Holt Castle, to which fortress he intended to convey the King. Thanks to this man's frauds on the Bristol Mint, my Lord of Sudeley got together money enough to raise an army of 10,000 men. In addition to all this, he was in league with no less than four distinct gangs of pirates or privateers, and had established a sort of dépôt for stolen property in the Scilly Isles, whither the cargoes of sea-plundered vessels were taken to await removal to London. Here, then, was an array of crimes and treasons enough to hang any man, even if he was the Lord Protector's brother! One fatal day Thomas made the egregious mistake of approaching Wriothesley on the subject of obtaining the Protectorship. He told him Dorset and Pembroke were on his side. "Beware what you are doing," replied Wriothesley gravely; "it were better for you if you had never been born, nay that you were burnt quick alive, than that you should attempt it." Sudeley, somewhat dashed by this rebuff, next sought the Earl of Rutland, and spoke to him in much the same impudent and imprudent fashion. Rutland, when his visitor departed, went straight to Wriothesley and told him what he had learnt. Both agreed to reveal all they knew of the conspiracy to the Council. Several meetings were held to inquire into the matter; and161 at length Somerset summoned his brother to appear before him. Sudeley sent a flat refusal. Early in the forenoon of 17th January 1549 Sir Thomas Smith and Sir John Baker proceeded to Seymour Place, and there arrested the Lord Admiral, who was conveyed by water to the Tower, after a passionate leave-taking with his aged mother.146

To Lady Jane the trial and subsequent execution of her guardian must have been a matter of intense and painful interest. She was still his guest at Seymour Place when he was arrested, and she must have witnessed the tragic parting of the unhappy mother from the son so remorselessly torn from her aged arms to meet his doom. Whatever his crimes and faults, the Lord of Sudeley had been a good son, and the old Lady Seymour mourned him deeply till she died of her sorrows, on 18th October in the following year. She was buried with scant pomp. The King, her grandson, and his Court did not even put on the customary mourning, on the plea that black gowns did not really signify respect to the dead, who were best remembered in the hearts and prayers of those who survived them—certainly not a popular or contemporary belief, for on the day following Lady Seymour's death two State funerals were celebrated with all those honours which were denied to the remains of the grandmother of the reigning sovereign. There was probably a political motive at the back of this want of respect, which may perhaps be ascribed to the evil influence of Warwick, who, in his desire to humiliate the Somersets, refused the honours due to the corpse of the Protector's mother.

Meanwhile, the destruction of Thomas Seymour was being prepared with skill and secrecy. Whilst the foredoomed Admiral had been boasting all over London of his immense influence, his foes, now that he was in their power, subtly compassed his ruin by buying witnesses against him and securing the goodwill of his numerous and venomous enemies. They had long been spreading a rumour that he had poisoned the late Queen Katherine in order to make an even higher alliance with one or other of the heiresses to the throne. His162 scandalous proceedings with regard to the Princess Elizabeth at Chelsea and Hanworth, and the unbecoming manner in which he had regained possession of Lady Jane, were brought up against him. Lady Tyrwhitt, one of the bedchamber ladies of the late Queen his wife, was called to give certain damaging evidence, pointing to a strong suspicion that Seymour had not only been most unkind to the deceased lady, but had actually poisoned her food during the last few days of her life, and set up the fever which carried her off within a week of her child's birth. Lord Latimer stated that Seymour, when Queen Katherine had prayers said in his house morning and afternoon according to the order of the Reformed Church, would get out of the way, and swear on his oath that "The Book of Common Prayer was not God's work at all." There was a merciless raking up of misdeeds, true or false, of the man's earliest youth—as, for instance, "that, in 1540, a woman who was executed for robbery and child-murder had declared that the beginning of her evil life was due to her having been seduced and desolated by Lord Thomas Seymour." The Dorsets were summoned from Bradgate to give evidence in the matter of the wardship of their daughter, and other witnesses were fetched from different parts of the kingdom to give damaging testimony.147

During, though not at, Seymour's trial, Elizabeth was subjected to a private inquiry at Hatfield, and personally asked whether Mrs. Ashley had encouraged her to marry the Admiral. This she declared she had never done, adding that she did not believe Mrs. Ashley had said the things attributed to her. The Princess also wrote the Lord Protector a letter, dated from her house at Hatfield, saying she had learned that vile rumours regarding her chastity were in circulation, and that people had even gone so far as to spread abroad that she was confined in the Tower, being with child by the Lord Admiral. The story, she protested, was an outrageous slander, and she demanded that she might be allowed to proceed to Court to disprove these evil reports. On this momentous occasion, Elizabeth, considering her youth, displayed no small amount of sagacity and also of that leonine spirit for163 which she was afterwards celebrated. When confronted, however, with Mrs. Ashley's written evidence, she blushed to the roots of her hair, and, abashed and breathless, returned the letter with trembling hands to her inquisitors. Curiously enough, Elizabeth does not seem to have resented Mrs. Ashley's outspoken condemnation of her conduct with the Lord Admiral. On the contrary, hearing of her arrest, she set to work to save her from the clutches of the law, declaring the lady had been in her service many years, and had exerted herself diligently to bring her up in learning and honesty.

Elizabeth told Sir Robert Tyrwhitt, who was sent by the Council to examine her on the subject of her intimacy with the Lord High-Admiral, "that voices, she knew, went about London that my Lord High-Admiral" should marry her, but added, with a smile, "It is but London news"—evidently London was as much a centre of gossip in those days as now. A little later she asserted that "she did not wish to marry him, for she who had had him [meaning Katherine Parr] was so unfortunate."

It would appear that Lady Browne (Surrey's "fair Geraldine") was also a friend of Seymour's, and that he went to her and asked her to break up her household and come to stay with the Princess Elizabeth, so that she might keep him posted as to what was going on in that Princess's circle. This the lady had agreed to do, but she was prevented by the sudden illness and death of her old husband, the famous Master of the Horse, Sir Anthony Browne. Parry, Elizabeth's comptroller, seems also to have favoured the Lord Admiral, although it was mainly owing to him that the revelations concerning his mistress's conduct with Seymour were made public. On one occasion, when Parry was advising the Admiral to leave off his attempt to court the Princess, he replied that "it mattered little, for, see you, there has been a talk of late that I should marry the Lady Jane," adding, "I tell you this merrily—I tell you this merrily."

As for the said Admiral, all the world now turned against him, excepting the late Queen's brother, the Marquis of Northampton, his other brother-in-law, Lord Herbert, and his deceased wife's two cousins, the Throckmortons, one of whom164 wrote the following homely lines on the wretched man's piteous plight:—

"Thus guiltless he through malice went to pot, Not answering for himself, not knowing cause."

No better proof can possibly be quoted in his favour, so far as the accusation of his having murdered Katherine Parr is concerned, than the fact that his wife's closest connections remained his only friends in his trouble.

Still Thomas Seymour stood out boldly for his innocence. He did not deny his flirtation with Elizabeth; it was a mere romp between a man and a child, with no harm in it beyond such as his enemies chose to impute. But the poor man's foes proved too much for him, and on 23rd February he was brought face to face with his accusers, and condemned by the Council without hearing or defence. The King, his nephew, seems to have made some effort to save him, but the Council forced the boy to sign the fatal warrant, which he delivered with a trembling hand, the tears standing in his eyes, and this despite the fact that the reference to Seymour's death in the King's *Journal* contains not a word of regret. Seymour had done him, personally, no great ill, and appears to have shown him kindness on more than one occasion. Cranmer, who ever ran with the hare and hunted with the hounds, hastened to affix his signature to the document ordering the Admiral's execution, and this, as Hume observes, "in contravention of the Canon Law, and in sheer spite." The Bishop of Ely informed Seymour that his earthly life was shortly to be ended, and a Catholic priest was sent to confess him; but he is said to have refused these ministrations, as well as those of a Protestant clergyman. He contrived, according to Latimer, to write letters to the Princesses Mary and Elizabeth denying the accusations against him, which letters he hid between the leather of one of his servants' shoe-soles. Suspected of serving his master too well, the poor faithful creature was arrested, the letters discovered, and the unfortunate man hanged without trial.

Without entering into any controversy as to the magnitude of Thomas Seymour's guilt, it may be admitted, in fairness to his brother of Somerset, that, if the misdemeanours of a personal165 character attributed to Sudeley rest on the gossiping evidence of women, the graver charges of collecting stores of arms, raising an army to strike a blow against his brother, and unscrupulously attempting to obtain funds even through pirates and notorious swindlers, do in a measure justify the severity of his punishment and excuse the infliction of an apparently unnatural and fratricidal sentence of death. Somerset, with all his faults, had a high sense of justice and of the responsibility of his exalted office. His brother had offended not only as an ordinary subject of the realm, but as a trusted servant of the nation, and his treason and unscrupulous abuse of his position were beyond all pardon. The voice of nature was stifled in the heart of the statesman, and thus the Duke, with a tolerably clear conscience, signed a death-warrant which must at the time have cost him a pang of horror and which has since branded him as a merciless fratricide.148

The Lord of Sudeley's rage against the Council, his brother, and his enemies in general, when he heard himself condemned, knew no bounds and admitted of no Christian forgiveness or resignation. He cursed them one and all with every terrible oath his tongue could utter. He was beheaded on Tower Hill on 20th March 1549, six months and some days after the death of Queen Katherine Parr. His demeanour on the scaffold caused great scandal: he refused to listen to the pastor deputed to minister to him, and the attendants had much difficulty in forcing him to kneel to receive the fatal stroke. He wrestled hard with the executioner, who, being a strong man, hurled him down on the scaffold and struck off his head at last, after a cruel hacking, due to his desperate struggles.

For nearly a week after the death of the Admiral, Lady[166] Jane remained alone with her attendants in the desolate house in the Strand. Then her father, Lord Dorset, came to London to take her back with him to Bradgate.

On the Sunday after the execution, Hugh Latimer preached a sermon at Paul's Cross which for bitterness and uncharitableness has never been surpassed. "This I say," he remarked, "if they ask me what I think of the Lord Admiral's death, that he died very dangerously, irksomely, and horribly." "He shall be to me," he furiously exclaimed, "Lot's wife as long as I live. He was a covetous man—a horrible covetous man. I would there were no mo' in England. He was an ambitious man. I would there were no mo' in England. He was a seditious man—a contemner of the Common Prayer. I would there were no mo' in England. He is gone. I would he had left none behind him."

The worst charge that posterity can bring against Somerset is not that he signed his brother's death-warrant, but that he seized the dead man's estates and even his wearing apparel, and despoiled his orphaned child, the infant daughter of Katherine Parr.[149]

[167] Princess Elizabeth learnt the death of the courtier she "loved most" with a composure singular for so young a lady, simply remarking that he was over clever—"a man of the greatest wit and the least judgment."

CHAPTER XI
THE EDUCATION OF LADY JANE

The extraordinary revival of letters in Italy, France, and Germany at the close of the fifteenth century did not fail to influence English education, and especially that of high-born women. In this department the exclusively classical culture then in vogue, which barred many subjects now held of far greater importance, would undoubtedly be deemed unpractical and excessive for women nowadays. Modern literature, however, was then in its infancy, and apart from the classics there was little to read but crude if noble poetry, and some historical, theological, and legendary works of a very primitive sort. These soon palled, whereas, to the cultured mind, the classic authors presented, then as now, an ever-varying and delightful fund of information and amusement. Science, in the modern acceptation of the word, was in its infancy, and, in the opinion of the most learned persons of the day, the secrets of theology and Nature, and those of art as well, were embodied in the works of the ancients, and above all in the Holy Scriptures. A knowledge of Greek and Latin was thus supposed to give the key to all science. It was the fashion, too, for princesses and women of noble birth to be, or to pose as being, learned; and notwithstanding the political and religious convulsions of the reign of Henry VIII, a number of English ladies of the highest rank, following the example of their French and Italian sisters, devoted their leisure to studies usually left nowadays to that class of pedantic females whom we somewhat scornfully dub "blue-stockings." This practice was not confined to women who had embraced the Reformed tenets. Many Catholics,—the daughter of Sir Thomas More and her learned friend, Margaret Clement, for instance,—deeply[169] versed in studies of this description, enjoyed the dialogues of Plato, and may have laughed over the scorching epigrams of Martial and the stinging satires of Juvenal in the original, and even recognised their applicability to the society of their own times. Most of the women who surrounded Lady Jane Grey were pedants, and even her shallow-hearted mother had presumably acquired a fair knowledge of classical literature.

But it was not till the young girl returned to Bradgate, after the death of Thomas Seymour, that the system of "cramming," which was to give her, at the age of seventeen, a reputation as a marvel of erudition, began in grim earnest.

Dorset, who had been summoned to London to attend the trial of his quondam friend, the Admiral, as a witness against him, retired to Bradgate in some despondency after its fatal termination. He and his wife felt they had been wasting their time over Thomas Seymour; they were conscious, too, that they were living under a cloud, for the revelation of their pecuniary interest in the transfer of their daughter to so notorious a scamp had produced a most damaging impression on the public mind. But the failure of their plans had not quenched their ambition. They took their luckless child back with them, and straightway set about preparing her to occupy the towering position they felt assured she would sooner or later be called to fill.

Her education was forthwith entrusted to the celebrated Aylmer, a native of Leicestershire, whom Elizabeth made Bishop of London, to reward him for his scathing answer to John Knox's pamphlet, *The First Blast of the Trumpet against the Monstrous Regiment* [*i.e.* regimen = régime or government] *of Women*. Aylmer, at this time a good-looking man in his early thirties, was, so Bacon tells us, engaged as tutor to the daughters of the Marquis of Dorset at Bradgate. The new preceptor was in close correspondence with the Genevan Reformers, and it must have been through him that Jane became acquainted with the celebrated Bullinger and with John ab Ulmis, better known as Ulmer, a learned but destitute Swiss Calvinist, who visited Bradgate as early as the summer of 1550. He mastered the English language, and having been170 sent to pursue his studies at Oxford at the Marquis of Dorset's expense, he spent his summer vacation at Bradgate, giving lessons in Greek and Latin to Lady Jane and her younger but less talented sister, Lady Katherine, and together with John Aylmer and Dr. Harding the Rector of Bradgate, superintended her classical and theological education. A somewhat crafty young man was Ulmer, skilled in the art of flattery, and much addicted to repaying solid benefits by empty compliments. He it was who urged Bullinger, his master, to dedicate his book, *The Holy Marriage of Christians*, to the Lord Marquis of Dorset, a rather venturesome act, seeing this nobleman was publicly credited with bigamy!150 Bullinger also presented the Marquis and the Lady Jane with a copy of his book, dedicated to Henry II of France, on Christian Perfection, for which the latter wrote to thank him in her father's name on 12th July 1551. Her epistle is written in Latin, and may have been suggested and even edited by Aylmer: it also contains a Biblical quotation in Hebrew. The following extract from it gives a fair idea of how this child of fourteen addressed one of the most learned men of his time:—

171

"From that little volume of pure and unsophisticated religion, which you lately sent to my father and myself, I gather daily, as out of a most beautiful garden, the sweetest flowers. My father also, as far as his weighty engagements permit, is diligently occupied in the perusal of it: but whatever advantage either of us may derive from thence, we are bound to render thanks to you for it, and to God on your account; for we cannot think it right to receive with ungrateful minds such and so many truly divine benefits, conferred by Almighty God through the instrumentality of yourself and those like you, not a few of whom Germany is now in this respect so happy as to possess. If it be customary with mankind, as indeed it ought to be, to return favour for favour, and to show ourselves mindful of benefits bestowed; how much rather should we endeavour to embrace with joyfulness the benefits conferred by divine goodness, and at least to acknowledge them with gratitude, though we may be unable to make an adequate return!

"I come now to that part of your letter," continues Lady Jane, "which contains a commendation of myself, which as I cannot claim, so also I ought not to allow; but whatever the Divine Goodness may have bestowed on me, I ascribe only to Himself, as the chief and sole author of anything in me that bears any semblance to what is good; and to Whom I entreat you, most accomplished sir, to offer your constant prayers in my behalf, that He may so direct me and all my actions, that I may not be found unworthy of His so great goodness. My most noble father would have written to you, to thank you both for the important labours in which you are engaged, and also for the singular courtesy you have manifested by inscribing with his name and publishing under his auspices your Fifth Decade, had he not been summoned by most weighty business in His Majesty's service to the remotest parts of Britain; but as soon as public affairs afford him leisure he is determined, he says, to write to you with all diligence."

Here follows an urgent request for a scheme for the study of the Hebrew language. She concludes:—

"Farewell, brightest ornament and support of the whole Church of Christ; and may Almighty God long preserve you to us and to His Church!—Your most devoted

"Jana Graia"[151]

Besides these visitors, the Lady Frances appears to have been the friend and patroness of a learned Protestant, Nicholas Udall, the famous stenographer. She was even guardian to his daughter, for a letter from her to Cecil still preserved at Hatfield begs she may be relieved of this responsibility, as the young lady is about to be married.

Late in the autumn of 1549, within six months of Seymour's execution, the celebrated Roger Ascham came on a visit to Bradgate. He too has been described as tutor to Lady Jane, but this is a mistake; he was preceptor to the Princess Elizabeth. As one of the leading lights of his time, he was already well known to the Marquis of Dorset, and passing through the neighbourhood on his way to attend Rutland and Morysone on an embassy to Charles V, conceived it his duty to pay his respects to the great man's family.

Walking through the beautiful park at Bradgate, on his way to the Hall, the visitor came upon the Marquis and his lady, with all their household, out hunting. When the cavalcade halted to greet him, Ascham inquired for the Lady Jane, and was told she was at home in her own chamber. He begged leave to wait upon her, a favour readily granted, and found her in her closet "reading the *Phædon* of Plato in Greek, with as much delight as gentlemen read the merry tales of Boccacio." Much surprised, he asked the young student "why she relinquished such pastime as was then going on in the park for the sake of study?"

With a smile, Jane replied, "I think all their sport in the park is but a shadow to that pleasure I find in Plato. Alas! good folk, they never felt what true pleasure means."

"And how attained you, madam," inquired Ascham, "to this true knowledge of pleasure? And what did chiefly allure you to it, seeing that few women and not many men have arrived at it?"

ROGER ASCHAM'S VISIT TO LADY JANE GREY AT BRADGATE

AFTER THE PAINTING BY J. C. HORSLEY, R.A.

"I will tell you," replied Lady Jane, "and tell you a truth which perchance you may marvel at. One of the greatest173 benefits that God ever gave me, is that He sent me, with sharp, severe parents, so gentle a schoolmaster [Aylmer]. When I am in presence of either father or mother, whether I speak, keep silent, sit, stand or go, eat, drink, be merry or sad, be sewing, playing, dancing, or doing anything else, I must do it, as it were in such weight, measure and number, even as perfectly as God made the earth, or else I am so sharply taunted, so cruelly threatened, yea, presented sometimes with pinches, nips and bobs and other things, (which I will not name for the honour I bear them), so without measure misordered, that I think myself in Hell, till the time comes when I must go with Mr. Aylmer, who teacheth me so gently, so pleasantly, and with such pure allurements to learn, that I think all the time of nothing whilst I am with him [that is to say, "the time passes pleasantly when I am with him"]. And when I am called from him, I fall to weeping, because whatever I do else but learning is full of great trouble, fear, and wholesome misliking unto me. And this my book, hath been so much my pleasure, and bringing daily to me more pleasure and more, that in respect of it, all other pleasures in very deed be but trifles and troubles to me."

Poor solitary little girl! We of this matter-of-fact age can but feel more of pity than admiration, as down the long vista of four and a half centuries we picture her sitting alone, poring over the *Phædon*—dull reading, one would imagine, for a child, even to one so harried by the ill-temper of her weak father and her sharp-tongued mother, "whether she stood still or moved about, was merry or sad, sewed or played," that she felt herself "in Hell" until Mr. Aylmer called her to her studies!

Ascham's story throws a very unpleasing sidelight on the conduct of Lady Jane Grey's parents and their harsh treatment of the child, and proves, moreover, the sort of forcing system to which she was being subjected. Ascham tells us that he mentions this interesting interview, which he introduces into his *Schoolmaster*, because it was the last time he ever saw "that sweet and illustrious lady," and also as a protest against the exceeding severity of the teaching of those times. It is curious to note, as her historian, Howard, observes, that whilst her parents were handling her like a froward child, this extraordinary[174] young lady was in active correspondence with such famous men as Ascham, Conrad Pellican, Bullinger, and Sturmius, who all treated her with the respect due to a grown-up woman of uncommon sagacity and experience. The only explanation of this fact is the supposition that these worthies, foreseeing Lady Jane might possibly occupy the throne, and anxious to promote the cause of the Reformation in every possible way, may have placed her on a higher pedestal than her immature talents deserved. They certainly flattered her father, of whom they spoke and wrote as being well-nigh apostolic in zeal and sanctity, and a marvel of light and learning to boot.

At the age of fourteen, then, Lady Jane was fairly conversant with Latin and Greek,[152] and with or without the aid of a dictionary managed to derive some entertainment from Plato. But when we are told that she had mastered Hebrew, and at the age of seventeen was forming the acquaintance of "the tongue of Chaldea" and "the language of Arabia," we are inclined, with Sir Harris Nicolas, to be sceptical. Her Greek and Latin may have been, and very likely were, thoroughly mastered. Several letters in these languages are attributed to her and are possibly of her own unaided composition, but even in these we note that her style and phraseology in many cases closely resembles that of Demosthenes or Cicero, whom she evidently imitated. In one of her letters, written on 12th July 1551, to Henry Bullinger, she says, "I am beginning to learn the Hebrew tongue," and asks him to give her a method whereby she may pursue her course of study in that language to the greatest advantage. Bullinger sent the plan, and in another letter she thanks him and says she will enter upon the study of the Hebrew language in the method which he so clearly directs. As this letter is dated July 1552, and her brief career ended in the following year, her proficiency in the language of the prophets was probably not very considerable.

That poor Jane Grey was "crammed" there can be no question, and the wonder is her weak health did not collapse altogether under the strain. The figurehead of a party she was to be, however, and it was necessary that extravagant[175] reports of her learning should be spread throughout her own country and among the Protestants in foreign lands.

Lady Jane Grey at this period, surrounded by learned men and women so much older than herself, appears strained, even artificial, but later, in her culminating misery, she displays a dignity, a sweetness of nature, and a pious sincerity which render her worthy of her fame. Her few compositions which have come down to us, most of them written during the last days of her life,—her prayer, for instance, the letter to her sisters, and the lines which, according to tradition, she scratched on the walls of her cell,—are full of feeling, and lead us to regret that so fine a nature should not have been spared to adorn mature womanhood as perfectly as its unaffected simplicity graced her short maidenhood. Yet there was a strain of obstinacy and even of coarseness in Jane's character which leads one to think that after all she might, had she remained Queen, have displayed in later life many of the less pleasing peculiarities of her Tudor ancestors.

A very curious letter, written to Lady Jane Grey by Ascham early in 1552, while he was still at the Court of Charles V, throws considerable light on the subject of her studies; it has also led some authorities to imagine the learned man had actually fallen in love with his fair pupil. "In this my long peregrination, most illustrious lady," says he, "I have travelled far, have visited the greatest cities, and have made the most diligent observations in my power on the manners of the nations, their institutions, laws, and regulations. Nevertheless, there is nothing that has raised in me greater admiration than what I found in regard to yourself during the last summer, to see one so young and lovely, even in the absence of her learned preceptor, in the noble hall of her family, in the very moment when her friends and relatives were enjoying the field sports, to find, I repeat—oh, all ye gods!—so divine a maid, diligently perusing the *Phædon* of Plato, in this more happy, it may be believed, than in her royal and noble lineage.

"Go on thus, O best adorned virgin, to the honour of thy country, the delight of thy parents, the comfort of thy relatives, and the admiration of all. Oh, happy Aylmer! to have such a scholar, and to be her tutor. I congratulate both you who176 teach and she who learns. These were the words to myself, as to my reward for teaching the most illustrious Elizabeth. But to you too I can repeat them with more truth, to you I concede this felicity, even though I should have to lament want of success where I had expected to reap the sweetest fruits of my labours.

"But let me constrain the sharpness of my grief which prudence makes it necessary I should conceal even to myself. This much I say, that I have no fault to find with the Lady Elizabeth, whom I have always found the best of ladies, nor indeed with the Lady Mary, but if ever I shall have the happiness to meet my friend Aylmer, then I shall repose in his bosom my sorrows abundantly.

"Two things I repeat to thee, my friend Aylmer [Aylmer was evidently at Bradgate at this period], for I know thou wilt see this letter, that by your persuasion and entreaty the Lady Jane Grey, as early as she can conveniently, may write to me in Greek, which she had already promised to do. I have even written lately to John Sturmius, mentioning this promise. Pray let your letters and hers fly together to us. The distance is great, but John Hales will take care that it shall reach me. If she even were to write to Sturmius himself in Greek, neither you nor she would have cause to repent your labour. [The "neither you nor she" points clearly to collaboration.]

"The other request is, my good Aylmer, that you would exert yourself so that we might conjointly preserve this mode of life among us. How freely, how sweetly, and philosophically then should we live! Why should we, my good Aylmer, less enjoy all these things, which Cicero, at the conclusion of the third book, *De Finibus*, describes as the only rational mode of life? Nothing in any tongue, nothing in any times, in human memory, either past or present, from which something may not be drawn to sweeten life!

"As to the news here, most illustrious lady, I know not what to write. That which is written of stupid things, must itself be stupid, and, as Cicero complains of his times, there is little to amuse or that can be embellished. Besides, at present, all places and persons are occupied with rumours of wars and commotions, which, for the most part, are either mere fabrications or founded on no authority, so that anything respecting177 Continental politics would neither be interesting nor useful to you.

"The general Council of Trent is to sit on the first of May," continues Jane's correspondent, "Cardinal Pole, it is asserted, is to be the president. Besides there are the tumults this year in Africa, their preparation for a war against the Turks, and then the great expectation of the march of the Emperor into

Austria, of which I shall, God willing, be a companion. Why need I write to you of the siege of Magdeburg, and how the Duke of Mecklenburg has been taken, or of that commotion which so universally, at this moment, afflicts the miserable Saxony? To write of all these things, I have neither leisure, nor would it be safe; on my return, which I hope is not far distant, it shall be a great happiness to relate all these things to you in person.

"Thy kindness to me, oh! most noble Jane Grey, was always most grateful to me when present with you, but it is ten times more so during this long absence. To your noble parents, I wish length of happiness, to you a daily victory in letters and in virtue, and to thy sister Katherine, that she may resemble thee, and to Aylmer, I wish every good that he may wish to Ascham.

"Further, dearest lady, if I were not afraid to load thee with the weight of my light salutations, I would ask thee in my name to salute Elizabeth Astley, who, as well as her brother John, I believe to be of my best friends, and whom I believe to be like that brother in all integrity and sweetness of manners. Salute, I pray thee, my cousin, Mary Laten, and my wife Alice, of whom I think oftener than I can here express. Salute, also, that worthy young man Garret and John Haddon.

"Farewell, most noble lady in Christ.

R. A."

"Augustæ"

"18th January, 1551"

When we consider that this letter was addressed to a girl who was not yet fifteen years of age, making due allowance for the high-flown style of the times, we can only conclude that there was some politic motive for a mode of address so injudicious in its flattery, so fulsome and so extravagant even for that age of courtly adulation.

178 Lady Jane Grey spent the better part of the years 1550–1551 and 1552 at Bradgate, improving her mind by hard study, and patiently submitting to the "nips" and petty tyranny of her mother. At one time she seems to have commenced the study of such music as was then in vogue. This, Ascham promptly assured her was a frivolous occupation, unworthy of a godly maiden. In a very curious letter, dated 23rd December 1551, Aylmer writes from London to Bullinger concerning the Lady Jane, begging him to write to her direct and seek to influence her to give up practising music so zealously.

"It now remains for me," writes the worthy Reformer, "to request that, with the kindness we have so long experienced, you will instruct my pupil in your next letter as to what embellishment and adornment of person is becoming in young women professing godliness. In treating upon this subject, you may bring forward the example of our King's sister, the Princess Elizabeth, who goes clad in every respect as becomes a young maiden; and yet no one is induced by the example of so illustrious a lady, and in so much Gospel light, to lay aside, much less look down upon, gold, jewels, and braidings of the hair. They hear preachers declaim against these things, but yet no one amends her life. Moreover, I would wish you to prescribe to her (the Lady Jane) the length of time she may properly devote to the study of music. For in this respect also, people err beyond measure in this country, while their whole labour is undertaken, and exertions made, for the sake of ostentation."

We can see by this letter, presumably written with a view to the great object all these men kept in their hearts,—that of influencing Jane in the event of her becoming Queen,—that they were endeavouring to make a narrow-minded bigot of her, and it is equally certain that the Princess Elizabeth was just then playing the part of the discreet and modest maiden. It is very amusing to find this wily Princess, whose reputation was already the reverse of good, held up as an example to innocent Jane Grey. The unhappy child was not even to practise on her virginals in peace, or dress as she chose, but to follow the example of Elizabeth, forsooth! Could Ulmer and Pellican have seen in a vision the three thousand dresses and179 the sixteen hundred wigs which were to adorn the wardrobe of the lady they were setting up as a model to their simple music-pupil! Even in matters of religion, Elizabeth at this early stage of her career showed a remarkable discretion, neither siding with nor offending either party. She was a pious Catholic in the company of her sister Mary, and an equally edifying Protestant at the Court of her brother, Edward VI.

In June 1551, after a lengthy absence, the Dorsets returned to their town mansion. They came to London for the purpose of examining the vast estate which the Lady Frances had inherited from the two sons of her father, Charles Brandon, Duke of Suffolk, by his fourth wife, Katherine Willoughby. These two brothers died at Bugden Hall, Cams., of the sweating sickness, within four hours of each other, and the bulk of their wealth, excepting the Duchess's dower, fell to the Lady Frances, whose husband, in September of the following year (1552), was raised to the rank of Duke of Suffolk. The Dorsets now lived very sumptuously in London, and with a view, perhaps, of pleasing the King and pushing forward the interests of the Lady Jane, whom they still fondly hoped would become Queen-Consort, they invited a number of English and foreign Reformers, at this time living in exile in London, to their house.

The Marquis, who was an enthusiastic admirer of Conrad Bullinger, had on more than one occasion exhorted him to correspond with his daughter, Lady Jane. In a letter addressed to that eminent Reformer in December 1551, he says: "I acknowledge myself also to be much indebted to you on my daughter's account, for having always exhorted her in your godly letters to a true faith in Christ, the study of the Scriptures, purity of manners, and innocence of life, and I earnestly request you to continue these exhortations as frequently as possible."

A letter of another Reformer—namely Ab Ulmis—gives us some interesting glimpses of the Reformation movement in England. He says: "You will easily perceive the veneration and esteem which the Marquis's daughter entertains towards you, from the very learned letter she has written to you. For my own part, I do not think there ever lived any one more deserving of respect than this young lady, if you180 regard her family; more learned, if you consider her age, or more happy if you consider both. A report had prevailed, and has begun to be talked of by persons of consequence, that this most noble virgin is to be betrothed and given in marriage to the King's Majesty. Oh! if that event should take place, how happy would be the union and how beneficial to the Church.... Haddon, a minister of the Word, and Aylmer, the tutor of the young lady, respect and reverence you with much duty and affection. It will be a mark of courtesy to write to them all as soon as possible. Skinner is at Court with the King. Wallack is preaching with much labour in Scotland," and so on. Ascham, in a letter to Sturmius, describes Jane as excelling in learning Lady Mildred, Cecil's accomplished wife. She is, says he, the most learned woman in England. "I hear you have translated the Orations of Æschines and Demosthenes into Latin. I pray you dedicate the work to this peerless lady."

These and other letters still extant prove, if proof were needed, that Aylmer, Ulmer, and Ascham, assisted by Pellican, Sturmius, and Bullinger, were at this time hard at work, preparing their future Queen and patroness for the position they fondly hoped she would one day occupy. Hales, too, was assisting them,— "Club-footed Hales," as he was called—an English lawyer who had visited Switzerland and adopted the tenets of the Geneva sect; he is described as "fanatical, learned, and ill-tempered." He was a frequent visitor at Suffolk House and Bradgate, and in after times was much involved in the troubles of poor Lady Katherine Grey, Jane's youngest sister. Further quotation from these letters is unnecessary; they are all written in the same style of pedantic flattery, and throw more light on passing events than most people would imagine, although the epistolary literature of this period is verbose, and as a rule uninforming. We can imagine, however, that the meetings at Suffolk House were exceedingly picturesque, and many will marvel that only one painter of note, M. M. P. Comte, has ever given us a picture of the youthful Lady Jane Grey seated among the doctors of the Reformed faith, in the noble Gothic hall of a mansion second to none in the old city for its architectural magnificence.153

181 The monotony of Jane's life of close study was frequently interrupted by long journeys on horseback, or in cumbersome waggons, to pay various country visits. Late in 1551, the Greys established, for some reason or other, a close intimacy with the Princess Mary, and this notwithstanding their religious differences. With increase of wealth and station, Jane's parents became more worldly than ever. Perceiving that Edward VI, who began to show signs of consumption, might not live long, and that the Crown might after all pass to her Catholic Grace, they wisely considered it prudent to be on the right side of a lady who was probably destined to become their sovereign. Accordingly they paid the Princess as many as four visits in a single year.

In the summer of 1551, Jane came very near losing her mother, Duchess Frances, who fell ill of a violent fever. The sick lady, who was at Richmond, sent for her daughter Jane from Bradgate, "to help nurse her." Suffolk describes her illness in the following quaint terms in a letter explaining her absence from Court addressed to the Duke of Northumberland's secretary, Cecil, whom he styles his "cousin Cycell": "This shall be to advertise you, that my sudden departure from Court was for that I have received a letter of the state my wife was in, and I assure you she is mo' like to die than not. I never saw sicker creature in my life. She hath three sicknesses, the first is a hot burning nague [ague] that doth hold her four and twenty hours, the other is the stopping of the spleen, the third is hypochondriac passion. These three being enclosed in one body, it is to be feared that death must needs follow." But it did not "follow"; by the beginning of October, the Lady Frances was better, and in November she was sufficiently convalescent to attend the entry into London of the Scottish Queen Regent, Mary of Guise, and be present at the festivities consequent on that rather unexpected royal visit.

Early in November 1551, Jane appeared at King Edward's Court for the first time, and took a prominent part in these merry-makings. The Scottish Queen-Regent, Mary of Guise, had recently arrived at Portsmouth from France, on her way to the dominions of her unfortunate daughter, Mary, Queen of Scots, and wrote begging the English King's licence to pass182 through his dominions. This was readily granted; and a pressing invitation to visit the Metropolis was sent to the Regent, and willingly accepted. On 2nd November, she proceeded by water to Paul's Wharf, and thence rode in great state through the City. She lodged in the Bishop of London's house, where she was entertained with regal hospitality, and, according to Stowe's *Annals*, was supplied with "beefs, muttons, veales, swans, and other kinds of poultry meates, with fuell, bread, wine, beare, and wax."

The first interview of King Edward VI with the Scottish Queen took place on 4th November, at Westminster Palace. She rode in her chariot from the City to Whitehall, attended by the Lady Margaret Douglas, cousin to the King, and Countess of Lennox, the Duchesses of Richmond and Suffolk, the Lady Jane Grey, and many other noble ladies, including the Duchess of Northumberland.

The Queen and the King dined alone together; but the Duchess of Suffolk, the Duchess of Northumberland, and the Lady Margaret Lennox, together with the Ladies Jane and Katherine Grey, dined, we are told, in the Queen's hall, and were sumptuously entertained. Neither the Princess Elizabeth nor the Princess Mary attended these festivities. They were not in favour at this time and had not been invited.

The banquet must have taken place at the hour we usually devote to luncheon, for at four the Queen, having visited the galleries and state apartments of the Palace, then considered "show places," left Westminster, and, accompanied by her escort of nobles and ladies, rode once more through the City to her lodgings in the Episcopal Palace.

On the following day (5th November), she made a solemn progress through the City, riding from St. Paul's, through Cheapside and Bishopsgate, to Shoreditch, whence she took the high road for her own dominions. She was accompanied by a great train of nobility, among them the Duchess of Suffolk and her daughter, the Lady Jane Grey, and that fateful Duke of Northumberland who was destined to bring ruin on the unfortunate Jane and her father. Northumberland had in his train one hundred horsemen, of whom thirty were gentlemen clad in black velvet, guarded with white, and wearing white hats with black feathers.

183 As soon as this state visit, mentioned with considerable delight by King Edward in his *Journal*, was over, the Lady Frances and her daughters returned to Bradgate.

In the middle of November the Ducal party set out again for Tylsey, the seat of Suffolk's young cousin and ward, the heir of Willoughby of Woollaton. From here they went on a visit to Princess Mary. A very curious MS. account book, still in the possession of the Willoughby d'Eresby family, shows that, on 20th November 1551, "ten gentlemen came from London to escort my Lady Frances's grace to my Lady Mary's grace, and they all left Tylsey after breakfast, the Lady Frances, accompanied by her daughters, the Lady Jane, the Lady Katherine and the Lady Mary, and repaired to my Lady Mary's grace." Whilst on this visit to Princess Mary, who was then at her town house, the former Priory of St. John of Jerusalem, in Clerkenwell, the Dorset family received handsome gifts, as appears from the Princess's expense book: "Given to my cousin Frances beads (*i.e.* 'rosary') of black and white, mounted in gold"; "To my cousin, Jane Grey, a necklace of gold, set with pearls and small rubies." In return, the Lady Jane presented Mary with a pair of gloves.

In the first days of December, the two younger daughters returned to Tylsey, but the Duchess and Lady Jane stayed on in London, for the Lady Jane, we are told, remained with the Princess at her house in Clerkenwell.

On 16th December, the Duke came to Clerkenwell to escort Jane and her mother back to Tylsey. There they seem to have spent a merry Christmas in the company of the Lords Thomas and John Grey. The Duke of Suffolk, in honour of his young wards the Willoughbys, and in their name, threw open the gates of Tylsey to all such of the county gentry as chose to seek hospitality within them. A company of players was ordered from London, together with a wonderful boy, who "sang like a nightingale," besides a tumbler and a juggler. These were presently supplemented by another band of players, belonging to the Earl of Oxford, who acted several pieces. Open house was kept until 20th January 1552, when the whole family proceeded to Walden, to spend some days184 with the Duke's sister, Lady Audley,154 whose husband, Lord Audley, or Audrey, was created Lord Chancellor by Henry VIII and presented with the house and property of the London Charterhouse, as an acknowledgment of his infamous treatment of Anne Boleyn. The record of the doings at Tylsey is in an account book kept by "old Mr. Medeley," husband of the heiress of Willoughby's grandmother and a trustee. This book was lent to Miss Agnes Strickland, who says—in her *Tudor and Stuart Princesses—Lady Jane Grey*—that Medeley "kept a very thrifty notation of all that was spent in 'man's meat' and 'horse's meat' on these journeys; likewise the payments of the players who were to assist in spending the Christmas with the 'godliness and innocence' dwelt upon with such unction" by Suffolk and by the Reformers.155 After the visit to Walden, the Lady Frances and her brood went back to Tylsey for about a week, at the end of January 1552.

These cross-country journeys, even if sometimes broken by two or three days' stay in one place, must have been extremely fatiguing to so young and delicate a girl as Lady Jane. The Duke of Suffolk and the Lady Frances being of the blood royal, travelled with a great escort, as many as a hundred to a hundred and fifty horsemen, scouts, etc., preceding and following their horses and waggons, otherwise called "chariots." If the weather was fine, equestrian travel was exceedingly pleasant: the canter through the leafy lanes, the midday picnic under the greenwood tree, and the evening meal in some picturesque inn, full of Shakespearean character, the bustling, bowing and curtseying host and hostess, the rustic waiters and grooms, the flicker of lamp and candle light, the glowing wood fire, the sanded floor, the shining pewter, and the savoury baked and roasted meats, all combined to make up a scene of primitive185 comfort, entirely absent from the great and sumptuous hostelries of our own time, in which luxury often predominates over more solid qualities of entertainment. But when pouring rain turned the ill-kept roads into quagmires, when the nipping airs of autumn and winter whistled through the skeleton branches of the trees, or the snow lay feet thick on the ground, and the keen wintry winds whistled over the frozen rivers and streams, then must the welcome glow cast by the crackling fires within the inn parlours have made them, however humble, appear so many havens of celestial refuge to the Lady Frances, her husband, her daughters, and her merry men and women. Since there were no other means of locomotion in those days, a specially swift and steady steed, or a particularly well-cushioned waggon, must have been considered with much the same sense of satisfaction as we bestow now on a new type of motor-car or a specially well-appointed railway train. Our immediate forbears were by no means dissatisfied with the old stagecoaches that transported them from one end of the kingdom to another in a week or ten days; sailing in luxurious airships which will have so reduced the bulk of the globe that from being "a vastie sphere" it will have become a mere overgrown orange—"from London to Rome in less than an hour; London to New York in three!"—our descendants will try to imagine how it was ever possible for us to travel by train and motor—so slow and uncomfortable! And thus we and our civilisation may presently come to be looked upon with the same sort of good-natured disdain we now bestow upon the social conditions and travelling arrangements of the days of "My Lord à Suffhoke."

It may well be that all this hard riding in bad weather and the unwonted dissipations of Christmas at Tylsey proved too much for Lady Jane, for in February 1552, Ab Ulmis writes to his friend Bullinger: "The Duke's daughter has recovered from a severe and dangerous illness. She is now engaged in some extraordinary production, which will very soon be brought to light, accompanied with the commendation of yourself. There has lately been discovered a great treasure of valuable books: Basil on Isaiah and the Psalms in Greek, ... Chrysostom on the Gospels, in Greek; the whole of Proclus; the Platonists, etc.... I have myself seen all186 these books this very day. The Duke of Suffolk, his daughter, (the Lady Jane), Haddon, Aylmer, and Skinner, have all written to you."156

These literary treasures were probably found in several parcels of old books purchased about this time by the Marquis from an Italian merchant.

In March 1552, Lady Jane, then at Bradgate, sent Bullinger's wife a present of gloves, and a ring. A month later, Ulmer returned from Switzerland, whither he had been sent on a mission, and brought with him a letter from Conrad Pellican, which Jane immediately answered. In Pellican's *Journal*, still preserved at Zurich, we find the following marginal note: "June 19th, 1552–3, I received a Latin letter, written with admirable elegance and learning, from the most noble virgin, Lady Jane Grey, of the illustrious house of Suffolk." This letter is lost.

Early in July 1552, Lady Jane went with her parents to Oxford,157 and, almost immediately afterwards, repeated her visit to Princess Mary, now at Newhall—a visit fraught with much evil, if we may believe the accounts which have come down to us, from, it must be admitted, rather suspicious sources; that is to say, from Aylmer and Ascham, both eager to represent Jane as even more Protestant than she really was.

Newhall Place, Princess Mary's chief country seat, had formed part, in days gone by, of the possessions of Waltham Abbey, and had been exchanged with Sir John de Shadlowe by the monks in the reign of Edward III for three other properties. Its most illustrious occupant in pre-Reformation times had been the unfortunate Margaret of Anjou. After her capture by the Yorkists it was confiscated by the Crown, and was eventually granted by Henry VII to Bottler or Butler, Earl of Ormond, who fortified the mansion and enlarged it. It187 passed, as a dower, to Sir Thomas Boleyn, grandfather of Queen Anne Boleyn, and he exchanged it with Henry VIII, who took a great fancy to the place, and changed its name to Beaulieu. The monarch stayed here on one occasion, at least, with Anne Boleyn, so that Mary Tudor may have found a few of the personal belongings of her mother's chief foe, when she took possession of the house which Henry bestowed on her towards the end of his reign. She made it her favourite abode, principally on account of its gardens, which are often mentioned in the Household Books of the period, as supplying the royal palaces of London with fruit and vegetables—the cherries and grapes being considered particularly fine. Elizabeth, who did not care for Beaulieu,—its association with her mother and sister must have been painful to her,—presented it to Radcliffe, Earl of Suffolk. He sold it to "Steenie," Duke of Buckingham, who let the place fall into such ruin that its value so decreased that Cromwell was able to buy it for "five shillings and no more!"

In Mary's day it was still a fine old Gothic mansion of the ecclesiastical type, with three lofty towers and a magnificent hall, containing a huge chimneypiece and a broad staircase leading to the upper apartments. In the chapel was that famous window made at Dort in Flanders by order of Henry VII, and now the chief ornament of St. Margaret's, Westminster. The furniture at Newhall, the inventory of which is still extant, was extremely magnificent, and included many sets of costly tapestries, hangings of velvet and Florentine brocades, Turkey carpets and inlaid bedsteads and chairs. The chief artistic treasure of the house, however, was a superb portrait of Mary herself by Holbein, and another of the King her father by the same great painter. These two portraits remained at Newhall until the beginning of the seventeenth century, when we lose trace of them, but the portrait of Mary is not improbably the one now in the possession of the Duke of Norfolk, and that of King Henry, that which is in the possession of Lord Leconfield at Petworth House.

A state visit to Newhall must have been conducted on similar lines to such a function at Sandringham or Windsor in our times, being a singular mixture of extreme simplicity and extreme stateliness. The Princess herself, who, had her188 life been cast in a less exalted sphere, would have been a kindly woman, had a deep hearty voice and a cheery welcome, which endeared her to all who approached her; yet an observation made by Lady Jane Grey to Lady Wharton proves that every time anyone passed before her Grace, they made obeisance by falling on one knee, as if she had been the Host on the altar. Meals were served somewhat after the French fashion: a very light breakfast at what we should consider an unearthly hour—six in summer, seven in winter—a heavy dinner at eleven, and supper at eight. All sorts of sports and pastimes—hawking, tennis, horse-riding, hunting—served to pass the intermediate time, and in the evenings there was card-playing, boisterous games, and dancing. Before retiring for the night, prayers were said, and a loving cup full of spiced wine was passed round, the Princess putting her lips to it before passing it, with a blessing, to her guests. We may take it for granted that during the visit of the Marquis and Marchioness, notorious Protestants, religious controversy did not enter into the conversation at Newhall. To do her justice, Mary at this time at least was very free from bigotry; two of her favourite ladies, Lady Bacon and Lady Brown, were Protestants, and her friendship for the imprisoned Duchess of Somerset and her daughters never failed so long as she lived—and yet the Duchess was an ardent "Gospeller." That the Princess enjoyed a little "flutter" at cards is proved by her household books, and as the Marquis was an excellent card-player, no doubt "Ombre"—a game introduced into England by the Spaniards whilst Katherine of Aragon was Queen—served to pass the evening, together with "Gresco," "Mountsaint," "Newcut," and "Lansquenet." Lady Jane and her little sisters may have joined in the romping game of "Trump," a noisy round game like our "Old Maid," in which, on the appearance of a certain card, everybody slapped their right hand on the table and cried out "Trump!" those who failed to do so paying a trifling fine. "Gleke," a primitive sort of whist, was also greatly in fashion; and at this game, we may be sure, the Lady Frances was prudent enough to lose fairly large sums to her august cousin, whose hot Spanish temper was apt to be ruffled when the tide of fortune turned against her.

189 It was during this visit that the Princess Mary presented the Lady Jane with a rich dress, and Jane, willing to practise some of the precepts which she had received from Zurich, asked the lady by whom her cousin sent the gown, what she was to do with it? "Marry," replied the lady, "wear it, to be sure!" "Nay," replied the Lady Jane, "that were a shame, to follow the Lady Mary, who leaveth God's Word, and leave my Lady Elizabeth, who followeth God's Word." This anecdote was recorded by her tutor, Aylmer, long years after this world had closed on Jane—at a moment, in fact, when Elizabeth did not thank him at all for reminding her subjects of the Puritan style she had affected in her youth. Another incident, which may be more certainly placed during this Newhall visit, shows the cousins at issue on those points of belief then so hotly debated. Lady Wharton, a fervent Catholic, crossing the chapel with Lady Jane Grey when service was not proceeding, made her obeisance to the Host as they passed the altar. Lady Jane asked "if the Princess were present in the chapel?" Lady Wharton answered that she was not.

"Then why do you curtsey?" demanded Jane.

"I curtsey to Him that made me," replied Lady Wharton.

"Nay," retorted the Lady Jane, "but did not the baker make him?"

Lady Wharton repeated this remark to the Princess, "who never after loved the Lady Jane as she did before."

Note.—The London residence of the parents of Lady Jane Grey was, in her early days, the house in Whitehall overlooking the Thames and known as Dorset Place; but, after the death of the two sons of the Duke of Suffolk, the Lady Frances inherited Norwich House, Strand, which Henry VIII had confiscated from the Bishops of Norwich, and exchanged with his brother-in-law for Suffolk Place, Southwark, which he converted into a mint. Norwich House now became generally known as Suffolk House. Here the Greys lived in great state, possibly abandoning their other residence in Whitehall for the larger and more sumptuous residence. The Lady Frances, after the execution of her husband, sold Suffolk House to the Percys and it presently became known as Northumberland House, and, altered from a Tudor to a Jacobean mansion, it remained a prominent feature of London street architecture until early in the second half of the last century, when it was pulled down for the improvements at Charing Cross.

CHAPTER XII
JOHN DUDLEY, EARL OF WARWICK

Immediately after the execution of Thomas Seymour, John Dudley steps forward on the lurid stage of this history. If Seymour was a rascal, Dudley, son of a rascal, was even worse. Divested of his magnificent habiliments and picturesque surroundings, this man was a far meaner and more sordid ruffian than was ever my Lord of Sudeley—more devilish in his cunning and, if anything, more unscrupulous.

John Dudley was the son of that notorious Edmund Dudley who, under Henry VII, had remorselessly plundered the public coffers, and so earned the execution which fell to his lot in the first years of Henry VIII's reign—on 28th August 1510, to be precise. In common justice, it is fair to say that this Dudley of evil repute was highly esteemed by his most illustrious contemporary, Sir Thomas More; and we may believe him to have been much calumniated, like many other men of his time. Dugdale says Edmund Dudley was the son of a carpenter,158 and the assertion is somewhat supported by191 the fact that although he was born twenty years before the death of the Lord Dudley whom he asserted to be his grandfather, that gentleman would never acknowledge him. His real patronym was Sutton, but he assumed that of Dudley after his acquisition of the ancient castle of that name, and the expulsion of its rightful owner, who fled abroad. On the gates of the Castle, Edmund affixed his own arms, together with those of the ancient houses of Someries and Malpas, from which he claimed descent. He was at one time Sergeant-at-Law and at another Speaker of the House of Commons, and married Lady Elizabeth, daughter and heiress of Edward Grey, Viscount Lisle, a collateral of the great house of Grey, and the same young lady to whom Charles Brandon was contracted and who, as we have seen, refused to carry out her side of the engagement.

The John Dudley of these pages was born about 1502, the eldest of three brothers, who, after their father's ignominious death, were placed under the guardianship of Sir Edward Guildford. The latter fought valiantly to obtain some part of the father's ill-gotten property for his wards, and their possessions were further increased at the death of their mother, a considerable heiress. Being a handsome, dashing young fellow, the father's bad reputation was soon forgotten, and his gay son John, as Viscount Lisle, was a prominent figure at Court in the last half of Henry VIII's reign. In his early years192 he was a good deal in France with Charles Brandon, Duke of Suffolk, the Lady Frances's father, who knighted him at Vian, in Normandy. John Dudley's wife, Jane Guildford, whom he married when he was a mere lad, contrived to absorb his affections so completely that his domestic life was remarkably respectable. She was a very beautiful woman, and part heiress of his former guardian, Edward Guildford, Lord Warden of the Cinque Ports. She bore him a numerous and handsome family, and her behaviour in clinging to her husband during his hour of danger, and making desperate efforts to save him, was rare at this strange period. With all her good qualities, however, she was cordially disliked by Lady Jane Grey, whom she treated with consistent harshness.

As Viscount Lisle,159 John Dudley worked his way up legitimately enough until he was nominated Lord High-Admiral and Master of the Horse (1542) to Henry VIII. Although at heart a Catholic, he sided with the Seymours against the Howards, and thus—for ambition's sake—came to be numbered among the chiefs of the Protestant party at Edward VI's coronation, and was then created Earl of Warwick. His ambition was now well fired—he must become *aut Cæsar, aut nullus*, and this he could only achieve by ousting the two Seymours and taking their place. Like most of his contemporaries, he was essentially an opportunist—*un arriviste*, as the French would say. For some years he worked like a rat in the dark, waiting his opportunity: first he nibbled at Thomas Seymour's good fame—what there was of it!—and then cunningly set brother against brother. Patiently, subtly, he gnawed on till he saw Thomas ascend the scaffold; then he promptly undermined Edward Seymour's credit with King and people. His aim was to become Lord Protector himself, to reach at supreme power by fair means or foul.

JOHN DUDLEY, DUKE OF NORTHUMBERLAND

FROM AN ENGRAVING BY G. VERTUE

Soon after the death of his brother, Thomas, Somerset began to totter. The Admiral's execution had produced a bad effect. Hardened as men were in those ferocious times, there were yet certain ties of consanguinity which might not be193 violated with impunity; and so, although Elizabeth did write to her sister Mary, that "had the brothers met, the Lord Admiral would have been saved," it was none the less the hand of Cain that signed his death-warrant. The people said so openly. They had not forgotten the dreadful carnage that had marked Edward Seymour's return, through Scotland into England, on the occasion of his first Scotch expedition.160

If the horrors perpetrated by Somerset himself during that expedition were execrable, those committed with his knowledge and connivance in the same forlorn country under Edward VI were even more atrocious. That "varmint" Lennox, the husband of the Lady Margaret, niece of Henry VIII, was his chief agent. Reeking corpses of men, women, and little children marked the passage of the English troops to and from the Border lands. Thus the Lord Protector's reputation in the North was of the worst—"his very name stank of blood."161

194 Dudley had not, therefore, so much difficulty as might be thought in undermining his formidable rival's position, towering though it was. In many ways, Somerset had proved himself a failure, and he had already lost much of his popularity, even among Protestants, who were none too sure of his loyalty—was he not the friend of Mary and the avowed enemy of Elizabeth? By the large Catholic party he was, of course, entirely and heartily detested.

He was not a Calvinist, although he maintained an active correspondence with Calvin, but a Church of England man of the "Low Church" description, a hater of ecclesiastical ritual and formality, and, incidentally, a born iconoclast. The statement that no man or woman was persecuted or burnt for religious opinions under his rule, is hardly exact. There are more ways than one of killing a dog—or of persecuting an opposing faith. True, the fires of Smithfield were quenched for the time being, but Catholics and Anabaptists were made to feel they were outside the law, and the prisons were crowded with men and women of those persuasions, and of every social grade.162 The cathedrals and parish churches were cleared of their sacred images, their plate, their rood-lofts, and their art treasures; even their frescoed walls were whitewashed. Stained glass was smashed, because it bore "idolatrous pictures," and replaced by plain glass or horn. Even dead men's tombs were overthrown, and the bodies cast "into filthy ditches and fields beyond the city."163 In a word, the artistic treasures of centuries were within a few months dispersed, destroyed, or sold to a throng of Jews, who flocked to England to seize so splendid an opportunity. Somerset pulled down three or four episcopal palaces, the beautiful North Cloister of St. Paul's Cathedral, and the Churches of St. Mary-le-Strand and St. John's, Clerkenwell, for the sake of their building materials, which he used for his own new and almost royal residence in the Strand. He gave orders for the demolition of St. Margaret's, Westminster, and but for the angry protests of the indignant parishioners, his command would have been obeyed. There was another195 cause of discontent, which has been much neglected by historians, namely, the doctrinal changes, which necessarily greatly altered outward observances, much to the disgust of the older generation, who saw the destruction of the cherished traditions of a thousand years, and the desecration of their most sacred social usages. Their pageants, pilgrimages, and processions were now paralysed; and it was an offence deemed worthy of imprisonment, ay, even of burning, to pray for the dead, or to retain the rosary the dying mother had given, with her last blessing, on her death-bed.

The average Englishman is apt to think of the Sixth Edward's reign as an era of peace and plenty, during which, to the applause of the entire nation, the Book of Common Prayer was formulated by Cranmer, and the churches emptied of "hated and idolatrous images and symbols." In reality, it was one of the most disastrous epochs in the whole of our history. Froude, in a passage of uncommon brilliance, sums up the appalling effect, after a lapse of fifteen years, of Henry VIII's dissolution of the monasteries and hospitals. With singular vividness he depicts the extreme misery to which the lower orders were reduced; the high roads and country lanes rendered dangerous by hordes of starving and half-naked men and women, who a few years previously had been in fairly comfortable circumstances, earning a living wage from the now banished masters of abbeys and priories. Now the poor wretches roved in fear and trembling, begging food and shelter; or, driven desperate by want, committing deeds of violence. Dr. Latimer, in his *Royal Sermons*, puts his unfailing finger on the right spot when he remarks that "the misery the people were enduring was entirely due to the new order of things. My father," he continues, "was a yeoman who lived comfortably, educated his children, served the King, and gave to the poor, on a farm the rent of which has been increased fourfold since, so that his successor in the farm has become a pauper in consequence." Then, turning upon the Seymours, the Pagets, and others of their kind, who had enriched themselves out of the ecclesiastical spoils, he thundered: "I fully certify you as extortioners, violent oppressors, engrossers of tenements and lands, through whose covetousness villages decay and fall down; and the196 King's liege people, for lack of sustenance, are famished and decayed.... You landlords, you rent-raisers, I may say, you step-lords, you unnatural lords, you have for your possessions yearly too much! The farm that was some years back from £20 to £40 by the year, is now charged to tenants at from £50 to £100.... Poor men cannot have a living, all kinds of victuals are so dear. I think, verily, that if it thus continue, we shall at length be obliged to pay twenty shillings for a pig. If ye bring it to a pass the yeomen be not able to put their sons to school, ye pluck salvation from the people, and utterly destroy the realm."... "In those days," he says in another sermon, "they [the monks] helped the scholars. They maintained and gave them living. It is a pitiful thing to see schools so neglected; every true Christian ought to lament the same. To consider what has been plucked from abbeys, colleges, chantries, it is a marvel that no more is bestowed upon this holy office of salvation.... Scholars have no exhibition. Very few there be who help poor scholars, or set children to school to learn the Word of God, and make provision for the age to come. It would pity a man's heart to hear what I have of the state of Cambridge.... I think there be at this day [1550] one thousand students less than were within twenty years, and fewer preachers."

The enclosure, too, by their new owners, of the vast tracts of lands, which had formerly belonged to the abbeys and priories, for the purpose of cattle rearing, instead of corn growing—as hitherto—(wool being at a premium) had thrown thousands of agricultural labourers out of employment; and soon the large cities, London, Bristol, and York, were crowded with poor creatures seeking work, only to meet with flat refusal from the citizens, who were angered and alarmed by so considerable an addition to that pauper population whose hapless descendants still form the bulk of the very appropriately styled "Submerged Tenth" of our times. This rapid increase of an undesirable class soon resulted in a marked debasement of the lowest orders, and so bad did the state of morals in the capital become, that Ridley, Bishop of London, preached more than one sermon on the subject, and, in a book entitled *The Lamentation of England*, gives a hideous picture of the rising tide of "immorality,197 crime, drunkenness, hatred and scorn of religion and its ministers amongst the people." Domestic chastity was held at a discount and reviled, and adultery was so common, even in the highest ranks, that the Privy Council spoke of bringing the question of prohibitive measures before Parliament. The Protector himself had set aside his first wife, Catherine Ffoliot, although she had borne him a son, on no valid pretext, legal or otherwise, in order to marry the higher born Anne Stanhope—the temper of this Stanhope lady was so peppery that he went in fear and trembling, and this led his contemporaries to say "he had got rid of a dove to saddle himself with a scorpion." Henry, son of William, Earl of Pembroke, divorced Katherine, daughter of Henry, Duke of Suffolk (Lady Jane's younger sister), to marry Mary, daughter of Sir Henry Sydney. The Earl of Northampton. Katherine Parr's brother, divorced Anne, daughter of the Earl of Essex, when he married Lord Cobham's daughter Elizabeth. Even Lady Jane Grey's own legitimacy was disputed; and the matrimonial adventures of her grandfather Brandon, Duke of Suffolk, have already been mentioned.

The wickedness of the upper classes164 spread downwards, and, coupled with intense poverty, made "London worse than Babylon of old."

Well might honest old Latimer cry out to the King, in one of his most interesting sermons (preached in 1550 at Paul's Cross), "For the love of God take an order for marriage here in England." Cecil also protests against the prevailing looseness of morals: "Sacrilegious avarice ravenously invaded Church livings, colleges, chantries, hospitals, and places dedicated to the poor, as things superfluous. Ambition and emulation among the nobility, presumption and disobedience among198 the common people, grew so extravagant, that England seemed to be in a downright frenzy." Hear Bishop Burnet also on the same subject: "This gross and insatiable scramble after the goods and wealth that had been dedicated to good designs, without applying any part of it to promote the good of the Gospel, and the instruction of the poor, made all people conclude that it was for robbery and not for reformation that their zeal made them so active. The irregular and immoral lives of many of the professors of the Gospel gave their enemies great advantage to say that they ran away from confession, penance, fasting, and prayer, only to be under no restraint, and to indulge themselves in a licentious and dissolute course of life. By these things, that were but too visible in some of the most eminent among them, the people were much alienated from them; and as much as they were formerly against Popery, they grew to have kinder thoughts of it, and to look on all the changes that had been made, as designs to enrich some vicious characters, and to let in an inundation of vice and wickedness upon the nation." To stem this rising tide would have been a task for a great statesman; Somerset was not a great statesman, for, though many of his intentions were good, his methods were primitively violent. He thought himself capable of repressing the inevitable result of the evil wrought by Henry VIII and his followers by force of arms, and by laws which, even in those days, chilled men with horror. To put down the vagabondage in the country districts,—a consequence of the disbanding of the great crowd of abbey retainers,—he signed a decree whereby "Any man or woman found suspiciously near any house, or wandering by the highways, or in the streets of any city, town, or village, for three days together, without offering to work, or running away from their labour, may be brought by the master, or any other person, before two justices of the peace [these] having the power of the statute law to exercise the said power by burning into his or her breast with a hot iron the letter V, and to adjudge him or her to be the slave of the informer, to have and to hold the said slave to him, his executors or assigns, for the space of two years, only giving the said slave bread and water." The "slave" was to be made to work by blows or chains. In the event of his disappearing for the space of fourteen days without[199] leave, he could be punished by chaining up and beating, "and if he [the owner of the slave] chose to prove the fault by two witnesses before the justices, they shall cause such slave to be marked on the forehead, or the ball of the cheek with a hot iron, with the sign of an S, that he may be known for a loiterer, and [the justices] shall adjudge the runaway to be the said master's slave for ever." The penalty of a second escape from slavery was death by hanging "from the nearest tree, if violent." Any one was permitted to take children between five and fourteen years of age from any wanderer, whether they were willing or not, and if the child ran away from his master the latter had the power "to keep and punish the said child in chains, or otherwise, and use him or her as his slave in all points," up to the age of twenty at least. The master of a grown-up slave had the right, under section 4 of this law, "To let, set forth, sell, bequeath, or give the service of such slaves to any person or persons, whatsoever." The law further empowered an owner of slaves "to put a ring of iron about his neck, arm, or leg, for a better knowledge and surety of keeping him." Aiding a slave to escape was punished by the forfeiture of ten pounds by the person so doing. These and other evils too numerous to detail helped to fan the flame of popular discontent.

Presently the counties began to rise, the people of Devonshire and Cornwall flew to arms to vindicate the rights of conscience. They would have back the religion which their forefathers had held for a thousand years. They demanded that the "Six Articles" should be put in force. The men of Cornwall refused the Book of Common Prayer, because, they alleged, they could not speak English, and could not understand it, while they were accustomed to the Latin Mass, which they had been trained from infancy to comprehend. Down into the West went Lord Russell ("Swearing Russell"), dispatched by the Lord Protector. He behaved "more like a wild beast than a human being"—as abominably as Lennox in Scotland. Hooper, who went with him to preach to the rebels, describes his massacres as "the most horrible butcheries of brave men that ever did happen in this world." Russell's dispatches do not in any way minimise the horrors he perpetrated, and "our men," he says, "are daily supplied with[200] large numbers of sheep and fowl from the places where the farmers and squires forfeited such property by their obstinate adherence to the Popish Mass, and other superstitions." Some three thousand men and several hundreds of women are said to have suffered death in the fight for freedom of conscience in Devonshire. The central counties rose too, and there were terrible riots in Gloucestershire, Wiltshire, Derbyshire, and Huntingdonshire.

But it was in Norfolk that the grandest demonstration against the tyranny of the central Government occurred. It commenced at Aldborough, and at first seemed a matter of little consequence; but the rumours of what had happened in Kent, where new enclosures had been broken down, greatly inflamed the people from one end to the other of the eastern counties. There was little of the religious element in the revolt, although two-thirds of the people, at least, still adhered to the old faith, but now religious differences were set aside, and Catholics and Protestants stood shoulder to shoulder in the fight for what we should call liberty. At first the mass of the people were without a leader, but they soon found one in the person of an honest tanner, named Robert Ket.165 It fell out on the 6th July 1549, at Wymondham, near Norwich,201 where many folk were watching, on a small stage erected in the market-place, a sort of "mystery," that the actors touched sarcastically upon the leading events and scandals of the day. Ket, who was present, leapt on to a barrel, and delivered a rough and ready oration on burning topics, every word of which told, and roused the enthusiasm of his audience to a very delirium. In a surging, motley crowd, his hearers followed him from Wymondham to Mousehold Heath, near Norwich, a desolate sweep of country commanding glorious views, immortalised in later times by a Crome or a Vincent. Hereabouts, on an elevation, grew a stalwart oak, beneath which Ket and his men encamped, and where he held Courts of Justice, of Common Pleas, Chancery and King's Bench, "even as in Westminster Hall." With a high and generous sense of freedom, he allowed the orators, not only of his own, but of the opposition party, to harangue the multitude from this tree of liberty, which was now called "the Oak of Reformation." The venerable tree had become a rostrum, and all who had anything to say scrambled into it. Aldrich, Mayor of Norwich, preached thence against the iniquities of Somerset's rule. Clergymen and priests, parsons and ex-monks, made a rough pulpit of it. Matthew Parker, afterwards Archbishop of Canterbury, climbed into its branches one day, and harangued the mob "on the unwisdom of their attempt," and the ruin they were sure to bring on themselves and their families. He would have done better to hold his peace; no one listened to him. So great was the crowd on Mousehold Heath, it looked on occasions like a surging sea of heads, and sometimes, as in Hyde Park in our times, separate groups of lecturers and hearers formed at a distance from the tree.

Suddenly, on July 31st, a glittering figure bearing the Royal Arms of England, rode into the midst of Ket's camp—his white horse sheathed like himself in steel, a plume of white feathers nodding on its head. In a loud voice the man in the "coat-of-arms" proclaimed a free pardon to all present in that multitude, if they "would depart to their homes." Some, weary of the business and only seeking an excuse, turned their backs on the oak, and trudged citywards; but Ket and the larger mass held their ground, saying they wanted no pardon, having committed no offence—they only craved justice, and202 that was the right of every Englishman. They were true subjects of the King, they said, and had done him no harm—all they needed was justice, justice! Turning his back on the tanner and the ancient oak, the glittering herald scattered the people right and left, as he galloped away across heath and common, dissolved into the mist like a meteor. When he had vanished, Ket, fearing a treacherous surprise, called his merry men together, and marched into Norwich, where they once more encountered the royal messenger, who again offered them his master's pardon. Ket replied as disdainfully as ever, and the gorgeous official departed, whilst the rebels, having seized all the arms and ammunition they could find, returned to their camp on Mousehold Heath. To Court sped the herald, and the Protector, alarmed at the turn of events, sent a force of fifteen hundred horsemen, under the Marquis of Northampton, and some Italians led by a *condottiére* named Malatesta, against the malcontents. These troops entered Norwich, but Ket and his men were able to drive both Northampton and the Italian out of the city, in a fight in which "fell Lord Sheffield and several gentlemen; so that now, blood being up on both sides, the town was set fire to and plundered." Hearing this news, the Protector ordered another army of eight thousand men, two thousand of whom were Germans, who were on their way to Scotland under the Earl of Warwick, to turn southward, march on Norwich, and disperse the rebels. After some resistance, Warwick entered the city, only to be so fiercely assailed on every side that it was as much as he could do to hold his ground. Ket galloped off towards Dossingdale; but Warwick's troopers came after him, and 3500 of his men were cut to pieces. Yet another massacre followed, in which many of the royal forces were killed. Ket was captured at last, and hanged without ado, on the walls of Norwich Castle, his brother William (who had been a black monk of the Hospitallers of St. John)166 was swung from the steeple of Wymondham Church, and nine of the ringleaders of the rebellion were203 hanged on the "Tree of Reformation." In the course of this expedition, Warwick saw enough to convince him that every town and village, farmstead and cottage, from the borders of Cambridge to the sea, was a hotbed of rebellion, and that the names of Somerset and Warwick had become loathed bywords.

Such a state of internal strife, combined with foreign defeat, made up an aggregate of confusion which only a statesman of the highest genius could attempt to quell. Somerset, a man of indifferent education, even if of the best intentions, was quite unequal to the task. His natural defects of character—his love of power and money, his contempt for the ancient traditions of the country, his hatred of the religion of his ancestors, his prejudices and his inveterate habit of scheming, now began to occupy the malicious attention of his enemies, who felt the time for striking the decisive blow, which should crush his power for ever, was drawing nigh.

Their plans were served by Warwick's reception in London as a conquering hero, recognised by the metropolis as a successful and able leader. His ambitious views were well seconded by old ex-Chancellor Wriothesley, who had a personal grudge against Somerset, and who now took up his would-be rival as a promising instrument for his revenge. Durham House presently became the rendezvous of a great number of the older nobility, who were discontented with the new régime; and here they plotted and schemed, with one great object in their hearts—the overthrow of Somerset and the exaltation of Warwick. The Londoners, too, were against the Protector. Boulogne had been lost mainly through his blundering policy, and the French war had been notoriously unsuccessful. Moreover, when Warwick demanded extra pay for some two hundred soldiers who had assisted in quelling the Ket rebellion, and other risings, Somerset, unconsciously playing into his enemy's hands, refused the request, and the mercenaries, naturally incensed against the Protector, held themselves ready to aid Warwick without compunction.

Realising in some measure—especially after the defection of Pembroke and Winchester to Warwick's party—that, unless he made some effort, his position would soon become altogether untenable, Somerset metaphorically entrenched204 himself and his family behind the person of the King at Hampton Court, and thence began to defy Warwick and his followers, so that, about September 1549, the Court of England was divided into two distinct camps—Warwick and the Council at Ely Place, Holborn; the Protector and the principal members of his party, Cranmer, Sir John Thynne, his secretary, Sir Thomas Smith, Cecil, Paget, and Petre, at Hampton Court, where King Edward was held in a state bordering on captivity. Then Somerset set to work to limit the power of his sovereign as much as possible, so as to have him on his own side in the struggle with Warwick, which was now beginning in earnest. On the ground that Warwick was bribing the Court lackeys to spy on the King, the royal attendants at Hampton Court were removed and replaced by Somerset's own men. No one could approach His Majesty's person save through the Protector. A stop was put to all those games and sports in which the little King delighted, on the score of his health, and the lad was made to feel himself so completely a prisoner, that he alludes sadly to the matter in his "Diary." Meanwhile the Duke himself assumed almost regal rank, styling himself "By the Grace of God Lord Protector of the Realm, Highness"; using a prayer in which he is described as being "called by Providence to rule"; addressing the French King as "brother," a title hitherto exclusively employed by the anointed monarch; and, as a climax, offending the nobility by taking a seat in the House of Lords above his peers. In October, he issued a proclamation, commanding all the King's loyal subjects "to repair with all haste to His Highness at His Majesty's Manor of Hampton Court, in most defensible array, with harness and weapons, to defend his most royal person, and his entirely beloved uncle the Lord Protector, against whom certain have attempted a most dangerous conspiracy. And this do in all possible haste. Given at Hampton Court the 5th day of October in the 3rd year of his most noble reign."167 Hundreds of copies of this document were distributed all over London; and Lord Edward

Seymour, the Protector's son, was dispatched with letters in the King's name to Lord Russell and Sir William Herbert, who were still in the West, stamping out the rebellion, commanding them to[205] hasten to the aid of the King and himself, with all the troops they could muster. These worthies, who would seem to have had personal grievances against Somerset,[168] promptly threw in their lot with Warwick's party, promising assistance, and sending to Bristol for cannon for that purpose. Somerset now set the printing-presses to work to distribute thousands of handbills, calling on townsfolk and villagers to rise and "protect the King and the Lord Protector," "because he [the Lord Protector] is the friend of the poor and the enemy of their oppressors." The Lord Mayor and Corporation were also commanded to dispatch a thousand men to Hampton Court, and the Lieutenant of the Tower received orders to close the gates of that fortress and refuse admission to members of the Council. On 5th October, Petre was sent to London to interview Warwick and the Council. He found them at Ely Place; but as Petre, thinking all lost, did not return to Hampton Court, the Protector never got any answer to his message. At the same time, the Council sent letters to the chief nobles throughout the country, demanding their aid and dilating on Somerset's misdeeds. Within a few days, the Lord Mayor, the Aldermen, and the Lieutenant of the Tower had all turned traitors to the Protector, and promised Warwick their support.

Hampton Court, put into a state of defence,[169] assumed the aspect of a fortress; the moat was filled up, the gates were fortified, and every battlement and tower was made ready in case of danger. Five hundred suits of armour were brought out of the armoury for the palace servants, much to the delight of King Edward, who watched the preparations. A vast crowd assembled round the palace, and in the neighbourhood; and the Protector, hoping that a sight of the King might rouse it to loyalty, led him into the Base Court, where[206] the soldiers were drawn up to receive him. The stricken youth[170] appeared, leaning heavily on his uncle's arm, with Archbishop Cranmer, Paget, and Cecil behind him; the heralds sounded their trumpets, and as the flare of the torches—for it was an autumn evening—flashed on their armour, the troops greeted his sickly Majesty with three times three cheers. From the Base Court the King and his escort passed over the stone bridge across the moat in front of the great gate, where a motley throng was gathered. Presently silence was obtained, and gradually the mumble of many voices was hushed, as the young King's feeble tones struck on the still evening air, asking humbly, "I pray you be good to us and to our uncle." Then Somerset made a speech, pleading in such stupid and selfish fashion for himself and the King that the rude crowd listened with impatience, and gave no cheers when he had finished. Mortified and disappointed, the Protector and the King turned their backs on the mob, and silently re-entered the palace. The people round Hampton Court were more bitter against Somerset than he imagined. Their grievance was not abstract and national, but local; they could not forget that it was Somerset who, in the first year of King Edward's reign, had dechased Hampton Court Chase.

Seeing himself unable to inspire the people with anything like enthusiasm for their sovereign (or for himself), Somerset determined on more vigorous action, and on 7th October, the King, despite his "rewme," was hurried to Windsor, at nine or ten o'clock at night. Thence the Protector wrote to the Council, asking what had become of Petre, and why no answer had been vouchsafed to his message, adding, "that if any violence was intended to the King's person, he would resist till death." Negotiations by letter continued for some days, and there was even an interview on 12th October at Windsor, between Warwick's group and the Protector. On the following day, a number of charges were promulgated against Somerset, and the once all-powerful "Lord Protector of these Realms" was arrested and confined for the night in Windsor[207] Castle. Next day he was conducted to the Tower, whither most of his adherents and associates in the Hampton Court adventure had preceded him; and he had the mixed pleasure of being received *en route* by his quondam friend the Lord Mayor, who had lately turned traitor to his cause. Meanwhile Edward, very glad, no doubt, to be rid of so austere and troublesome an uncle, returned from Windsor to Hampton Court, and appointed Warwick Lord Great Master and Lord High-Admiral. So far, John Dudley's plot had prospered.

CHAPTER XIII
THE FALL OF THE HOUSE OF SOMERSET

In the earlier stages of his struggle for power, when he felt himself insecure with the Protestant party, Warwick had endeavoured to secure Catholic support by promising the old religion a satisfactory amount of freedom; but no sooner was he safe in his saddle, during Somerset's imprisonment (1549–50), than he became its inveterate enemy. The Protector had made an effort to liberate Gardiner, but Warwick kept him more closely confined than ever. During the new ruler's term of office, the internal disorders of the country continued as acute, in every detail, as under Somerset's régime; all military works fell into decay, no new ships of war were built, fortifications came to a standstill, and many troops were disbanded. The coinage was debased, though the Protector had worked hard to improve it; the tribunals were as corrupt as at any period. To ensure the passing of his vigorous religious measures, and carry on his administration, Warwick "packed" both Parliament and Council with his own staunchest followers. It was almost a piece of good fortune for him when Somerset was released from the Tower, for so great was the general dissatisfaction with his administration that he would probably have been overthrown in his turn.

EDWARD SEYMOUR, DUKE OF SOMERSET

FROM AN ENGRAVING AFTER THE PAINTING BY HOLBEIN

During the winter of 1549–50, Somerset, confined in the gloomy old fortress, was striving to retrieve his tottering fortunes. His first move was to sign (in December) a confession of "his guilt, presumption, and incapacity." Early in January 1550, a bill, brought before Parliament and passed in both Houses, promised him his life, on condition that he forfeited his estates to the King, gave up his positions, and paid a fine of £2000 a year in land. He attempted to appeal against the extent of the forfeiture, but the Council grew so menacing209 that the fallen Protector, with visions, it may be, of Tower Hill and the block before his eyes, thought it best to pocket his grievance. So on 2nd February he wrote to the Council expressing his gratitude to the King for sparing his life and treating him so leniently. According to a letter from Ab Ulmis to Bullinger, dated from Oxford, 4th December 1551, Warwick generously made an effort to save the Duke by imploring him in court to throw himself upon the mercy of the King, which he did. On the 4th of that same month he was released, after giving a bond of £10,000 as a guarantee of good behaviour, and on the peculiar conditions that he should not go more than four miles away from the Council, nor yet come to the meetings unless summoned; further, if the King went near the palace at Sheen or Somerset's own house at Sion (in one or other of which two places he was to abide), the former Protector was to depart instantly. The Duke's full pardon was given on 16th February. At the same time, all those who had been imprisoned with him were released, after being mulcted in heavy fines.

Immediately after his liberation Somerset joined the Court at Greenwich, and was shortly afterwards made a Privy Councillor! Indeed, before many months were over he had regained his former position and influence over the King so completely that Warwick considered it safer to become, at least publicly, reconciled to him. For this purpose he arranged a marriage between John, Viscount Lisle,171 his own eldest son, and the Lady Ann Seymour, Somerset's eldest daughter. This marriage took place on 3rd June (1550) at the royal palace at Sheen, and in the King's presence. On the following day occurred yet another aristocratic wedding, also attended by His Majesty, that of Warwick's third son, Sir Robert Dudley, afterwards famous as the Earl of Leicester of Elizabeth's reign, with that renowned heroine of romance, Amy Robsart. Sir Walter Scott, in his *Kenilworth*, falls into the error—unless, indeed, he wilfully disregarded facts for the sake of artistic effect—of placing the scene of this marriage in Devonshire, and of describing it as clandestine. On the contrary, it was210 quite an open affair, mentioned by King Edward in his *Diary* in the already quoted entry for 4th June 1550, relating to the cruel sport of duck-pulling. The King seems to have attended this wedding, but he was too ill to be present at the far more important marriages of his two cousins three years later. About this time, the summer of 1550, the ex-Protector's forfeited lands were restored to him, and he was allowed to reconstitute his household as in the past.

In February 1550 a proposal was brought before Parliament for the restoration of Somerset to the office and title of Lord Protector, and was only quashed by the prorogation of that body. He seemed in a fair way of regaining his old position of power, and the Dorsets, thinking no doubt that it would be well to be on friendly terms with him, began to bethink themselves once more of the old project of marriage between their eldest daughter, Lady Jane Grey, and young Hertford, who had once been on such intimate terms in their family circle that, as we have seen, the Lady Frances had on more than one occasion called him her "son." She now wrote to Cecil172 referring to some service Somerset had rendered her—this may have been her reason for reviving the matrimonial project—and stated incidentally that she much desired a match between his (Somerset's) son and her daughter, but "that she wished to let the parties have their free choice." Somerset does not, however, appear to have approved of the plan, for there is no evidence that he did anything now to further it, and when it was originally proposed he had allowed the matter to fall into abeyance. It is not at all improbable that the lady's letter, if communicated to him, put him on his guard against traps such as the wily Dorsets might set for him and his son. The incident is not devoid of interest, as demonstrating how the Dorsets never ceased their intrigues and matrimonial schemes, and also how even Warwick's best friends were none too sure of his eventual success, now his rival was again at large. The Dorsets were evidently anxious to have a foot in each camp; but this time they failed, and ended by falling back on Northumberland's youngest son as a husband for the much-enduring Jane.

211 Meanwhile, Warwick was contemplating, by no means complacently, the honours and favour heaped upon the rival for whose ruin he was only awaiting some favourable opportunity. His first chance of proving his unvarying hatred of the Protector came on 15th October of the year 1550, on the occasion of the death of the aged Lady Seymour. This event placed her son, as we have already seen, in a quandary—a State funeral, such as was due to the King's grandmother, would have enabled Warwick to accuse him of a fresh assumption of regal dignity; a private funeral, on the other hand, might be maliciously construed into disrespect shown to the sovereign. Wherefore Somerset consulted the Council as to what should be done. The reply, as already mentioned, was that a State funeral was not at all necessary, nor even any formal Court mourning, since such observances served "rather to pomp than to any edifying," an opinion peculiar to the Council, for in the preceding August a State funeral (that of Lord Southampton) had been organised with all possible "pomp." This denial of the honour due to Lady Seymour's remains did not, of course, proceed from any idea of economy or Puritanism, but merely from the Council's desire to insult Somerset and his family. It was an opportunity neglected, for if Seymour had insisted upon a State funeral, the events of the following year might have been anticipated, and the accusation of usurping regal honours brought against him at once. Another curious fact in connection with this funeral is that Somerset—a shining light amongst Reformers—wrote to ask Gardiner to "offer up Mass for the health of his mother's soul after her death" (!)173

Another method adopted by Warwick was that already employed by Sudeley in his struggle with his elder brother, of spreading calumnies against his rival through the agency of a third person, and ensuring their reaching the King's ears. After a time these tales began to make their impression on his juvenile Majesty, though Somerset, for his part, was working hard to recover the King's favour entirely, and consolidate his own position. Rich, the Lord Chancellor,212 an infamous traitor, gave him his aid and acted as his spy, keeping him informed of every movement made by Warwick and his party. One of Rich's letters on this subject, addressed merely "To the Duke," was handed by mistake to the Duke of Norfolk, next to Warwick, Somerset's bitterest enemy; thus each opponent had some idea of his adversary's plans. Still, so subtle was Warwick's work that there was no movement against Somerset visible enough to justify him in taking open measures; there was nothing for it but to bide his time, and do his best, meanwhile, to ingratiate himself with the King. In public, the rivals appeared the best of friends, and, to maintain this pleasant fiction, Somerset, on 11th October 1551, attended what must have been a painful ceremony to him—the investiture of Warwick with the title of Duke of Northumberland in the Great Hall of Hampton Court.174 The mortification caused by this evidence of his rival's growing power, a power he could not openly attack, must have been bitter indeed.

Side by side with Northumberland's intrigues, the national discontent, of which we have already given instances, and which had been intensified by Northumberland's brief term of office, was a potent factor in the eventual ruin of the Protector: for we may be sure Somerset's enemies took good care to father Northumberland's misrule on his rival. It would be useless for our purpose, though easy indeed, to cite further and numerous instances of the universal disorder into which the realm had fallen. Suffice to say that the England of this period strongly resembled France under the Directory. Everything was upside down. The faith of the people had received a staggering blow, from which it would take nearly a hundred years to recover, and then only in a measure, for to this day the masses of the lowest class of the people of England remain in terrible darkness, alike indifferent to influences religious and moral. In the213 reign of Henry VII, and in the first years of Henry VIII, no hale man or woman dreamt of missing Mass on a Sunday: under Edward VI, Latimer complained that the churches were deserted, and Gardiner describes the lower classes as gradually falling into a state of paganism. This relaxation of religious observance influenced the popular morals, and in every class the domestic habits of the country were most disreputable. So bad was the condition of things, in fact, that Northumberland and his party came to realise that Somerset's worst enemy was himself; in other words, that the general discontent and misery arising from his maladministration—or, to be just, in some cases from causes over which he had no control—furnished a more powerful argument against him than the spiteful inventions of his opponents. They must have felt confident that any blow they struck at him would meet with little or no opposition, but rather with encouragement from the people, who had turned the cold shoulder on his appeal at Hampton Court some two years previously.

Accordingly, on 16th October 1551, the Duke of Somerset was suddenly re-arrested in the Council Chamber175 at Hampton Court, and taken to the Tower to await his trial on charges made against him to Northumberland by Sir Thomas Palmer, "a brilliant but unprincipled soldier." Palmer asserted that Somerset and his friends had plotted to raise the North of England against Northumberland; that he had intended to secure the Tower, to incite the populace of London to revolt, to seize the Great Seal, with the aid of the City apprentices, and, finally, to murder the Duke and his principal supporters at a supper in Lord Paget's house. There would seem to have been but little truth in these charges; Northumberland at a later date, at any rate, confessed that they were fabrications, and Palmer, before his death, described them as the products of Northumberland's fertile imagination. This second trial of the Lord Protector took place on 1st December in Westminster Hall. The judges were seven and twenty peers, amongst214 them all the prisoner's enemies—Northumberland, Northampton, and Pembroke, with the Marquis of Winchester as President. The business was conducted with the unfairness which distinguished nearly all the political trials of this period; no witnesses for the prosecution were produced in person, but their depositions were read. The indictments accused Somerset of plotting to lay hands on Northumberland and others, to seize the Great Seal and the Tower, and to deprive the sovereign of his kingly power; he was also charged with having incited the citizens of London to rebel against the King. The official indictment made no mention of his supposed intention of assassinating Northumberland; neither was Paget, in whose house it was alleged the murder was to have taken place, ever tried for his share in the plot. This melodramatic accusation would, in fact, seem to have been entirely dropped at the last moment. Somerset, who denied the charges, was acquitted of treason on the first count, but found guilty on that of felony for inciting the citizens to revolt. There is ample evidence that he never did anything of the kind. Winchester, a few months back his enthusiastic ally, pronounced the death sentence on the unhappy man. Its effect upon him was sudden and staggering. He became pale, and fell upon his knees before Northumberland, Northampton, and Pembroke, who turned their backs whilst he besought the people to pray for him and his family. And so he was ordered back to the Tower to prepare for death. The count of treason not having been proved, the axe did not face the prisoner on the way back to his cell, and "the people, supposing he had been clerely quitt, when they see the axe of the Tower put downe, made such a shryke [shriek] and castinge up of caps, that it was heard into the Long Acre beyonde Charing crosse."176 This must have cheered him greatly. He may have thought and hoped that the people loved him still.

King Edward is said to have expressed considerable anxiety on his uncle's account, but his distress did not prevent him from indulging, according to his own statement, notwithstanding his delicate health, in exceptionally riotous Christmas215 festivities.177 The popular joy over his acquittal on the charge of treason proved fatal to Somerset, for it convinced Northumberland more than ever of the necessity of destroying his rival. Holinshed sarcastically informs us that "Christmas being thus passed and spent with much mirth and pastime, it was thought now good to proceed to the execution of the judgment against the Duke of Somerset." Notwithstanding the frequency of such events, the execution of so great a nobleman produced a considerable impression throughout London. Though every precaution was taken to prevent the assembling of an unusual crowd, Tower Hill was black with people long before dawn on 22nd January 1552, the day of doom. The vast assembly had gathered in the expectation of the Duke's reprieve rather than of his death. There was an extraordinary muster of halberdiers, men-at-arms, sheriffs and their officers. At eight o'clock Somerset was brought forth. He faced the axe manfully, knelt down and said his prayers, and then, rising to his feet, made a speech. Unlike most of his peers, he did not deny with his last breath the religion he had helped to promulgate; there was nothing he regretted less, said he, when on the brink of his bloody fate, than his endeavours "to reduce religion to its present state, and he exhorted the people to continue steadfast in the Reformation principles, and thereby escape the wrath of God." Just as he was about, according to custom, to take formal leave of the crowd, great confusion was caused by the arrival of a body of soldiers with bills and halberds, who had received orders to attend the execution. Arriving late, these men dashed towards the scaffold, and their onrush, combined with some noise as of thunder,—"a great sound which appeared unto many above in the element as it had been the sound of gunpowder set on fire in a close house bursting out,"—terrified the mob, and an awful panic ensued: spectators standing on the edge of the Tower moat lost their balance and fell into the water, and not a few were216 trampled underfoot and others broke their necks. Presently, in the midst of the hubbub, during which Somerset was left so unguarded that, it is said, he might easily have escaped, Sir Anthony Browne was seen riding towards the spot. The mob, somewhat recovered from its consternation, imagined he was bringing a reprieve, and shouted, "A pardon, a pardon!" casting their caps and cloaks into the air. But Sir Anthony brought no message of mercy with him. The doomed Duke had been standing quietly on the edge of the scaffold, watching the turmoil. He too, when he heard the shouts of "Pardon!" imagined his nephew had remembered him; but he soon realised his error. The hectic colour which for a moment had flushed his cheeks with the gleam of hope faded as, in a ringing voice, he concluded his interrupted speech; and that done, he bestowed his rings on the headsman, said a few words to the Dean of Christchurch, bared his neck, knelt on the straw, and laid his head on the block. Another instant and the axe had fallen. Edward Seymour, Duke of Somerset and first Lord Protector of England, was buried in the Church of St. Peter-ad-Vincula within the Tower on the north side of the choir, between the coffins of the Queens Anne Boleyn and Katherine Howard; the funeral rites were those of the Church of England, as then constituted, "but hurried and simple as for a pauper."178

The character of Edward Seymour has been the subject of much discussion; but it would seem fair to seek a *via media* between the over-severe condemnation of some historians and the exaggerated praise of others. If we cannot exalt him to the high pedestal upon which he has been set by Mr. Pollard, we need not fall into the error of degrading him to the low level assigned him by eighteenth-century historians. Somerset must not be judged by modern standards. If the balance of good and evil in his character is considered, and we contemplate him by the light of the middle sixteenth century, we may217 even come to share the opinion of a large section of the London populace of his day—mostly those of the Protestant party, be it said—who looked on him as an admirable and God-fearing man,179 who did his best to free the people from much of the superstition, oppression, and injustice from which it suffered. His faults, his ambition and lust of power, were very human; and the evils of his administration were largely due to the condition to which Henry VIII's misrule had reduced the country. The age in which he lived was very unpropitious to statesmen and leaders of men, for, no matter how intelligent they might be, some rival lurking in the shade was sure to be ready to trip them up and take their place at the first opportunity. On the whole, Somerset seems to have worked for what he believed to be the interests of his King and the good of the Protestant religion, to which he was consistently faithful. His domestic life was clean, and in an age of place-hunters and libertines Edward Seymour was one of the most respectable men. Neither entirely mediocre nor altogether great, the Duke of Somerset may be described as *un grand homme manqué*—one who just missed greatness.

* * * * *

Note.—A long letter from a Reformer named Francis Burgoyne, written from London to John Calvin on 22nd January 1552, gives a most detailed account of the Duke of Somerset's execution, and an analysis of his character which is of great interest. He says: "Hence arise our tears, hence arises the all but universal distress, that on this very day, about 9 o'clock, the Duke of Somerset of pious memory, when218 hardly any person looked for or suspected such an event, was led out publicly to execution. I myself was not present at the sight ... but many of my friends related to me what they had seen and heard." Then follows a long account, given to Burgoyne by Utenhovius, of Somerset's last speech, continuing that "he spake all this ... with a look and gesture becoming the firmness of a hero, and the modesty of a Christian; (they say) that he was splendidly attired, as he used to be when about to attend upon the King, or to appear in public on some special occasion; that he gave the executioner some gold rings which he drew from his fingers, together with all his clothes; only to a certain gentleman, the Lieutenant of the Tower of London ... he gave his sword and upper garment. What weeping, and wailing, and lamentation, followed upon the death of this nobleman, it is as difficult to describe as to believe. It is stated by some persons who belong to the household of some of the Councillors ... that by the Royal indulgence the capital punishment had been remitted, with a free pardon, while the Duke was yet in prison, and that whole Council sent to inform him of it more than once; but when he rejected with contempt the grace that was offered to him, (I know not whether in reliance on his own innocence, or on the favour of the King and some other parties, or on his own influence, and wealth, and rank, or on some other delusive persuasion), the whole Council were at length so irritated by this conduct, that they determined that they would no longer endure that excessive arrogance of the man.... It is quite evident, in my opinion, that the deceased nobleman, like other men, was not without his faults, and those perhaps more grievous than could be passed over by God without punishment in this life.... This man was endowed and enriched with most excellent gifts of God both in body and mind, but is not that the best gift, that God has chosen the light of the Gospel to shine forth by his instrumentality throughout this Kingdom.... I do not now mention how God had so exalted him, from being born in a private station, that as the late King's brother-in-law, the brother of a Queen, the uncle of the present King, he had no one here superior to him in any degree of honour, and then especially, when appointed Lord Protector of the Realm, he was all but King, or rather esteemed by everyone[219] as the King of the King." Burgoyne then passes to the subject of Somerset's religion: "During almost the whole time when we were both of us here, he had become so lukewarm in the service of Christ as scarcely to have anything less at heart than the state of Religion in this country. Nor indeed did he retain in this respect anything worthy of commendation, excepting that, as far as words go, he always professed himself a Gospeller when occasion required such acknowledgement." "It is notorious to every one in this Kingdom," he continues, "that he was the occasion of his brother's death, who, having been convicted on a charge of treason which no one could prove against him by legal evidence, and of which when brought to execution he perseveringly denied the truth, was beheaded owing to his information, instigated by I know not what hatred and rivalry against his brother.... In fine, that very act, for which he was last of all thrown into prison, was both unworthy of a Christian such as he professed himself to be, and also sufficiently shews that the most part of the crimes which I have laid to his charge, have their foundation in truth. For he was himself the head and author of a certain conspiracy against the Duke of Northumberland, lately called the Earl of Warwick, whom he pursued with the most unrelenting hatred, as having been foremost in depriving him of the rank of Protector, and being himself regarded from that time by the King's Councillors as occupying that office; the Duke of Somerset, I say, gained over some accomplices in this conspiracy even from among the Council itself (who are now in prison awaiting the King's pleasure respecting them), by which it was agreed among them, that on the Duke of Northumberland being dispatched (together with any of his friends who should oppose their views) either by violence, or in secret, or in any other way, they should place the entire administration of the Kingdom in their own hands, but that the Duke of Somerset should be invested with the chief authority, or even be restored to the order of Protector." The writer, after saying that "at his death he manifested some favourable marks of Christian penitence," concludes: "Two reasons are present to my mind which increase my regret; one of them is, that we have lost so great a man, and one who was not so entirely corrupted but that there[220] remained some hope both of his reformation, and also that the interest of the Gospel would in any case be advanced by his authority and protection, since there is certainly the greatest scarcity and want of such characters in this country."[180]

CHAPTER XIV
THE LADY JANE MARRIES THE LORD GUILDFORD

The execution of the Duke of Somerset left the stage clear for Northumberland, who was now all-powerful.181 More cunning than his predecessor, he avoided offending the nation by assuming the title of "Protector," and rousing his colleagues' jealousy by styling himself "Highness." Little cared he whether he sat on the King's right hand or on his left, so long as his young sovereign obeyed him implicitly—on this point he was resolved. His ambition was sordid enough: he had no care for the people, but a great deal for his own advancement to wealth and power; and his wife and children were as greedy and ambitious as himself. He had flattered the Catholics, and if Princess Mary had been younger, and willing to marry one of his sons, the religious history of England might have been different. Somerset had always entertained a friendly feeling for Mary, who was kind to his wife, while he hated Elizabeth; Northumberland loathed both Henry VIII's daughters equally. Almost his first act on entering222 office, nominally as Great Master of the Household or Lord High Steward, but virtually as Lord Protector of the Realm, was to annoy Mary by opening up the question of her chaplains, and her right to have Mass said in her private chapel—a blunder which nearly resulted in a war with the Emperor, her cousin, to whom the Princess appealed. Then he lent Cranmer a hand in persecuting the Anabaptists. The fires of Smithfield flared up once more. Joan Bocher, and Peter of Paris a Dutchman, were put to death, though Cranmer found it hard to get Edward VI to set his hand to the warrant for Joan's execution. With great alacrity, then, Northumberland pushed on Somerset's iconoclastic vandalism, till he made our glorious cathedrals and churches as bare as meeting-houses. Shiploads of holy images, chalices, pictures, and painted windows were carted out of the churches, defaced, destroyed, or sold, and carried abroad, even as far as Constantinople, where a cargo of "imaugys" from England fetched a high figure among the Catholics of Pera and Galata. So wanton was the destruction of Church linen at this time that the citizens, disgusted at seeing it burnt at the street corners, petitioned Northumberland to hand it over to the hospitals.

The Catholics, perceiving they had gained nothing in return for the help they had given Northumberland, retired into obscurity, to wait for better days; whilst the Reformers acclaimed the zeal of a man who fought so fiercely against the faith in which he eventually elected to die. It presently occurred to the Lord High Steward that the young King was failing fast. The servants about the Court saw death in the boy's pale face and shrunken form, and heard its stealthy advance in his feeble voice and hacking cough. To curry favour for himself, Northumberland allowed the dying monarch greater freedom than he had hitherto enjoyed. Sports and pastimes were arranged for his amusement, and if we may believe his *Journal*, he enjoyed them after his own fashion. Nobody had been so kind to him since his uncle Thomas's death! But sports and pastimes could not galvanise the attenuated lad into fresh vigour, and he grew worse every day, watched with anxious eyes by Northumberland and Suffolk, and above all by Cranmer, whose hopes were concentrated in him.

223 Since his accession to great wealth the Duke of Suffolk had gradually abandoned Bradgate for London and fixed his family's abode at Sheen,182 in the abbot's buildings of the once opulent Carthusian monastery, which he had adapted as a private residence.183 Here the Suffolks resided towards the end of the year 1552 and during the early part of the momentous year 1553. The house, a large and noble structure, with a long Gothic gallery running from end to end, stood close to the venerable palace built by Edward the Confessor. It was supposed to be haunted—the place was often disturbed after dark by the sound of footsteps, the rustle of ghostly garments, and the mutter of unearthly voices; but the most ghastly incident of all was one which struck sudden terror into the hearts of the Duke and Duchess as they paced

the gallery in the gloaming. All at once a skeleton hand and arm thrust itself from the wall, and brandished in their faces a sword, or, as some said, an axe, dripping with blood. It224 should be remembered that the Lady Frances was now in possession of nearly all the Carthusian property in and about London, which had been granted by Henry VIII to her father, Charles Brandon, and which she had lately inherited from her stepbrothers; and this spectre may have been contrived by some friend of the exiled Brotherhood to impress on the Duchess and her brood the sacrilegious origin of this wealth, which certainly did not bring them good luck.

Nearly opposite to this uncanny residence stood Syon or Sion House, an ancient Bridgetine convent which had been presented at the Dissolution to the late Duke of Somerset, and which his rival, the Duke of Northumberland, had filched from his widow. As the scene of the most dramatic event in Lady Jane Grey's short life, it still retains considerable historical interest; but although much of the old convent is standing, the cloisters and other portions have been hidden under the plaster and stucco of an exceedingly ugly structure of the debased Victorian villa type.184

Northumberland, although he had not yet evolved the scheme of marrying his only bachelor and youngest son to Jane Grey, none the less considered the amity of the Suffolks too valuable an asset to be neglected. At this time Northumberland's power and certainly his secrets were largely shared by his ally, the Duke of Suffolk, who never took any initiative or made a step in any direction without the consent of his all-powerful friend, who knew him to be a "weakling."185

SUPPOSED PORTRAIT OF LADY JANE GREY, FORMERLY IN THE COLLECTION OF COL. ELLIOTT, AND NOW AT OXFORD UNIVERSITY

FROM AN ENGRAVING AFTER THE PAINTING BY HOLBEIN

Northumberland, it would seem, did not at first intend Guildford for Lady Jane Grey, but for the Lady Margaret Clifford, whose right to the throne was at this time considered less disputable, she being Henry VIII's own grand-niece, eldest daughter of the Lady Eleanor Brandon, the younger sister of the Duchess of Suffolk. Born after the nullification of Charles Brandon's marriage with Lady Mortimer, her legitimacy was indisputable, whereas the enemies of the Suffolks were busily engaged about this time (1552) in spreading a report that Jane225 was illegitimate, her mother, the Lady Frances, having come into the world during the lifetime of the said Lady Mortimer. This insinuation was probably made by Lady Powis, Brandon's eldest daughter by his second wife, Anne Browne. At one moment this matter of Lady Jane's illegitimacy came very near saving her life, but Queen Mary, to whom the matter was represented, refused, it is said, to take such a possibility into consideration, out of respect for the memory of her aunt, the Queen-Duchess of Suffolk, whose marriage would have been invalidated if this assumption had been proved. Among Catholics, however, Lady Jane's legitimacy was much disputed, and the Lady Eleanor prudently refused to encourage any great intimacy between her daughter and Northumberland's son; she and her family, indeed, kept themselves in the background as much as they possibly could. At last, even though the boy-King had been induced to take an interest in the projected marriage, and had written both to Northumberland and to the Earl of Cumberland on the subject, the Duke altered his mind, and in 1553, with the casual fashion of those days, having decided to marry Guildford to the Lady Jane, he "offered" the Lady Margaret Clifford to his own younger brother, Sir Andrew Dudley.186

Perhaps that which finally decided Northumberland to abandon his first project was the unguarded and compromising language used by a certain Mrs. Huggones, a former servant of the widowed Duchess of Somerset. This good woman's tongue having been loosened on one occasion by too liberal potations—the conversation is said to have taken place during supper—openly lamented the Duke of Somerset's misfortunes (the incident occurred about August 1552), called the young King an unnatural nephew, and vivaciously remarked she wished226 she "had the jerking of him." She added that Lord Guildford Dudley was to marry the daughter of the Earl of Cumberland, the match having been planned by the King, and finally, "with a stoute gesture," she cried, "have at the Crown, with your leave." Further, she used "unseemly saiyenges, neither meet to be spoken, nor conseyled of any hearer." Sir William Stafford, in whose house at Rochford, in Essex, the affair apparently occurred, wrote to the Privy Council an account of these injudicious remarks. On 8th September, Mrs. Huggones was arraigned before Sir Robert Bowes, Master of the Robes, and Sir Arthur Darcy, Lieutenant of the Tower, acting for the Privy Council. She denied what had been said of her, and expressed great admiration for Northumberland. "And, moreover, she being examined of the last article concerning the marriage of the Lord Guildford Dudley with the Earl of Cumberland's daughter, she deposeth that she heard it spoken in London (but by whom she now remembereth not) that the King's ma^{ty} had made such a marriage, and so she told the first night that she came to Rochford to supper, showing herself to be glad thereof, and so she thought that all the hearers were also glad at that marriage."187 Maybe the fact that her daughter was becoming the subject of popular gossip was another incentive to the proud Lady Eleanor to place obstacles in the way of Northumberland's proposal.188

There is no evidence that any of the Reformers visited the Suffolks at Sheen, but it is probable they did so, for the success of the Northumberlands' scheme depended on the zeal of Lady Jane for Protestantism being kept at fever heat; and we may therefore conclude her Reforming friends were frequent guests at the ex-monastery.

The foreign Reformers were at this time very active all over227 England. Cranmer was particularly engaged with them, sending the smartest among them to lecture at Oxford and Cambridge, and inviting the great Melanchthon, and even Calvin himself, to visit England and preach, although the religious opinions of both were very different from his own. He even proposed to Calvin the formation of a sort of Protestant œcumenical council in London in opposition to the Council of Trent. In March 1552, he wrote to Calvin: "Our adversaries are now holding their Council at Trent for the establishment of their errors. Shall we neglect to call together here in London a godly synod for restoring and propagating the truth?"

There is nothing in Reformation correspondence so interesting or so curious as the *Zurich Letters*—no writings so rich in details and revelations. The tone of these old letters, of Melanchthon, Calvin, Cranmer, Hooper, Conrad Pellican, Œcolampadius, Hilles, Hales, Gualter, Fagius, Stumphius, Ab Ulmis, Bullinger, Bucer, etc. etc., is strangely modern. It is easy to imagine oneself to be reading the documentary evidence of some great modern revolutionary scheme for "the betterment of humanity." All these worthies held themselves in a "godly" light uncommon to the rest of mankind. They, and they only, brandished the torch of truth, albeit they did not by any means hold identical views on even the most vital points of Christian faith—but they were as one when face to face with their common enemy, the Pope, and the religion he represented, and any blow dealt at Lutheranism was an equal joy to them. Cranmer would have burnt half of them to cinders for their "heresies" had they been Englishmen—he sent Anne Askew and Joan Bocher to the stake for holding "errors" which coincided with those of some of his foreign friends, Stumphius, Fagius, and Calvin, for instance! He would have hanged a Briton for stating in plain English his belief in predestination—but none the less invited over to a synod the great teacher of that desperate doctrine. These men were, no doubt, in earnest, and have left some strange details of their doings which throw floods of light on the history and mentality of the times in which they lived. They believed themselves to be so many God-appointed apostles, and addressed each other as "father in Christ," even substituting for their common Teutonic names rich-sounding classical228 ones—Œcolampadius, Stumphius, Massarius, Utenhovius, Terentianus, Vadianus, Osiander, Dryander, Ochianus, etc. They would willingly have suffered death heroically and patiently for what they believed to be the truth. On the other hand, they could hate like very devils; Mary to them was Jezebel or Ataliah, Philip, Satan, Pole, a hell-hound, and the Pope, the Scarlet Whore and worse than the Devil. They could not speak decently of their adversaries; and it is precisely here that we see their influence on the youthful Jane—the reason why, if she really wrote the letter to Harding after his reversion to Catholicism, she employed a viragoish language unworthy of so gentle a Christian.

We have no positive proof of how the two families, of Northumberland and Suffolk, passed their time in the more genial months of the years 1552–3, when the Thames is pleasantest, especially in the neighbourhood where they had elected to pitch their respective camps. The two Dukes and their Duchesses cannot always have been engaged in political intrigues; they must have given themselves some occasional recreation, and we may imagine that archery, tennis, and other sports, dancing, music, and such amusements, were frequently indulged in at Sheen and Sion, the two state barges incessantly crossing and recrossing the river, from one mansion to the other. We can picture the scene on the lawn in front of Sion, down which the handsome Duchess of Northumberland often went to welcome the Lady Frances and her daughters as they landed from their barge, leading them, with the stately ceremony of those days, from the water-gate to the terrace in front of the former convent, and so into the cloisters along which the sisterhood of St. Bridget had so often and so recently passed in solemn procession to their now ruined chapel. And then came the gay romp in the hall and the merry games of the young folk, in which even the austere little Lady Jane would condescend to mingle, to the righteous consternation, doubtless, of her friends from Zurich and Geneva. Here, too, must have come the handsome Ambrose Dudley, lately married to the Lady Anne Seymour;189—229but did that lady visit the house of the man who had compassed the ruin and death of her father? And here Robert Dudley, afterwards the famous Earl of Leicester, may have brought his affianced wife, the fair Amy Robsart of *Kenilworth* fame. And the Lady Mary Sidney, Northumberland's elder daughter, and wife of Sir Henry Sidney, soon to become the mother of one of the most illustrious men of the Elizabethan age, no doubt joined the circle with her clever young husband. In these hours of relaxation, when the dark undertakings to which the politics of those bloody days forced them were forgotten, these youths overflowed with animal spirits, and it is more than likely that Jane and her sister Katherine, and even the little Lady Mary, romped merrily with their guests. It was a romping age, the good old healthy country dances were in high favour, and the best performer was he who could lift his lady highest off the ground, or could cross his legs twice in a pirouette before he touched the floor again! Northumberland himself was famous as a dancer of extraordinary elegance and skill. That the Calvinism in which they had dabbled had not as yet stirred up

Henry of Suffolk and his Tudor consort to a proper pitch of "godliness" is evident, for a company of players who had enacted comedies, tragedies, and tragi-comedies at Tylsey in the previous year, repeated their performances at Sheen in the winter of 1552–3, and brought a smile, perchance, to the pale lips of the studious Lady Jane, and evoked a hearty laugh from her materialistic mother, who, for aught we know to the contrary,—let us hope it was not so!—may already have begun to allow a certain ginger-headed Master Adrian Stokes, His Lordship's Groom of the Chambers, to pay her compliments which a great Princess and an honest woman ought to have nipped in the bud. Tradition has it that Northumberland and his colleague of Suffolk often played a game of chess together, and that Suffolk would wax irritable if Northumberland won more often than himself.

No doubt, as soon as the Cumberland affair was broken off, and Northumberland had decided to marry his son to Lady Jane, Guildford was thrown as much into the young230 girl's society as was possible in those days of rigid etiquette, when maidens of rank were not often allowed out of the sight of their parents and governesses. But there is no record of any love-making between the young folk: on the contrary, there is plenty of evidence that the girl disliked her suitor. About a week before the wedding her parents ordered her to marry the young gentleman, and, according to Baoardo,190 she at first stoutly refused, "her heart," she said, "being plighted elsewhere." The Duke harshly reiterated his command and, according to the Italian chronicler, even struck his daughter several hard blows, whilst the broad red face of the Lady Frances purpled threateningly. The Duke told Jane her marriage had been ordained by no less a person than King Edward himself, and sharply inquired "whether she intended to disobey her King as well as her father?" Poor Jane, aching from his blows, could scarcely stammer her reply, "that she could not marry with Guildford since she was already contracted to another" and that with her father's consent,—she doubtless alluded to the young Earl of Hertford, the late Duke of Somerset's son. But what could a forlorn little girl of less than sixteen do, surrounded, as Jane was, by people whom she believed to be all-powerful? She had been so "nipped and pinched and bobbed" in her youth for an ill-constructed Latin verse or a faulty translation of a Greek sentence,191 that her spirit was already more or less broken; she gave a reluctant consent at last; and straightway the two Duchesses began their wedding preparations. Milliners and haberdashers, glove-makers, embroiderers and Italian silk merchants flocked to Sion and Sheen to display their gewgaws and rich stuffs. Let us hope the little bride-elect derived some childish pleasure from all this finery, the ostentatious display of which must have thrown her Calvinistic friends into hysterics of righteous indignation.231 And thus, long before she went to the Tower and thence to her unmerited doom, Jane's life was made a burden to her. Like the forlorn bride of Lammermoor, she was the victim of cruel parents, and one only wonders her young mind did not totter under the weight of so much woe!

Lord Guildford Dudley was born about 1533, and was consequently not yet of age, as Queen Mary afterwards remarked to the Imperial Ambassador. He was in his nineteenth year at the time of his ill-omened marriage. The Duchess of Northumberland, his mother, was granddaughter of that Lady Guildford who had been governess to Mary Tudor, sister of Henry VIII, and to whom occasional allusion is made in early Tudor documents as "Moder Guildford." This lady had contrived to offend Louis XII of France, who packed her off to England the day after he married the English Princess. Thus the great-grandson of the governess and the granddaughter of the royal pupil eventually became man and wife. Lord Guildford Dudley's case is believed to be the first instance, in this country, of the bestowal of a family instead of a Christian name at baptism; in stricter Catholic times it had been illegal to baptize a child by any name but that of a saint. Guildford was a tall, well-built youth, of very fair complexion.192 In contrast with his splendid colouring and light-brown hair, he had the soft brown eyes which lend so peculiar a charm to the authentic portraits of his father, whose darling he was.193 The Northumberland family was proverbially beautiful;—232Robert, the famous Earl of Leicester and lover of Queen Elizabeth, was considered the handsomest man of his time. Guildford Dudley had a second name, James or Diego, received at his christening from a Spanish194 nobleman, the famous Diego Hurtado de

Mendoza, a trivial circumstance, apparently, but fatal in its consequences, for, as we shall see, it was largely a foolishly worded letter from this godfather that brought Guildford to the block.

It is uncertain whether Jane's wedding was celebrated towards the end of May or in the beginning of June195 (1553), but the former is the date generally received. Three marriages occurred on the same day: the first that of Lady Jane Grey and Guildford Dudley; the second between Lord Herbert,196 eldest son of the Earl of Pembroke, and the Lady Katherine Grey, younger sister of Guildford's bride; whilst the third was between Henry, Lord Hastings, eldest son of the Earl of233 Huntingdon, and Lady Katherine, the young sister of Lord Guildford Dudley. On the same day, little Lady Mary Grey, barely eight years of age, was solemnly betrothed to her equally youthful kinsman, Arthur, Lord Grey of Wilton.

Lady Jane Grey's wedding seems to have been exceptionally magnificent. Strype tells us that to increase its splendour and solemnity, the Master of the Wardrobe, Sir Andrew Dudley, had orders to deliver to the various parties much rich apparel and jewels out of the royal wardrobe.197 As the King's "table diamond" was delivered to the Princess Mary about this time, it seems probable that she also attended the wedding. These articles were not new, but consisted of velvets, brocades, pieces of cloth of gold, of silver, etc., the property of the late Duke of Somerset and of his Duchess, who was still a prisoner in the Tower; which had been forfeited to the King, on their attainder. Thus was poor Jane's bridal party bedecked with the finery of her father's victim, who preceded her by a few months only on the road to the bloodstained scaffold. The French Ambassador also mentions the exceptional pomp displayed at this wedding, but gives no details.

No contemporary account of this particular ceremony is234 in existence,198 but the general custom was for the bride, attired in a dress highly ornamented with gold and embroidery, her hair hanging down, curiously waved and plaited, to be led to the church "between two sweet boys, with bride laces, and rosemary tied about their silken sleeves." Before the bride was carried "a fair bride cup, of silver gilt," "therein was a goodly branch of rosemary, gilded very fair, and hung about with silken ribbands of all colours; next there was a noise of musicians, that played all the way before her."199 Then followed a train of virgins in white, crowned with fresh flowers, with their hair hanging loose, some bearing bride cakes, and others garlands, adorned with gold. Last came the bridegroom, splendidly apparelled, with young men following close behind. There were scarves and gloves, an "epithalamium" and masques and dances; and "all the company was decked out with the bride's colours, in every form and fantasy."

When Jane's marriage took place, the populace, though far from pleased with the exorbitant pretensions of the Duke of Northumberland, could not forbear admiring the bridegroom's extreme beauty of person. The bride was considered pretty, but small and freckled. She must have come, in all her bridal bravery, from Suffolk House in the Strand to Durham House, for it was the custom then, as it is still, for the bride to start from her paternal roof, and meet the bridegroom at the church door or even at the altar. The Church of St. Mary-le-Strand having been destroyed by Somerset, the service was undoubtedly held in the private chapel of the ex-palace of the Bishops of Durham, then the town residence of Northumberland.

Edward VI was too ill to attend the wedding, and there is no direct evidence that either of the Princesses, his sisters, were present; though, as we have already said, Princess Mary may have been. Their absence, however, points to their fear of Northumberland's sinister intentions. The young King235 made his cousin, Jane, and Lady Katherine Grey some wedding gifts of jewels and plate.

Burke says in his *Tudor Portraits*, though on what authority he does not tell us, that on the morning of her fatal marriage, "Lady Jane's headdress200 was of green velvet, set round with precious stones. She wore a gown of cloth of gold, and a mantle of silver tissue. Her hair hung down her back, combed and plaited in a curious fashion 'then unknown to ladies of qualitie.' This arrangement was said to have been devised by Mrs. Elizabeth Tylney, her friend and attendant, who was with her to the end. The bride was led to the altar by two handsome pages, with bride lace and rosemary tied to their sleeves. Sixteen virgins, dressed in 'pure white,' preceded the bride to the altar. Northumberland and his family were remarkable on this occasion for the splendour of their costumes. We have seen that they were jays in borrowed plumes. A profusion of flowers was scattered along the bridal route, the church bells gave a greeting, and the poor received beef, bread and ale for three days."

Ascham reports that the wedding was "conducted much in the old Popish fashion," and adds, curiously enough, as a rider to this observation, that "Northumberland, notwithstanding his pretended zeal for the Reformation, was a Papist at heart." He was quite right, as events proved, though it should be remembered that at this time of transition the order of the marriage ceremony, unlike that for funerals, had not yet been formulated according to the Reformed rite.

Every item in this tragic story would seem predestined to increase its fateful horror. Part of Jane's wedding dower was the estate of Stanfield in Norfolk,201 which has more than once236 been associated with scenes of horror, not the least dreadful being the Rush murder, in the second half of the last century. This property belonged at one time to the Robsart family, and was believed by many to be the birthplace of the fair Amy, Countess of Leicester, who was really, however, born at Syderstone, an adjacent manor.

In the letter to Queen Mary, dated August 1553, quoted by Pollino,202 and written, according to him, from the Tower, Jane Grey relates the manner of her existence between her marriage and Edward's death. "The Duchess of Northumberland," she says, "promised me at my nuptials with her son, that she would be contented if I remained living at home with my mother. Soon afterwards, my husband being present, she declared that it was publicly said that there was no hope of the King's life (and this was the first time I heard of the matter), and further she observed to her husband, the Duke of Northumberland, 'that I ought not to leave her house,' adding 'that when it pleased God to call King Edward to His mercy I ought to hold myself in readiness, as I might be required to go to the Tower, since His Majesty had made me heir to his dominions.' These words told me off-hand and without preparation, agitated my soul within me, and for a time seemed to amaze me. Yet afterwards they seemed to me exaggerated, and to mean little but boasting, and by no means of consequence sufficient to hinder me from going to my mother." Evidently Jane expressed these sentiments very frankly, for she proceeds: "The Duchess of Northumberland was enraged against my mother and me. She answered 'that she was resolved to detain me,' insisting, 'that it was my duty at all events to remain near my husband, from whom I should not go.' Not venturing to disobey her, I remained at her house four or five days." These days were most likely spent at Durham House. "At last," continues Lady Jane, "I237 obtained leave to go to Chelsea for recreation" (meaning perhaps change of air), "where I very soon fell ill." Her illness was a struggle for life or death, the suffering so acute as to lead her to imagine she had been poisoned. The mention of this attack of what we should now call nervous breakdown, lends an indisputable air of authority to Jane's letter as given by Pollino. There was really no earthly reason why anybody should attempt her life—it was certainly too precious to the Dudleys for the Duchess, an eminently respectable if an autocratic woman, to wish to see it prematurely ended. It is well known that this fear of being poisoned frequently seizes on people in time of distress.

Chelsea Manor House, which had lately been in the possession of the Duke of Somerset, had fallen, with other property, into the hands of Northumberland, and thence he dates certain letters to Cecil and his other colleagues.203 Lady Jane apparently preferred going to Chelsea to stopping at Durham House; and so departed without her husband, although so recently married. Guildford was not present at the scene at Sion (on 9th July) when the Crown was offered to his wife, which points to his having been left in bachelor solitude at Durham House. Possibly the absence of her mother-in-law from the Chelsea establishment accounts for the bride's preference for that suburban residence; and having married Guildford without entertaining the least affection for him, she probably did not desire his presence either.

The pomp and splendour of these nuptials were the last gleam of gaiety in the reign of Edward VI. A very short time afterwards, the poor young King grew so pitifully weak that Northumberland thought it was time to carry his great projects into execution. Otherwise, as he clearly saw, he and his friends must not expect to continue long in power, or even in security: all his efforts, his overthrow of Somerset, and the rest, would be rendered useless if his royally born daughter-in-law was not named by the King himself as the lawful successor to the throne.

CHAPTER XV
ON THE WAY TO THE TOWER

The Duke of Northumberland is accused, even by almost contemporary authorities, of having forged the will of King Edward VI; but, as we shall presently see, that King never made a will, but left a sort of tentative document called a "Devise" for the succession, written in his own hand; though maybe it was suggested or even dictated by the Duke. By an Act—the XXVIII of Henry VIII, cap. 7—it was enacted that, failing issue of Queen Jane Seymour, "Your Highness (Henry) shall have full and plenary power and authority to give, dispose, appoint, assign, declare, and limit by your letters-patent under your great seal, or else by your last will made in writing, and signed with your most gracious hand, at your only pleasure, from time to time hereafter, the Imperial Crown of this Realm." Other Acts had recapitulated this; and King Henry, acting on the same principle, made a will in his thirty-fifth year, under the terms of which the Crown was to pass, firstly to his son Edward and his heirs; secondly, to his own heirs by the then Queen, Katherine Parr, "or any other wife I may have"; thirdly, to his daughter Mary; fourthly, to his daughter Elizabeth; fifthly, to the heirs of the body of his niece, the Lady Frances; sixthly, to those of her sister, Eleanor; seventhly, to the next rightful heirs, meaning the heirs of his sister, the Queen of Scots. It was also stipulated that if either of his daughters married without the consent of the Privy Council, they were to be passed over "as if dead."

Both Edward VI and his father seem to have wished for a male successor, for in the latter's enactments limiting the succession, all the female heirs are set aside in favour of their as yet unborn male issue. King Edward's "Devise" for the239 limitation of the succession makes no allusion to his two sisters, the Princesses Mary and Elizabeth. On the other hand, in the letters-patent for this limitation of the succession, which were based on the "Devise," the Princesses' claim is ruled out for three reasons: that they were illegitimate; that they were of half-blood to the King; that there was a chance of their marrying foreigners. Besides, as we have said, the King, like his father, was anxious for a male successor; in fact, this desire is on the very surface of the "Devise," wherein much stress is laid on the "issue masle," since for the one living male descendant of Henry VII—that is, Edward himself—there were as many as seven ladies (even excluding the Scotch line) potential to the English Crown.204

The first limitation decided upon by the young King was to the Lady Frances's issue male, born before the King's death, and, failing them, the Lady Jane's issue male. This scheme suited Northumberland, for if Jane had a son by Guildford the Duke would become the grandfather of the King of England and proportionately powerful. But as time went on it became evident that the King was doomed to an early death, and therefore a swifter and more practical solution of the succession problem had to be arrived at. The next best arrangement would have been the nomination of the240 Lady Frances;205 Northumberland, however, could not approve of such a scheme, since it would have placed the weight of power in the hands of the Duke of Suffolk, her husband. At last, all plans failing, Edward decided to nominate the Lady Jane Grey as his successor to the throne—and thereby the Duke gained his point. The words in the "Devise," "to the L'Janes heires masles," were now changed to "*to the L'Jane and her heires masles*": in the copy of the document bearing the King's signature which is still extant, it can be seen that a pen has been drawn through the "s" at the end of Jane's name, and the words "and her" have been written above. Thus was manufactured206 the ladder by which Northumberland, by becoming the father-in-law of a Queen, hoped to reach the summit of his ambition.

Northumberland had a great deal of trouble to get his scheme legalised. Edward was not unpliable, and indeed attributed Northumberland's intense desire to see the "Devise" carried into effect entirely to his zeal for the Reformed religion; but Archbishop Cranmer, Sir Edward Montagu, Lord Chief Justice, Sir James Hale, Secretary Cecil and others, either because they saw through Northumberland or else because they really had qualms of conscience as to its legality, opposed the plan, taking their stand on the fact that the nomination of Jane Grey, being contrary to the older "Statute of Succession," would be illegal. Cranmer, as the result of an interview with the King, was finally converted to his views. Lord Darcy, the Lord Chamberlain, and the Marquis of Northampton were present at this meeting, much to the Archbishop's disgust. "I desired to talk with the King's Majesty alone," says Cranmer, "but I could not be suffered: and so I failed of my purpose. For if I might have communed with the King alone, and at my good leisure, my trust was, that I should have altered him from his purpose; but they241 (the above-mentioned noblemen) being present, my labour was in vain. And so at length I was required by the King's Majesty himself to set my hand to his will (that is, the scheme for the succession) saying that he trusted that I alone would not be more repugnant to his will than the rest of the Council were. Which words surely grieved my heart very sore. And so I granted him to subscribe his will, and to follow the same. Which when I had set my hand unto I did it unfainedly and without dissimulation."207

Directly Northumberland was satisfied that the young King would not depart from the decision to which he had forced him, he summoned Lord Chief Justice Montagu to attend at the Royal Court at Greenwich, on 11th June 1553, with Sir John Baker, Mr. Justice Bromley, Attorney-General Gosnold and Solicitor-General Griffin. This command was the first step towards officially depriving Mary of her inheritance, and the letter was signed by Secretary Petre, Sir John Cheke, and strange to relate, by Cecil, which is surprising when taken in conjunction with his subsequent conduct in the matter. The Lord Chief Justice, coming into the royal presence, found the King very ill, lying on a couch, surrounded by Lord Winchester, Lord Treasurer, the Marquis of Northampton, Sir John Gates, Sir John Palmer, and others. Raising himself, Edward declared, in the verbose language of the time, that he had summoned his Council to hear from his own lips that he had appointed the Lady Jane Grey his heiress, as the Lady Mary might change her faith, and "his Highness's proceedings in religion might be altered.208 Wherefore his pleasure was that the state of the Crown should go in such form, and to such persons, as his Highness had appointed in a bill of articles [*i.e.*, the "Devise"209] now signed with the King's hand, which were read, and commanded them to make a book thereof accordingly with speed." Montagu refused to do this, saying the nomination242 of Lady Jane would be illegal and against the already mentioned "Statute of Succession," which had passed Parliament. Edward, or rather Northumberland, became so irritable, that the Lord Chief Justice finally acquiesced so far as to ask for time to deliberate and consult the laws; whereupon the King gave him the "Devise" to study, and dismissed all present, Northumberland alone remaining. On the following day (12th June), Secretary Petre sent for the Lord Chief Justice to Durham House, Northumberland's palace in the Strand, and told him the matter must be executed off-hand. Montagu immediately went to Ely Place, Holborn, where he found the Council sitting, but Northumberland absent; which emboldened him to warn the Council of the exceeding danger of the matter they were about to approve. "In God's name, my Lords," cried he, "think twice what you do—it will be treason to us all who have a hand in it." Hardly had he spoken ere Northumberland, who was, of course, aware of his opposition, burst, as white as a sheet, into the room like a whirlwind, "before all the Council there," says a contemporary account, "being in a great rage and fury, trembling for anger; and, amongst his ragious talk, called Sir Edward Montagu traitor, and further said that he would fight in his shirt [sleeves] with any man in that quarrel." No one took up the challenge, and Montagu withdrew in some dismay—thankful, no doubt, that there had been no actual blows given or received.

Nothing was signed or done that day, but on the next, Montagu received a fresh order to repair immediately to Court with the same companions as before. On arrival at Greenwich, the party was ushered into a room filled with the notables of the Court, who "looked upon them with earnest countenance, as though they had not known them, so that they might perceive there was some steadfast determination against them"; which treatment, combined with uncertainty as to whether the all-powerful Northumberland might not persuade the King into punishing them for not preparing the "book" of the King's scheme as he had wished, made the poor gentlemen feel very uncomfortable. Edward also (on 15th June), received the Lord Chief Justice and his colleagues haughtily; His Majesty was apparently better, and seated in his chair. Montagu's party endeavoured to excuse themselves243 by using the same arguments against the scheme of succession as they had previously put before the Council. They said that, by reason of the "Statute of Succession," the plan would be null and void after Edward's death; and that the only power which could remove the said Statute was Parliament, which had made it, and which was not then sitting. Thereupon the King said he would summon a Parliament, but, all the same, the drawing up of his scheme must be proceeded with. He further commanded Montagu to obey his order, and "make dispatch." At last Montagu, "in great fear as ever he was in his life before, seeing the King so earnest and sharp, and the Duke so angry the day before—who ruled the whole Council as it pleased him, and they were all afraid of him (the more is the pity)210 so that such cowardliness and fear was there never seen amongst honourable men—being an old man and without comfort, he began to consider with himself what was best to be done for the safeguard of his life." Accordingly he agreed to comply with his sovereign's command, provided Edward granted him (as a sort of protection) his commission under the Great Seal, enjoining him to draw up the instrument of succession, and that a general "pardon" for having signed it should be made out at the same time. The King acceded to these terms; and so the letters patent nominating Jane Grey as King Edward's successor received the Great Seal on 21st June, and over a hundred signatures, including those of the Lord Mayor, the Sheriffs of Middlesex, Surrey, and Kent, the officers of the Royal Household, and of Thomas Grey, the Duke of Suffolk's younger brother, were affixed to the document. It took so long to collect all the signatures that the work was not finished until the 8th of July, that is, after Edward's death. Stowe records the attendance of the "chief citizen" of the metropolis on that day in the following terms: "The 8. of July the lord mayor of London was sent for to the court then at Greenwich, to bring with him six aldermen, as many merchants of the staple, and as many244 merchant adventurers, unto whom by the council was secretly declared the death of King Edward, and also how he did ordain for the succession of the crown by his letters patent, to the which they were sworn, and charged to keep it secret." Sir James Hale, however, refused his signature with great dignity; Cecil slipped out of the difficulty on a pretext of sudden illness. Foreseeing, even before 11th June, the rocks ahead, he wisely retired from Court after a well-acted scene of simulated faintness, so realistic as to mislead the shrewd Lord Audley, who, being a great believer in his own prescriptions, sent the disordered Secretary the following delightful receipt:—

"Take a sow-pig of nine days old, and flea him and quarter him, and put him in a stillatory with a handful of spearmint, a handful of red fennel, a handful of liverwort, half a handful of red nepe [turnip], a handful of celery, nine dates clean picked and pared, a handful of great raisins, and pick out the stones, and a quarter of an ounce of mace, and two sticks of good cinnamon bruised in a mortar; and distill it together, with a fair fire; and put it in a glass and set in the sun nine days; and drink nine spoonfuls of it at once when you list.

"A Compost

"*Item.*—Take a porcupin, otherwise called an English hedgehog, and quarter him in pieces, and put the said beast in a still with these ingredients and boil together; item, a quart of red wine, a pint of rose-water, a quart of sugar, cinnamon and great raisins, one date, twelve nepe. Pass the whole through a sieve and drink at night, a full cup thereof warm."211

Possibly his Lordship intended this epistle as a fine piece of sarcasm, for if Cecil was only to partake of the "sow-pig" and raisin remedy nine days after it was concocted, there was every chance of his dying or getting well in the interval.

The fact that so many persons were found to sign the fateful document is another proof—even if we make allowance for the majority of the Council being time-servers—that Edward's "Devise" for the succession, though evidently245 suggested and forwarded by Northumberland, was not a forgery.

On 6th July212 (1553), whilst the newly-made bride was peacefully resting at Chelsea, King Edward VI passed away at Whitehall Palace. He had been taken out of the hands of his physicians, Drs. Owen213 and Wendy, old and trusted Court doctors, and put into those of a female quack, who soon extinguished the feeble ray of life that still flickered in his wasted body. An hour before Edward passed away, Dr. Owen, who had been recalled in a hurry, bent over him, saying, "We heard you speak to yourself, but what you said we know not?" The weary lad answered, smiling faintly, "I was praying to God." A little later he was heard to murmur, "Lord have mercy upon me, and take my spirit." He never spoke again—he was very tired, and needed rest!

The people had shown their anxiety for Edward's health by assembling daily in front of Greenwich Palace to ascertain how he was, and to convince the mob that he was still alive246 it had become necessary to make the royal lad show his sickly person, robed in velvet and ermine, and his poor wasted face—crowned with the delightful little velvet cap with the white feathers, so familiar to us in his portraits—at the window. The received version among all classes was that the King was being slowly poisoned by the Duke of Northumberland, whom they also accused of having forged Edward's "Devise" for the succession in favour of Lady Jane. The Swiss Reformers, in their letters to Strasburg and Zurich, did not hesitate to give currency to the report that Northumberland, whom a few weeks earlier they had called the "illustrious" and the "noble," had murdered his nephew. "That monster of a man," says John Burcher to Henry Bullinger (letter dated from Strasburg, 16th August 1553), "the Duke of Northumberland, has been committing a horrible and portentous crime. A writer worthy of credit informs me, that our excellent King has been most shamefully taken off by poison. His nails and hair fell off before his death, so that, handsome as he was, he entirely lost all his good looks. The perpetrators of the murder were ashamed of allowing the body of the deceased King to lie in state, and be seen by the public, as is usual: wherefore they buried him privately in the paddock adjoining the palace, and substituted in his place a youth not unlike him.... One of the sons of the Duke of Northumberland acknowledged this fact. The Duke has been apprehended214 with his five sons, and nearly twenty persons; among whom is master [Sir John] Cheke, doctor Cox, and the Bishop of London, with others unknown to you...."215 Burcher does not tell us which son of the Duke made this confession; nor is there evidence that any of Northumberland's boys ever accused their father of regicide. Besides, Burcher was somewhat addicted to putting his faith in the reports of untrustworthy people. A few years earlier (in 1549) he had written Bullinger a letter in which he repeated the sensational story of an attempt to murder King Edward made by his uncle, Thomas Seymour, a crime frustrated by the vigilance of the King's lap-dog, which seeing the murderer suddenly appear, flew at him and247 made such a yelping that the bodyguard was in time to save their sovereign. This story may or may not be true; but is as unauthenticated as the other. There is just one point, however, that supports the poison theory; which is that the young King's old and competent nurse, Mrs. Sybil Penn, was suddenly relieved of her duties, and replaced by a woman who was an acknowledged quack, and declared she could cure the lad by a sort of faith-healing not unknown in our own times. On the other hand, Edward was suffering from such a complication of diseases that there was no reason why Northumberland should have troubled to burden his soul by hastening an end that would in any case have come before long.216 Born of a debauched father and a sickly mother, the "second Josiah" never throve, and never could have thriven, for he bore in his puny frame the seeds of early death from his birth.

EDWARD VI

FROM AN ENGRAVING BY G. VERTUE

King Edward VI lived exactly fifteen years, eight months, and six days. We can easily believe Strype's assurance that his wonderful and almost preternatural sagacity was merely the result of skilful prompting. He informs us that whenever the young King was about to attend the Council, Northumberland carefully rehearsed with him both how he should behave and what he was to say. Yet the boy does not appear to have been devoid of exceptional intelligence. It may be doubted whether his affections were very deep; he certainly did not hesitate to bastardise his two sisters at the bidding of their common enemy. It has been stated that Lady Jane Grey was devotedly attached to her young cousin; that there had even been love passages between them. The King's youth should mark this report as the veriest gossip. Not a248 tinge of affection or regret for her cousin is expressed in any of Lady Jane's letters, and we have no proof whatever that she was specially affected by his early death. There is but little evidence, indeed, of her having been much in his company, nor any proof that he, on his side, held her in exceptional esteem.

Nature added a warning note to the horror of the approaching tragedy. "Several women were delivered of monsters on the day of the King's death, one of an infant with two heads and four feet, and another of a child whose head was planted in the centre of his body." The ghost of Henry VIII was reported to have been seen stalking along the battlements of Windsor and at Hampton Court and Whitehall—so that even the supernatural stimulated popular imagination. The hour of the young King's death, too, was ushered in by a tempest of such appalling violence, that heaven and earth seemed to menace the city. A terrible hailstorm swept over London and its outskirts, and the ruined gardens and devastated orchards for miles round were heaped with hailstones "as red as blood." Cataracts of water deluged the lower parts of the city: trees were torn up, and the steeple of the church in which the first Protestant service was held was shattered by forked lightning. The people, terrified at the universal havoc, believed, when they learnt of the King's death, that this storm was the forerunner of fresh disasters and terrible crimes, and so indeed it proved to be—for the death of Edward VI was the signal for the outbreak of the long contemplated revolution so skilfully prepared by Northumberland.

CHAPTER XVI
THE LADY JANE IS PROCLAIMED QUEEN

No sooner had King Edward VI given up the ghost, than Northumberland devised a cunning attempt to obtain possession of the person of Princess Mary, then at Hunsdon. The Duke persuaded the Council to address a treacherous letter to her, after Edward was actually dead, but before his decease was divulged to the public, in which they gave no hint that her brother was dead, and informed her he was only very ill, and "prayed her to come to him, as he earnestly desired the comfort of her presence." Touched by this exhibition of brotherly affection, Mary fell into the trap, and, returning a loving answer, started immediately for London; but a timely warning prevented the whole course of our history being changed. The plot was to seize her on the high road near the metropolis, and convey her a prisoner to the Tower.

A young brother of Sir Nicholas Throckmorton, however, who was in Northumberland's service, and in attendance upon him at Greenwich Palace, was surprised to see Sir John Gates come, on the morning after the King's death, to the Duke's chamber before he was dressed. They discussed the movements of the Princess, and young Throckmorton overheard Gates exclaim angrily, "What sir! will you let the Lady Mary escape, and not secure her person?" Acting upon this hint, he forthwith galloped to Throckmorton House, where he found his father and his brothers, together with Sir Nicholas, who had just come to inform them of the King's death, of which he had been a witness, and also of Northumberland's schemes concerning the proclamation of Lady Jane. On this the youth related what he had overheard that morning in Northumberland's bedroom; and Sir Nicholas, who, although250 a Reformer, was none the less loyal to Mary, instantly dispatched her goldsmith, a trusty servant, who met her at Hoddesden, and informed her both of her brother's death and of the danger in which she stood. Even yet she doubted the genuineness of the warning, and remarked to the goldsmith that "If Robert217 had been at Greenwich, she would have hazarded all things, and gaged her life on the leap." Sir Robert Throckmorton,218 however, arriving on 7th July, confirmed the goldsmith's message, and Mary and her retinue, in consequence, left the London road and struck off into Suffolk, reaching her manor of Kenninghall after a two days' hard gallop. Almost as soon as she arrived there, she addressed the Council a comparatively mild remonstrance, and at the same time confirmed her claim to the throne. Mary prized the fidelity of the Throckmortons so highly as to bestow upon the chief of that ancient house the position of chief-justice of Chester, which act of kindness he repaid in after times, when Mary was long dead, by praying for her soul whenever he said his mealtime grace.

Lady Jane Grey meanwhile remained at Chelsea until she was sent for: "There came unto me," she continues in her letter[251] to Queen Mary, "the Lady Sidney, the daughter of the Duke of Northumberland, who told me she was sent by the Council to call me before them, and she informed me that I must be that night at Sion House, where they were assembled, to receive that which was ordained for me by the King."

The two young ladies went that afternoon (9th July 1553) by river from Chelsea to Sion House, which they reached towards nightfall:—

"On arriving at Sion," writes Lady Jane, "I found no one there. But presently came the Marquis of Northampton, the Earls of Arundel, Huntingdon, and Pembroke, who began to make me complimentary speeches, bending the knee before me, their example being followed by several noble ladies, all of which ceremony made me blush. My distress was still further increased when my mother (the Lady Frances), and my mother-in-law (the Duchess of Northumberland), entered and paid me the same homage. Then came the Duke of Northumberland himself, who, as President of the Council, declared to me the death of the King, and informed me that every one had good reason to rejoice in the virtuous life he had led, and the good death he had. He drew great comfort from the fact that, at the end of his life, he took great care of his kingdom, praying to our Lord God to defend it from all doctrine contrary to His, and to free it from the evil of his sisters. He signified to the Duke of Northumberland 'that he (the said Majesty of Edward VI), had well considered the Act of Parliament, in which it had been already ordained that, whoever shall recognise Mary, or Elizabeth her sister, as heir to the Crown, were to be considered traitors, seeing that Mary had disobeyed the King, her father, and her brother (Edward VI) and was, moreover, a chief enemy to the Word of God, and that both were illegitimate. Therefore he would not that she and her sister be his heirs, but rather thought he ought in every way to disinherit them.' And before his death, he 'commanded his Council, and adjured them by the honour they owed him, by the love they bore their country, and by the duty they owe to God, that they should obey his will and carry it into effect.' The Duke of Northumberland then added that I was the heir nominated by His Majesty, and[252] that my sisters, the Lady Katherine and the Lady Mary Grey, were to succeed me, in case I had no issue legitimately born, at which words all the lords of the Council knelt before me, exclaiming, 'that they rendered me that homage because it pertained to me, being of the right line,' and they added, that in all particulars they would observe what they promised which was, by their souls they swore, to shed their blood and lose their lives to maintain the same. On hearing all this, I remained stunned and out of myself, I call on those present to bear witness, who saw me fall to the ground weeping piteously, and dolefully lamenting, not only mine insufficiency, but the death of the King. I swooned indeed, and lay as dead, but when brought to myself I raised myself on my knees, and prayed to God 'that if to succeed to the Throne was indeed my duty and my right, that He would aid me to govern the Realm to His glory.' The following day, as every one knows, I was conducted to the Tower."

Lady Jane's own version as given above differs materially from the one of this famous scene of the recognition of Jane as Queen edited by Foxe; the two are, however, identical in the main facts, but the bombastic speech put into the mouth of his heroine by the author of the *Book of Martyrs* is much less natural than Pollino's version. *The Grey Friars' Chronicle* corroborates in every particular both narratives, and adds that, "on 10th July, the Lady Jane came from Richmond to Westminster by water,[219] whither she came to robe herself before proceeding to the Tower." On her way from Westminster, she stopped at Durham House, her father-in-law's palace on the Thames, where she dined. Lady Jane afterwards proceeded by the State barge to the Tower, where she landed about three o'clock in the afternoon, the weather being exceedingly fine.

In the Genoese Archives there is a letter from a member of the Spinola family,[220] who was then in London, giving details of that day's doings:—

253

"To-day [the date is not given, but possibly it figured on the cover, now lost: it was, of course, 10th July 1553] I saw Donna Jana Groia [an Italianisation of Grey] walking in a grand procession to the Tower. She is now called Queen, but is not popular, for the hearts of the people are with Mary, the Spanish Queen's daughter. This Jane is very short and thin, but prettily shaped and graceful. She has small features and a well-made nose (*ben fatta ha il naso*), the mouth flexible and the lips red. The eyebrows are arched and darker than her hair, which is nearly red. Her eyes are sparkling and red (*rossi*—a sort of light hazel often noticed with red hair). I stood so long near Her Grace, that I noticed her colour was good, but freckled. When she smiled she showed her teeth, which are white and sharp. In all, a *graziosa persona* and *animata* [animated]. She wore a dress of green velvet stamped with gold, with large sleeves. Her headdress was a white coif with many jewels. She walked under a canopy, her mother carrying her long train, and her husband Guilfo [Guildford] walking by her, dressed all in white and gold, a very tall strong boy with light hair, who paid her much attention. The new Queen was mounted on very high *chopines* [clogs] to make her look much taller, which were concealed by her robes, as she is very small and short. Many ladies followed, with noblemen, but this lady is very *heretica* and has never heard Mass, and some great people did not come into the procession for that reason."

Queen Jane was received by Sir John Brydges, Lieutenant of the Tower, and his brother, Mr. Thomas Brydges, Deputy-Lieutenant, and walked in procession from the landing-place to the Great Hall, a crowd of spectators lining the way, all kneeling as the new Queen passed. The Lady Frances, Duchess of Suffolk, to the surprise of every one, carried her daughter's train. Pollino informs us that universal indignation was expressed by the onlookers when they beheld the Duchess-mother, who was rightful heiress, playing the part of train-254bearer to her daughter, and describes as theatrical in the extreme the obsequious manner in which the Duke of Suffolk and his consort treated their own child, kneeling to her and walking backwards before her, "the which was a most despicable and humiliating sight."

* * * * *

Note.—The following is the full text of the celebrated "Devise," drawn up by Northumberland and approved by Edward VI.

Deuise for the succession.

1. For lakke of issu (masle *inserted above the line, but afterwards erased*) of my body (to the issu (masle *above the line*) cumming of thissu femal, as i haue after declared (*inserted, but erased*). To the L. Fraūceses heires masles (For lakke of *erased*) (if she have any *inserted*) such issu (befor my death *inserted*) to the L'Janes (and her *inserted*) heires masles, To the L. Katerins heires masles, To the L Maries heires masles, To the heires masles of the daughters wich she shal haue hereafter. Then to the L Margets heires masles. For lakke of such issu, To th'eires masles of the L Janes daughters. To th'eires masles of the L Katerins daughters, and so forth til yow come to the L Margets (daughters *inserted*) heires masles.

2. If after my death theire masle be entred into 18 yere old, then he to have the hole rule and gouernaūce therof.

3. But if he be under 18, then his mother to be gouuernres til he entre 18 yere old, But to doe nothing w'out th'auise (and agremēt *inserted*) of 6 parcel of a counsel to be pointed by my last will to the nombre of 20.

4. If the mother die befor th'eire entre into 18 the realme to be gouuerned by the coūsel Prouided that after he be 14 yere al great matters of importaunce be opened to him.

5. If i died w^tout issu, and there were none heire masle, then the L Fraunces to be (regēt *altered to*) gouuernres. For lakke of her, the her eldest daughters, and for lakke of them the L Marget to be gouuernres after as is aforsaid, til sume heire masle be borne, and then the mother of that child to be gouuernres.

6. And if during the rule of the gouuernres ther die 4 of255 us doo assent to take, use, and repute hym for a breaker of the common concord, peax, and unite of this realme, and to doo our uttermost to see hym or them so varying or swarving punisshed with most sharpe punisshmentes according to their desertes.

```
T. CANT    T. ELY, CANC    WINCHESTER    NORTHUBRLAND
J. REDFORD    H. SUFFOLK
          W. NORTHT
            F. SHREWESBURY    F. HUNTYNGDON
                                  (PEMBROKE.
            E. CLYNTON    T. DARCY    G. COBHAM
          R. RYCHE        T. CHEYNE
            JOH'N GATE    WILL'M PETRE
                              (JOAN.' CHEEK
  W. CECILL    EDWARD MOUNTAGU.
                              JOHN BAKERE
  EDWARD GRYFFYN    JOHN LUCAS
  JOHN GOSNOLD
```

CHAPTER XVII
THE NINE DAYS' REIGN

As soon as Jane Grey and her escort had entered the royal apartments of the Tower, the heralds trumpeted, and a few minutes later (it was close on six o'clock), four of them read the new Queen's proclamation, one of the most tedious State documents in existence, and the first in which a woman claims the title of "Supreme Head of the Church."221 The ceremony of solemn proclamation within the precincts of the Tower once over, other heralds proceeded for the same purpose to Cheapside and the Fleet. In Cheapside, a potboy who was heard to disapprove of the wordy document, and of the expression "bastard" applied to the Lady Mary, was arrested, and treated after a fashion quaintly described by Machyn,222 who says, "there was a young man taken that time for speaking of certain words of Queen Mary, that she had the right title. The xj day of July, at viij of the clock in the morning, the young man for speaking was set on the pillory, and both his ears cut off; for there was a herald, and a trumpeter blowing; and incontinent he was taken down, and carried to the Counter; and the same day was the young man's master dwelling at Saint John's head, his name was Sandor Onyone, and another, master Owen, a257 gun-maker at London Bridge was drowned, dwelling at Ludgate."223

It is curious that the original of this unique proclamation should have passed into the hands of Cecil, who endorsed it with the significant words—"*Jana non Regina.*"

From every point of view, Queen Jane's proclamation was ill-advised. It was prodigiously long-winded, even for that period, and the manner in which it dealt with the claims of Mary and Elizabeth, brutal in frankness, was well calculated to offend the Catholic Powers, and cruelly wound the personal feelings of the late King's sisters. Queen Mary's resentment is proved by the stern simplicity of the language of the death-warrant of Northumberland, Lady Jane, and Guildford, which allows none of them the vestige of a title. Elizabeth, in later life, never alluded to her cousin Jane without bitterness. Jane was, of course, perfectly innocent of the offensive wording of this document,224 but it nevertheless bore her signature. The sentence which infuriated the Princesses ran as258 follows: "And, forasmuch as the said limitation of the Imperial Crowne of this Realme, being limited as is aforesaid to the said Lady Mary and the said Lady Elizabeth, being illegitimate the marriage between the said King Henry VIII our progenitor and great uncle, and the Lady Katherine, mother to the said Lady Mary, and also the marriage between the said late King Henry VIII and the Lady Anne, mother to the said Lady Elizabeth, being very clearly undone by sentence of divine, according to the word of God, and the ecclesiastical laws. The Ladies Mary and Elizabeth are to all intents and purposes divested to claim or challenge the said Imperial Crown or any other honours, etc., appertaining thereunto, etc."

This proclamation, as well as most of the other official documents of Jane's reign, which are generally attributed to Northumberland, was, we may take it for granted, edited by the celebrated Sir John Cheke, who entered the Tower at the same time as Lady Jane and was her Secretary throughout the whole of her nine days' reign. We have already mentioned in more than one place this distinguished Greek scholar, who had been for a time tutor to Edward VI, over whom he had a great influence, and by whom he was knighted at the same time that the Marquis of Dorset was elevated to the Dukedom of Suffolk in 1551. At the period of Jane's misfortunes he was between thirty-nine and forty years of age, greatly in favour with his royal pupil, and holding the office of Clerk to the Council; so that when there was a talk of Cecil resigning his secretaryship, Cheke was, on 2nd June 1553, appointed a principal Secretary of State, Cecil however continuing in office; and on 11th June, Cheke sat in the Council for the first time as Secretary. It is probable that Northumberland suggested his nomination to the King, for the express purpose of interesting a diplomat of such ability in the forthcoming conspiracy to place Jane on the throne. He was far too high-minded a man to be influenced by pecuniary motives, but undoubtedly his zeal for the Reformation was such that he desired the advent of Jane, which meant a continuance of the Reformation, rather than the coming of Mary, which he fully realised would be disastrous to it. Cheke's appointment to the office of Secretary of State gave great joy259 to the Reformers, and Ascham, then in Brussels with our Ambassador, Morysone, wrote him a laudatory letter, in which he congratulates England, the State, Cambridge, and St. John's College on having produced so learned and worthy a man! Great must have been Cheke's delight when he beheld Queen Jane, the hope of Protestantism, actually enthroned in the Tower; and it must have been a consolation to Lady Jane to have about her so capable and at the same time so upright a man—one devoted, not only to her personally, but especially to the cause she represented. Cheke tried to induce the cunning Cecil to take an active part in the Government; Strype says, "He checked his brother Cecil who would not be induced to meddle in this matter, but endeavoured to be absent."

Before this, the first day of her reign, came to a close, Jane signed a letter to William Parr, Marquis of Northampton, Lord Lieutenant of Surrey, informing him of her entry into the Tower "this day." After the usual preamble concerning the death of Edward, the document proceeds: "we are entered into our rightful possession of this kingdom, as by the last will of our said dearest cousin our late ancestor ... now therefore do you understand we do this day make our entry into our Tower of London as rightful queen of this realm, and have accordingly set forth our proclamation to all our loving subjects, giving them thereby to understand ... their duty of allegiance which they now of right owe unto us ... nothing doubting, right trusty and well beloved counsellor, but that you will endeavour yourself in all things to the uttermost of your power, not only to defend our just title, but also assist us ... to disturb, repel, and resist, the feigned and untrue claim of the Lady Mary, bastard daughter to our great uncle Henry th' Eight, of famous memory."

This missive was later on shown to Mary, and increased her resentment against Jane, whose signature it bore, and also against Northumberland, who drew up the original draft, though the copy Jane signed was made by some clerk, perhaps by Sir John Cheke. Cecil was, therefore, wise to number the composition of this compromising epistle among the many dangerous offices out of which he contrived to shuffle;260 for it is certainly to this letter to Northampton that he refers in his "Submission," by the words, "I eschewed the writing of the Queen's Highness, *bastard*, and therefore the Duke (of Northumberland) wrote the letter himself which was sent abroad in the Realm." The Duke so fully appreciated the dangerous nature of the document, that later on he endorsed the clerk's copy of it with the words, "*Jana non Regina*"—just as Cecil did with the proclamation.225

All her State duties over, the young Queen supped in state at a small table on a dais, the Duke of Suffolk on her right, the Duke of Northumberland on her left, and the two Duchesses opposite to her. She was indisposed, and retired early, the whole company rising as she left her seat.

The following morning (11th July) there was a violent scene226 between Jane, her husband, and his mother. So far as can be ascertained, the marriage had not hitherto gone beyond the stage of ceremony, and Guildford Dudley and his bride had never lived as man and wife. The Duchess of Northumberland insisted that this state of affairs should cease, resolving that "her son should share the new Queen's bed and throne, and forthwith assume the title of King Consort." With this object, the ambitious parent and her docile son made a sudden incursion into Jane's chamber, whilst she was still seated at her toilet. The Duchess vituperated her daughter-in-law, using coarse and violent language; the would-be King was noisy and impertinent! But Jane stoutly refused to grant the latter part of the Duchess's request. "The Crown," she said, "was not a plaything for boys and girls. She could make her husband a Duke, but only Parliament could make him a King."227 On these words the Duchess burst into a fury, and paced angrily up and down the floor, swearing her strongest oaths, that her son should be King, whether Jane would or261 not. Guildford, who was boyish, began to cry, and left the room. Jane had to endure another scene of the most unpleasant description with the Duchess, in the midst of which Guildford, still sulking, returned. His mother presently caught his hand and drew him out of the room, saying "she would not leave him with an ungrateful wife."

Thereupon Jane sent for the Earls of Arundel and Pembroke, and asked their advice. They apparently approved of the line she had taken, and going to young Guildford, informed him he must on no account leave the Tower, nor agree to the Duchess's proposal that he should separate from his wife, and return with her (*i.e.* his mother) to Sion House. It is quite probable that if he had done so, his life would have been spared.

Lady Jane's account of this stormy interview is as follows: "The Lord High Treasurer, Winchester," says she, "brought me the regalia and the Crown, the which were neither demanded by *me* nor by any one in *my name*228; he desired to place it on my head to see how it fitted. This I declined with many protestations; but he said, 'I might take it boldly, for that he would have another made to crown my husband with.' Which thing I certainly heard with infinite grief, and displeasure of heart. As soon as I was left alone with my husband I reasoned with him, and after we had had a great dispute he consented to wait till he was made King by me and Act of Parliament." Jane then relates what we have already said—how she sent for the Earls of Arundel and Pembroke, and the scene with the Duchess and her threat of carrying Guildford off to Sion; also how the two Earls were charged to keep Guildford from going there. "And thus," concludes the narrative, "I was compelled to act as a woman who is *obliged* to live on good terms with her husband; nevertheless I was not only deluded by the Duke and the Council, but maltreated by my husband and his mother."

Disregarding Jane's prudent advice, her ambitious young husband nevertheless did his best to get himself recognised King of England. In the minutes of a dispatch which must262 have been written during the nine days' reign of his wife, and is addressed to the Duchess-Regent of the Netherlands by Guildford's directions, he recalls Sir Thomas Chamberlayne (English Minister in that country) and desires that "in all *his* (Guildford's) affairs" full credit be given to Sir Philip Hoby.229 One of the first acts, therefore, of Jane's Council was to nominate Sir Philip, then at Brussels, as successor to Chamberlayne; this nomination is signed "Jane the Quene." Jane herself, true to what she said to her mother-in-law and to Guildford, does not appear to have recognised her husband as King, for no mention of him appears in such of her official documents as have come down to us. All the same, Guildford contrived to get his claims accepted by some Continental notabilities. On learning of the death of Edward VI, Sir Philip Hoby and Sir Richard Morysone,230 the English Commissioners in Flanders,—who had doubtless been primed beforehand by Northumberland,—wrote from Brussels to the Privy Council (under date of July 15th) that "The xiii[h] of this presente, Don Diego found me Sir Phillipe Hobby (Hoby), and me Sir Richard Morysone, walkyne in our hostes gardene." This Don Diego Mendoza231 was a member of the Spanish administration in the Low Countries, an old personal friend of the Dudley family, and,263 as already stated, godfather to young Guildford, who had, of course, been baptized a Catholic. On the occasion of this meeting with the Englishmen, the Spaniard, after the usual condolences on the death of Edward VI, passed to praises of that monarch's wisdom in providing England with so good a King, meaning not "Jane the Quene," the rightful heiress of the Realm, but Guildford Dudley.232 The truth may be that Diego said nothing of the kind, and that the English diplomats simply put these words into his mouth, to confirm the Council in its allegiance to Jane, and make it look on Guildford as the King, by creating an impression that his right to the throne was admitted by leading men on the Continent. Don Diego Mendoza told the Commissioners (they said) that his condolences on the occasion of the death of King Edward and his offers of service "to the kyng's majestie" (Guildford) had been retarded, by the advice of the Bishop of Arras, a member of the Ministry at Brussels. "Therefore says he (*i.e.* Don Diego, quoted by the Commissioners) do I (feel) sorry that you lose so good a King, so much do I rejoice that ye have so noble and toward a *Prince* to succeed him, and I promise you, by the word of a gentleman, I would at all times serve His Highness myself if the Emperor (Charles V) did call me to serve him (*i.e.* "allow me to do so")." The English Envoys inform the Council that they told Don Diego "they had received the sorrowful news (of the death of Edward VI) but the glad tidings (of the "accession" of Guildford) were not as yet come unto us by letters"—which was probably true, so far as official intimations of them went. Upon this Don Diego replied: "I can tell you this much. The King's Majesty (Edward VI), for discharge of his conscience, wrote a good piece of his testament with his own hand, barring both his sisters of the Crown, and leaving it to the Lady264 Jane, near to the French Queen (that is to say, "related to Mary Tudor, Queen of Louis XII of France"). Whether the two daughters be bastards or not or why it is done, we that be strangers have nothing to do. You are bound to obey and serve His Majesty (Guildford Dudley), and therefore it is reasonable (that) we take him for (*i.e.* "to be") your King, whom the consent of the nobles of your country have declared for ("to be") your King, and," he continued, "for my part of all others, I am bound to be glad that His Majesty is set in this office. I was his godfather, and would as willingly spend my blood in his service as any subject that he hath, as long as I shall see the Emperor willing to embrace (His) Majesty's amity." "Don Francisson (Francesco) de Este, general of all the footmen Itallyanes (Italian Infantry)," the Commissioners add, "is gone to his charge in mylland ("Milan"), who, at his departure, made the like offer, as long his master and ours should be friends, which he trusted should be ever, praying us at our return to utter it to the King's Majesty (Guildford), and will (we) humbly take our leave of your honours."

It is obvious that, if Diego de Mendoza ever really used the words attributed to him in this letter, and did not merely lend his name to the English Commissioners, he must have been well "coached" by the Dudleys in what he was to say, though his close connection with Guildford as his godfather would naturally incline him to credit anything in his favour. Still, knowing Northumberland and Suffolk's deep scheming, one cannot suppose that Mendoza's enthusiasm for Guildford's illegal claim to royal honours and his haste to admit it was entirely uninspired by outside influences. It is, indeed, a significant fact that Ascham, a great friend of the Duke of Suffolk, and very intimate with the inner workings of English politics, who had been sent abroad as Secretary to Morysone in 1550, was still in Brussels with that knight in the summer of 1553. It is more than probable, therefore, that Ascham, being in correspondence with Suffolk, knew beforehand of the forthcoming elevation of Jane to the throne, and, on behalf of the Duke, advised Hoby and Morysone as to what they should say and do when that event took place, and also had an interview with Don Diego to the same end. We may be certain,265 however, that Ascham did not countenance the Catholic side of the question.

This letter from the Commissioners was not written until 15th July, and by the time it reached England the political scene had changed. It damaged Guildford's position seriously by its revelation of the schemes of the Dudleys and their party, who, not content with placing Northumberland's daughter-in-law on the throne, were also seeking to crown that nobleman's youngest son. From certain documents in the Belgian and Viennese Archives it would appear that Diego de Mendoza went so far as to address the Emperor directly on the subject of Guildford's right to the throne, even assuring him that his godson would become a Catholic.

A strong searchlight has been thrown on this hitherto rather obscure passage in the history of this period by the learned Editor of this work, in his interesting volume, *Two Queens and Philip*.233 The author, it is true, had suspected that Northumberland must have had some strong foreign support in his audacious attempt to usurp the throne, ostensibly for Lady Jane, though in reality for his own son, Guildford, but Major Martin Hume's researches in the Spanish Archives have proved beyond a doubt that Charles V was backing him throughout in his perilous undertaking, and this against the interests of his own cousin, Mary Tudor.

The Swiss Reformers, and especially Bocher, doubted the sincerity of Northumberland's Protestantism, and it is not at all improbable that he had promised the Emperor that, should he succeed in placing Guildford Dudley on the throne and Jane as Queen-Consort, he would veer round to the Catholic party and re-establish papal supremacy in England.

The Emperor had sent the Sieurs de Courrières and Renard as Ambassadors to our Court in the last year of Edward VI. Whether they were deceived by Northumberland or were genuinely of the opinion that the chances of Mary's succession were very remote and that Jane's party was infinitely the strongest, we know not, but the Emperor, acting on their advice, backed Northumberland for all he was worth up to the very day that he was captured at Cambridge and conveyed a266 prisoner to London. Bearing these facts in mind, the almost incredible story which we have just related concerning Guildford's attempt to secure the throne for himself becomes intelligible.

On the other hand, Northumberland had apparently done nothing to obtain favour for poor Jane's own Envoys, sent to announce her accession to the Courts of Paris and Vienna, for no sooner had those gentlemen reached the cities in question than they were refused recognition and turned back. The elder Dudley, selfishness incarnate, cared little for the dignity of his daughter-in-law, if only his son might be proclaimed King.

In the Museum at Hastings there is the impression of a hexagonal seal which was to have figured on the State documents of "Queen Jane and King Guildford Dudley." Under an arched crown, between the initials "G. D." (Guildford Dudley)—a striking proof of the extent to which his claims to the Crown were carried—are two escutcheons, one to the left bearing the royal arms of England, lions and fleurs-de-lys, and the other to the right, two animals, probably bears, grappling a ragged staff, the arms of the Dudleys. Properly speaking, according to heraldic rule, the royal arms should be on the right and the family arms on the left. Doubtless the mistake was due to the haste with which this seal was prepared. Under the escutcheons are the words "Ioanna Reg," and on either side the date 1553. The matrix of this seal seems to have been lost; at least, its present whereabouts are unknown.

On the 11th of July the Council wrote afresh to the Commissioners (Hoby and Morysone) telling them of the "signification of our sovereign lord's death," and remarking that, "although the Lady Mary hath been written unto from us (*i.e.* in answer to her letter of the 9th), yet nevertheless we see her not so weigh the matter that if she might she would disturb the state of this realm, having thereunto as yet no manner apparent of help or comfort but only the connivance of a few lords and base people: all others the nobility and gentlemen remaining in their duties to our sovereign lady Queen Jane. And yet, nevertheless, because the conditions of the baser sort of people is understood[267] to be unruly if they be not governed and kept in order, therefore for the meeting with all events, the Duke of Northumberland's grace, accompanied with the Lord Marquis of Northampton, proceedeth with a convenient power into the parts of Norfolk, to keep those countries in stay and obedience, and because the Emperor's ambassadors here remaining shall on this matter of the policy not intermeddle, as it is very likely they will and do dispose themselves, the Lord Cobham and Sir John Mason repaireth to the same ambassadors, to give them notice of the Lady Mary's proceeding against the state of this realm, and to put them in remembrance of the nature of their office, which is not to meddle in these causes of policy,[234] neither directly nor indirectly, and so to charge them to use themselves as they give no occasion of unkindness to be ministered unto them, whereas we would be most sorry, for the friendship, which on our part, we mean to conserve and maintain. And for that grace the ambassadors here shall advertise the others what is said to them.... The xi[th] of July, 1553."

This document was followed, next day, by an official letter to the Commissioners, signed by Jane, and outlining what they were to say to the Emperor as to the foreign policy to be pursued hereafter:—

"Trusty and well-beloved,—We greet you well. It hath pleased God of his providence, by the calling of our most dear cousin of famous memory, King Edward the VIth, out of this life, to our very natural sorrow, that we both by our said cousin's lawful determination in his lifetime, with the assent of the nobility and state of this our realm, and also as his lawful heir and successor in the whole blood royal, are possessed of this our realm of England and Ireland."

Then comes a recommendation of the bearer of the letter, a Mr. Shelley; the confirmation of Hoby's appointment—"the whole number of our ambassadors shall there remain to[268] continue to dwell in the former commission which ye had from our ancestor the King," and an order that Hoby shall make this clear to the Emperor, and assure him that the friendship between England and the Emperor shall be continued as hitherto.

Worry, anxiety, and annoyance soon brought on a relapse of the illness from which Jane had lately suffered. Her pains at last grew so acute that she again fancied the Duchess of Northumberland had poisoned her. Possibly this illness accounts for our hearing so little of her doings during the second, third, and fourth days of her short reign (11th, 12th, 13th of July). "Twice," she writes, "was I poisoned, once in the house of my mother-in-law,[235] and afterwards in the Tower; the venom was so potent that all the skin came off my back." This idea was evidently only the result of the fever, which caused the skin to peel. Trouble had so reduced the poor girl, no doubt, that she fell an easy prey to the fevers so prevalent in and about the Tower, as long as the moat remained uncovered.

On the 11th the Council received a letter from Mary, dated from Kenninghall 9th July, stating she had heard of her brother the King's death, and was surprised that she had not known it sooner, and adding her intention to cause her right and title to be published, and proclaimed accordingly. The letter declared the

Princess aware of the Council's desire to undo her claims, but added that she was willing to grant pardon, and closed with an order to the Council to have her proclaimed in the City of London and other places. The Council's reply was a masterpiece of "bluff." It ran as follows:—

"Madam,—We have received your letters (of) the 9th of this instant, declaring your supposed title ... to the Imperial Crown of this Realm, and all the dominions thereunto belonging. For answer whereof, this is to advertise you, that for as much as our Sovereign Lady, Queen Jane is after the death of our Sovereign Lord Edward the 6th, ... invested and possessed with the just and right title in the Imperial Crown[269] of this Realm, not only by good order of ancient laws of this Realm, but also by our late Sovereign Lord's letters-patent, signed with his own hand, and sealed with the Great Seal of England, in presence of the most part of the nobles, councillors, judges, with divers other grave and sage personages, assenting and subscribing to the same. We must, therefore, of most bound duty and allegiance assent unto her said Grace, and to none other, except we should, which faithful subjects cannot, fall into grievous and unspeakable enormities. Wherefore we can no less do, but for the quiet both of the Realm and you also, to advertise you, that forasmuch as the divorce made between the King of famous memory, Henry VIII and the Lady Katherine, your mother, was necessary to be had, both by the everlasting laws of God, and also by the ecclesiastical laws, and by the most part of the noble and learned universities of Christendom, and confirmed also by the sundry acts of Parliament, remaining yet in their force, and thereby you justly made illegitimate and unheritable to the Crown Imperial of this Realm ... you will, upon just consideration hereof, and of divers other causes lawful to be alleged for the same, and for the just inheritance of the right line and godly order, taken by the late King our Sovereign Lord King Edward the VI, and agreed upon by the nobles and great personages aforesaid, surcease by any pretence, to vex and molest any of our Sovereign Lady Queen Jane her subjects, from their true faith and allegiance unto Her Grace; assuring you, that if you will ... show yourself quiet and obedient, as you ought, you shall find us all and several ready to do you any service that we with duty may.... And thus we bid you most heartily well to fare.

"Your ladyship's friends, showing yourself an obedient subject."

This document was signed by the following members of the Council: "Thomas Canterbury, the Marquis of Winchester, John Bedford, Will. Northampton, Thomas Ely, Chancellor; Northumberland, Henry Suffolk, Henry Arundel, Shrewsbury, Pembroke, Cobham, R. Rich, Huntingdon, Darcy, Cheney, R. Cotton, John Gates, W. Peter, W. Cecill, John Cheeke, John Mason, Edward North, R. Bowes." Of[270] all the signatories of this letter, not more than four, if so many, remained true to Jane to the last!

LADY JANE GREY, BY WYNGARDE

THE EARLIEST ENGRAVED PORTRAIT OF HER, FROM A PICTURE SAID TO BE BY HOLBEIN, NOW LOST

On 12th July, the second day after Jane's entry into the Tower, the Marquis of Winchester brought her unwilling Majesty a curious collection of miscellaneous articles of jewellery, the contents of sundry boxes and caskets, deposited at the Jewel House in the Tower, and which had belonged to Henry's six queens. Jane, despite her poor health, was constrained to examine these things. The caskets contained, amongst other articles, "A fish of gold, being a toothpick. One dewberry of gold. A like pendant, having one great and three little pearls. A newt of white silver" (that is to say, a silver ornament wrought in the form of a lizard or eft). "A tablet of gold with a white sapphire and a blue one, a balas ruby, and a pendant pearl. A tablet of gold hung by a chain with St. John's head, and flat pearls. A tablet with our Lady of Pity, engraved on a blue stone. A pair of beads of white porcelain, with eight gauds of gold, and a tassel of Venice gold. Beads of gold with crymesy (crimson) work. Buttons of gold with crimson work. Six purse hangers of siver and gilt" (these were to hang purses or trinkets to the girdle, like the modern chatelaine). "Five small agates with stars graven on them. Pearls in rounnels of gold between pivots of pearls. Pipes of gold. A pair of bracelets of flaggon chain (pattern), connecting jacinths of orange coloured amethysts.

Many buttons of gold worked with crimson, and in each button set six pearls. Thirty turquoises of little worth. Thirteen table diamonds set in collets of gold. An abiliment set with twelve table diamonds" (these were the borderings of the caps like those of Anne Boleyn, or even of the round hood which was the fashion that succeeded them). "Forty-three damasked gold buttons, and a clock or watch set in damasked gold, tablet fashion," close the list,236 but Winchester affirms that he delivered to Jane, on 12th July, not only these, but the regalia237 and other jewels, together with a supply of cash, books, and even clothes.

271 About this date, too, Lord Guildford Dudley was sent a quantity of the Crown jewels, possibly as an earnest of his future dignity. They certainly cost him dear!

A curious inventory exists at Hatfield, of stuffs delivered to "the Lady Jane Grey, usurper, at the Tower by commandment over and above sundry things already delivered to her by two several warrants." These goods were her own personal property, evidently left by her at Westminster Palace on the occasion of some visit, of which no record now exists. The stay in question must have occurred very shortly before Edward's death, and the things may have been forgotten in the confusion attendant upon his last illness. The inventory is endorsed by Sir Andrew Dudley and Sir Arthur Sturton, deceased, Keeper of the Palace at Westminster, and was made, according to custom, on the day of the King's death, when seals were put on the doors of every apartment in the royal palaces, not to be lifted till the King's burial, after which such articles as belonged to persons in waiting or servants were delivered, after verification, to their various owners. The list of goods and chattels belonging to Lady Jane is a very lengthy one, and we will only make a few quotations, to give a glimpse of the contents of her wardrobe and her minor possessions:—

"Item, a muffler of purple velvet, embroidered with pearls of damask gold garnished with small stones of sundry sorts and tied with white satin.

"Item, a muffler of sable skin with a head of gold with 4 clasps set with five emeralds, four turquoises, six rubies, two diamonds and five pearls, the four feet of the sable being of gold set with turquoises and the head having a tongue made of a ruby.

"Item, a hat of purple velvet embroidered with many pearls.

"Item, a hat of black velvet laced with aglets (tags), enamelled, with a brooch of gold.

"Item, a cap of black velvet, having a fine brooch with a square table ruby with divers pictures enamelled in red, black and green.

"Item, eighteen buttons with rubies.

"Item, eighteen gold buttons.

272 "Item, a helmet of gold with a face, and a helmet upon its head and an ostrich feather.

"Item, three pairs of garters having buckles and pendants of gold.

"Item, one shirt with collar and ruffles of gold.

"Item, three shirts—one of velvet, the other of black silk embroidered with gold, the third of gold stitched with silver and red silk.

"Item, a piece of sable skin.

"Item, two little images of wood, one of Edward VI, and the other of Henry VIII.

"Item, a dog collar wrought with red work with gold bells.

"Item, a picture of Lady of Suffolk in a gold box.

"Item, a picture of Queen Katherine Parr that is lately deceased."

This list also contained some articles which must have belonged to Guildford, for it is not probable that Lady Jane ever possessed "a sword grille of red silk and gold" or "a Turkey bow and a quiver of Turkish arrows," or "a white doublet and hose of silk and velvet." The number of clocks contained in this list is very remarkable:—

"One fair striking clock standing upon a mine of silver; the clock being garnished with silver and gilt, having in the top a crystal, and also garnished with divers counterfeit stones and pearls, the garnishment of the same being broken, and lacking in sundry places.

"One alarum of silver enamelled, standing upon four balls.

"One round striking dial, set in crystal, garnished with metal gilt.

"One round hanging dial, with an alarum closed in crystal.

"One pillar, with a man having a device of astronomy in his hand, and a sphere in the top, all being of metal gilt.

"One alarum of copper garnished with silver, enamelled with divers colours having in the top a box of silver, standing upon a green molehill a flower of silver, the same altar standing upon three pomegranates of silver.

"One little striking clock, within a case of letten, book fashion, engraven with a rose crowned, and *Dieu et Mon Droit*."

273 The articles enumerated were brought to Lady Jane at the Tower, during her imprisonment, after her brief reign was over, and having ascertained their agreement with the Inventory, she signed that document, which was returned, and came into the possession of Cecil, and now lies, as we have said, among the State Papers at Hatfield. The fact that the list contains a reference to articles evidently belonging to Guildford Dudley points to his having accompanied Lady Jane to Court, and shared his wife's apartment. Probably the object of the visit had been to bring Jane under the King's immediate notice, and influence him to name her in his will, as his chosen successor.

It had evidently been decided that the young Queen was not to tarry long in the gloomy palace prison, for some of the documents drawn up during the "nine days" have spaces left blank for the insertion of some other royal residence. Besides, when Jane appointed her brother-in-law, Lord Ambrose Dudley, to be her palace-keeper at Westminster, in lieu of his uncle, Sir Andrew Dudley, one of his first wardrobe orders was for twenty yards of purple velvet, twenty-five of Holland cloth, and thirty-three of coarser lining to make her robes, "against her removal from the Tower."

On the night of 12th July, according to Machyn, "was carried to the Tower iij carts full of all manner of ordnance, as great guns and small, bows, bills, spears, mores-pikes, arnes [harness or armour], arrows, gunpowder, and wetelle [victuals], money, tents, and all manner of ordnance, gun-stones a great number, and a great number of men of arms; and it had been for a great army toward Cambridge;"238 in other words, all these things were provided for the use of a great army, to proceed to Cambridge. These warlike preparations were made none too soon, for on the following morning, 13th July, news reached the Tower that the rival Queen was at Kenninghall, on the borders of Suffolk and Norfolk, and that the men of Norfolk, knights and squires alike, were scurrying in their hundreds along the dusty lanes, to offer Mary their lives and service. In brief, the guilty inmates of the Tower, the would-be rulers of the realm, learnt to their consternation that throughout the length and breadth of the274 kingdom the people were against Queen Jane, and for Queen Mary. The Council was hastily assembled, and it was at once decided that the Lords Robert Dudley and Warwick were too young and inexperienced "for such difficulties as these." The first proposal was, that the Duke of Suffolk should leave the Tower, and take command of the troops; but Queen Jane, alarmed for her own safety, insisted she needed her father, and could not do without him. His age and bad health were also factors in the final decision that Northumberland would, after all, be the best man to send.239 The Duke left Her Majesty in charge of the Council, and swore one of his big oaths that when he came back "Mary should no longer be in England, for he would take care to drive her into France, or——" He took a passionate leave of his son Guildford, holding him in a long and tender embrace, pressing his head in his hands, and kissing him again and again. Did it flash across the father's mind that he might never see his darling son again?

Northumberland ordered the troops he was to command, which were to be raised by the various noblemen adhering to Jane's party, to meet him at Newmarket. He gave a sort of farewell dinner to the Council in the Tower on the 13th, opening the banquet with a threatening speech to his guests. "If you do not keep your oath, or if you turn traitor to Jane," said he, "God shall [will] not acquit you of the sacred and holy oath of allegiance, made freely by you to this virtuous lady, the Queen's Highness, who by your and our enticement is rather of force placed therein [*i.e.* "in the position of Queen"], than by her own seeking and request. But if ye mean deceit, though not herewith but hereafter, God will revenge the same. I can say no more." This was perhaps fortunate, for some of the assembled gentlemen certainly did "mean deceit." The Duke concluded by asking the Council to "wish him no worse speed in his journey than they would have themselves."275 One of the members of that august body replied in the following terms: "My Lord, if ye mistrust any of us in this matter [the forcing Jane to become Queen], Your Grace is far deceived; for which of us can wipe his hands clean thereof? And if we should shrink from you, as one that is culpable [of having forced Jane to assume the crown], which of us can excuse himself as guiltless? Therefore herein your doubt is too far cast." Northumberland was not offended by these ambiguous remarks, and merely added, "I pray God it be so. Let us go to dinner." When this—as we should imagine—rather gloomy banquet was over, Northumberland sent a messenger to Jane at the Tower, and received by his hand his commission as "Lieutenant of the Army." As he passed through the Council Chamber on his way to Durham House for the night, he encountered the Earl of Arundel, "who prayed God to be with His Grace, saying he was sorry it was not his chance to go with him and bear him company, in whose presence he could find in his heart to spend his blood even at his feet; and, taking Thomas Lovel, the Duke's boy, by the hand, he added, 'Farewell, gentle Thomas, with all my heart.' Then the Duke, with the Lord Marquis of Northampton, the Lord Grey, and divers others, took barge and went to Durham Place and to Whitehall, where they mustered their men."240 Next morning, Friday, 14th July, the Duke and his followers rode proudly forth,241 with a train of guns and a body of six hundred men, led by some of the greatest in the land; such as Lord Edward Clinton, the Marquis of Northampton, the Earls of Warwick, Huntingdon, and Westmoreland, the Lords Grey de Wilton, Ambrose and Robert Dudley, Sir John Gates, and a score of others, equally influential, the majority already tried in war. As the glittering troop, armed with the motley collection of weapons brought to the Tower two days before, passed through the city and along Shoreditch, Northumberland noticed that, great as the crowd was, it was sullen, no one greeting the troops and their leaders with anything like276 enthusiasm. "The people," he remarked surlily to Sir John Gates, "press to see us, but no one bids us God speed."

On the day her father-in-law left the Tower, only to return as a condemned prisoner, the Lady Jane—whose occupations from the time of her stormy interview with her mother-in-law up to this point are nowhere recorded, except for her inspection of the Crown jewels—signed a number of letters and documents of considerable importance. She wrote to the Duke of Norfolk, for instance, demanding his allegiance and commanding him to come to her Court as Earl Marshal, and confirming his titles and honours if he proved loyal to her. The original of this letter is in the possession of Mr. Wilson of Yorkshire. The body of the document is in Northumberland's hand, and must have been drafted some days previously, but the signature is Jane's. She next signed a warrant for the appointment of Edward Baynard as Sheriff of Wiltshire in lieu of our old friend, Sir William Sharington, "lately deceased." This curious and little-known document is in the possession of Mrs. Alfred Morrison, and is exceedingly curious. The body of the text is in the hand of a Secretary, but the name is in Lady Jane's handwriting and the signature is an autograph. Curiously enough, on 6th July Queen Mary had made the same appointment: later, she issued a proclamation to the effect that "no document, appointment, payment, or gift of land or money made by Jane Dudley,242 usurper," should be considered valid; but Baynard's nomination, however, held good, as we find from the Pipe Rolls of the County of Wiltshire for 1553. It is strange that Baynard should have been appointed by both the rival Queens, though this may be accounted for by the fact that he is said to have been a Wiltshire man and popular in his neighbourhood.

Bad news reached London that evening, and before Queen Jane retired to rest she knew her fortunes were in jeopardy and she herself rapidly ceasing to be Queen, even in name. Presently a messenger informed the Council that the men of277 Bucks, under Lord Windsor and Sir Edward Hastings, were rising for Queen Mary. Still worse news flew Londonwards on Saturday, the sixth day of Jane's disastrous reign. Queen Mary had been proclaimed at Framlingham and Norwich. Northumberland, perceiving his weakness, had sent to London for fresh troops, and was himself speeding as fast as horse could gallop towards Cambridge, which he reached at midnight.

So complete and rapid was the collapse of Jane's cause that even the most carefully planned precautions taken in her interest ended by serving her foes. Her partisans, for instance, fearing Mary might escape by sea, had ordered six men-of-war to cruise off the east coast, intercept her flight, and bring her back a prisoner. The weather suddenly became so stormy that the vessels were driven into Yarmouth Roads just as a body of men was being levied in that town for Mary's support. The sailors of the squadron, who had landed, bribed with money and strong ale to abandon their ships and join the levy, handed over their vessels to Sir Henry Jerningham, one of the staunchest supporters of the Tudor Princess, who, being thus supplied by her enemies with money, ammunition, and a train of artillery,243 marched forthwith against Northumberland, who was soon fain to fall back towards Cambridge, where he fancied himself safe in Trinity College, with his friends Drs. Sandys, and Parker, and Dr. Bill. As a matter of fact, his enemies, declared and secret, were as numerous and formidable in Cambridge as elsewhere; but during the momentary lull which ensued he flattered himself with false hopes, and plied the Council with demands for money and men, many of his followers having deserted him at Bury to join the enemy. Yet all the time Cecil244 was betraying him at every point. Nothing can278 exceed the cunning and treachery he displayed—so deep and cruel that one cannot but feel some pity for Northumberland, notwithstanding his many crimes and faults. When Cecil was forced to order his horsemen to take the field against Mary, he contrived to have them ambushed and attacked, and thus rendered quite useless to the Duke and harmless to his opponents. The Council informed Northumberland of the miscarriage of Cecil's men; but the letter fell into the hands of Mary, who inquired of Roger Alford, Cecil's confidential servant in attendance on her, why her master, whom she evidently knew to be playing traitor to Jane, had sent troops against her. Alford, so he says, "being privy to the matter before (hand), laughed, and told her [Mary] the matter,"—

that Cecil had never intended his men should do any harm to her cause, but had simply sent them as a "blind" to make Northumberland think the Council was doing all in its power to send him reinforcements, and thus spur him forward to his ruin. Under such circumstances, the Duke's position soon became desperate. "He would sit moodily in his chair lost in thought, then starting up, would pace the room, muttering to himself."

Dr. Sandys and several of his friends in Cambridge asked him to sup with them on the Saturday night, and spoke in a very friendly manner about Lady Jane. He shook his head, rose from the table, and seated himself in a vacant chair; remained there a long time in silence, and in deep depression; and, when his entertainers bade him good-night, took their hands in his, and begged them severally to pray for him, "for he was in great distress."

Sandys had been appointed to preach before the Duke on the following morning (Sunday, 16th July). Before retiring279 to rest, the learned Doctor, intending to choose a text, took up a Bible, which fell open at the first chapter of Joshua, the verse that met his eye being, "All that Thou commandest we will do, and wheresoever Thou sendest, so will we go." "Upon which text he preached the next day with such discretion that he [Northumberland] got not such full advantage of him as he had hoped." On the Monday the Duke went with his men to Bury. Their "feet marched forward, but their minds moved backwards"; in other words, they were but a half-hearted set, and one by one they deserted all through the day, hiding behind hedges and in ditches, till when evening came, the Duke, heart-sore and heavy, rode back to Cambridge almost alone, "with more sad thoughts than valiant soldiers about hym." Realising that all was lost, he bethought him of a dramatic, or rather theatrical, trick to save himself. He conceived the idea that if he went to London and fell at the Queen's feet, she would welcome and forgive him. Had she not pardoned many rebels? and was he worse than any of these?

Presently, considerably cheered by his own but erroneous reflections, he betook himself, accompanied by the Mayor and Dr. Sandys, to the market cross, where the crowd greeted him in silence, "more believing the grief in his eyes, when they let down tears, than the joy professed by his hands, when he threw up his cap," full of gold coins, into their midst. This show of tardy loyalty—produced by the arrival of the news of Mary's growing power—having failed in its effect, Slegg, the Sergeant-at-Arms, accused him of treason, and brought him back a prisoner to King's College.245

On the morning of the 21st of July, according to Machyn, the Earl of Arundel, as treacherous a man as any in that nest of vipers, who, a week before, had knelt before Northumberland and sworn to shed his blood for him and for Queen Jane, came rapping at his door before he was up. The Duke, huddling on a cloak, went out to him, and seeing him look so280 threatening, fell on his knees, praying him to be good to him and merciful. "For the love of God, my lord," said he, "consider that I have done nothing but by consent of the Council." "My Lord Duke," quoth the Earl of Arundel, "I am hither sent by the Queen's Majesty, and in her name I arrest you." Whereupon the Duke, rising, said, "I obey; but I beseech you, my Lord Arundel, have mercy towards me, knowing the case as it is." "My good lord," quoth the Earl, "you should have sought for mercy sooner. I must do according to the commands that have been given to me," and upon this he took the Duke's sword and committed him in charge of the guard and other gentlemen that stood by. The miserable Duke went to breakfast with not much appetite, looking as white as a ghost and feeling most wretchedly ill. Towards evening, under an escort of eight hundred men, he left Cambridge with Sir John Gates and Dr. Sandys—both prisoners—still wearing his red cloak wrapped about him and suffering agonies from gout in the feet. As night fell, it began to rain; and down long country roads, under the lowering clouds, went the weird procession of rough troopers on horseback, footmen with their pikes, and in their midst the tall, gaunt, grim figure of the Duke, his soaked and tattered red cloak clinging about his bent shoulders. He is said to have spent the night in a barn, to be moved on to London the next day, entering the city early in the morning, 25th July, just as the shopkeepers were taking down their shutters. His plight must have been pitiable, for in the streets men, recognising him, jeered at him as a "Traitor," threw mud on his red cloak and scowled at him, calling him Somerset's murderer, and so scaring him that he was almost thankful to reach the Tower and its comparative safety. He had gone forth in proud security, certain of success, sure he was about to punish his enemies and reward his friends. He came back, cold and miserable, knowing he had sacrificed his youngest son to his ambition; that the fate of his other children and of the unhappy Jane hung in the balance; and that the only friend left him in the world was his faithful wife, who was at that moment on her knees to Queen Mary, pleading for mercy and receiving none, her husband's offence being deemed too great for pardon. That night surely, in the solitude of his281 prison in the Beauchamp Tower,246 the Duke flung himself on his knees, and prayed the long-neglected prayers of his childhood, the *Pater Noster* that was now said in English, and the *Ave Maria* that had gone out of fashion altogether!

Meanwhile, on Sunday the 16th (the seventh day of Queen Jane's reign) there was no rest throughout the whole length and breadth of England; everywhere the people were rising for Queen Mary. In the streets of the metropolis there was great cheering and rioting, even bloodshed. Bonfires were lighted in the streets, and crowds of rough men and loose women whirled round the lurid flames shouting, "Queen Mary! Queen Mary!" In the churches, the claims of the rival Queens and rival Creeds occupied the preachers. At Paul's Cross, Bishop Ridley preached against Queen Mary247 and the Scarlet Woman, and in favour of Jane and the Reformation. At St. Bartholomew's, a Catholic priest told his congregation to kneel down and thank God that the victory was with Queen Mary; while at Amersham, in Buckinghamshire, John Knox thundered forth in favour of Queen Jane—but all his eloquence, and that of her other defenders, was in vain: the people would have Queen Mary, and Queen Mary only. Late this Sunday night a curious incident occurred. The Tower had been shut up for the night, when suddenly Jane, dreading perhaps some unexpected rising, ordered the outer gates to be locked and the keys carried up248 to her chamber.282 Then the guards were informed that one of the Royal Seals was missing; and Jane had the lately closed gates unbarred, to send a body of Archers of the Guard after the Marquis of Winchester, who had left the precincts about seven o'clock for his house in Broad Street. They found him in bed, forced him to rise and dress himself, and brought him back about midnight to the Tower, where, it is said, he had to explain matters to Lady Jane, who connected him with the loss of the Seal. The whole incident is somewhat mysterious. Did the poor little Queen fancy Winchester was contemplating some move like that of Somerset when he practically assumed the Kingship at Hampton Court? Winchester undoubtedly bore Jane no particular good-will, and the interview, if it occurred, was probably somewhat stormy.

The eighth day of the reign, Monday the 17th, opened with a violent scene in the early morning between the Duchesses of Northumberland and Suffolk, who wrangled over Guildford and his Kingship. Poor Jane was most miserable: her eyes were red with weeping, and she looked more dead than alive as she endeavoured to calm her belligerent Grace of Northumberland and reason with her own headstrong and domineering parent. By this time everything and everybody in the Tower were at sixes and sevens. No one seemed to know what to do or say. In the midst of it all came bad news from the country, where the peasants, notwithstanding the threats of their lords and masters, were refusing to take arms against Mary. Trouble283 was drawing unpleasantly near.249 On the previous day (Sunday, 16th) some ten thousand of Mary's adherents, many of them county notables, had assembled at Lord Paget's house at Drayton, and marched to Westminster Palace, which they sacked of its arms and ammunition, "for the better furnishing of themselves in the defence of the Queen's Majesty's person and her title." Paget, whose house was this army's headquarters, was at this time, be it observed, amongst the party in the Tower and ostensibly loyal to Jane! Meanwhile, the people, at one with that section of the nobles who would have none of poor Jane, were shouting, in London and all over the land, "God save Queen Mary!"—whilst poor Jane's name was never heard except to be scoffed at. The "nine days' Queen" was now nothing but "a mock."

On Tuesday (the 18th) it was patent that the drama—or rather, tragi-comedy—was drawing to a close. Of all Queen Jane's Council only two men, Cranmer and her own father, remained true to her; and the former left that afternoon for Lambeth and Croydon. Winchester, Arundel, Pembroke, Paget, and Shrewsbury, to save their necks, had by this time definitely decided to betray the cause of the girl whom they had helped to put on the throne—and of these men, two, Arundel and Pembroke, only nine days before, had knelt before her at Sion House, protesting their loyalty and belief in her right to the crown! This day, however, Jane signed an order to Sir John Brydges and Sir Nicholas Poyntz that those officers should raise forces, "with the same to repair with all possible spead towardes Buckinghamshire, for the repression and subdewing of certain tumultes and rebellions moved there, against us and our Crowne by certain seditious men." This order is now to be seen in the British Museum, Harleian MSS, No. 416, f. 30.

On Wednesday, 19th July, the short reign ended—"Jane the Quene" became "*Jana non Regina.*" Yet still there was a flicker of Queendom, for that morning, information being received from the Lord Lieutenant of Essex, Lord Rich,[284] that the Earl of Oxford, who was then in Essex, had thrown in his forces with Mary, Sir John Cheke, Queen Jane's Secretary of State, wrote a letter, to which the treacherous Lords of the Council affixed their signatures, requiring Oxford "like a noble man to remain in that promise and stedfastness to our sovereign Lady Queen Jane, as ye shall find us ready and firm with all our force to maintain the same: which neither with honour, nor with safety, nor yet with duty, we may now forsake." This morning, too, commenced the betrayal, when Winchester, the Lord Treasurer, the Lord Privy Seal, Arundel, Shrewsbury, Pembroke, Sir Thomas Cheney, Sir John Mason, and Sir John Cheke waited on Suffolk, as the principal leader in Northumberland's absence, and desired leave to depart from the Tower so as to confer with the French Ambassador about the foreign mercenaries[250] who were to come over and aid Northumberland[251]—at that moment awaiting arrest at Cambridge! Their zeal evidently touched Suffolk, who granted them leave to depart. No sooner had they left the grim fortress behind them than they proceeded straight to Baynard's Castle,[252] where, having sent for the Lord Mayor, they[285] were presently joined by that dignitary, with the Recorder and some of the Aldermen. The proceedings of this improvised Council opened with an attack on Northumberland's ambition and scheming, delivered by Arundel,[253] and then Pembroke drew his sword, and cried out, "If the arguments of my Lord Arundel do not persuade you, this sword shall make Mary queen, or I will die in her quarrel." This speech was much applauded, and Mary's proclamation was signed by all present. The conspirators then had Mary publicly proclaimed Queen at the Cross in Cheapside by four trumpeters and two heralds in their gorgeous coats. This took place about five or six in the evening—the very hour at which Jane's accession had been published nine days earlier! The proclamation in the Chepe concluded, the Councillors proceeded to St. Paul's for evensong and the singing of the *Te Deum*, whilst Cecil,[254] Arundel, and Paget were sent to pay the Council's homage to Mary. Now that the people had absolutely nothing to fear from the broken power of Jane, they gave wild vent to their feelings. The bells of the city churches, swung with a right good will, sounded a welcome to the coming reign; bonfires blazed in every street. One of those attacks of spontaneous feverish enthusiasm which seize nations from time to time, even in these prosaic days, took hold of London.[286] Tables were dragged into the thoroughfares, that all might sit down and drink to the health of her Catholic Majesty. Money was dispensed freely by the rich; and "the number of cappes that weare throwne up at the proclamacion wear not to be tould." Most enthusiastic and excited of all was my Lord Pembroke, who filled and refilled his cap with small coin to be scrambled for by the mob. He could afford to be liberal: he knew Mary would reward him well for his share in her proclamation. London was a very pandemonium that night. "For my tyme," says a contemporary news-letter,[255] "I never saw the lyke and by the reporte of otheres the lyke was never seen.... I saw myself money was thrown out at windows for joy. The bonefires were without number; and what with shouting and crying of the people, and ringing of bells,[256] there could no one man hear what another said; besides banketyng [banqueting] and skipping the street for joy."[257]

Archbishop Cranmer is said to have been the last of Jane's Council, then resident in the Tower, to leave it, which he did in the course of 19th July, after a sad leave-taking with Lady Jane. His position in the

Janeite conspiracy has been severely criticised by more than one historian, and by none more than by Lord Macaulay. He had been instrumental in aiding Northumberland to overthrow Somerset, probably because he disliked the latter's Calvinistic tendencies, and regarded him as a stumbling-block in the way of his proceedings for the establishment of a more moderate and orthodox Church of England. After the death of Somerset, the Archbishop[287] became one of Northumberland's chief supporters, and, as Macaulay points out, covered himself with lasting obloquy by his attempt to seduce an innocent girl into a treasonable career which was to lead to her ruin. In her eyes he was something more than a political Councillor—an Apostle of the Lord—and his advice no doubt told with her above that of any one else. The next time they met, Cranmer was a prisoner on his way to Guildhall,[258] whither she too was tramping on foot to hear her doom, approved of by most of the men who had been her chief Councillors, read out before the multitude of Queen Mary's friends and supporters.

There was little joy and much grief within the Tower. Presently a messenger to Suffolk from Baynard's Castle came to tell him that the nobles there assembled required him to deliver up the Tower, and proceed to the Castle to sign Mary's proclamation. They also ordered Lady Jane to resign the title of Queen. Instantly Suffolk abandoned the unequal struggle; leaving the Lieutenant in charge of the Tower, he went out, telling his men to leave their weapons behind them. He himself announced Mary's accession on Tower Hill, and then, going to Baynard's Castle, he signed her proclamation. This done, the wretched man returned to the Tower to tell his daughter that her Queenship was a thing of the past. Jane, meanwhile, having promised Edward Underhill, the famous "Hot Gospeller," then on duty in the Tower, that she would act as godmother that day to his infant son, who was to be christened Guildford, and being herself too ill to attend the baptism, commissioned Lady Throckmorton to go in her stead. Lady Throckmorton left the royal apartments and proceeded to St. John's Chapel (some[288] say All Hallows', Barking), leaving Jane surrounded by the insignia of royalty—the cloth of estate, the throne, and all that marked her position as Queen. When her ladyship returned, these had all been removed; for *the* Queen of England had not yet arrived in London, and her subject, "Jane, the usurper," no longer sat on the throne. During the absence of Lady Throckmorton Suffolk had rushed back to his daughter. He found her alone in the Council Chamber, seated, forlorn, under her canopy of State. "Come down from that, my child," said he; "that is no place for you." Then he gently told her all; and gladly did poor Jane rise and quit her hateful office. For a moment father and daughter stood weeping, locked in each other's arms, in the centre of the deserted hall, through the open windows of which, borne on the summer air, came the exulting shouts of "Long live Queen Mary!"

Then, after a pause, Jane Grey spoke four simple words, sublime in their pathos. "Can I go home?" she asked ingenuously. God help her! what a world of innocence was in that little sentence, "Can I go home?" Alack! alas! poor little victim of so much ambition and such damnable intrigue, there is no more earthly home for thee!

CHAPTER XVIII
THE LAST DAYS OF NORTHUMBERLAND

All through the night of Queen Mary's proclamation, Jane Grey was abandoned in the great fortress to the care of her personal attendants; and bitter must have been her distress, as she realised the cruel plight to which the mad ambitions of others had brought her. Everything helped to heighten her terror—the changed attitude of the guards, and other Tower officials, who a few brief hours before had treated her with obsequious deference, and who now marked their loyalty to Mary by an ostentatious display of scorn for the fallen majesty of the "Nine Days' Queen"; the tears of her women, their whispered talk, the brooding and ominous silence of the palace, broken only by the distant shouts of revellers, who acclaimed the triumph of her successful rival, all combined to increase the nervous and hysterical agitation into which the poor girl's recent illness had already thrown her. Her mother, the Duchess, compelled by circumstances beyond her control, most probably, had left the Tower, and hurried back to Sheen, after having obtained Queen Mary's pardon for her husband. The Duchess of Northumberland, white with horror, and trembling with anxiety for her wretched husband and children, had likewise departed with her attendants up the river to Sion: so that of all Jane's Court none remained to help and comfort, except her faithful women and servants. Suffolk's movements at this time are not quite clearly recorded. That he retired to Sheen immediately after Mary's proclamation, appears certain; and also that, on the 27th July, he was arrested and committed to the Tower, to be released at the intercession of the Duchess his wife, on his own bail, on the 31st of the same290 month.259 Yet a contemporary letter, dated August 11th, says: "The Duke of Suffolk is (as his owne men report) in prison, and at this present in suche case as no man judgeth he can live." An explanation of these conflicting statements may be, that the Duke, when officially released, was for some days too ill to leave the Tower.

There is reason to believe that Lady Jane remained in the State apartments till late in the evening of the 19th July, when she was transferred to the rooms above the Deputy-Lieutenant's, recently vacated by the Duchess of Somerset. The Deputy-Lieutenant of this period was Thomas Brydges or Bridges, brother of Sir John Brydges, Lieutenant of the Tower. This last gentleman attended Jane on the scaffold, in discharge of his duty; but Thomas Brydges figures a good deal in the narrative of the last months of Jane's life. There has been much dispute as to the exact situation of the rooms in the Tower in which the innocent prisoner was confined, and the absolute identity of her keeper. But it is now pretty clearly established that the first period of her detention was not spent, as so often stated, in the Brick Tower, but in the modernised house of the Deputy-Lieutenant, which stands next door to the Lieutenant's or the King's House. Later—we do not know the precise date of her removal—she was lodged in a house, also on the Green, adjacent to the Lieutenant's dwelling, and which then belonged to the Gentleman Gaoler, Mr. Nathaniel Partridge.260 Earlier historians have denied the existence of Partridge, and even Harris Nicholas thought he was Queen Mary's goldsmith; but his identity is now conclusively proved, and he is admitted to have been a well-known figure in and about the Tower at this period. He died in February 1587, and is buried in St. Peter-ad-Vincula in the same vault as his illustrious guest. During her incarceration, Jane was allowed to walk in the Queen's Garden, and "on the hill within the Tower precincts."261

291 Several persons attended on Lady Jane in the Tower, among them Elizabeth Tylney,262 "a beautiful young woman of good birth," Lady Throckmorton, wife of Sir Nicholas Throckmorton, and "Mrs. Ellen." Some light has been thrown upon the identity of the last-named lady by Lady Philippa de Clifford, Lady Jane's cousin, whose curious account of her unhappy kinswoman's last hours was published in Brussels in 1660; from this we learn that "Mrs. Ellen, an elderly woman," was Lady Jane's nurse. There were also two waiting-maids, and a lad, in the suite of the Princess, as we glean from *The Chronicles of Queen Jane and Queen Mary*. Thus she was no "solitary prisoner," but served by gentlewomen, and in comparative comfort. We must, therefore, dismiss the old idea that Lady Jane Grey was ever relegated to a "dungeon deep," to pine in darkness and in loneliness. That she was not fed on bread and water is proved by the Privy Council records, from which we learn that ninety-five shillings a week was allowed for her maintenance whilst in captivity, and twenty shillings for each of her attendants, six in number—a very handsome allowance in those days, and equivalent, in modern coinage, to about fifteen times the amount.

It must be clearly understood that Lady Jane was never even formally arrested, as were Henry VIII's Queens. No armed guard took her captive, after the reading of a solemn warrant. She was simply detained in the Tower,263 partly as a hostage for the good behaviour of her father, and partly to prevent her being once more the tool of those who might attempt to place her on the throne, and make her the figure-head of a politico-religious party. Northumberland and his followers had claimed honours for her which rightly belonged to Mary,292 and when Mary gained the upper hand, "Jane the usurper" had, *ipso facto*, to be kept in retirement.

There is no trace of any independent movement on Guildford's part, during the nine days of his wife's reign, except to assist his mother in pushing his "claim" to the throne. Either he sulked, because Jane had refused to make him King Consort on the day following her entry into the Tower; or else Northumberland advised him to keep out of the way as much as possible, so as to escape the blame of having taken an active part in the usurped administration. Be this as it may, we have no news of his doings, from the first day or two of the nine days' reign, until after its termination, when he was parted from his wife, and sent to the Beauchamp Tower, whither, on the 25th July, his brothers, Lord Warwick and Lord Ambrose Dudley, followed him, to be joined the next day by Lord Robert Dudley.

Jane's peaceful seclusion was of very short duration. On the day following her deposition (20th July), the Marquis of Winchester, Lord High Treasurer,264 came to ask for the return of the Crown Jewels and other articles delivered to her on the second day of her Queenship. A parcel or so was missing, it would seem, and Winchester, when he commanded Jane to restore the Crown Jewels, desired she should also make good the alleged deficiency. Astonished at this demand, she declared she knew nothing of the missing articles, but agreed293 to give up all the money she had in her possession, and on 25th July she consigned to the Treasury an extraordinary assortment of coins—angels of the reign of Edward VI, gold coronation medals of Henry VIII and Edward VI, some shillings and half shillings, as well as some deteriorated coinage of Edward VI, of no value. The whole of her available assets did not amount to more than £541, 13s. 2d. The missing valuables, it would appear, had not been returned two months later, or else Queen Mary had not been informed of their receipt, for on 20th September she writes to Winchester requesting him immediately to order Lady Jane to give up the jewels and "stuffs," which had been delivered to her "on July 12th," and which were still missing. The inventory of these mislaid "stuffs" includes a most curious assortment of odds and ends, which one would think it hardly worth Queen Mary's while to reclaim. First we have a large leather box, marked with Henry VIII's broad arrow, containing "two old shaving cloths, and thirteen pairs of old leather gloves, some of them worn." Another "square coffer" missing, and described as being covered with "Naples fustian," contained a collection of old Catholic prayer books, rosaries, and other odds and ends, which had probably remained among the Tower stores since Katherine of Aragon had last kept court there, and which were, needless to say, of no use to Lady Jane Grey! The first article in this collection is the half of a broken ring of gold, perchance some forgotten love-token. Then comes "a book of prayers, covered with purple velvet, and garnished with gold. A *primer* [or Catholic prayer book] in English. Three old halfpence in silver, seven little halfpence and farthings. Item, sixteenpence, two farthings and two halfpence. A purse of leather with eighteen strange coins of silver. A ring of gold with a death's head. Three French crowns, one broken in two. Item, a girdle of gold thread. A pair of twitchers [tweezers] of silver. A pair of knives in a case of black silk. Two books covered with leather. Item, a little square box of gold and silver with a pair of shears [scissors] and divers shreds of satin. A piece of white paper containing a pattern of gold damask." The third coffer was "Queen's jewels," and contained chains of gold studded with rosettes of pearl and other valuables. The fate of this curious294 collection of gewgaws is unknown. About the same time, Winchester made an exploration of the contents of Guildford's pockets, which resulted in the discovery that he possessed exactly £32, 8s., in the debased coinage of Edward's reign. Miss Strickland, in mentioning this incident, says: "Thus the prisoners were left entirely without the means of bribing their gaolers." This is not the case, for Lady Jane appears to have made a will (which may still be in existence, though for the time being it has disappeared) in which she left certain jewels, clocks, and valuables to her sisters, her women, and her servants, and, strange to relate, a gold cup or chalice to Queen Mary. Wherefore we may conclude she was allowed to retain the articles brought her from Westminster Palace, some of which served, no doubt, to decorate her apartment in the Tower. We possess no record, unfortunately, of the sort of food provided for the prisoner and her husband; we can only guess at its nature by consulting the bills of fare, still extant, provided for the Duchess of Somerset during her imprisonment in the Tower: from the fact of the prices of the various dishes being appended, we may conclude that the wealthier political prisoners were allowed to pay for their meals. Her Grace's bill for "dynner" was as follows:—

"Mutton stewed with potage	viijd.
Beef boiled	viijd.
Veale, rost	xd."

"Suppr" consisted of:—

"Slyced beef	vjd.
Mutton rost	viijd.
Bred	xd.
Bere	viijd.
Wyne	viijd."

"Wood, coills (coals) and candull by the weke," cost "xxd."

In the meantime, the Council had retired to Westminster, whence, as is generally believed, it sent Northumberland orders to disband his army and await Mary's pleasure before returning to London; the herald who bore this order being commissioned to proclaim, in certain places *en route*, that if the Duke refused to submit he should be arrested as a traitor. Before this, as we have said (on the 19th instant), the Earl of[295] Arundel and Lord Paget had been dispatched to offer the Council's homage to Mary, bearing with them the following letter—a good specimen of the barefaced hypocrisy practised on Lady Jane. "Our bounden duties most humbly remembered to your most excellent majesty, it may like the same to understand, that we your most humble, faithful, and obedient subjects, having always (God we take to witness) remained your Highness's true and humble subjects in our hearts, ever since the death of our late sovereign Lord and Master, your Highness's brother, whom God pardon; and seeing hitherto no possibility to utter our determination herein, without great destructions and bloodshed, both of ourselves and others till this time, have this day proclaimed in your city of London, your majesty to be our true natural sovereign, liege Lady and Queen, most humbly beseeching your Majesty to pardon and remit our former infirmities, and most graciously to accept our meaning which have been ever to serve your Highness truly, and it shall remain with all our powers and forces to the effusion of our blood. These bearers, our very good lords, the Earl of Arundel and Lord Paget, can and be ready now particularly to declare, to whom it may please your excellent Majesty, to give firm credence; and thus we do and shall daily pray to Almighty God for the preservation of your most royal person long to reign ... from your Majesty's city of London this ... (19th) day of July, the first year of your most prosperous reign." This letter needs no comment; Paget's treachery towards his late patron is particularly diabolical. He seems to have behaved throughout with Mephistophelian cunning and falseness. There is something absolutely Satanic in the hypocritical manner in which this letter asserts that the Council had hitherto had no opportunity to express its "determination" in the matter of Mary's right to the Crown—this in the hope of leading Mary to think it had been acting under compulsion! If Jane's friends *had* succeeded in establishing her on the throne, and Mary had been killed or driven out of the country, these Councillors, the latter's "most humble, faithful, and obedient subjects," would, no doubt, have rallied about her rival— provided always it paid them so to do; Mary being victorious, they saved their necks and kept their positions by embracing her cause.[296] Like the Vicar of Bray, no matter who was King, or what were the social and religious conditions of the country, these gentlemen were resolved to cling to their offices, and accommodate their opinions and actions to those of the party in power.

It was about this time that Mary received another abject document of the same sort—the already quoted "Submission" or *apologia* of Cecil, whose conduct throughout had been as tortuous as that of any of Eugene Sue's Jesuits.

A previous chapter has touched upon the singular intrigues of the Commissioners in Brussels, who conveyed Diego Mendoza's acclamation of Guildford, as King of England, to the Council. We must now relate the sequel. On the 20th July, these gentlemen followed up their letter of the 15th, by another, stating that they had vainly endeavoured to obtain an interview with the Emperor, who was exasperated by what had happened in England, and had even refused to receive Mr. Shelley, the bearer of the Council's letter of the 12th July. His Imperial Majesty held that Jane's assumption of the Crown would lead to trouble with France; Mary Stuart, Queen of Scots, at this time consort of the Dauphin of France, having a claim to the English throne prior to that of Lady Jane. He does not seem to have approved—or else he feigned disapproval—of Mary Tudor's succession, but desired the matter should be settled by Parliament in accordance with the will of the English nation. Within a few days, probably, the Commissioners, hearing of Jane's downfall, and realising their own danger, promptly submitted—like the Council at home—to Mary, and enclosed the letter brought by Shelley in one of their own dated 29th July to the Council at Westminster, "for that it hath pleased God to call my Lady Mary her grace to the State and possession of the realm, according to the King's majesty her father's last will and the laws of the realm." Not quite sure, however, as to what has taken place, they ask the Council to let them have all news to date, and desire to know "her maj^{tys} pleasure what we should do, wherunto we shall conform ourselves most willingly according to our most bounden duty.... Sir Philip Hoby, etc., to the Council."265 In spite of their forethought, Hoby297 and Morysone were recalled by an order of 5th August, their place at Brussels being taken by Dr. Wootton, Bishop of Norwich; and the fact that in the said order they are described as "*Mr.*" Hoby and "*Mr.*" Morysone suggests that they were in dire disgrace. Most likely their letter about Guildford rankled in Mary's mind! Their attempt to shelter themselves behind a show of loyalty, at all events, was not as successful as that of the Council at home, but they richly deserved any punishment their duplicity received; for, like the rest of the Janeite conspirators, they supported her cause as long as it seemed likely to profit them, and abandoned it, as if it were plague-stricken, directly the tables were turned.

None the less, the Emperor Charles V (who dropped the cause of Northumberland the moment he perceived that Mary had won the day), wishing "to show his great love for that Queen his most dear cousin," requested the Governess of the Netherlands, Mary, Queen of Hungary, to entertain the above-named gentlemen, as well as the newly dispatched Ambassador, Bishop Wootton of Norwich, "to such a banquet as they had never partaken of before, for such carvings, and sumptuous dishes, and frequent changing of wines." The Emperor's Embassy, which included the Sieur de Courrières, already mentioned, Simon Renard, and several other noblemen, was amongst the first of the numerous Envoys sent from all parts of Europe to congratulate the Queen on her victory, and, as if to emphasise his affectionate interest in the Royal cousin whose cause he had so lately abandoned in favour of that of her chief enemy, the negotiations for the marriage of the Queen of England with the young widowed Prince, afterwards King Philip of Spain, were pushed forward with the utmost alacrity.

The mere idea of a union with her very Catholic cousin inflamed the imagination of the old maid sovereign with so ardent a passion as to absorb her whole being, and to bring about the sad catastrophe of her tragic life. She now "could think and speak of Philip, and of Philip only." The most affectionate solicitude was displayed on the part of Queen Mary for the welfare and comfort of her future Consort, so that even a special clause was included, allowing him to land at the most convenient port he should choose, for he was "apt298 to be very sick on the sea, and most eager to be on land again."266

In some way or other Lady Jane must have been kept informed of the current events and gossip of the day. Some one probably gave her an account of Elizabeth's ride through London on 31st July, from Somerset House to Wanstead, where she joined her sister. The astute Princess had at first hesitated as to what course she should pursue, but at last, seeing Jane's position was hopeless, she made up her mind to side with her sister, and pass through the City and Aldgate with a numerous escort. The royal prisoner must have heard of the gay decorations of the streets, brilliant with flags, and streamers, and splendid tapestries, and how wild was the popular enthusiasm for Queen Mary.

The foredoomed prisoners must have received a rude shock on 1st August, when the monotony of their existence was suddenly broken by the appearance of the Constable of the Tower, Sir John Gage, and his officials, who repaired to them severally, and read out to them the solemn indictments made against them in the Queen's name. These indictments—the originals of which will be found in the Baga de Secretis, pouch xxiii., at the Public Record Office—were dated 1st August, and had been previously read out and endorsed at Guildhall, with all due ceremonial, earlier in the day, in the presence of Thomas White, Lord Mayor of London; Thomas, Duke of Norfolk, Earl Marshal; the Earls of Derby and Bath; Richard Morgan, Chief Justice of Common Pleas; and other noblemen and gentlemen, not all of whom were, however, actually present, but represented by deputies. The first document, divested of its legal verbosity, declares Lady Jane Grey, Guildford Dudley her husband, Cranmer, Archbishop of Canterbury, and the Lords Ambrose and Henry Dudley, guilty of treason, for having seized the Tower of London,267299 on 11th July; having sought to depose their rightful sovereign, Queen Mary; and having "acknowledged and proclaimed Jane Dudley, wife of Guildford Dudley, Esq., of the parish of St. Martin's by Charing Cross, Queen of England." The address is curious, as it indicates that the town residence of the unfortunate couple was still Durham House, the Duke of Northumberland's palace in the Strand.

The second indictment concerns John, Duke of Northumberland, William, Marquis of Northampton, Francis, Earl of Huntingdon, and others, for having, "between the 10th and the 17th July, first of Mary, levied men at Cambridge to march against the Queen."

Yet a third indictment is of even greater historical interest, and charges Thomas Cranmer, Archbishop of Canterbury, as "a false traitor to the Queen," with providing arms for twenty men, under Barnaby Boylot, Walter Morford, and Robert Durant of Westminster, and dispatching them to Cambridge, in aid of John, Duke of Northumberland. This proves that the original indictment against Cranmer did not charge him with heresy, but merely as a political offender. Undoubtedly, as Macaulay points out, by making himself the accomplice of Northumberland in endeavouring to overcome the scruples of so amiable a young woman as Lady Jane Grey, and seducing her into treason, Cranmer committed an act of most unjustifiable wickedness.

A little later, in the early twilight of 3rd August, the flickering of hurrying lights, and the boom of cannon—"the loudest that ever was heard"—could not fail to apprise the State prisoners in the Tower that some unusual event was happening, and that the Queen and Princess Elizabeth had entered its precincts, to prepare for the obsequies of Edward VI. From her windows Lady Jane noted the flaring torches,300 moving hither and thither, in unwonted chambers and courtyards, and heard the tramp of feet, the heavy tread of the guards, the changing of sentinels, and the coming and going of the Ambassadors and courtiers hurrying to pay their homage to the new Sovereign—amongst them, doubtless, most of those very men who had solemnly sworn allegiance to herself!

The Protestant funeral service of Edward VI took place on 8th August, the King's body having been removed, on the preceding evening, from Greenwich to Whitehall. A great number of children in surplices were gathered together to attend his obsequies in the Abbey, and this gave a touch of poetry to a ceremony described by Noailles as "a very shabby one, badly attended, without any lights burning, and no official invitations sent to the Ambassadors." Archbishop Cranmer, who had organised the function, read the plain English service, from the Book of Common Prayer. Round about the coffin were a great number of standard-bearers with their standards, conspicuous among them being those of his mother, Queen Jane Seymour, and of his grandmother, Lady Seymour, as well as one with a white dragon on a red background, and yet another with a very large white greyhound, the emblem of the house of Tudor. All the banners were bowed as the little coffin was lowered into the vault in Henry VII's Chapel, and the wands were broken and cast in upon the lid. Cranmer gave a heavy sigh as he watched it pass into the gloom, knowing full well that with that little corpse passed away all his hopes and power—that the vengeance of the Queen whose mother he had outraged was near at hand. He never officiated again at any State function; his day was over! Lady Jane heard of this particular service with considerable pleasure, for it was celebrated in accordance with her own religious views; but the details of another ceremony in suffrage of King Edward's soul, according to the ritual and doctrine of the Church of Rome, celebrated in the Queen's presence in the Royal Chapel of the White Tower, must have pained her not a little. 268301 Mary, in residence in the Tower at this time, had organised this special Requiem Mass with all permissible pomp and ceremony, and we may take it for granted that Jane saw from her windows a good deal of the coming and going of royal personages, officials, and servants, consequent upon so elaborate a function. Pained indeed must have been the Reforming Princess to learn that Dr. George Day, the very Catholic Bishop of Chichester, had been selected to preach before Her Majesty the panegyric of her very Protestant brother!

We must now turn our attention to the Duke of Northumberland. Soon after entering the Beauchamp Tower on 25th July, he collapsed, and had to take to his bed. The fates were not, indeed, propitious to Northumberland in this respect, for his health broke down when he most needed all his physical as well as moral strength to help him through his tremendous task. Even as far back as 1550, John ab Ulmis, in a letter to Bullinger, mentioned "the Earl of Warwick's very dangerous illness." He would seem to have never quite recovered from this attack, for in the following August he was very ill, and again, late in September 1552, he wrote Cecil that he was "fevrish and unable to sleep." In January 1553, Warwick told Petre or Cecil that he was much alarmed about himself, and feared he was "going to be very ill." Throughout the year 1553 he was observed to look pale, and to walk with difficulty, but his indomitable will held him up, and he was able to do the work of a dozen men, for his energy was as admirable as its object was detestable. Northumberland is scarcely a commendable character, but there is none the less a pathos in the fact that his health was giving way under the terrible strain that crushed him. He does not deserve much sympathy, but it is impossible not to pity him in his extremity, abandoned by every one, a doomed prisoner, his last card played and lost. To his insane ambition he had sacrificed his youngest and best-loved son, and the young creature the lad had so recently married, and now an unnatural death faced him in stark horror. What nights he must have spent, hopeless and helpless, alone in that prison on every gate of which the great302 Italian might have written, *Lasciate ogni speranza voi ch'entrate*. He knew the Queen hated him with the intense and unforgiving hatred of a Spaniard. Had he not sided against her mother, and framed the pitiless and insulting documents he had forced his helpless daughter-in-law to sign, stigmatising Mary and Elizabeth as "bastards"? Reflecting on these, and a hundred other offences, he realised his case was hopeless. So bitterly did the Queen loathe him, as a matter of fact, that she actually requested Comendone, the Papal Envoy, to put off his departure for a few days, so as to witness the execution of her chief foe, and give a personal account of it to the Pope!

The trial for treason of John Dudley, Duke of Northumberland, took place on August 18th in Westminster Hall. The Marquis of Northampton, and the Earl of Warwick, Dudley's son, were arraigned at the same time. Thomas, Duke of Norfolk, sat as High Steward of England; this was, indeed, one of his last official appearances. He died in the following year (on 24th August) at Kenninghall. Several of those men who sat in Jane's Council, and had only saved their necks by addressing their hasty submission to Mary, figured at this trial. Northumberland was very obsequious to his judges, and "protesting his faith and obedience to the Queen's Majesty, whom he confessed grievously to have offended, said that he meant not to speak anything in defence of himself." He then demanded of the court, first "whether a man doing an act by the authority of the Prince and Council, and by warrant of the Great Seal,269 and doing nothing without the303 same, may be charged with treason for anything which he might do by warrant thereof?" and secondly, "whether any such persons as were equally culpable in that crime, and those by whose letters and commandments he was directed in all his doings, might be his judges, or pass upon him his death?" The answer returned was that the Great Seal to which he appealed was not that of the lawful Queen of the realm, but was the seal of a "usurper," and as such had no authority; also, that though some of his judges might be equally guilty with himself, they had no attainder against them, and therefore were as fit to try him as any one else, provided the sovereign gave permission. Finding they were bent on his destruction, the unhappy man pleaded guilty, and besought the Duke of Norfolk to obtain the Queen's pardon for him. Following suit, the Marquis of Northampton and the Earl of Warwick also pleaded guilty; the former urged, that "after the beginning of these tumults he had forborne the execution of any public office, and that all the while he, intent to hunting and other sports, did not partake in the conspiracy," whilst Warwick begged the Queen would have his debts paid out of his confiscated goods. They were both sentenced to death, "to be had to the place that they came from, and from thence to be drawn through London unto Tyburn, and there to be hanged, and then to be cut down, and their bowels to be burnt, and their heads to be set on London Bridge and other places."270 When he heard this horrible sentence of death, Northumberland asked that, as a nobleman, he might be beheaded, and "begged that his children might be kindly treated." He had the grace also to confess that Jane, so far from desiring regal honours, was only induced to accept the Crown "by enticement and force"—which confirms what we have said of her parent's ill-treatment of her. The Duke also requested that a "learned divine" might be sent to him; and that he might have an interview with four members of the Council, "for the discovery (*i.e.* revelation) of some things which304 might concern the State."271 What these mysterious "things" may have been, is now unknown. Lingard says Gardiner and another member of the Council visited Northumberland in prison, and that the former interceded for him with the Queen; but there is no documentary evidence as to the purport of the State secrets the Duke had promised to divulge.

On the following day, 19th August, four of the chief of those who had ridden out of London with Northumberland against Mary—Sir Andrew Dudley,272 Sir John Gates, Sir Harry Gates, and Sir Thomas Palmer—were sentenced to death in Westminster Hall.

Next day Northumberland made a public renunciation of the Protestant religion, either in the Church of St. Peter-ad-Vincula, or else in the chapel in the White Tower; the former place is more generally accepted. Some forty of the principal citizens of London were present; and the Marquis of Northampton, Sir Andrew Dudley, Sir Henry Gates, and Sir Thomas Palmer, were also reconciled to the Latin Church at the same time. The ex-conspirators knelt during Mass, saying the *Confiteor* after the celebrant, who was probably Gardiner. When the Mass was concluded, they one after another asked each other forgiveness, kneeling as they did so. After this they all went in front of the altar, where, on bended knees, they confessed to Gardiner, that "they were the same men in the faith, according as they had confessed to him before, and that they all would die in the Catholic faith." Having received the Eucharist, the Duke turned to the congregation and said, "Truly, good people, I profess here before you all that I have received the sacrament, according to the true Catholic faith; and the plague that is upon this realm, and upon us now, is, that we have erred from the faith these sixteen years, and this I protest unto you all, from the bottom of my heart." Northampton, Andrew Dudley, Gates, and Palmer made the same statement, and they were all conducted back to their respective prisons.273 There can305 be no doubt, that, if this ceremony took place in St. Peter's, Lady Jane must have seen, from the windows of the Deputy-Lieutenant's house, the procession of her father-in-law and his followers on their way to hear Mass, and her grief on learning that they had abandoned Protestantism was, as we learn from her own lips, intense.

The evening of the 21st August, Northumberland was informed by the Lieutenant of the Tower that he was to die next day, whereupon he wrote the following abject letter to his brother-in-law and captor, the Earl of Arundel:—

"Hon[ble] lord, and in this my distress my especial refuge, most woeful was the news I received this evening by Mr. Lieutenant, that I must prepare myself against to-morrow to receive my deadly stroke. Alas, my good lord, is my crime so heinous as no redemption but my blood can wash away the spots thereof? An old proverb there is, and that most true, that a living dog is better than a dead lion. Oh! that it would please her good grace to give me life, yea, the life of a dog, if I might but live and kiss her feet, and spend both life and all in her honourable services, as I have the best part already, under her worthy brother, and most glorious father. Oh! that her mercy were such, as she would consider how little profit my dead and dismembered body can bring her; but how great and glorious an honor it will be in all posterity when the report shall be that so gracious and mighty a queen, had granted life to so miserable and penitent an object. Your hon[ble] usage and promise to me since these my troubles, have made me bold to challenge this kindness at your hands. Pardon me if I have done amiss therein, and spare not, I pray, your bended knees for me in this distress. The God of Heaven, it may be, will requite it one day, on you or yours; and, if my life be lengthened by your mediation, and my good lord chancellor's (to whom I have also sent my blurred letters), I will ever owe it to you, to be spent at your hon[ble] feet. Oh! my good lord, remember how sweet life is, and how bitter the contrary. Spare not your speech and pains; for God, I hope, hath not shut out all hopes of comfort from me in that gracious, princely and womanly heart; but that, as the doleful news of death hath wounded to death, both my soule and body,306 so the comfortable news of life, shall be a new resurrection to my woeful heart. But if no remedy can be found, either by imprisonment, confiscation, banishment, and the like, I can say no more, but, God grant me patience to endure, and a heart to forgive the whole world.

"Once your fellow, and loving companion, but now worthy of no name but wretchedness and misery.

J. D."274

It must have cost the haughty Northumberland dear, to write so humble a supplication; but he was a man of strong domestic affections, and realised that if he were spared, his children and brothers might also be saved. But Mary's hate, thoroughly Spanish in its intensity, was implacable; and if, as some historians seem to think, the prisoner hoped to obtain his freedom by returning to the religion of his ancestors,275 he made a terrible mistake. The Queen may have rejoiced that the chances of his eternal salvation were enhanced, according to her views, by his conversion, but none the less did the outraged sovereign and woman claim the head of her arch-enemy, and worst detractor.

Machyn tells us of a strange incident, in connection with the Duke's execution, which tends to prove it was to have taken place on the 21st August, and to have been accomplished by the common hangman. Says the chronicler in question: "The xxj of August was, by viij of the clock in the morning, on the Tower hill about XM (*i.e.* "about ten thousand") men and women for to have seen the execution of the Duke of Northumberland, for the scaffold was made ready and sand and straw was brought, and all the men that belong to the Tower,276 as Hoxton, Shoreditch, Bow,307 Ratclyff, Limehouse, Saint Katherines, and the waiters [attendants] of the Tower, and the guard, and sheriff's officers, and every man stand in order with their halbards, and lanes made (*i.e.* barriers placed so as to admit of the free passages of the troops and officials) and the hangman was there, and suddenly they were commanded to depart."277 The fact that the hangman was present seems to denote that the order, changing the sentence from hanging and disembowelling, to decapitation, had not yet been made. Northumberland had given way at his trial to an unusual display of emotional terror, as the barbarous details of the sort of death to which he was condemned were read out to him, and probably efforts were therefore made, and not in vain, to spare him so atrocious an ordeal and substitute the more merciful and dignified death by the axe. Maybe it was this which occasioned the postponement of the grim ceremony.

According to a MS, now in the Brussels Archives, entitled, *Les événements en Angleterre*, 1553–4, the Duke of Northumberland was allowed to take a pathetic leave of his youngest son, "whom he pressed again and again to his breast, sighing and weeping a deluge of tears, as he kissed him for the last time."

The executions of Northumberland, Sir John Gates, and Sir Thomas Palmer, took place on 22nd August, on Tower Hill. The prisoners were first delivered over to the Sheriffs of London by the Lieutenant of the Tower. As soon as the Duke was confronted with Sir John Gates, he exclaimed, "Sir John, God have mercy on us, for this day shall end both our lives, and I pray you forgive me whatsoever I have offended, and I forgive you with all my heart. Although you and your counsel was a308 great occasion thereof (*i.e.* "of my troubles"). "Well," returned Gates, "I forgive you all, as I would be forgiven, and yet you and your authority was the original cause of it, altogether, but the Lord pardon you, and I pray you forgive me." They then bowed to each other, and the Duke, who was garbed in "swan-coloured (*i.e.* grey) damask," went forward to the scaffold, looking dejected. Bishop Heath, crucifix in hand, walked with him. On the way, when they were outside the Tower gates, a woman rushed forward, and waving in his face a handkerchief, which had been dipped in the blood of Somerset, cried out, "Behold, the blood which thou did cause to be unjustly shed, does now apparently begin to revenge itself on thee!" The guards dragged her away, and the condemned proceeded on their way to Tower Hill. On the scaffold, the Duke took off his outer cloak, and leaning over the rail, on the east side, made his farewell speech to the people, of which several versions exist. He admitted that he had been "an evil liver"; begged the Queen's forgiveness, kneeling; alluded to his accomplices, and would not name them; regretted his religious errors; professed his attachment to the Catholic Church, asking the Bishop of Worcester, Heath, to bear witness to his sincerity, to which the prelate answered "Yea"; and finally, asking all to pray for him, he knelt down, and recited the *De Profundis*, after which he made the sign of the cross, in the sawdust of the scaffold, and stooped and kissed it. Then, rising, he bared his neck, tied the handkerchief over his eyes, and, turning to the executioner, said he was ready. The fellow, who was lame in one leg, took good aim— and in a flash, John Dudley, Duke of Northumberland, was no more. Sir John Gates would not have his eyes bandaged, and died a fearful death, after three blows from the axe. Palmer was beheaded at one stroke. Both made lengthy speeches, in which they styled themselves staunch Catholics. It is said that when the horrible scene was over, children came and dipped cloths in Northumberland's blood, to be preserved as a memorial of him, and this despite his unpopularity.278

309 A pathetic incident occurred in connection with the burial of the Duke's remains. One of his servants, John Cock, sufficiently attached to his memory to have a care for the whereabouts of his last resting place, waited upon Queen Mary and prayed her to command that his master's head should be given to him. "In God's name," answered Her Majesty, somewhat irate, "take the whole body as well, and give your lord proper burial." Acting on this permission, Cock took Northumberland's corpse and laid it to rest in the Church of St. Peter-ad-Vincula, beside the coffin of the Duke of Somerset!

CHAPTER XIX
THE TRIAL OF QUEEN JANE

The writer of the *Chronicle of Queen Jane and Queen Mary* relates that he dined with Queen Jane in "Partridge's House," on 27th August, and incidentally mentions her evident resentment at her father-in-law's apostacy. This chronicler appears to have been a resident in the Tower, and a friend of Partridge. He writes: "I dined at Partridge's house with my Lady Jane being there present, she sitting at the board's end, Brydges, his wife, Sarah, my lady's gentlewoman and her man, she commanding Brydges and me to put on our caps [*sic*]. Amongst our communications at this dinner, this was to be noted. After she had once or twice drunk to me and bade me heartily welcome, saith she: 'The Queen's Majesty is a merciful Princess; I beseech God she may long continue, and send His bountiful grace upon her.'

"After that we fell to discussing matters of religion, and she asked, 'What he was that preached at Paul's on Sunday before———' [a blank], and so it was told her. 'I pray you,' quoth she, 'have they Mass in London?'

"'Yea, forsooth,' quoth I, 'in some places.'

"'It may be so,' quoth she. 'It is not so strange as the sudden conversion of the late Duke, for who would have thought he would have so done?'

"It was answered her, 'Perchance he thereby hoped to have had his pardon.'

"'Pardon,' quoth she, 'Woe worth him. He hath brought me and our stock in most miserable calamity, and misery by this exceeding ambition. But for the answering that he hoped for life by turning, though others be of the same opinion, I utterly am not, for what man is there living, I pray you, although311 he had been innocent, that would hope of life in that case—being in the field against the Queen, in person as general, and after his taking, so hated and evil spoken of by the Commons, and at his coming into prison, so wondered at, as the like was never heard by any man's time? Who was judge that he should hope for pardon, whose life was odious to all men? But what will ye more? Like as his life was wicked and full of dissimulation, so was his end thereafter. I pray God I, nor no friend of mine, die so. Should I, who am young and in the flower of my years, forsake my faith for love of life? Nay, God forbid. Much more he should not, whose fatal course, though he had lived his just number of years, could not have long continued. But life was sweet, it appeared, so he might have lived, you will say, he did not care how. Indeed, the reason is good, for he that would have lived in chains to have had his life, belike would leave no other means attempted. But God be merciful to us, for He sayeth, 'Whoso denieth Him before man, He will not know him in His Father's Kingdom.'

"With this and much other talk, the dinner passed away, which ended, I thanked her Ladyship that she would vouchsafe to accept me in her company, and she thanked me likewise, and said I was welcome. She thanked Brydges also for bringing me to dinner. 'Madam,' said he, 'we are all somewhat bold, not knowing that your Ladyship dined before, until we found your Ladyship there.'"

A little later, that is, at the end of September and in October, Lady Jane's hopes of release may have risen, for Mary had returned from St. James's Palace to the Tower, for the Coronation. There is no evidence that she ever came into personal contact with Lady Jane Grey after the friendly visit to Newhall in the summer of 1552. If so interesting an event had taken place, there would surely be some trace of it; some account, however brief, of the broken words poor Jane's trembling lips uttered, when she, the Queen-usurping, and Mary, the Queen-Regnant, stood face to face. But since there is no contemporary mention of such a meeting, we must conclude it never occurred, even at this time, when Jane was awaiting an uncertain fate in one corner of the Tower, while Mary was receiving the homage of the hypocrite Councillors in its State chambers.

312 A wave of unusual heat swept over England during the summer of 1553, accompanied by storms of extreme violence. Jane must have felt the sultriness in her prison, and have gladly accepted the refreshing walks in the Queen's garden, which not only brought her amid the last roses of summer,279 but into

contact with the busy life of the Palace-fortress, so that she must have seen many of the preparations for the forthcoming Coronation. It may well have occurred to her that, had fate been less cruel, all this coming and going might have been in her honour, and she, instead of the triumphant Mary, might have gone forth to Westminster, the first Protestant Queen of England. And the Coronation ceremony itself—surely some gossip told her all about that? How stately was the procession of 30th September, in which nearly all the erstwhile ardently Protestant Privy Council of King Edward, now staunch Papists every one, surrounded the most Catholic Mary, garbed in their official bravery, and proclaiming themselves more orthodox than her Papistical Majesty herself; Lord Russell with his big beaded rosary at his waist—that rosary, which on a famous occasion, hearing Mary might very likely order his share of the Church lands to be handed back to the monks, he cast, with a fierce oath, upon the fire! They must have told the Lady Jane how fair and gracious Elizabeth looked in her golden chariot lined with crimson, her robes of pale blue velvet threaded with silver; how Anne of Cleves scintillated with jewels, and how sixty grand dames, in ruby velvet and ermine, with coronets on their heads, rode in the gorgeous procession to Westminster. They must have told her, too, how the charity children, who had sung Calvinistic hymns a week or so ago, now tunefully invoked the blessings of the Saints upon their Catholic Sovereign; how the French Ambassador, Noailles, rode near to the famous Renard, the sly fox who represented the Emperor, and contributed to bring about Jane's death; how my Lady of Sussex carried the Queen's crown and the Lord Mayor her sceptre; how the people thought the old Duke of Norfolk looked much changed since he had last appeared in his official robes; how my Lord Edward Hastings had been made Master of the Horse, and313 led the Queen's milk-white palfrey; how the Protestant Mrs. Bacon had obtained Cecil's pardon, and how Mrs. Barnett, Sir Thomas More's granddaughter, helped to robe the Queen; how Gog and Magog had condescended to leave Guildhall and go to the Tower gates, where they saluted the Queen, and how Gog's head had nearly wobbled off his gigantic shoulders; how three thousand yeomen, in the apple green and white of the House of Tudor, and three hundred Beefeaters from the Tower, in scarlet and black, had added a brilliant touch to the sumptuous procession; how there were so many giants in the wayside pageantry, along the route from the City to Westminster, that people talked about it as a weird contrast, since the Queen was of such low stature as to be almost a dwarf; how among these giants was a colossal angel ten feet high, all clothed in gold foil, sent by the Florentine merchants to grace a triumphal arch in Fenchurch Street; and how, in conclusion, Noailles, true Frenchman as he was, had waxed excited over the splendours of the Queen's jewels, and annoyed because Elizabeth walked next to her! And the scene in the Abbey next day, surely Lady Jane heard all about that?—how Gardiner, fresh from the Tower, crowned the Queen—which was deemed an ugly omen, for both Canterbury and York were in prison, and no King of this land had ever yet been crowned by a mere Bishop! They must have told the young prisoner how brilliantly the banquet went off; how Dymoke, hereditary champion of England, rode into the Hall, armed *cap-à-pie*, and championed the Queen's right; how, no one taking up the challenge, the Queen drank to him; how the old Duke of Norfolk, in true mediæval fashion, rode into the Hall, too, and ushered in the first course of the elaborate meal; how Anne of Cleves, weighed down with heavy pearls, rubies and emeralds, sat next Elizabeth, who had precedence of everybody after the Queen; and how Heywood, the dramatist, had returned from exile to superintend the revels and masques. All that holiday, poor Jane's ears must have ached with the boom of cannon,280 and the pealing of bells, and the shouts of the guards and servants, as they sang and banqueted and drank, and lighted a big bonfire on Tower Hill. Probably the gossips314 told her too of the scandals, the tales of petty intrigues, quarrels, and heart-burnings, the little shames and mortal sicknesses, which the Muse of History has disdained to record, but which were of greater interest, one fancies, to the fair prisoner, than the broader effects of the gorgeous pageant which boded so little good for her.

Jane's parents and friends, were buoyed up with the hope that soon after her Coronation, Mary would liberate her young cousin, and her husband; and the Queen, her detractors to the contrary, did make a strong effort to save Lady Jane Grey and Guildford. When, either late in July or in August 1553—very soon after Jane's fall—Renard, the Imperial Ambassador, had an audience with the Queen (probably at Newhall or Wanstead), and opened the question as to what was to become of the little usurper, the Queen answered, "she never could be induced to have her executed, because three days before she left Sion House, she had deemed herself to be the victim of intrigues." Neither, said she, was Jane the daughter-in-law of Northumberland, because she had been validly contracted to another person; and had taken no part in the Duke's enterprise, and was "innocent." The wily Renard, who had formerly backed Jane's party, but now wished to destroy her, answered that very probably the contract of marriage had been invented as an excuse, and that she must at least be kept a prisoner, as her liberation would give rise to a great deal of trouble and endanger the Realm, and the Catholic religion. The Queen's answer was, that Lady Jane would not be liberated, without every necessary precaution having been taken to avoid all difficulties. Upon this speech being reported to the Emperor, he reiterated his advice—given in a letter of 20th July—that *all* who were implicated in Northumberland's plot should be put to death.281

315 Noailles, also, spoke to Her Majesty about Lady Jane's position, and she repeated that she "intended to spare her." "After all," said she, "the marriage with Guildford is invalid, since she was already contracted to a youth in the employ of the Bishop of Winchester"—*ung serviteur de l'Evêque de Wincestre*. Was Hertford ever in Dr. Gardiner's employ? Even after she had received the Emperor's despatch, crying for vengeance on all the participants in the late usurpation, Mary wrote, on 29th August, to Dr. Wotton, our Ambassador to France, "that she would see Jane was kept safe, and that before giving her liberty, she would see that she was innocuous"; but on 19th September, the Imperial Ambassadors wrote rather jubilantly that at last the Queen is determined to execute "the five sons of Dudley and Jane of Suffolk." There was still hope, however, for on 5th November, Renard writes that being at supper with the Venetian Ambassador, he heard it said that "the four sons of Northumberland, were to be executed, but that Robert might be pardoned, and that he thought Jane, too, would not be executed." This was as it should be, for Robert Dudley was of all Northumberland's sons, the least guilty, his share in the conspiracy being a very light one. We may add that in a letter preserved in the Corsini Library at Rome, Cardinal Pole says he has lately heard that Queen Mary was desirous of saving "Lady Jane Suffolk," as he calls her. There is not a tittle of evidence that Mary at any time gave it to be understood, either to Lady Jane or to others, that she would be pardoned if she embraced316 the Roman Catholic religion. Religion had little or nothing to do with the matter; the charge against Jane was, that she had usurped the throne—treason—and treason to the Queen was a purely secular offence. The Emperor's desire for Jane's death, was actuated by a fear that if she were set at liberty, she might once more be used as an instrument against Mary's legitimate pretensions, since the late King had named her his successor in his "Devise." The reason why the Council shared the Emperor's opinion, and had urged Mary to sign Lady Jane's death-warrant was, that it was anxious to show its whole-hearted zeal for Mary, and entirely dissociate itself from Jane's claims. Let it not be forgotten by those who would blame our severe judgment of the Council's behaviour, that the very men who now urged the Queen to destroy Jane282 and her husband, and who attended Masses with the utmost unction, had not only been staunch Protestants a few months previously, under Edward VI, but Janeites of the hottest during the first two or three days of Jane's brief reign. Beset on all sides, Mary Tudor yielded at last, and, when the sentence had been passed, reluctantly signed the death-warrant.

Before that, however, a Writ of *Habeas Corpus* was issued on the evening of 11th November, commanding John Gage, Constable of the Tower, "to bring up [*i.e.* to Guildhall, two days later, for their trial] the bodies of the accused, to wit, Thomas, Archbishop of Canterbury, Jane Dudley, Guildford Dudley, Ambrose and Henry Dudley." The document bore the signatures of Thomas White, Mayor, and Thomas, Duke of Norfolk.

On 13th November 1553, Jane Grey, Guildford Dudley, Thomas Cranmer, Archbishop of Canterbury, and the Lords Ambrose and Henry Dudley, were arraigned at Guildhall for the offences cited in the official indictment already mentioned. The accused left the Tower on foot early in the day, in the company of Sir Thomas Brydges. Lady Jane was attended by her women, and together with her companions[317] in misfortune, was escorted through the thronged streets by four hundred halberdiers. She was dressed in a black cloth gown, the cape lined and edged with velvet. Her coif was of black velvet made like a hood, after the French fashion; a book bound in black velvet—probably it was a Bible or prayer book, hung by a chain from her girdle. She held another open in her hand, on the pages of which she constantly kept her eyes fixed. Her two women, also dressed in black, walked behind her. Cranmer led the procession, walking between two gentlemen, and immediately behind, the Gentleman-Chief Warder, who bore the axe; Guildford, in a black velvet suit slashed with white satin, followed his wife, and with him were the two Lords Ambrose and Henry Dudley, though separated from him by officials and guards. Florio, an Italian writer, who witnessed Jane's trial, declares her behaviour to have been most dignified. Even the ordeal of passing on foot through the densely-crowded streets did not affect her composure. Within Guildhall there was a great array of lords, prominent among them the old Duke of Norfolk, who after his long and enforced absence from official life, once more enjoyed the privilege of sitting on the Bench as High Steward and Earl Marshal. His aged eyes had mirrored, not only the State trials of two previous Queens of England, Anne Boleyn and Katherine Howard, but also the bloody death of the first-named, whilst his ears had heard the fire crackling round Anne Askew.

On entering Guildhall, the prisoners and their attendants and guards were conducted by an usher with the usual ceremony, to the upper part of the fine old hall, where Lady Jane, owing to her royal rank, was granted the privilege of a chair draped with scarlet cloth, and a footstool; her women stood beside her. Cranmer was placed, according to regulation, in a railed-off pew or box by himself, which separated him by a light barrier from the Lords Guildford, Ambrose and Henry Dudley. The "innocent usurper," although naturally awed by the stately dignity of the scene, may have sought among the many faces present those of not a few she had known all her brief life, and who had even caressed her in her childhood, or been obsequious to her in her ominous Queendom. There sat the aged head of the house of Howard;[318] then came the Earls of Derby, Bath, and Hastings; Sir Richard Morgan, Chief Justice of the Common Pleas,[283] who sat with the other Judges and men of law in their furred robes of office; Nicholas Hare, Master of the Rolls; a little further on, the Lord Mayor and Sheriffs, in their crimson satins and velvets, and their costly sables and glistening chains; then, a crowd of noblemen and gentlemen and officials, filling up nearly the whole of the space at the top of the hall, the body of which was reserved for privileged persons, whilst the lower part nearest the entrance was given over to the mob, with difficulty kept in order by the halberdiers and other guards. The sacred emblems of the ancient Faith, which had been cast out under Edward VI, were restored by this time; and before a small altar, on which stood a crucifix, and six golden candlesticks, the Lord Mayor's Chaplain opened proceedings, whilst all knelt, with the "*Veni, Sancte Spiritus*," and other prayers[319] in Latin. The reading of the indictments followed, and after a pause between each, the prisoners were arraigned to plead guilty or otherwise; but Cranmer, crying out in a loud voice, "Not Guilty!" the other prisoners also pleaded "Not Guilty!" As the counts of the indictment were matters of general knowledge, no witnesses were brought forward on either side, nor were the prisoners cross-examined, nor was any defence made. A jury, consisting of citizens of Middlesex, was empanelled and sworn. After an absence of about twenty minutes they returned, giving as their verdict that the "sufficient and probable evidence" was in favour of the Queen's Grace, and that they therefore returned a verdict of guilty. On this, Archbishop Cranmer, standing up, reversed his previous plea, and admitted his offence—an example which was speedily followed by the other prisoners, who one and all pleaded "Guilty!" Then sentence was pronounced by Chief Justice Morgan, whose voice is said to have trembled considerably, especially as he came to that fearful portion of it, in which Lady Jane was condemned to be burnt alive, or beheaded, "as the Queen shall please." The luckless victim heard her doom with sublime meekness and dignity. Cranmer and Guildford were condemned to be hanged at Tyburn, but a pardon was extended to the Lords Ambrose and Henry Dudley. Then, after the recitation of the *De Profundis*, the Court rose,[284][320] the prisoners were ceremoniously re-conducted to the door of the hall, and escorted back to the Tower, in much the same order as that in which they had come thence— but the axe was reversed; a sign of condemnation which deeply moved the populace, especially with pity for young Dudley and his consort. How weary must have been that tramp back to the fortress, especially to one so young, and in such frail health, as the unfortunate Lady Jane! To Guildford Dudley, too, the journey must have been exceeding painful, for he was in the full vigour of early youth; and the terrible words of the sentence presented to his imagination that awful final scene with which, like most men of his time, he was but too familiar. Cranmer must long since have realised that his days were numbered; but he was as yet mercifully spared the knowledge of the gruesome nature of the end in store for him.

There is, however, no indication that Jane and her husband were treated with any greater severity than hitherto, and Mary, even after the condemnation, was certainly still unwilling to put her cousin to death. She might, in fact, have been saved even then from capital punishment, at all events, if not from imprisonment, if the Wyatt rebellion and the Duke of Suffolk's indiscreet behaviour had not given colour to the opinion entertained by the Emperor and the Council, that Jane's freedom and very existence were a menace to Mary's safety, and compelled the unwilling sovereign to inflict the utmost penalty of the law.

In December, Guildford and his brother Robert were321 "allowed the liberty of the leads" of the Bell Tower: which most likely means that they were permitted to walk on the terrace-like space on the ballium wall between the Bell and the Beauchamp Tower. Cranmer and Ridley—because they had been "evill of their bodies for want of ayre"—shared the right of walking in the Queen's Garden with Lady Jane, and Ridley even dined with the Lieutenant; but it is unlikely that either he or Cranmer were allowed converse with Jane Grey, whose spiritual adviser, we know, was Dr. Feckenham—not Abbot of Westminster at this time, as generally stated, but Dean of St. Paul's,285—whom the Queen had expressly delegated to attend on her unfortunate cousin, in the hope of converting her to the Catholic faith.

Towards the end of the year 1553, Lady Jane is said to have written that coarsely violent epistle to Dr. Harding, once her tutor and her father's chaplain, which will be found in Foxe's *Acts and Monuments*, vol. iii., p. 27. Harding was a most unblushing turncoat; a Protestant and leading Reformer under Edward VI, under Mary—when his old patron's power was broken—his Popish opinions were as extreme as his Protestantism had been fierce. According to some historians, this letter is wrongly attributed to Lady Jane, and certainly its wording, of a vulgar polemic type, has nothing in common with the Christian forbearance and piety of her undisputed compositions. It is difficult to believe Jane Grey can have used such expressions as "thou deformed imp of the Devil," "sink of sin," "white-livered milksop," and even worse, hurled at Harding by the writer of this virulent epistle, more likely to have been the production of Hales, that stalwart hater of "Rome," than of the gentlest of princesses.

Christmas must have been a dismal season for the poor prisoners, whose hopes of pardon were failing, and who realised that the New Year about to open would be their last on earth. Jane's thoughts flew back, in the long dull evenings, to the merry scenes of her Yuletide at Tylsey, two years previous, and to the cheery games and sports at her father's mansion at Sheen, only twelve short months ago! And beautiful Bradgate with its lovely park, the scenes of her childhood,322 her happy lessons with Aylmer, all must have come back to the lonely captive. Before the New Year was a week old, stirring events were happening in the great world beyond the Tower walls. The Queen's early popularity was already on the wane. Her obstinate determination to marry Philip of Spain had sore offended her people, who, in the Midland counties, began to rise openly against the "Spanish match." The Duke of Suffolk, thanks to his wife's intercession, and his own zeal in proclaiming Mary, had been set free after three days' imprisonment, and was residing at Sheen. Bethinking herself that he would make a good leader of her troops against the rebels, Mary sent for him to take command.286 The Queen's messenger reached Sheen on 25th January 1554, and summoned the Duke to Court. His answer was, "Marry, I was coming to her Grace. Ye may see, I am booted and spurred, ready to ride, and I will but break my fast and go." He then gave the messenger a present and some refreshment, and himself departed, accompanied by his brothers, the Lords John and Leonard Grey,287—but instead of going to the Queen in London, he galloped with some fifty followers into Leicestershire and Warwickshire, and made an attempt to rouse the population into open revolt against the Queen's marriage. That he "proclaimed Jane in every town he passed through" is not true. He swore he had never swerved from his loyalty to Mary, and it seems certain that he told the Mayor of Leicester the Queen was "the mercifullest prince that ever reigned." He rebelled against the Spanish marriage and against that only. The people of the Midlands, however, notwithstanding his bribes, did not rally to him to any extent—his own men deserted him. The Earl of Huntingdon took the field against him, and after a defeat near Coventry, he had to fly for his life. He reached his own estate of Ashley, and threw himself on the mercy of Underwood, his park-keeper, who saved him, for a few days, by hiding him in a hollow tree in the park, where, according to Pollino, he was nearly starved to death. One of his brothers, who had managed to escape with him, was hidden under a pile of grass or hay. At last, thanks to Underwood's treachery and to the noise made323 by a dog which persisted in barking at the foot of the tree where the unhappy Duke was concealed, the two brothers were delivered up to Warner, Mayor of Coventry, who handed them over to the Earl of Huntingdon.288 They were brought to London, and reached the Tower on 6th February,289 towards the conclusion of the Wyatt rebellion. As he passed through London the Duke looked, we are told, more dead than alive, "pale as a ghost and shivering."

QUEEN MARY AT THE PERIOD OF HER MARRIAGE

FROM THE PAINTING BY ANTONIO MOR IN THE PRADO MUSEUM

Some mystery surrounds the motives of Suffolk's misguided action. He does not seem to have intended, as has been frequently but wrongly represented, to reconstruct a party in favour of his daughter, Lady Jane.290 Perhaps, after all, he was sincerely incensed at the Spanish match, fearing it would undo all the work of the Reformation, to which he was honestly attached. It is presumable, too, that a conspiracy existed to place Princess Elizabeth on the throne,291 which, Suffolk may have hoped, would lead to the release324 of his daughter and son-in-law. The result, however, was entirely opposite. The knowledge of this movement, combined with Wyatt's rebellion, enabled the Spanish party to force Mary's hand and oblige her to put Lady Jane and her young husband to death.292 Mary affixed her signature to the "Nine Days' Queen's" death-warrant on the very day which saw Suffolk led a prisoner into the Tower.

The terror and anxiety with which Jane received the news of her father's arrest and imprisonment may be better imagined than described. Did she ever see him again? There is no trace of such an interview, but we possess the MS. of a letter she wrote him on the fly-leaf of a prayer book. She was certainly very much attached to her father, but it is significant that she never attempted to see her mother, nor wrote, nor even alluded to her. And whereas the petitions of the wives of the Dudleys—including, by the way, that of Amy Robsart, wife of Lord Robert Dudley—to see their husbands in the Tower, are still extant, and were readily granted—no document exists to prove that the Duchess of Suffolk ever made any attempt to visit either her daughter or her son-in-law in their prison. Perhaps she was otherwise and more agreeably engaged!

There was a great commotion and consternation in the325 Tower during the Wyatt rebellion, when London presented a spectacle not unlike that of Paris during certain of the greatest outbursts of the Reign of Terror. Lady Jane and the other State prisoners, most of whom had attendants, who, after due ransacking of their persons, were allowed to pass in and out of the Tower and its wards, were well acquainted with the details of that extraordinary attempt on the part of a youth of only twenty-three summers, not to overthrow the legitimate sovereign indeed, but to prevent her marriage with Philip of Spain, soon to be called King of Naples. The Queen's courage in risking her person in defence of her rights had won the hearts of the people, opposed though they were to the Spanish alliance, and the Wyatt crusade was, in every sense, a useless and a foolish one. Never, however, since the tumultuous days of Jack Cade had London been so disturbed as during the early months of the year 1554. On 7th February Wyatt and his men were as near the Tower as Southwark, where they sacked the shops and destroyed Bishop Gardiner's library, so that they stood "knee deep among the tattered leaves of his precious volumes." Later in the day, when the rioting had got as far as Charing Cross, so great and shrill was the noise of the shouts of men and of the cries of frightened women and children, "that it was heard to the top of the White Tower; and also the great shot was well discerned there out of St. James's field."293 "There stood upon the leads there [*i.e.* of the White Tower]," continues the same Chronicler, "the Lord Marquess [of Northampton], Sir Nicholas Poyns, Sir Thomas Pope, Master John Seamer and others. From the battle, when one came and brought word that the Queen was like to have the victory, and that the horseman had discomfited the tale of his enemies, the Lord Marquess for joy gave the messenger ten shillings in gold, and fell in great rejoicing."

We may imagine the anxiety of the condemned prisoners in the Tower. If Wyatt were victorious, they might yet be saved by a change of administration, that would send Mary flying abroad for her life, and bring Princess Elizabeth to the throne. Wyatt's object was to seize the Tower, but alas! poor man, when he had approached it as near as the Belle326 Sauvage Yard, on Ludgate Hill, he collapsed on the bench of a fishmonger's shop, was swiftly seized and cast into durance, in that very fortress whence he hoped to proclaim his victory over "Spanish tyranny." The prisoners in the Tower must have heard a hundred tales of the appalling retaliation practised on the promoters of the rebellion; of the scores of men hanged in bunches at the street corners294; of the bloody heads stuck on London Bridge, and even in front of the Queen's palace at St. James's. They may even have seen Wyatt and his fellows enter the Tower. Guildford, too, since he had the same privileges as Northampton, may have heard the cries of the frightened populace in those days of hot rebellion, from the leads of the White Tower, where he was allowed to take the air, and whence he could see beyond the precincts over on to Tower Hill without.

Jane may likewise have learnt with considerable distress that the Earl of Huntingdon and many other Catholic courtiers—all the Spaniards, for instance—were permitted to attend Mass in the Tower chapel; and that this, to her, idolatrous ceremony had replaced the plain Communion service of Edward VI in most of the churches of London, and indeed, throughout the length and breadth of the kingdom. She must also have heard with disgust that half London was going in procession nearly every day, with banners, copes, "imauges," and lights, praying for fine weather.

Unfortunately little is known about the death-warrant of Lady Jane Grey and her husband. The date of its signature would seem to have been 6th February—the very day, as we have said, that Suffolk was brought back a prisoner into the Tower—a confirmation of the statement that it was his indiscreet action which eventually decided Queen Mary to put Lady Jane to death. The warrant itself and the text have disappeared. All we know is that the document unceremoniously described the unfortunate young couple as "Guildford Dudley[327] and his wife"; and named Friday, 9th February 1554, as the day of execution. The Queen signed the document at Temple Bar, whither it was brought by the Lord Mayor and Sheriffs. How Mary came to be at Temple Bar on this occasion is not clear, but as Her Majesty is not likely to have performed her dread duty in the middle of the street, it is probable that the warrant received her signature in the office of the Duchy of Lancaster, just beyond Temple Bar. If this is the case, the actual chamber in which the dramatic event occurred still exists, in the upper storey of the quaint old house now used as a barber's shop and recently restored (externally) to its original condition by the removal of a lath and plaster façade, dating from the early eighteenth century, which masked the fine Tudor front that now lends so picturesque a note of mediævalism to modern Fleet Street. For a long time this chamber was believed to have been of the reign of James I, but a close examination of the scheme of decoration revealed the monogram of Prince Arthur, younger brother of Henry VIII, and from this we may conclude the building to have been the office of the Duchy of Lancaster, of which this young Prince was treasurer, and which is known to have stood hereabouts. This is the origin of the tradition so popular in London a generation ago, that the house in question was "the palace of Henry VIII and Cardinal Wolsey"; who may indeed have forgathered there for business purposes, but who certainly never inhabited the building.

CHAPTER XX
THE SUPREME HOUR!

To Dr. Feckenham Mary assigned the melancholy task of announcing her hopeless position to Jane Grey. This duty he performed on 8th February, the day before that originally fixed for the execution, at the same time exhorting her to prepare for death. The little victim of great iniquity is said to have learnt her doom with Christian resignation and princely dignity. She did not fall into a consternation as when her accession to the throne was announced to her at Sion, but listened, dry-eyed, to the worthy prelate's awful words. The call to another world was more welcome, doubtless, to her weary spirit than had been that other summons to an earthly throne. Her life, she told Feckenham, had long been a living death, and the sooner it ended the better—"I am ready to receive death patiently," she said, "and in whatever manner it may please the Queen to appoint. True, my flesh shudders, as is natural to frail humanity, at what I have to go through, but I fervently hope the spirit will spring rejoicingly into the presence of the Eternal God, Who will receive it." She pleaded for her husband; "he was innocent," she said, "and had only obeyed his father in all things." Finally, she expressed her desire to see a minister of her own religion, and prayed that during her last hours she might not be troubled by the presence of any Roman Catholic priest or prelate, since "she had no time for that." Mary, however, was resolved that no minister of the Reformed religion should visit her cousin, but she had made a judicious choice in sending Dr. Feckenham, a liberal-minded man of the gentlest manners,[295] to minister spiritual consolation to[329] her. Though the numerous pictures representing the tragic scene of Jane's death generally depict Feckenham as a dignified old man with a long white beard, he was in reality a short, stout, "comfortable-looking" elderly gentleman, with a close-shaven red face, and twinkling eyes. A devout Catholic, he desired, no doubt, to convert his illustrious prisoner to his own faith, and even Pollino, who must have been well acquainted with all that the Catholic party had to say on the subject, says that Lady Jane and Feckenham held long conversations on the subject of the Eucharist, one on which Lady Jane held distinctly Protestant views: but there is no evidence that, as some historians allege, she ever engaged in a discussion on matters of faith and doctrines with Feckenham in a hall of the Tower set apart for that purpose, and in the presence of an assembly of learned Catholic prelates and theologians. We may be sure that any controversy between Lady Jane Grey and Dr. Feckenham, either in the last week of her life or at any other time, took place in the privacy of her own apartment. Florio, the Protestant Italian historian, who has written a life of Lady Jane Grey—concocted out of Foxe's *Book of Martyrs* and other similar works,—prints at the end of his book a dialogue between Lady Jane and Feckenham on the subject of Transubstantiation, and this conversation is also given in Harris Nicholas's *Literary Remains of Lady Jane Grey*. This is most likely a report dictated by some one to whom Jane communicated the substance of what passed between herself and the Benedictine. Dr. Feckenham has left his own account of what took place, and admits that in the course of several lengthy conversations with Jane on matters of dogma, by means of which he had hoped to convert her to Catholicism, he had been deeply impressed by her gentleness, her dignity, and her evident sincerity.

Feckenham obtained the respite of three days, generally given in such cases, and the execution was postponed until Monday, 12th February. On his informing Jane of what he had done, she is said to have replied, "Alas, sir! I did not intend what I said to be reported to the Queen, nor would I have you think me covetous for a moment's longer life; for[330] I am only solicitous for a better life in Eternity, and will gladly suffer death, since it is her Majesty's pleasure." Feckenham, it appears, had misunderstood the phrase, "she had no time for that," as meaning that Jane might be disposed to listen to his religious teaching if allowed more time for its consideration; and had therefore requested the respite granted by the Council. But she proved no more amenable to the worthy priest's arguments on the last day than on the first.

Lord Guildford Dudley, unlike his stoical wife, received his sentence with a flood of tears. Of all the victims of this terrible tragedy, he was, in truth, the most inoffensive. The poor lad had done no harm, except to obey the instructions of his father and mother—especially in respect to his foolish attempt at Brussels, which was probably the real cause of his condemnation—and there was nothing, now that his father was removed, to be gained by putting him to death. Except by his marriage, he was not connected with the royal family; he was therefore not in the line of succession, and his liberation would not have involved the slightest danger to Queen Mary or her throne. His execution may be described as a useless murder, even a darker stain on Mary Tudor and her advisers—the Emperor Charles V, his agent Simon Renard, and the Council—than that of Lady Jane Grey, who certainly might have been used again, in the near future, as the tool of some unscrupulous statesman. Mary, as we have said, was herself perfectly willing, almost to the last, to spare both Guildford and his wife, but their chance of pardon was ruined by the Duke of Suffolk's abortive rebellion. Had he obeyed Mary's orders, put himself at the head of her troops, remained loyal, and defeated the rising in the Midlands, as Huntingdon eventually did, his children's lives would doubtless have been spared by the grateful sovereign.

The original order, as we have seen, was that Jane and Guildford should perish together on Tower Hill. Harris Nicholas seems to think the plan was abandoned because the Council dreaded the effect of the prisoners' youth and innocence on the populace. This view has been adopted by other writers, but the real motive of the change was a matter of political etiquette. Lady Jane was of the Blood Royal, and[331] therefore entitled to be executed within the precincts of the Tower, on the Green where the two Queens of

Henry VIII and the old Plantagenet Princess, Margaret of Salisbury, had been beheaded. Guildford, on the other hand, on the paternal side of even plebeian origin, could only be decapitated without the Tower.

On the evening of the day originally fixed for the execution (Friday, 9th February), Jane wrote the following letter to her father, in which she herself holds him responsible, through his rashness, for her death:—

"Father,—Although it hath pleased God to hasten my death by you, by whom my life should rather have been lengthened, yet can I patiently take it, that I yield God more hearty thanks for shortening my woeful days, than if all the world had been given into my possession, with life lengthened at my own will. And albeit I am well assured of your impatient dolours, redoubled many ways, both in bewailing your own woe, and especially, as I am informed, my woeful estate; yet, my dear father, if I may without offence rejoice in my own mishap, herein I may account myself blessed, that washing my hands with the innocence of my fact, my guiltless blood may cry before the Lord, 'Mercy to the innocent.' And yet, though I must needs acknowledge that being constrained, and, as you know well enough, continually assayed; yet, in taking [the Crown] upon me, I seemed to consent, and therein grievously offended the Queen and her laws, yet do I assuredly trust, that this my offence towards God is so much the less, in that being in so royal estate as I was, my enforced honour never mixed with mine innocent heart. And thus, good father, I have opened unto you the state in which I presently stand, my death at hand, although to you it may seem woeful, yet to me there is nothing that can be more welcome than from this vale of misery to aspire to that heavenly throne of all joy and pleasure, with Christ our Saviour: in whose steadfast faith (if it be lawful for the daughter so to write to the father), the Lord that hitherto hath strengthened you, so continue to keep you, that at last we may meet in heaven with the Father, Son, and Holy Ghost. Amen.—I am, Your obedient Daughter till death,

Jane Dudley"

332 Jane probably spent Sunday (10th February) in prayer and meditation; or perhaps as an unwilling listener to Feckenham's exhortations. The next day Gardiner, preaching before the Queen, then at Whitehall, blamed her for what he considered her leniency. He "axed a boon of the Queen's Highness, that like as she had before extended her mercy particularly and privately, so through her lenity and gentleness much conspiracy and open rebellion was grown, according to the proverb *nimia familiaritas parit contemptum*; which he brought then in, for the purpose that she would now be merciful to the body of the commonwealth, and conservation thereof, which could not be, unless the rotten and hurtful members thereof were cut off and consumed."296

Some communication seems to have reached Jane from her ruined home on this Sunday, for in consequence of the transports of grief into which her sister, Lady Katherine, was plunged, she wrote that evening the following beautiful letter, on the blank pages at the end of her Greek Testament:—

"I have sent you, good sister Katherine, a book, which, although it be not outwardly rimmed with gold, yet inwardly it is more worth than precious stones. It is the book, dear sister, of the laws of the Lord; it is His Testament and last Will, which He bequeathed unto us wretches, which shall lead you to the path of eternal joy, and if you, with a good mind, read it, and with an earnest desire follow it, shall bring you to an immortal and everlasting life. It will teach you to live, and learn you to die; it shall win you more than you should have gained by the possession of your woeful father's lands,297333 for as if God had prospered him, ye should have inherited his lands, so if you apply diligently [to] your book [*i.e.* the Bible], trying to direct your life after it, you shall be an inheritor of such riches as neither the covetous shall withdraw from you, neither the thief shall steal, neither yet the moth corrupt. Desire, sister, to understand the law of the Lord your God. Live still to die, that you by death may purchase eternal life; or after your death enjoy the life purchased [for] you by Christ's death; and trust not the tenderness of your age shall lengthen your life, for as soon, if God will, goeth the young as the old; and labour alway to learn to die. Deny the world, defy the devil, and despise the flesh. Delight yourself only in the Lord. Be patient for your sins, and yet despair not. Be steady in faith, yet presume not, and desire with St. Paul to be dissolved and to be with Christ, with whom even in death there is life. Be like the good servant, and even at midnight be waking; lest when death cometh and stealeth upon you, like a thief in the night, you be with the evil servant found sleeping, and lest for lack of oil ye be found like the first foolish wench,298 and like him that had not on the wedding garment, and then be cast out from the marriage. Resist [sin] in ye [yourself] as I trust ye do, and seeing ye have the name of a Christian, as near as ye can, follow the steps of your master Christ, and take up your cross; lay your sins on His back, and always embrace Him; and as touching my death, rejoice as I do, and assist [perhaps, 'consider'] that I shall be delivered of this corruption, and put on incorruption, for I am assured that I shall for losing of a mortal life find an immortal felicity. Pray God grant you [and] send you of His grace to live in His fear, and to die in the love [here is an illegible passage, perhaps made so by fast falling tears], neither for love of life, nor fears of death. For if ye deny His truth to lengthen your life, God will deny you, and shorten your days; and if ye will cleave to Him, He will prolong your days, to your comfort and His glory, to the which glory God bring mine and you hereafter, when it shall please God to call you.

334 "Farewell, good sister, put your only trust in God, who only must uphold you.—Your loving sister,

"Jane Dudley"

The precious volume containing this letter is fortunately the property of the nation, deposited in the MS. department of the British Museum.

In the British Museum299 there is also a small and beautiful MS. vellum prayer book, imperfect in one or two pages. Four inches in length, and nearly two inches thick, bound in red morocco, and richly ornamented, it contains thirty-five distinctly Protestant prayers. The catalogue of the Harleian Collection states that it "was perhaps written by the direction of Edward Seymour, Duke of Somerset and Protector of England, upon his first commitment to the Tower of London; and that the last five prayers were added after his second commitment, which ended in his execution." On the margin of several pages, not more than three lines occupying the same leaf, are a series of interesting autographs. The first of these is in the hand of Lord Guildford Dudley, and runs as follows:—

"Your loving and obedient son wisheth unto your grace long life in this world, with as much joy and comfort as ever I wish to myself; and in the world to come, joy everlasting.—Your most humble son till his death,

"G. Dudley"

It has been conjectured from this inscription that Guildford presented the book to his father-in-law, on the occasion of his wedding with Lady Jane; unless the inscription was addressed to his father, Northumberland. It is also supposed that the Duke of Suffolk, having received it from Guildford, left it behind him after his release from his three days' imprisonment in the Tower. Others say that Sir John Gage, Constable of the Tower, gave it himself to his prisoners, so that they might write something in it for him to keep in remembrance of them. It was certainly in Jane's possession for some time, for she carried it with her to the scaffold; and it contains in her hand, a solemn farewell to, and prayer for, her father, in the following terms:—

335

"The Lord comfort your grace, and that in his word, wherein all creatures only are to be comforted. And though it hath pleased God to take ij of your children, yet think not, I most humbly beseech your grace, that you have lost them; but trust that we, by leaving this mortal life, have won an immortal life. And I, for my part, as I have honoured your grace in this life, will pray for you in another life.300—Your grace's humble daughter,

"Jane Dudley"

Shortly before proceeding to her execution, Jane's kindly jailor, Sir Thomas Brydges, begged her to give him something to keep in memory of her; whereupon she offered him this very prayer book, and at his request wrote in a third sentence:

"Forasmuch as you have desired so simple a woman to write in so worthy a book, good master Lieutenant, therefore I shall as a friend desire you, and as a Christian require you, to call upon God, to incline your heart to His laws, quicken you in His ways, and not to take the word of truth utterly out of your mouth. Live still to die, that by death you may purchase eternal life; and remember how the end of Methuselah, who as we read in the Scriptures was the longest liver that was of a manner, died at the last. For, as the preacher saith, there is a time to be born and a time to die; and the day of death is better than the day of our birth.—Yours as the Lord knoweth as a friend,

"Jane Dudley"

Finally, at some time or other during her imprisonment, Jane wrote three further inscriptions on the last page of this book in Latin, Greek, and English, which run as follows:—

The Latin—"If justice is done with my body, my soul will find mercy with God."

The Greek—"Death will give pain to my body for its sins, but the soul will be justified before God."

336 The English—"If my faults deserve punishment, my youth at least and my imprudence were worthy of excuse. God and posterity will show me favour."301

It was on this, the last Sunday evening of her unhappy life, that Jane wrote the well-known prayer, which, although quoted in full by Foxe and Howard, is not now extant in Lady Jane's own hand, and may therefore, like several letters, etc., attributed to her, be apocryphal.302

The few details we possess as to the acts of other State337 prisoners, implicated in Northumberland's plot, on the day of their execution, are lacking in the case of Lady Jane; no record has come to us of how she slept on her last night of life; of those who were present at her last mournful meal. However, enough has been reported by contemporary writers to enable us to reconstruct the events of the later portion of the day, when the hour of the execution drew near. It is clearly stated that Lord Guildford Dudley made an attempt to see his wife before his death, and even informed his guards of his desire to do so. Hearing of this, Mary sent word, on the very morning of the fatal day, that "if it would be any consolation to them, they should be allowed to see each other before their execution." When this concession was communicated to Lady Jane she declined it, saying "it would only disturb the holy tranquillity with which they had prepared themselves for death"; and unnerve them for the supreme moment. At the same time she sent a message to Guildford to the effect that such a meeting "would rather weaken than strengthen him"; that he ought to be sufficiently strong in himself to need no such consolation; that "if his soul were not firm and settled, she could not settle it by her eyes, nor confirm it by her words; that he would do well to remit this interview till they met in a better world, where friendships were happy and unions indissoluble, and theirs, she hoped, would be eternal." But Jane took her stand at the window of her room to watch her husband pass, a little before ten o'clock, to his doom on Tower Hill. Sir Thomas Brydges stood by her, as she waved her hand to Guildford. Burke (*Tudor Portraits*) says, but without naming his authority, that "like his father and brothers," Guildford Dudley, "recanted his supposed Protestantism whilst in the Tower"; and that "he was attended to the scaffold by two Benedictine Fathers." Other and earlier writers do, indeed, declare that Guildford received Communion according to the rites of the Roman Catholic Church before his death; but *The Chronicle of Queen Jane and Queen Mary* makes no mention of this recantation, and clearly says no minister of any religion attended at Guildford Dudley's execution.303 At the Bulwark Gate of the Tower (its outside338 entrance), Guildford was met by Sir Anthony Browne and Sir John Throckmorton, and several other gentlemen who had assembled to bid him farewell, and with whom he shook hands "pleasantly." Here, too, Sir Thomas Offley, the Sheriff of Middlesex, in accordance with precedent,304 took charge of the prisoner. The mob that in those days invariably assembled to witness such sinister functions, was on Tower Hill in its hundreds, nay thousands, to see the poor boy beheaded. He looked very handsome, in his suit of black velvet slashed with dark coloured cloth: his tall and youthful figure impressed the people most favourably, and a murmur of sympathy ran through the motley throng. Guildford did not attempt to make a speech. He knelt down and said his prayers—simple prayers he had learnt as a child—and, it was said, he shed some tears at the thought of dying so young. But despite the youth's natural emotion, he faced death bravely. He begged the "good people" to pray for him; took off his doublet himself, unfastened his collar with his own hands, knelt on the straw, stretched out his graceful limbs, laid his head on the block; and in an instant, with one stroke of the axe, his spirit passed into Eternity.305 His blood-stained corpse, covered with a sheet, was thrown into a tumbril or handcart filled with straw, and his head, wrapped in a cloth, was cast at its feet.

And now a horrible incident occurred. Whether by accident or design,306 Jane caught a glimpse of her husband's339 mutilated remains as they were carried into the Tower for interment. We have several versions of this story: some say she saw the body taken out of the cart307 and carried into St. Peter's Chapel, whilst a passage in Grafton308 lends colour to the belief (adopted by many historians, including Turner and Nicolas) that she met the corpse as she was herself proceeding to the scaffold. What most likely happened is, that she was waiting to be summoned by the Lieutenant of the Tower and the Sheriffs, when she heard the rumbling of cart wheels, and before her attendants could prevent her, rushed to the window, and beheld the hideous sight, without, however, it seems, expressing any great emotion. "Oh Guildford, Guildford!" we are told she exclaimed, "the antepast that you have tasted, and I shall soon taste, is not so bitter as to make my flesh tremble; for all this is nothing to the feast that you and I shall partake this day in Paradise."

The direful procession which was to conduct a young and innocent Princess of the Blood Royal, of barely seventeen summers, to the foot of an ignominious scaffold, was formed according to established precedent. But for some unexplained reason, it was nearly an hour late in starting from Partridge's house to the place of execution, opposite the Church of St. Peter-ad-Vincula, where, since that day, countless pilgrims from the Old and New Worlds have paused to ponder a moment over the fate of Lady Jane Grey, and have learnt to hate Mary Tudor with an almost personal detestation. The delay may have resulted from the state of nervous prostration into which the unfortunate Princess had been thrown by the sight of her husband's mangled remains. It would have been impossible, even in those hard times, to convey the victim to execution if she had swooned. It was nearly340 eleven o'clock, then, before the drums began to beat, and the procession fell into order.

The morning had dawned grey and misty, heavy clouds veiling the sun that now and then shone feebly athwart them, but it was fairly fine for London at that early season, and no rain fell throughout the day. The bells of St. Peter-ad-Vincula, and of All Hallows', Barking, tolled at regular intervals, whilst the grand outline of the White Tower stood out luminous against the threatening sky, as the dread procession wended slowly onwards. First, came a company of two hundred Yeomen of the Guard; then, the executioner, in a tight-fitting scarlet worsted and cloth garment, displaying the swelling muscles of his chest, arms, and legs;309 his face was masked, and his head hooded in scarlet. Beside him marched his assistant, a rough-looking man, who carried the axe over his shoulder; then Sir John Brydges, Lieutenant of the Tower, with Sir Thomas Brydges, Deputy-Lieutenant, and between them Sir John Gage, Constable of the Tower, with two Sheriffs, in their robes of office. Lastly, the young prisoner herself, dressed as on the occasion of her trial at the Guildhall in the same black cloth dress, edged with black velvet, a Marie Stuart cap of black velvet on her head, with a veil of black cloth hanging to the waist, and a white wimple concealing her throat; her sleeves edged with lawn, neatly plaited round the wrists. Not wearing *chopines* to increase her height, as on the occasion of her State entry into the Tower, the people who had not seen her since were greatly surprised at her diminutive stature. On her right walked Abbot Feckenham, in his black robe, without a surplice, and carrying a crucifix in his hand. Behind him came the Chaplains attached to the Chapel Royal of the Tower. Lady Jane's ladies, Mrs. Tylney and Mrs. Ellen, and Mrs. Sarah; two other women and a man-servant, all in deep mourning, and weeping bitterly, closed the doleful procession. The route was a short one, and the crowd of spectators—about five hundred—allowed to be present at the execution, was silent and respectful. From Partridge's house to the scaffold, the Lady Jane continued to read the open Prayer-Book in her hand—it was that containing the various inscriptions already341 mentioned—and paid little or no heed to Feckenham's pious exhortations, if, indeed, he made any.

At the foot of the scaffold stood a jury of forty matrons, who had been previously called upon to testify that the Princess was not with child; a rumour that she was in this condition was so widespread as to be mentioned by Radcliffe—who says, "Lady Dudley was very brave, considering the condition she was in"—and by Fuller, Pomeroy, Challoner, and Fox. The presence of these matrons is also mentioned by Bishop Godwin. There is no record of the presence of the Duke of Norfolk in his usual seat as Earl Marshal, but no doubt he was there with Lord Mayor White and several Aldermen, Sheriffs, and noblemen. Before ascending the three or four steps that led to the scaffold, the Lady Jane took leave of her ladies, who sobbed bitterly; Mrs. Ellen and Mrs. Tylney followed her on to the platform, ominously littered with fresh straw. Here Feckenham, the executioner, and his assistant also took their stations, with Sir Thomas Brydges. "When she appeared on the scaffold," writes a contemporary, "the people cried, and murmured at beholding one so young and beautiful about to die such a death." Nevertheless, though the writer of *The Chronicle of Queen Jane and Queen Mary* says "her countenance [was] nothing abashed, neither her eyes misted with tears," there can be little doubt but that the long spell of anxiety had left some trace on Jane's sweet face. She advanced to the edge of the scaffold, and in the dead silence spoke in a distinct voice: "Good people, I am come here to die, and by a law I am condemned to the same. My offence against the Queen's Highness was only in consenting to the device of others, which is now deemed treason; but it was never of my seeking, but by the counsel of those who should seem to have further understanding of such things than I, who knew little of the law and less of the title to the Crown. The part, indeed, against the Queen's Highness was unlawful, and so the consenting thereunto by me; but touching the procurement and desire thereof by me, or on my behalf, I do wash my hands thereof in innocency before God and in the face of you, good Christian people, this day," and therewith she wrung her hands in which she had her book. Then she continued, "I pray you, all good Christian people, to bear342 me witness that I die a true Christian woman, and that I look to be saved by none other means, but only by the mercy of God, in the merit of the blood of His only Son Jesus Christ; and I confess that when I did know the Word of God, I neglected the same, loved myself and the world, and therefore this plague of punishment has worthily happened into me for my sins; and yet I thank God of His goodness that He hath thus given me a time and respite to repent. And now, good people, while I am living, I pray you to assist me with your prayers."

Lady Jane's relative, Lady Philippa de Clifford, in her little known report,310 adds that, "After a pause, and wiping343 her eyes, she (Jane) said in a firmer voice, 'Now, good people, Jane Dudley bids you all a long farewell. And may the Almighty preserve you from ever meeting the terrible death which awaits her in a few minutes. Farewell, farewell, for ever more.' Jane, when she had finished speaking, was much affected, and hid her face upon the neck of the old nurse who attended her on the scaffold." This nurse must have been Mrs. Ellen, into whose arms she threw herself when she first perceived the towering figure of the masked executioner, garbed from head to foot in scarlet. Clinging to the aged woman, the poor girl sobbed convulsively. Growing calmer, after a while, she knelt down, and asked Feckenham what prayer she should recite—"Shall I say this Psalm?"—probably pointing to her prayer-book as she did so. "Yes," answered he; and then, as she and many of the people knelt, he said the fifty-first Psalm, the *Miserere*, in Latin, Jane repeating it after him in English. This done, she rose, and said very courteously to Dr. Feckenham, "God will abundantly requite you, good sir, for all your humanity to me, though your discourses gave me more uneasiness than all the terrors of approaching death." Bishop Godwin says, "Just before she knelt down, Lady Jane embraced the venerable prelate and thanked him for his kindness to her." She then gave her handkerchief and gloves to Mrs. Tylney; and turning to Sir Thomas Brydges, said gently, "You asked me for a parting memory of me," and handed him the prayer-book which she had been using and in which she had written her farewells.

The supreme moment had arrived. Without the assistance of her two female attendants, who were too completely overcome to assist her, she untied the collar of her gown. The executioner offered to help her, but she curtly desired him to desist, and turning to her ladies, spoke a few words to them. Mastering their emotion, they took off her outer dress, leaving her in her kirtle, or under gown with close-fitting sleeves. They also removed her headdress (described by the old chroniclers as a "frose paste") and kerchief, giving her at the same time a handkerchief to tie over her eyes. Then the executioner knelt and besought her pardon; she replied344 simply, "Most willingly." Now came what was perhaps the most painful episode of the horrible ceremony—the pause of five minutes "for the Queen's mercy." The poor girl had to stand, with the ghastly preparations for her approaching death about her, for a space of time which, brief as it really was, must have seemed an eternity to her, waiting for a clemency she no longer expected nor desired. But no white wand was waved—there was no mercy for Jane Grey! The five minutes ended, the executioner motioned the unfortunate Princess to take her place upon the straw, and she, noticing the block for the first time, began to tremble a little, and said, as she knelt down, "I pray you dispatch me quickly," adding, "Will you take it off before I lay me down?"311 "No, madam," replied the executioner. With her own hands she bound the handkerchief about her eyes, and being now in that darkness from which death would soon release her, lost consciousness of where she was, and groping about for the block, asked eagerly, "Where is it? What shall I do? Where is it?" Someone guided her to the fatal spot, and the "Nine Days' Queen," laying herself down with her fair head upon the block, stretched out her body, and cried aloud that all might hear her, "Lord, into Thy hands I commend my spirit!"312 A flash, a thud, a crimson deluge on the straw-strewn scaffold—and, as the cannon boomed, an innocent soul was borne towards a Throne more high, and a Justice more sure than those of Queen or Emperor!313

345 There are several conflicting accounts of what subsequently happened. The more generally received version is that the body was handed over to Lady Jane's women, who reverently placed it in a common deal coffin, and conveyed it to St. Peter-ad-Vincula, precisely as the women of Anne Boleyn and Katherine Howard had conveyed the mangled remains of those slaughtered Queens. But on the other hand, Antoine de Noailles,314 the French Ambassador, who had arrived346 in London early in the morning, passing that way about three o'clock in the same afternoon (he was living at Marillac's old house on the Tower Green), saw Lady Jane's half-naked body lying abandoned on the scaffold, and was amazed at the immense quantity of blood that had poured out of so small a corpse.315 Peter Derenzie tells us her remains "were left for hours half naked on the scaffold streaming with blood, and were placed in a deal coffin." It would seem indeed that, in death as in life, Lady Jane Grey, the moment fortune turned against her, was abandoned by all those, even by her own mother, who by reason of natural ties should have rallied round her in the hour of need. Thus after death her bleeding remains were treated with corresponding neglect; the puppet which was to have made Northumberland's fortune was thrown aside,

with none to care for it, when once its purpose failed. This unusual treatment of the body may not, however, have proceeded entirely from heartlessness; but from the difficulty and uncertainty as to the nature of the religious service to be said over the remains of one who, though born a Catholic, had died a "heretic"; St. Peter's Chapel having been lately restored to the Catholics, Jane could not be buried there without ecclesiastical licence, and to obtain this, Feckenham probably had to see Queen Mary, or get some sort of "permit" from Archbishop Heath. But, granting all this, the corpse might, at least, have been decently covered. The delay as to the burial of Jane Grey's corpse may have given rise to the popular report that it was transported to Bradgate, and interred there. There is no question, however, that the body was eventually conveyed into the Church of St. Peter-ad-Vincula and buried in the vault which already contained the mangled remains of so many of her contemporaries.316 Many years ago, a very small and347 broken coffin was discovered in this vault, containing the remains of a female of diminutive stature, with the head severed from the body. The skeleton, which crumbled to ashes immediately it was exposed to the effect of the atmosphere, was surmised to be that of Lady Jane Grey, and the dust was enclosed in an urn and placed immediately under the oval inscription in the chancel above, which records her death. Yet in Leicestershire, the tradition still persists that the body was brought to Bradgate late at night, and secretly interred in the parish church. And with this tradition, of course, is connected the legend of the coach with the headless occupant, said to appear before the gates of Bradgate on the anniversary of Lady Jane's death.

Thus, in blood and in neglect, ends the tragic story of Lady Jane Grey, one of the most popular heroines in our history, the helpless victim of circumstance, and of the soaring ambition of a singularly masterful and unscrupulous man.

CHAPTER XXI
THE FATE OF THE SURVIVORS

The Reforming Leaders, who had so flattered Lady Jane Grey when they saw a chance of her becoming Queen, do not seem to have felt much concern at her death. In a letter of 3rd April 1554, addressed to Bullinger, Peter Martyr says, "Jane, who was formerly Queen, conducted herself at her execution with the greatest fortitude and godliness"; Burcher, writing on 3rd March 1554 to Bullinger, casually remarks, "I have heard, too, that the Queen has beheaded his [Suffolk's] daughter Jane, together with her husband; that Jane, I mean, who was proclaimed Queen"; lastly, a less well-known Reformer named Thomas Lever wrote to Bullinger in the April of 1554, that Jane had been beheaded.317 As to the Imperial Ambassadors, Montmorency Marnix, Jehan Schefer, and Simon Renard, they were one and all jubilant over the death of Lady Jane, her father, and Northumberland. There was not much sympathy ever expressed for Lady Jane among the people. No doubt her execution was the main topic of chatter in all the taverns of London, as well in the little darksome dens, down by the wharves, where seafaring men congregated, as in the luxurious hostelries in Cheapside, the Strand, Holborn, and Westminster, where rich gossips forgathered; but of demonstrative sympathy there was none. Yet the erection on that fateful Monday of some fifty gibbets intended for the hanging of the Wyatt rebels did impress the hardened populace with a sense of horror and anxiety. It marked the beginning of the reaction against Mary, which set in violently a few months later on with the burnings in Smithfield, to blast her name for ever by the fearful epithet of—"Bloody."

Let us give a parting glance to the remaining actors in349 this tragedy. Jane's father, Henry Grey, Duke of Suffolk, was brought to trial for high treason in Westminster Hall on 17th February. The indictment was for levying war against the Queen, adhering to Sir Thomas Wyatt, in order to depose the Queen and set the Crown on his daughter Jane; and having opposed the Earl of Huntingdon when the latter was in command of the Queen's forces.318 The Duke's defence was, that he had not attempted to proclaim Jane during his expedition of January 1554, and had only gone out to rouse the people against the Spaniards, which, as a peer of the Realm, he claimed he was entitled to do. As to the accusation of opposing Huntingdon, he answered that he did not know that nobleman was acting under the Queen's orders: he also took refuge behind his brother Thomas, who, he said, had advised him to go into the country, where he would be safe among his tenants, whereas if he remained in London he would be sent to the Tower again. This feeble defence was not accepted; and Henry Fitzallan, Lord Maltravers (Lord Arundel), the Queen's Lord Steward, who had brought the record into court, pronounced sentence of death, as a traitor, on that Henry Grey who had so greatly injured his sister, Lady Katherine Fitzallan, his first and neglected wife, from whom he was never legally divorced. He had his hour of revenge at last! The Duke was "much confounded at his condemnation"; contemporaries inform us that when he left the Tower he went "stoutly and cheerfully enough," but when he re-entered Traitor's Gate "his countenance was heavy and pensive." He had not to wait long for his *coup de grâce*. On the following Friday (23rd February) he was brought out of the Tower, between nine and ten in the morning, to be executed on Tower Hill. He had some trouble with Dr. Weston, the Roman Catholic priest Mary had appointed to accompany him to the scaffold. When they arrived at its foot, the Duke refused to listen to him, and even went so far as to prevent his ascending350 the steps. Dr. Weston, however, insisted in the Queen's name; whereupon, with an expressive gesture of resignation, Suffolk submitted to his presence, but the attempt to change his religious convictions failed utterly. Dr. Weston told him in a loud voice that the Queen forgave him, to which the Duke replied, "God save her Grace!" and the people murmured, and some said they hoped he (Weston) would have a like pardon. The Duke at last made a brief speech, saying simply, "Masters, I have offended the Queen, and her laws, and thereby I am justly condemned to die, and am willing to die, desiring all men to be obedient; and I pray God that this my death may be an example to all men, beseeching you all to bear me witness that I die in the faith of Christ, trusting to be saved by His blood only, and by no other (*sic*) trumpery: the which died for me, and for all men that truly repent and steadfastly trust in Him. And I do repent, desiring you all to pray to God for me, that when ye see my breath depart from me, you will pray to God that He may receive my soul."319 After this, kneeling and raising his hands in supplication to Heaven, he repeated the *Miserere*—the very Psalm his daughter had said under like circumstances a week or so before. Then, rising, he continued—also as she had done—saying, "Into Thy hands, O Lord, I commend my spirit." Just as he was about to make his final preparations for death a very human incident occurred. A man to whom he was deeply in debt stood up and asked him, "Who will now pay me my money?" "Well," quoth the Duke, "ask not me now, but go and see my officers, who will, I doubt not, satisfy you." On this the man departed, saying, "God save your soul, Sir!" Suffolk now removed his cap and neck-cloth, and to the headsman's usual appeal for forgiveness, replied, "God forgive thee, and I do; and when thou dost thine office, I pray thee, do it quickly, and God have mercy on thee."320 Lastly, having tied a handkerchief over his eyes, he knelt down and recited the Lord's Prayer aloud, and appealing for mercy to the Throne of Grace, Henry Grey laid his head on the block, and on the stroke of the headsman's axe expired. Suffolk's body was laid to351 rest in St. Peter's Chapel; but his head, for some reason which has never been explained, was sent to the Church of the Holy Trinity in the Minories.321 Here it was embalmed after a fashion, by being placed in a small vault by the altar, in the dust of oakwood, which, as it contains a quantity of tannin, is a strong preservative; and when unearthed about fifty years ago, it was sufficiently perfect for the mark of a blow made by the axe above the actual place of severance (rather low on the neck), to be still visible. Sir George Scharf was greatly struck by the resemblance between this head and the portrait of Suffolk now at Hatfield and the copy of it in the National Portrait Gallery. The author has himself inspected the relic closely, and recognised the resemblance to the portrait: the exceedingly arched eyebrows and the rather weak chin are identical: three of the teeth are perfect, the eyes are closed, the mouth open, the head beardless and bald.

Lady Jane's uncle, Lord Thomas Grey, shared the fate of his brother of Suffolk and of Lord Leonard Grey. At the time of the Duke's rising, he attempted to escape to the Continent by way of Wales; but he got no farther than the borders of the Principality, where he was captured, according to a contemporary, "through his great mishap and folly of his man who had forgot his cap case with money behind him in his chamber one morning at his inn, and, coming for it again, upon examination what he should be, it was mistrusted that his master should be some such man as he was indeed, and so he was stopped, taken, and brought up to London." Lord Thomas, however, took no very prominent part either in the rebellion in Warwickshire, or in the previous attempt to establish Lady Jane on the throne; and it is difficult to understand why he should have been sacrificed, especially when Lord John Grey, who had been caught as it were red-352handed in hiding with the Duke of Suffolk at Ashley, was released after two trials.322 However, the mention of the Lord Thomas by Suffolk at his trial was distinctly damaging to him; perhaps also Mary had some personal grudge against him, or his unloving sister-in-law, the Duchess of Suffolk, who, despite her husband's action, was much in favour with Mary, may have prejudiced the Queen against him. According to Noailles, Thomas Grey frankly avowed his determination to see Courtney, Earl of Devonshire, King, or to be King himself. He did not explain how this was to be achieved; but added, "If I am not King, I'll be hanged." He was beheaded instead! This reference to Courtney gives support to Suffolk's admission, that the Wyatt rebellion and his own expedition had for their immediate object the proclamation of Elizabeth as Queen. Curiously enough, Lord Thomas Grey, unlike his relatives, always remained a Catholic, and is said to have asked for a confessor before he died. After being brought to trial at Westminster on 9th March 1554, as Machyn says: "The xxviij day of April was beheaded on Tower hill, between ix and x of the clock before noon, my lord Thomas Gray, the Duke of 'Suffoke-Dassett['s]' brother, and buried at Allalow's [All Hallows'], Barkyne, and the head ..." (the sentence is unfinished).323

THE LADY FRANCIS BRANDON, DUCHESS OF SUFFOLK, AND HER SECOND HUSBAND, ADRIAN STOKES, ESQ.

PROBABLY BY CORVINUS. PROPERTY OF COL. WYNN FINCH

The Duchess of Suffolk, Lady Jane's strange and untender mother, did not, as might have been expected, even in those unfeeling times, go into retirement after the bloody deaths of her daughter, son-in-law, husband, and brother-in-law, but within a fortnight, and on the very day that Lord Thomas Grey was arraigned (9th March 1554, not, as some writers say, the day he was executed), she married her late husband's Groom of the Chambers, a red-haired lad of middle-class origin, fifteen years her junior, one Mr. Adrian Stokes. She received a reminder of "the dear departed" on this her wedding-day, in the shape of a demand to deliver, "unto the[353] Lord-Admiral the Parliamentary robes, lately belonging to the Duke her husband; or, if she had them not, to let the Lord-Admiral understand where they remain, to the end he may send for the same." This widow of Ephesus was not in the least disturbed by the message, and after returning the paraphernalia in question, gaily proceeded with her nuptial preparations! To account for so extraordinary and apparently heartless a proceeding, we must remember the position in which the Lady Frances now found herself. She realised that unless she was married, and that speedily, to some one much beneath her station, she might be proposed by the Protestant party as one of its candidates for the succession, and her life and tranquillity be thus endangered. Her marriage with one who was little better than a menial[324] rendered this impossible; and besides (she was a Tudor), she may have been really in love with her red-haired Mr. Stokes. That Queen Mary did not resent the match is evident, for throughout her reign the Lady Frances occupied a towering position at Court, with precedence of all other peeresses, sometimes even of Princess Elizabeth herself. Her daughters, the Ladies Katherine and Mary Grey, were appointed Maids-of-Honour to the Queen who had so lately signed the death-warrants of their father, sister, brother-in-law, and uncles, and seem to have been very much attached to their mistress. They probably convinced themselves that the recent tragedies had been purely political, and not the least domestic or personal. The lives of these two young ladies were not a jot happier than that of their sister; but this was due to Queen Elizabeth, who played with them both much as a cat plays with a mouse, and literally worried them into early graves. Lady Frances and her youthful husband had their portraits taken the very year of their marriage, both in one panel; the picture was lately in[354] the possession of Colonel Wynn Finch. The Duchess appears as a buxom, puffy-looking dame of thirty-six,—the age given on the margin of the picture,—whilst her sheepish-looking, ginger-headed husband is put down as twenty-one. He is represented in a superb costume of black velvet, edged with ermine and sparkling with jewels. The lady wears black satin cut somewhat after the fashion of the year 1830. Her garment is edged with ermine, and she wears two wedding-rings on the fourth finger of her fat hand, and several handsome chains and carcanets about her short neck. A close examination of this picture reveals the extraordinary breadth of the Duchess's face. Divested of her feminine head-dress, and with a very little "make up," she might easily be the very image of her uncle, King Henry VIII. Lady Jane's mother lived happily enough with Mr. Stokes, to whom she bore a daughter so soon after her marriage—a little under nine months—that if she had visited her husband in the Tower (which she did not) the question of her paternity might have been raised. This child, baptized Elizabeth, died the day it was born. The Lady Frances herself died in October 1559, leaving most of her fortune—by this time considerably reduced—to her husband, and very little to her two surviving daughters. She was buried in Westminster Abbey in great pomp on 5th December 1559. Elizabeth, out "of the great affection she bore the Duchess and because of her kinship," ordered that the Royal Arms should be borne at her funeral, which was attended by Garter-King-at-Arms and by Clarencieux. Her monument, still in existence, occupies the exact site of the shrine of St. Edmund in the chapel of that saint, and is a fine specimen of the early and best period of Elizabethan art. The inscription is in old English, and, modernised, runs as follows: "Here lieth the Lady Frances, Duchess of Suffolk, daughter to Charles Brandon, Duke of Suffolk and Mary the French Queen; first wife to Henry, Duke of Suffolk, and after to Adrian Stokes, Esq." This is followed by a few lines of high-flown panegyric in Latin. After the death of his Duchess, Mr. Stokes obtained a new lease of twenty-one years of "her Highness's manor of Beaumanor," in Leicestershire. About 1571 he was returned as M.P. for Leicestershire, and took as his second wife Anne, relict of Sir Nicholas Throckmorton.[355] Mr. Adrian Stokes died on 30th November 1586, leaving his brother William as his heir.[325]

The widow of the once all-powerful Duke of Northumberland spent some months with her daughter, Lady Mary Sidney, endeavouring to restore her shattered health and to recover some shreds of the property taken from her at the time of her husband's condemnation. It was mainly through the instrumentality of Don Diego de Mendoza, or "Damondesay," as she styles him, whose imprudent conduct had brought such misfortune on her luckless son, that Philip II was led to solicit the restoration of a considerable part of the Duchess's fortune. She also obtained permission to inhabit the empty Manor House at Chelsea, where she endeavoured to collect some of the magnificent furniture which had once adorned the royal mansion, Durham House, in the Strand, recovering, amongst other things, a set of green curtains shot with gold thread and certain carved chairs and tables. But peace and shelter, even combined with a measure of comfort and independence, availed not to restore her broken health, and on 22nd January 1555 the famous Duke of Northumberland's widow died broken-hearted at Chelsea Manor in her forty-sixth year. Her will is one of the most curious extant. After declaring it written entirely in her own hand, without the advice of one learned in the law, she bequeaths to "the Lord Diegoe Damondesay, that is beyond the sea, the littell book clock that hath the moon in it, etc.," and her dial, "the one leaf of it the almanac and the other side, the Golden Number in the middle." What would we not give for a glimpse of this curious little clock or dial? To Sir Henry Sidney she leaves the gold and green hangings in the gallery at Chelsea; to her daughter, Mary Sidney, her gown of black barred velvet, furred with sable; to her daughter, Katherine Hastings, a gown of purple velvet, and a summer gown; to the Duchess of Alva, her green parrot, "having nothing else worthy of her"; to Elizabeth, wife of Lord Cobham, a gown of black barred velvet, furred with lizards. The document ends with the following quaint directions: "My will is earnestly and effectually, that little solemnities be made for me, for I had ever have a thousand folds my debts to be paid, and the356 poor given unto, than any pomp to be showed upon my wretched carcase; therefore to the worms will I go, as I have afore written in all points, as you will answer it afore God; and you break any one jot of it, your will hereafter may chance be to as well broken.... After I am departed from this world, let me be wound up in a sheet, and put into a coffin of wood, and so laid in the ground with such funerals as pertaineth to the burial of a corpse. I will at my year's mind (*i.e.* anniversary of her death) have such divine service as my executors shall think meet, with the whole arms of father and mother upon the stone graven; nor in any wise to let me be opened after I am dead. I have not loved to be very bold afore women, much more would I be loth to come into the hands of any living man, be he physician or surgeon." She was buried in Chelsea Parish Church on 1st February 1555, two heralds attending the funeral, at which there was a brilliant display of escutcheons and banners, etc. Her tomb is against the south wall of the church, and is under a Gothic canopy, supported by pillars of mosaic. It bears a long inscription, together with effigies of the Duchess and her five daughters, kneeling: a similar plate with her eight sons on it has been torn off.326

357 The Duchess of Somerset, the Protector's widow, followed the example of my Lady of Suffolk, and ensured her personal tranquillity by contracting a *mésalliance* with Mr. Newdigate, son of that Mr. Newdigate to whom, as recorded in an early chapter of this work, Lord Latimer, Katherine Parr's second husband, used to let his house furnished. The Duchess had been released from the Tower with other notable prisoners when Mary first entered its precincts. She was much beloved by that Queen, who used to address her as "my good Nan," and this despite the fact that the Duchess was an ardent Protestant. She died in her ninetieth year, and was laid to rest under a monument which is reckoned as one of the finest in Westminster Abbey.

Katherine, Dowager Duchess of Suffolk, Charles Brandon's fourth and last wife and Lady Frances' stepmother, had followed the prevailing custom and married her secretary, Mr. Bertie or Bartie, "a gentleman of fair family and little means." Her Grace was one of the first Englishwomen of noble birth to embrace the principles of the Reformation, and greatly incensed Queen Mary by doing so. This lady's mother, Lady Willoughby d'Eresby, was Queen Katherine's closest friend, and a staunch Catholic, a fact that probably increased the Queen's resentment against the Duchess and her second spouse; and a hint that he might be arrested on a charge of heresy sent Mr. Bertie flying to Flanders. He had not the kindness to inform his wife of his intended flight, and she, feeling herself forsaken and in danger in London, escaped one foggy morning from her house in the Barbican and followed in the wake of the truant, whom she found at Wesel, where their famous son, Peregrine, the brave Lord Willoughby, was born. After Elizabeth's accession, the Duchess returned to London with her children by Mr. Bertie and that gentleman himself. She was favourably received by the Queen,358 who saddled her, however, with many unwelcome obligations among them the custody of her step-granddaughters, the Ladies Katherine and Mary Grey. The Duchess, who was on friendly terms with Cecil, kept up a constant correspondence with him; and even after the lapse of nearly five hundred years, her humorous descriptions of people and things raise not a smile only, but a hearty laugh—she was, in fact, considered the wittiest woman of her day. Katherine, Dowager Duchess of Suffolk, died late in the reign of Elizabeth.

Queen Jane's Secretary, Sir John Cheke, was arrested on 27th or 28th July 1553 (Strype says, "together with the Duke of Suffolk") and committed to the Tower. There he remained a close prisoner. On 12th or 13th August an indictment as a traitor was made out against him, which brought forth a private letter to him from Cranmer, with whom he was on intimate terms. In this epistle Cheke is described as "one who had been none of the great doers in this matter [*i.e.* of the accession of Jane] against her [Queen Mary]." In 1554 Sir John Cheke was, after his estates had been confiscated, released from the Tower and given a licence by the Queen to travel abroad,327 whereupon he made no delay in getting to Switzerland and thence to Italy.328

APPENDIX
ICONOGRAPHY OF LADY JANE GREY AND HER FAMILY, ETC.

The painted portraits of Lady Jane Grey are exceedingly scarce, and probably not a single one of them is authentic; on the other hand, very early and almost contemporary engraved portraits are fairly numerous. The oldest of these latter is one by E. V. Wyngaerde. It bears a certain resemblance to the portrait of her grandfather, the Duke of Suffolk, by Jacobus Corvinus, in the possession of Sir Frederick Cook at Richmond. Although Wyngaerde engraved it in the middle part of the reign of Elizabeth, when many persons were still living, the Queen herself included, who had seen Jane Grey, and who could have set him right, he attributes the original to Hans Holbein, who died in London of the plague, according to recent discovery, in 1543, that is to say, when Jane was but six years old, a fact which renders it impossible for him to have painted any of the numerous portraits attributed to him of Edward VI as a lad in his teens, Edward being born in the same year and month as Lady Jane. The portrait of Jane Grey from which Wyngaerde engraved is evidently by some other artist who painted in the style of Holbein, presumably one of his pupils. It must be remembered that in our own time people are constantly attributing to Gainsborough and Reynolds portraits they could not have painted, so in the seventeenth century it was the fashion to attribute every portrait of the early part of the preceding century to Holbein, whose great name was remembered, whilst those of his lesser contemporaries were forgotten.

(2) In the Earl of Stamford and Warrington's collection there is a very ancient portrait of Lady Jane Grey, engraved by Lodge. It is not well painted, but is none the less extremely interesting. The features are small and delicate. The costume360 is rich but simple, and the pretty neckerchief is fastened at the bosom by a bunch of flowers.

(3) Another frequently engraved portrait of Jane Grey, also attributed to Holbein, and engraved in George Howard's *Life of Lady Jane Grey*, was for many years in the possession of the late Mr. Wenman Martin, of Upper Seymour Street. The costume is exceedingly rich.

(4) Probably on account of its excessive prettiness, the celebrated picture called "Jane Grey," in the possession of Lord Spencer, at Althorpe, is likely to remain the most popular likeness of Lady Jane. It represents a sweet-looking young woman of about sixteen, seated by a window, reading an illuminated missal. By her side, on a table, stands a richly chiselled goblet or chalice. The dress is of ruby velvet, made very plain, and with hanging sleeves of a darker material. It was engraved in the last century by Dibden, as the frontispiece of the *Decameron*, a work which certainly has no association whatever with the poor little "Nine Days' Queen." By its general neatness and vivid colouring, this picture may very reasonably be attributed to Luca Penni, an Italian and pupil of Raphael, who painted a good deal in England under Henry VIII, Edward VI, and Mary. There is a very singular fact connected with this Althorpe picture. The noble Milanese family of Trevulzio has possessed for many generations an almost identical picture which has always been known as a portrait of Lady Jane Grey. A photograph of this picture is in my hands, and certainly the resemblance between it and the Althorpe picture is remarkable. Lord Spencer has most kindly afforded me some interesting details connected with his own picture. "It has been," he said, "for many generations in our family, and can be traced as a portrait of Lady Jane Grey as far back as the seventeenth century." Some years ago, Lord Spencer took it down from its place in his gallery, and found on the back of it an inscription in the handwriting of his grandmother, Lavinia, Countess Spencer, to the effect that the picture was a portrait of the Lady Jane Grey, and that what she had written was copied from a much older inscription, which had been nearly obliterated by time. Lord Spencer many years ago saw at Milan the picture above-mentioned, and was struck by its likeness to his own, of which it might have been a copy. Sir George Scharf, although an authority on portraiture, was apt at times to have prejudices and to cast doubt on those historical portraits which have been handed down as authentic for many generations; and his singular ignorance or rather disregard of the value of costume in determining the period of a picture often led him into ludicrous errors of361 judgment. His reason for discarding the Althorpe portrait of Lady Jane Grey appears rather unreasonable. He objected to it because a tall standing goblet or chalice figures conspicuously on the table beside the lady, such a chalice being, according to him, an attribute of St. Mary Magdalen, and so, too, is the skull, which is not present in this picture. However, an extraordinary number of Tudor portraits represent great ladies with a similar goblet standing beside them. These gold and silver chalices or cups were a common gift from royal god-fathers and mothers in Tudor times, and were frequently stolen from the churches. Lady Jane, we know from the inventories of her effects, had several in her possession.

(5) An exceedingly beautiful portrait, said to represent Lady Jane Grey, is at Madresfield, Lord Beauchamp's seat in Worcestershire. The face bears a resemblance to that in the engraving by Wyngaerde, and the costume is undoubtedly one that Lady Jane might have worn, and consists of a rich velvet gown, cut square at the neck and filled in with soft lawn and lace. Her head-dress is very elaborate and graceful. Her expression is sweet and noble. This picture is wrongly ascribed to Lucas Van Heere, and is more likely to have been painted by Streete. Independently of its historical interest, it is a beautiful picture. On the other hand, its companion, supposed to represent Lord Guildford Dudley, is absolutely wrong. It represents a tall young gentleman with strongly-marked features and a vapid expression. It is the costume that gives the lie to the tradition that it is the portrait of Lady Jane's husband, for the dress, with its voluminous ruff, is of the mid-Elizabethan period, and at least twenty-five years later than the death of the unfortunate young gentleman it is said to represent; but, on the other hand, the little velvet cap, with its two plumes, is certainly of the time of Edward VI. The ruff may have been added at a later date by an ignorant restorer.

(6) There is a curious portrait, probably of Lady Jane Grey, in the possession of J. Knight, Esq., of Chawton House, Alton.

(7) A very remarkable portrait, called "Jane Grey," was formerly in the possession of Colonel Elliot; said to be now in one of the Colleges at Oxford. It was, however, engraved in 1830, and has lately been reproduced in colour by Messrs. Graves of Pall Mall. The face is that of an older person than Lady Jane, but the features are small and pretty, the expression being rather defiant and world-wise. She wears a turban-shaped hat of velvet, studded with immense pearls, which was certainly not in fashion in the days of Edward VI, or even in362 the last years of Henry VIII. Here again is an instance of costume giving the lie to tradition. Lady Jane could no more have worn such a hat and costume than a lady in 1909 could be painted as wearing the crinoline and spoon-shaped bonnet of mid-Victorian days.

(8) The small semi-miniature in the National Portrait Gallery is wrongly attributed to Lucas Van Heere, who was born in the year of Jane's execution, and could therefore neither have painted the portrait in question nor any one of the numerous likenesses of Queen Mary ascribed to him, since he was only five years of age when that Queen died.

(9) A small portrait called "Jane Grey" is in the possession of Lord Hastings at Melton Constable, Norfolk.

(10) "A splendid portrait of Jane Grey" was exhibited at the Derby Art Exhibition in 1841—mentioned by Howard. It belonged to a Mr. Harrington, who inherited it from two ancient ladies, the Misses Gray of Derby, in the possession of whose family this picture had been for many generations.

(11) There is a sweetly pretty contemporary Tudor portrait, reputed to be that of Lady Jane Grey, in the possession of Colonel Horace Walpole, at Heckfield Place, Hants.

The Wyngaerde engraving has been frequently reproduced. In the Print Room at the British Museum there are no less than six variations of it. There are also engravings, more or less apocryphal, of Lady Jane by G. W. Krauss and G. C. Schmidt, 1782.

Engraved and fanciful portraits:—

Jane Grey, by G. Smerton, 1824.

Lady Jane Grey, by G. Buckland, 1776.

Lady Jane Grey, by Sherwin.

Lady Jane Grey presenting her prayer-book to Sir Thomas Brydges. Engraved by Wells. 1786.

Lady Jane Grey as Queen. By J. P. Simons.

Lady Jane Grey "From a contemporary miniature at Strawberry Hill," by Vertue. (The original is now in the National Portrait Gallery.)

Lady Jane Grey. From a portrait in the possession of the Marquis of Buckingham. No name of engraver. She wears a velvet gown open at the throat to display a double chain with pendant cross. On table, large gold chalice.

Paul Delaroche has painted two famous historical pictures, representing events in the last days of Lady Jane Grey's life—her farewell to Guildford and her execution. They have been frequently engraved.

363

Portraits of Lady Jane's Mother, Father, and Grandfather

"Frances Brandon, Duchess of Suffolk, and her second husband, Adrian Stokes" (dated 1554). Small half-lengths of the Duchess of Suffolk on the left, and Adrian Stokes on the right. She wears a black dress with tags and jewels, gold-edged ruffs at neck and wrists, black jewelled hoods, two necklaces of pearls, one with pendants, right hand resting on cushion and holding glove, left holding ring. He wears a light-coloured embroidered doublet, black fur-lined surcoat slashed and with tags, ruffs at neck and wrists edged with pink, chain round neck, right hand on hip, left holding gloves, sword at his side. Above her head, *Ætatis* xxxvi: above his, *Ætatis* xxi. Dated MDLIV. Panel, 19½ × 27 in. Probably by Corvinus. This picture was engraved by Vertue. Colonel Wynn Finch.

Frances, Marchioness of Dorset. A superb Holbein drawing. H.M. the King, at Windsor.

Frances Brandon, Duchess of Suffolk. Miniature. Was lent to the Tudor Exhibition by Lord Willoughby d'Eresby.

There are fine portraits of Charles Brandon, Duke of Suffolk, in the National Portrait Gallery, and in the possession of Sir Frederick Cook. There is also a fine portrait by Corvinus of Henry Grey, Marquis of Dorset, in the National Portrait Gallery, and another in the possession of G. P. Boyce, Esq.

A portrait of Katherine, Baroness Willoughby d'Eresby, and Duchess of Suffolk, is in the possession of her descendant, Lord Willoughby d'Eresby.

Bibliography of Lady Jane Grey

In literature, Lady Jane Grey has been a popular heroine. She figures in: *The Tower of London*, by Harrison Ainsworth. *Jane Grey* (French novel), by Alphonse Brot. *Lady Jane Grey*, by Philip Sidney. The life story of Lady Jane is told in *Jeanne Grey*, by Mdme. de Genlis. *The Chronicle of Queen Jane and Queen Mary*. *Lives* of Lady Jane Grey, by Howard, Agnes Strickland (in *Tudor and Stuart Princesses*), and Dr. Harris Nicholas.

There is a fine elegy of Lady Jane Grey by Sir Thomas Chaloner, one of the best Latin writers of the reign of Elizabeth, the original of which is preserved in the Bodleian Library. It is contained in the collection called the Illustrium, Jan. II. 68. p. 33.

364

"Jana luit patriam profuso sanguine culpam, Vivere Phœnicis digna puella dies. Illa suit Phœnix, merito dicenda manebat; Ore placens Venerio, Palladis arte placens.
Culta fuit, formosa fuit: divina movebat Sœpé viros facies, sœpé loquela viros. Vidisset faciem? porterat procus improbus un: Audisset cultæ verba? modestus era," etc.

Lady Jane Grey's tragic fate has been several times dramatised:—*John Dudley, Duke of Northumberland*, a tragedy, by Scriptor Ignotus. London, 1686. *Lady Jane Grey*, by J. W. Ross, 1882.

Independently of Rowe's tragedy, *Lady Jane Grey*, there is the German tragedy of Von Sommer, entitled *Johanna Grey*; and *Jane Grey*, an opera-epilogue, acted 25th February, 1723, for the benefit of Mrs. Sterling at Dublin.

The literary works attributed to Lady Jane Grey are:—

1. Four Latin epistles—three to Bullinger, and one to Lady Katherine Grey. The originals of the first three are preserved at Zurich, the other is in the King's Library, British Museum.

2. Her conference with Feckenham (probably apocryphal), although quoted by such early writers as Foxe and Florio.

3. A letter to Harding (doubtful).

4. A prayer for her own use in prison.

5. Four Latin verses scratched on her prison walls with a pin. These will be found on p. 336.

6. Her speech on the scaffold.

7. *The Complaint of a Sinner.*

8. *The Duty of a Christian.*

9. The annotations in the famous prayer-book.

10. A fragment of a letter has been recently found, and is printed in volume vii of the State Papers; Edward VI. Domestic Series. Addenda.

Hollingshead and Sir Richard Baker state "that she hath wrotten other things," but they do not tell us where they are to be found. Several of her letters, notably the one to Sudeley and the famous letter to Queen Mary, are not extant in her own handwriting.

Lady Jane's fine autograph signature figures on a number of contemporary documents. It is nothing like so elaborate as that of Elizabeth, but it is easy to see that the two Princesses received lessons in Italian caligraphy from the same teacher, probably Castiglione.

Printed in Great Britain
by Amazon